Minorities in international law

An introductory study

Gaetano Pentassuglia

Council of Europe Publishing

Cover design: Mediacom
Cover photo: © Council of Europe
Layout: Pre-press unit, Council of Europe

Edited by Council of Europe Publishing
http://book.coe.int
F-67075 Strasbourg Cedex

ISBN 92-871-4773-6
© Council of Europe, November 2002
Printed in Germany by Koelblin-Fortuna-Druck

CONTENTS

FOREWORD

Walter Schwimmer, Secretary General of the Council of Europe

The 1990s, a decade marked by the resurgence of ethnic and regional conflicts, especially following the collapse of communism, saw the emergence of a large corpus of texts and measures relating to the protection of minorities, at both European and global level. In view of its prominent role in the human rights field, the Council of Europe has been particularly active in this regard, as can be seen from this publication.

The protection of minorities remains one of our Organisation's priorities, not only out of a constant concern to uphold the equality and dignity of all human beings and promote tolerance, but also with the aim of contributing, through the protection of fundamental values, to the fight against terrorism.

It was for these reasons that the Council of Europe readily agreed to a partnership with the European Centre for Minority Issues (ECMI) for the production of a series of reference publications on the protection of minorities. This, to our knowledge, unprecedented work should make it possible to catalogue and analyse the entire range of legal instruments, mechanisms and practical measures existing at European and global level to protect minorities. The publications in this series are aimed at legal experts and practitioners, government officials, NGOs, representatives of minorities and journalists, as well as at a less specialised readership with an interest in these issues. They also constitute an excellent introduction to the question of the protection of minorities for students of international law, political science and international relations.

I welcome this practical co-operation with the ECMI and thank its Director, Mr Weller, and the author of this publication, Dr Pentassuglia, for their contribution to the project.

PREFACE

Marc Weller, ECMI Director

Issues of minority-majority relations have dominated the politics of the wider Europe over the past decade. The Council of Europe, in tandem with the Organisation for Security and Co-operation in Europe, has taken a lead in providing some answers to the complex challenges and opportunities that arise in this context. The Council of Europe, in particular, has been a unique focus of action in generating the first set of comprehensive, legally binding rules on minority governance in general and also in relation to minority and regional languages more specifically. This has been backed up by the first dedicated implementation monitoring mechanism, staffed by leading international and independent experts, and a very efficient international secretariat. It is therefore no exaggeration to say that it was the Council of Europe that has pioneered important developments affecting minority governance and minority rights. It has done so in a way that covers all of Europe, East and West, thus answering the criticism of selectivity in the approach to minority issues of European institutions.

Of course, while a great deal has been achieved, an even greater amount of work remains to be done. The standards contained in the Council of Europe documents are at times quite general in their formulation and it may be difficult to derive concrete entitlements from them. Some issues are not, at present, covered at all. There is implementation monitoring, but no enforcement. Not all states of the wider Europe have signed and ratified the relevant conventions. It is also disappointing that other regions of the world have not yet followed suit and developed their own sets of standards and implementation processes. Minority rights legislation at the universal level remains rudimentary.

Given the impressive set of achievements in some areas, and the lack of progress in others, this is an appropriate time to review the field of minority rights in a comprehensive and yet concise way. With this aim in mind, the European Centre for Minority Issues (ECMI) commissioned Dr Gaetano Pentassuglia to write what is, in effect, the first textbook on minorities in international law. However, the task set for Dr Pentassuglia was somewhat more difficult than simply generating a basic text. In addition to introducing the reader to the principal instruments and mechanisms in the area of minority protection, this book also serves a more ambitious intellectual agenda. It identifies key themes of discourse in the area of minority-majority relations and traces these themes through the corresponding legal debates. Important issues, such as the definition of minorities, the issue of

11

sovereignty and self-determination, problems of standard setting and inter-pretation, implementation mechanisms and the relationship of international and domestic systems, are all covered. This is achieved in a way that makes these problems relevant to the non-expert, while still managing to make an important contribution to scholarship in this area.

The European Centre of Minority Issues owes a significant debt of gratitude to Dr Pentassuglia for having undertaken this difficult task and for having completed a manuscript of this quality in a short period of time. We hope that this book will become a standard work of reference in the field. In view of the pioneering role of the Council of Europe in addressing diversity in all its aspects, it is only too fitting that this book is published under its auspices, furnishing yet another example of the close co-operation between the European Centre for Minority Issues and the Council.

LIST OF ABBREVIATIONS

AJIL	*American Journal of International Law*
CBSS	Council of Baltic Sea states
CDL	(European) Commission of Democracy through Law
CEI	Central European Initiative
CERD	Committee on the Elimination of Racial Discrimination
CFSP	Common foreign and security policy
CPR	Civil and political rights
CSCE	Conference on Security and Co-operation in Europe
DR	Decisions and Reports
EC	European Community
ECHR	European Convention on Human Rights
ECJ	European Court of Justice
ECOSOC	Economic and Social Council
EHRR	European human rights reports
EPC	European political co-operation
ECRI	European Commission Against Racism and Intolerance
ESCR	Economic, social and cultural rights
EU	European Union
EurCommHR	European Commission of Human Rights
EurCtHR	European Court of Human Rights
FRY	Federal Republic of Yugoslavia
FYROM	"the former Yugoslav Republic of Macedonia"
HCNM	High Commissioner on National Minorities
HRC	Human Rights Committee
ICCPR	International Covenant on Civil and Political Rights
ICERD	International Convention on the Elimination of All Forms of Racial Discrimination
ICESCR	International Covenant on Economic, Social and Cultural Rights
ICJ	International Court of Justice
ILM	International legal materials
NGO(s)	Non-governmental organisation(s)
OAS	Organisation of American States
OJ	Official Journal
ODIHR	Office for Democratic Institutions and Human Rights
OSCE	Organisation for Security and Co-operation in Europe
PCIJ	Permanent Court of International Justice
TEU	Treaty on European Union
UDHR	Universal Declaration of Human Rights
UN	United Nations
YBECHR	Yearbook of the European Convention on Human Rights

LIST OF ABBREVIATIONS

TABLE OF CASES

PCIJ

Acquisition of Polish Nationality, Advisory Opinion, PCIJ Series B, No. 7, 1923.

Interpretation of the Convention between Greece and Bulgaria Respecting Reciprocal Emigration (Greco-Bulgarian Communities), Advisory Opinion, PCIJ Series B, No. 17, 1930.

Minority Schools in Albania, Advisory Opinion, PCIJ Series A/B, No. 64, 1935.

Rights of Minorities in Upper Silesia (Minority Schools), PCIJ Series B, No. 15, 1928.

ICJ

Application of the Convention on the Prevention and Punishment of the Crime of Genocide (Preliminary Objections), *Bosnia and Herzegovina v. Yugoslavia*, ICJ Reports 1996.

Application of the Convention on the Prevention and Punishment of the Crime of Genocide, Croatia v. Yugoslavia, Application of 2 July 1999.

Barcelona Traction, Light and Power Company, Limited (Second Phase), *Belgium v. Canada*, ICJ Reports 1970.

East Timor, Portugal v. Australia, ICJ Reports 1995.

Frontier Dispute, Burkina Faso v. Republic of Mali, ICJ Reports 1986.

Legal Consequences for States of the Continued Presence of South Africa in Namibia (South West Africa) notwithstanding Security Council Resolution 276 (1970), Advisory Opinion, ICJ Reports 1971.

Legality of Use of Force, Yugoslavia v. Belgium, Yugoslavia v. Canada, Yugoslavia v. France, Yugoslavia v. Germany, Yugoslavia v. Italy, Yugoslavia v. Netherlands, Yugoslavia v. Portugal, Yugoslavia v. United Kingdom, Orders of 2 June 1999.

Military and Paramilitary Activities in and against Nicaragua (Merits), *Nicaragua v. United States*, ICJ Reports 1986.

Nottebohm (Second Phase), *Liechtenstein v. Guatemala*, ICJ Reports 1955.

Reservations to the Convention on the Prevention and Punishment of the Crime of Genocide, Advisory Opinion, ICJ Reports 1951.

South West Africa Cases (Second Phase), *Ethiopia v. South Africa, Liberia v. South Africa,* ICJ Reports 1966.

Western Sahara, Advisory Opinion, ICJ Reports 1975.

ECJ

Angonese v. Cassa di Risparmio di Bolzano SpA, Case 281/98, (2000) All ER (EC) 577.

Bickel and Franz, Case C-274/96, *Criminal Proceedings against Bickel,* (1998) ECR I-7637.

Friedrich Kremzow v. Austria, Case-C/299/95, (1997) ECR I-2405.

Nold v. Commission, Case 4/73, (1974) ECR 491.

Opinion 2/94 on accession by the EU to the ECHR (1996) ECR I-1759.

European Court and Commission of Human Rights

Abdulaziz, Cabales and Balkandali v. United Kingdom, EurCtHR, Judgment of 28 May 1985, Series A, No. 94.

Airey v. Ireland, EurCtHR, Judgment of 9 October 1979, Series A, No. 32.

Artico v. Italy, EurCtHR, Judgment of 13 May 1980, Series A, No. 37.

Beard v. United Kingdom, Application No. 24882/94, EurCtHR, Judgment of 18 January 2001.

Bideaut v. France, Application No. 11261/84, EurCommHR, Decision of 6 October 1986, DR 48, 1986: 232.

Buckley v. United Kingdom, EurCtHR, Judgment of 25 September 1996, Reports 1996-IV: 1271; EurCommHR, Report of 11 January 1995, EHRR CD 19, 1995: 20.

Buscarini and Others v. San Marino, EurCtHR, Judgment of 18 February 1999, Reports 1999-I: 607.

Case Relating to Certain Aspects of the Laws on the Use of Languages in Education in Belgium (Merits), EurCtHR, Judgment of 23 July 1968, Series A, No. 6.

Chapman v. United Kingdom, Application No. 27238/95, EurCtHR, Judgment of 18 January 2001.

Coster v. United Kingdom, Application No. 24876/94, EurCtHR, Judgment of 18 January 2001.

Cyprus v. Turkey, Application No. 25781/94, EurCtHR, Judgment of 10 May 2001; EurCommHR, Report of 4 June 1999.

Fryske Nasjonale Partij and Others v. Netherlands, Application No. 11100/84, EurCommHR, Decision of 3 October 1985, DR 45, 1986: 240.

G and E v. Norway, Application Nos. 9278/81 and 9415/81, EurCommHR, Decision of 12 December 1985, DR 35, 1994: 30.

Grande Oriente D'Italia di Palazzo Giustiniani v. Italy, Application No. 35972/97, EurCtHR, Judgment of 2 August 2001, Decision of 21 October 1999.

Informationsverein Lentia and Others v. Austria, EurCtHR, Judgment of 28 November 1993, Series A, No. 276.

Isop v. Austria, Application No. 808/60, YBECHR 5, 1962: 108.

Jane Smith v. United Kingdom, Application No. 27238/95, EurCtHR, Judgment of 18 January 2001.

Lee v. United Kingdom, Application No. 25154/94, EurCtHR, Judgment of 18 January 2001.

Lindsay and Others v. United Kingdom, Application No. 8364/78, EurCommHR, Decision of 8 March 1979, DR 15, 1979: 247.

Mathieu-Mohin and Clerfayt v. Belgium, EurCtHR, Judgment of 2 March 1987, Series A, No. 113.

McCann and Others v. United Kingdom, EurCtHR, Judgment of 27 September 1995, Series A, No. 324.

McGuinness v. United Kingdom, EurCtHR, Decision of 8 June 1999, Reports 1999-IV: 483.

Plattform "Ärtze für das Leben" v. Austria, EurCtHR, Judgment of 21 June 1988, Series A, No. 139.

The Liberal Party, Mrs R. and Mr P. v. United Kingdom, Application No. 8765/79, EurCommHR, Decision of 18 December 1980, DR 21, 1981: 211.

Thlimmenos v. Greece, Application No. 34369/97, EurCtHR, Judgment of 6 April 2000.

X and Y v. Belgium, Application No. 2332/64, YBECHR 9, 1966: 418.

X v. Austria, Application No. 8142/78, EurCommHR, Decision of 10 October 1979, DR 18, 1980: 88.

Young, James and Webster v. United Kingdom, EurCtHR, Judgment of 13 August 1981, Series A, No. 44.

HRC

Antonina Ignatane v. Latvia, Communication No. 884/1999, Views of 25 July 2001, CCPR/C/72/D/884/1999.

Apirana Mahuika et al. v. New Zealand, Communication No. 547/1993, Views of 27 October 2000, CCPR/C/70/D/541/1993.

Bernard Ominayak, Chief of the Lubicon Lake Band v. Canada, Communication No. 167/1984, Views of 26 March 1990, (1990) Annual Report II: 1.

Broeks v. Netherlands, Communication No. 172/1984, Views of 9 April 1987, (1987) Annual Report: 139.

Dominique Guesdon v. France, Communication No. 219/1986, Views of 25 July 1990, (1990) Annual Report II: 61.

Gordon McIntyre v. Canada, Communication No. 385/1989, Views of 31 March, (1993) Annual Report II: 91.

Hopu and Bessert v. France, Communication No. 549/1993, Views of 29 July 1997, (1997) Annual Report II: 70.

I. Länsman v. Finland, Communication No. 511/1992, Views of 26 October 1994, (1995) Annual Report II: 66.

Ivan Kitok v. Sweden, Communication No. 197/1985, Views of 27 July 1988, (1988) Annual Report: 221.

J.G.A. Diergaardt et al. v. Namibia, Communication No. 760/1997, Views of 25 July 2000, CCPR/C/69/D/760/1996.

J. Länsman v. Finland, Communication No. 671/1995, Views of 30 October 1996, (1997) Annual Report II: 191.

John Ballantyne, Elizabeth Davidson v. Canada, Communication No. 359/1989, Views of 31 March, (1993) Annual Report II: 91.

M.K. v. France, Communication No. 222/1987, Views of 8 November 1989, (1990) Annual Report II: 127.

Marshall et al. v. Canada, Communication No. 205/1986, Views of 4 November 1991, (1992) Annual Report: 201.

R.L. et al. v. Canada, Communication No. 358/1989, Views of 5 November 1991, (1992) Annual Report: 358.

Sandra Lovelace v. Canada, Communication No. 24/1977, Views of 30 July 1981, (1981) Annual Report: 166; (1983) Annual Report: 248.

T.K. v. France, Communication No. 220/1987, Views of 8 November 1989, (1990) Annual Report II: 118.

Waldman v. Canada, Communication No. 694/1996, Views of 3 November 1999, CCPR/C/67/D/694/1996.

Zwan De Vries v. Netherlands, Communication No. 182/1984, Views of 9 April 1987, (1987) Annual Report: 160.

CERD

L.K. v. Netherlands, Communication No. 4/1991, Opinion of 16 March 1993, CERD/C/42/D/4/1991.

Inter-American Commission on Human Rights

Report on the Situation of Human Rights of a Segment of the Nicaraguan Population of Miskito Origin and Resolution on the Friendly Settlement Procedure regarding the Human Rights Situation of a Segment of the Nicaraguan Population of Miskito Origin, Case No. 7964 (Nicaragua), OAS Docs. OEA/Ser.L/V/II.62, Doc. 10, rev. 3, 1983; OEA/Ser.L/V/II.62, Doc. 26, 1984.

Case No. 7615 (Brazil), Resolution No. 12/85, 5 March 1985, OAS Doc. OEA/Ser.L/V/II.66, Doc. 10, rev. 1, 1985 (concerning the *Yanomami of Brazil*).

National cases

Reference re Secession of Quebec from Canada, Canadian Supreme Court, Opinion of 20 August 1998, Supreme Court Reports (1998), 2: 271.

AUTHOR'S INTRODUCTION

In recent years, minorities issues have regularly come up in activities within international forums, such as the UN and several European institutions. The "old" problem of minorities is one of the most delicate challenges posed to the human rights and institutional framework of the post-cold war era. Far from showing a lack of applicable standards, the current international scene presents a large set of provisions relevant to the situation of minorities, couched in a plurality of forms and reflecting varying degrees of legal significance. A variety of international techniques of supervision are directly or indirectly concerned with their implementation. They generate patterns of scrutiny, providing guidance to a forward-looking assessment on state compliance. Moreover, domestic systems and other *ad hoc* arrangements supplement the overall picture, highlighting models or otherwise means of protection and control to be viewed in the light of the relevant international instruments.

The basic aim of this book is to provide an introductory survey on the protective regimes which have developed in the main international institutions (namely, UN, Council of Europe, OSCE and EU), as well as within special treaty co-operation frameworks, in response to the needs and demands of minority groups. Following from a concise introduction to the issue of minorities in historical perspective (Chapter I) and a general discussion of the understanding of minority rights and "minority" within the corpus of international human rights law (Chapters II and III), the book indeed examines major international standards (Chapters IV to IX) and supervisory methods (Chapter X), and briefly explores particular (adopted or attempted) minority arrangements in European country contexts (Chapter XI). The final part offers some thoughts on the current international system of minority rights protection and the prospects of its evolving architecture. The review seeks to achieve three separate, and yet interrelated, objectives: to outline the substantive entitlements available to minorities and their members, pointing to the distinctiveness of minority rights within the wider human rights frame; to appreciate the role of the institutional work in the field; and to single out special problems and contexts where the minority question arises.

Although this book does not pretend to offer an in-depth analysis of all relevant issues, it nevertheless tries to combine a description of basic conceptual, substantive and procedural aspects with a relatively extensive critical assessment. In doing so, a fundamental concern is to identify ways of enhancing the effectiveness of international law in general and international human rights law in particular, in tackling the complexities of the minority question. Consequently, a good deal of practice is considered in the various chapters, encompassing the jurisprudence of both judicial and quasi-judicial bodies. It also follows that general legal aspects are addressed only where they are deemed to be relevant to the structure and scope of the present work.

Given the introductory nature of the study, enough references to the literature have been included at the end of each chapter to enable the reader to follow-up any specific points of interest. With a similar objective, an appendix sets out partially or in full some of the documents discussed in the text. The material used is generally updated as of the autumn of 2001, but exceptionally data are provided regarding later developments.

I wish to thank the European Centre for Minority Issues (ECMI) for its efforts leading to the publication of this book, and in particular its director Marc Weller, who persuaded me to undertake the project. I am grateful to the University of Munich, where I have been teaching over the last few years, benefiting from a valuable academic environment within which to complete this volume, and to Bruno Simma for his constantly friendly support. My thanks are also due to the secretariats of the Framework Convention for the Protection of National Minorities (Directorate General II – Human Rights) and the Venice Commission, as well as the Directorate General I – Legal Affairs/European Charter for Regional or Minority Languages, at the Council of Europe, for producing useful and updated information about their respective areas of concern. Needless to say, the views expressed in the book are mine alone and do not engage any of the people, institutions or bodies mentioned. Finally, special thanks go to Marita Lampe at the European Centre for Minority Issues and the staff at the Council of Europe for the technical layout of the manuscript, and to my partner Sofia, whose encouragement, as always, was invaluable.

Part A

The minority question in context: background and concepts

CHAPTER I

INTERNATIONAL CONCERN FOR MINORITIES IN AN HISTORICAL PERSPECTIVE

1. Sketch of major stages

In ancient and medieval societies there existed a fragmentation of local power centres. City-states, districts, towns, etc., were regulated on the basis of functional principles and legal systems, mostly in connection with the status of certain segments of the population (the clergy, nobility, landlords, merchants, etc.). The Magna Carta of 1215 well reflected this approach in early thirteenth-century England. There were no specific majority-minority relationships or dynamics.

The Roman Empire was broadly tolerant of religious communities. The liberal pattern reflected the pagan background of the ruling élites and, more importantly, the political expectation of fostering loyalty to the emperor among the communities concerned. Still, the question of religious toleration arose as the Catholic Church gained a prominent status in the empire (Jews, Muslims and heretics were among the main victims of discrimination).

The Protestant Reformation and the Thirty Years War which broke out in the sixteenth century resulted in the end of the Roman Catholic Church's monopoly of religion in Europe, thereby paving the way for the first attempts to use religious toleration as a basis to resolve potentially destructive conflicts. Yet, this did not lead to developing a general theory of rights, let alone a theory of minority rights, but rather reflected new political realities. The Peace of Westphalia (1648), based on the Treaties of Münster and Osnabrück between France, the Roman Empire and the respective allies, confirmed the principle *cuis regio eius religio* (his land, his religion) set out by the Peace of Augsburg (1555), recognised the three major religious communities (Catholic, Protestant and Calvinist), and provided for specific entitlements in the sphere of not only religion but also political participation.

The treaty guarantees were related to either comprehensive regimes of territorial redistribution (for example, the Westphalia peace settlements) or to specific cessions of territories (for example, the Treaty of Paris of 1763 between Great Britain and France, which contained guarantees for the Catholic community living in territories formerly under French sovereignty, and ceded to Great Britain under that treaty). Thus, in most cases their scope of application was confined to the relevant, transferred territory. By contrast, the treaties between Christian powers and the Sublime Porte provided for protection of the Christian groups throughout the Ottoman Empire. The traditional *Millet* system under Ottoman law, granting religious freedom and personal autonomy to non-Muslim communities in the whole of the empire, may have constituted one reason for such a discontinuity.

The American Revolution in the late eighteenth century brought to the fore the notion of individual rights and the consent of the governed, whereas the later French Revolution highlighted the notion of fundamental rights as combined with the concept of nation state as a culturally homogeneous polity. Such events were largely to influence the development of modern states and their problematic dynamics in multinational contexts.

The Congress of Vienna (1815) redrew the European boundaries following the demise of the Napoleonic regime. As a result of the progressive rise of "national identities" in Europe, the concept of national guarantees made its first appearance particularly in connection with the partition of Poland among Austria, Prussia and Russia. While the treaty provisions agreed upon in Vienna were rather vague and their implementation was left to the discretion of the governments concerned, the protection to be afforded to minorities set out by the Congress of Berlin (1878) featured prominently as a corollary of the rise of new states and thus as part of the price of the Great Powers for their acquiescence to border changes in the Balkans (for this and earlier stages, see also *infra*, Chapter IX).

The first genuine "system" of minority rights protection was set up by the League of Nations in the aftermath of the first world war. Again, the redrawing of boundaries prompted by the disintegration of three multinational empires, Austria-Hungary, Prussia and the Ottoman Empire, posed the question of national groups which could not be accommodated through giving each of them a state of its own, but which had to be protected within the newly emerged or enlarged states where such groups found themselves in a non-dominant position. Although a proposed provision on minorities was in the end omitted from the League Covenant, a new system was established consisting of a set of treaty- and declaration-based obligations, the "guarantee" of which was vested in the league instead of the Great Powers. That was one important difference between the new treaties and previous agreements, such as the Treaty of Berlin. The league system entailed the active involvement of the League Council and the PCIJ to enable impartial decisions. Still, for reasons outlined below, the system eventually collapsed along with the League of Nations itself.

The period between 1945 and 1989 (namely, the cold war era) witnessed little attention to minority issues. Kunz spoke of "fashions in international law just as in neckties" (Kunz, 1954: 282), to describe the marked decline in scholarly (but also political) interest in minority rights in the years following the ending of the second world war; "[t]oday" – he wrote – "the well-dressed international lawyer wears 'human rights'" (*ibid*). The emphasis on human rights "for all" was the dominant theme, in line with the basic tenets of liberal individualism. The absence of need for border changes, the bad experience of the use of the minority question by nazi Germany as a tool for aggressive policies, and a general inclination by states to assimilate minority groups into their own societies were also conducive to discarding the League of Nations experiment. The Potsdam Protocol of 1945 (in line with earlier precedents) even envisaged population transfers as a viable means of "solving" minority questions. The record of major international organisations or institutions (for example, UN, Council of Europe and CSCE) did not reveal any particularly notable leap in substance in the field of minority rights, except for, *inter alia*, the adoption of Article 27 of the 1966 ICCPR. Still, even Article 27 was drafted in a tentative language, due to perceived frictions with the classical individualistic pattern.

The upsurge of ethnic tensions following the break up of the Soviet Union and Yugoslavia and in states of other continents, prompted to seriously reconsider the minority question at the universal, regional and sub-regional level, a process which is still underway. Bengoa has recently spoken of "ethno-genesis", to describe the reconstruction of lost or partially lost ties by what he identifies as "third generation" minorities (Bengoa, 2000: 8-11). As will be shown later in this book, the international protection of minority rights in the post-cold war era reveals constructive approaches (for example, greater emphasis on non-forced assimilation, positive measures and group dimension), combined with remarkable weaknesses (for example, substantively or geographically limited impact of the applicable regimes and "hard law-soft law" dichotomy arising from such regimes).

The following describes in more detail the essential elements of legal development affecting minorities and their members as they occurred during the main historical phases just indicated.

2. The League of Nations system

After the first world war, arrangements set out under the aegis of the League of Nations took four forms: special treaties on minorities between the principal allied and associated powers, on the one hand, and Poland (Versailles, 1919), Czechoslovakia (Saint-Germain-en-Laye, 1919), and others, on the other; special chapters in the peace treaties with Austria (Saint-Germain-en-Laye, 1919), Bulgaria (Neuilly-sur-Seine, 1919), Hungary (Trianon, 1920) and Turkey (Lausanne, 1923); special conventions relating to Upper Silesia (Geneva, 1922) and the Memel Territory (Paris, 1934); and declarations entered before the Council of the League of Nations by Finland (1921), Albania (1921), Lithuania (1922), Latvia (1923), Estonia (1923) and Iraq (1932) as a condition of their admission to the league. Four main types of provisions may be discerned in such arrangements (the Polish Minorities Treaty of 1919 largely constituted the "model" for the other treaty- and declaration-based regimes):

- provisions on acquisition and loss of nationality;

- provisions recognising to all inhabitants basic rights to life, liberty and free exercise of any creed, religion or belief not incompatible with public order or morals;

- provisions according nationals equality before the law and equal enjoyment of CPR; and

- provisions setting forth guarantees for the benefit of "nationals who belong to racial, religious or linguistic minorities" (see e.g. Article 8 of the

Polish Minorities Treaty), namely equality in law and in fact with the other nationals; right to establish and run at one's own expense charitable, religious and social institutions, schools and other educational establishments, with its attendant language and religious freedoms; adequate facilities enabling the use of the minority language, either orally or in writing, before the courts; adequate facilities ensuring instruction through the medium of this language in the public primary schools, in towns and districts with a "considerable proportion" (see e.g. *idem:* Article 9) of minority members; and "equitable share" (see e.g. *ibid*) of public funds to benefit the minorities living in those towns and districts for educational, religious or charitable purposes.

Exceptionally, the treaties and declarations went further in that they granted forms of political or cultural autonomy to specific groups, for example the Szeklers and Saxons of Transylvania under the Treaty between the Powers and Romania (Paris, 1919), and the Vlachs of the Pindus under the Treaty concerning the Protection of Minorities in Greece (Sèvres, 1920), or other advanced entitlements which could be interpreted as implying legal recognition of groups *per se* (Mandelstam, 1923). However, such provisions were generally limited in scope and did not affect the league arrangements as fundamentally a product of the individualistic point of view.

In its 1935 advisory opinion in the *Minority Schools in Albania* case (PCIJ Series A/B, No. 64, 1935: 17), the PCIJ so brilliantly captured the essential aim of the system by stressing the interplay of anti-discrimination and cultural identity obligations, and their relation to conflict-prevention purposes. Such obligations were indeed intended to ensure:

> the possibility of living *peacefully* alongside the population and *co-operating amicably* with it, while at the same time preserving the characteristics which distinguish them from the majority, satisfying the ensuing special needs. (Author's emphasis.)

The league "guarantee" was both internal and external. Internally, the state concerned undertook to confer on the treaty provisions the status of fundamental laws, invalidating all contrary laws or regulations. The external "guarantee" applied only to the extent that the various rights affected persons belonging to racial, religious or linguistic minorities – they indeed constituted "obligations of international concern". The League Council and the PCIJ were the pillars (political and judicial) of the machinery. The treaty provisions could not be amended without the approval of a majority of the League Council. Council members could draw the attention of the council to actual or potential infractions of minority obligations, while the council could thereupon take such action as it deemed proper and effective in the circumstances, including having recourse to the PCIJ. The PCIJ was indeed made competent to exercise contentious and advisory jurisdiction over differences of opinion on questions of law or fact arising out of the treaty regimes, but it was not open to the minorities themselves. Rather, the latter and states not represented in the council could petition the league, though not the council directly. The usual procedure was that, where the case was considered admissible by the secretary general, the council appointed an *ad hoc* minorities committee to investigate the matter and try to reach a friendly settlement. A remarkable exception was envisaged in the German-Polish Convention relating to Upper Silesia of 1922, which established the right to directly petition, individually or collectively, the council (and the mixed commission set up by this treaty, before which the petitioners could also appear for oral hearings), foreshadowing later procedural developments regarding complaints procedures under international human rights law. The PCIJ played a major role by delivering a number of advisory opinions. It gave judgment only in one contentious case, in 1928, concerning *Rights of Minorities in Upper Silesia (Minority Schools)* (PCIJ Series B, No. 15, 1928).

The above references to the network of minority obligations clearly indicate that the system was not intended for general application – it only applied to certain states where "owing to special circumstances, [minority problems] might present particular difficulties" (Claude, 1955: 16-17). The states concerned resented this approach from the very beginning, considering the underlying double standard (essentially based on a distinction between Western and Eastern Europe) as an attack on their sovereign independence. As a result, they displayed an unco-operative attitude in respect of the implementation of the treaties. Poland denounced the 1919 treaty in 1934 – a step which went largely unchallenged. The minorities, for their part, levelled criticism at the petition procedure which, apart from the arrangement for Upper Silesia, did not have sufficient regard to an effective representation of their claims (they had no *locus standi* vis-à-vis the council, nor could they appear before it or the other competent bodies for oral hearings). Finally, some "kin-states" (notably nazi Germany) exploited the minority question for the purpose of revising the 1919 Versailles settlement (as well illustrated by the Munich Four Power Agreement of 1938), sometimes with the backing of some – though by no means all – of the respective minorities.

Bagley (1950: 126) situates the collapse of the system within a wider international context of considerable retrogression. He observes that the rise of dictatorships, the flourishing of hate and intolerance, and passionate nationalism made it inevitable that minorities should be the main victims of the new climate.

3. After the second world war: context and beyond – the UN approach

A study of the UN secretariat from 1950 concluded that the minorities treaties had generally ceased to exist. The *rebus sic stantibus* clause (now embodied in Article 62 of the 1969 Vienna Convention on the Law of Treaties, regarding "fundamental change of circumstances") was referred to as a ground for the above effect of extinction. Some commentators also speak of termination by "desuetude" (Capotorti, 1997). The Åland Islands regime was one of those thought to be still in place, based on a settlement reached in 1921 between Sweden and Finland (see *infra*, Chapter XI). The League of Nations system did not generate international customary rules. On the contrary, the population transfers which took place in the aftermath of the second world war gave evidence of a wide discretion of states in the treatment of minority groups. While reflecting a specific European experience, that system, legally grounded on the notion of equal treatment, largely fitted the later individualistic paradigm of international human rights protection, and was designed to meet concerns for stability, just as the contemporary regimes do. According to Thornberry, what was rejected was, in fact, the league system as "symbol and spectre" (Thornberry, 1991: 117) rather than the expression of specific legal norms or broad peace preservation goals. The frequent reference to major PCIJ pronouncements and key assumptions of the league system in the subsequent discourse of minority rights, seem to confirm it.

The UN Charter does not contain a specific minority provision – the emphasis is on human rights in general. Still, the charter may now be read as including minority rights by implication (namely, as part of human rights). Certainly, the general formula of human rights without distinction as to race, sex, language, or religion (Article 1, paragraph 3, and Article 55, sub-paragraph c), reflected the dominant post-war pattern, as indirectly confirmed by the subsequent work of the relevant UN bodies (see *infra*). The peace treaties of 1947 featured the same approach, occasionally adding a special prohibition of discrimination among nationals on various grounds, including race, language and religion. The theme of minority rights was not completely absent at the international level: the Paris Agreement of 5 September 1946, concluded between Austria and Italy (the so-called "De Gasperi-Gruber Agreement"), and annexed to the peace treaty between the allies and associated powers and Italy, dealt with important minority issues (see *infra* in the text, and Chapters IX and XI).

Preference was also expressed for including a minority provision in the UDHR. A draft article was prepared by the secretariat and another, revised draft was submitted by the Drafting Committee of the Commission on Human Rights and this latter's sub-commission. In the final draft, the previous reference to "an equitable proportion of public funds" to be made available for the benefit of minority schools and cultural institutions (which somewhat echoed the earlier clause on public funds contained in the minorities treaties after the first world war) was dropped, and a personal restriction to "well-defined" and "clearly distinguished" ethnic, linguistic or other minority groups was included, an element which was to re-emerge in later discussions about the notion of minority (see *infra*, Chapter III). The rights envisaged allowed persons belonging to such groups to establish and maintain their own schools and cultural or religious institutions, and to use their own language in the press, in public assembly and before the courts and other authorities of the state, if they so chose and to the extent compatible with public order and security. The proposal met with opposition. Further proposals were submitted by the Soviet Union, Yugoslavia and Denmark in the General Assembly, but they fared no better. The "new" states from North and South America favoured "melting pot" and assimilation. The "old" states were largely dominated by the homogenising ideology of nation-state. The Eastern bloc was more sensitive to minority issues, in line with the Soviet model of group accommodation based on cultural-territorial decentralisation (but paradoxically resisted by strong political centralisation). In the African and Asian continents there were not many independent states – only India took a stand in favour of a minority article. However, it eventually joined the

UK and other Western countries in proposing that general prescriptions of equality and non-discrimination would suffice for securing effective protection for minorities. Upon adoption of the UDHR in 1948, the General Assembly recognised, however, that the UN could not "remain indifferent" to the fate of minorities (Resolution 217 A (III) of 1948); it referred the matter to the ECOSOC with a view to producing a "thorough study" of the problems of minority groups.

Thus, the minority question remained on the UN agenda. Standard-setting and institutional developments pointed in the same direction. The 1948 Convention on the Prevention and Punishment of the Crime of Genocide clearly benefited minorities – many decades later the upsurge of ethnic conflicts (and "ethnic cleansing") was sadly to confirm this. In terms of UN institutional action, the mandate of the Commission on Human Rights included proposals, recommendations and reports on the protection of minorities (Resolution 5 (I) of 1946). Resolution 9 (II) of 1946 authorised the commission to establish a Sub-Commission on Prevention of Discrimination and Protection of Minorities made up of independent experts elected by the commission. The sub-commission elaborated an instructive distinction between "prevention of discrimination" and "protection of minorities" (see *infra*, Chapter IV), attempted to define "minority", and prepared the draft text of Article 27 of the ICCPR. Yet, "prevention of discrimination" rather than "protection of minorities" was the dominant concern: the sub-commission was actively engaged under the "ECOSOC 1503 procedure", concerning patterns of gross violations of human rights, and in assessing country-specific discriminatory practices (for example, the apartheid regime in South Africa). In 1971, the same body, through special rapporteur Francesco Capotorti, undertook a comprehensive study on the rights of persons belonging to ethnic, religious and linguistic minorities, which was completed in 1978. The aim was to assess the application of the provisions set out in Article 27 of the covenant.

The United Nations also addressed some concrete cases of group protection. The Cyprus and South Tyrol situations (the former concerning the position of the Greek and Turkish communities in Cyprus, and the latter involving the German-speaking minority in the South Tyrol, which had been ceded to Italy under the Treaty of Saint-Germain-en-Laye of 10 September 1919) were brought to the attention of the General Assembly. In the South Tyrol case, centred on the statute of autonomy recognised for the benefit of the South Tyrol's German-speaking element in the Paris Agreement of 5 September 1946, the assembly recommended Austria and Italy to resume negotiations to give effect to the agreement, and, if necessary, to have recourse to the ICJ (Resolutions 1497 (XV) and 1661 (XVI), adopted in 1960 and 1961 respectively). The Cyprus case only initially posed, *inter alia*, a genuine minority issue, namely the question of protecting the minority population of Turkish origin in Cyprus in connection with the decolonisation of the latter; no specific measure was, however, recommended by the General Assembly. The Cyprus problem took on far more complex features following the independence of Cyprus and the recognition of the Turkish population as an ethnic (as opposed to minority) group on an equal footing with the island's population of Greek origin. Other country-situations were considered, among others, by relevant UN treaty bodies.

In terms of standards, and apart from Article 27 of the ICCPR discussed in Chapter V, the Unesco Convention Against Discrimination in Education adopted in 1960 came to recognise in Article 5, paragraph 1, sub-paragraph c, the right of members of national minorities to carry on their own educational activities, including the maintenance of schools and, depending on the educational policy of each state, the use or the teaching of their own language, provided that this right did not prevent such minority members from understanding the majority culture and language, did not prejudice national sovereignty, did not offer a standard of education which was lower than the one approved by the competent authorities, and the attendance at the minority schools was optional. Further steps forward were taken as cold war polarities came to an end. In 1989 a provision was introduced in the widely ratified UN Convention on the Rights of the Child, combining rights of indigenous and minority children in a text that adapts Article 27 of the ICCPR. The Declaration and Programme of Action of the World Conference on Human Rights held in Vienna in 1993 reaffirmed the right of persons belonging to ethnic, linguistic or religious minorities to enjoy their own culture, to profess and practice their own religion and to use their own language in private and in public, freely and without interference or any form of discrimination (Part II.B.2).

4. Introductory overview of contemporary instruments and institutions

As noted earlier, the post-cold war era reveals a strong move towards developing international minority rights regimes. In the UN context (see *infra*, Chapter V), the most important contemporary non-treaty text devoted to minority rights is the UN Declaration on the Rights of Persons Belonging to National or Ethnic, Religious and Linguistic Minorities, adopted by the General Assembly in 1992. The declaration is "inspired" by Article 27 of the ICCPR, though it is not necessarily to be linked to the limitations of this article.

At the European level, the Council of Europe and the (now) OSCE have been most active in recent years as regards the promotion and protection of minority rights (see *infra*, Chapters VI and VII). As for the Council of Europe, the 1950 ECHR does not contain any specific minority rights provisions. Still, it prohibits discrimination in the enjoyment of the rights and freedoms recognised therein on any ground such as "association with a national minority" (Article 14). The prohibition of discrimination has been further expanded under Protocol No. 12 to the ECHR, opened for signature in November 2000. In fact, such a prohibition is not limited to the rights and freedoms contained in the ECHR. The Council of Europe Framework Convention for the Protection of National Minorities, opened for signature in 1995, is the first multilateral treaty on the protection of national minorities in general, while the European Charter for Regional or Minority Languages produced in this same context two years earlier affects to some extent the specific position of minorities. In addition, useful minority rights texts were produced by respectively the European Commission for Democracy through Law (hereinafter the "Venice Commission") in 1991, and the Parliamentary Assembly in 1993. Recommendation 1201 (1993) adopted by this latter body contains standards which are being referred to as "commitments" in Assembly opinions on the admission of new member states to the Organisation.

The OSCE, too, has taken important steps. In contrast to the limited scope of the minority clause in Principle VII of the 1975 Helsinki Final Act (concerning equality before the law, actual enjoyment of human rights, and protection of legitimate interests in this sphere), the document of the Copenhagen Meeting on the Human Dimension of 1990 provides for a wide range of minority rights provisions and remains the most complete OSCE document elaborating commitments in the field.

Although the EU has not developed an instrument on minority rights, general and specific elements of protection can be found in this framework as well, in relation to an increased attention to human rights matters (see *infra*, Chapter VII). The EC Treaty (as subsequently amended) contains references to respect for cultural diversity within the Community context (notably in Article 151, ex Article 128), and a new anti-discrimination clause covering minority components (Article 13, ex Article 6a). The recently adopted Charter of Fundamental Rights of the EU, contains equality and non-discrimination provisions (Article 20 and Article 21, paragraph 1), as well as references to respect by the EU for cultural diversity (including religious and linguistic diversity, under Article 22), in accordance with earlier developments.

Two 1999 council regulations laying down the requirements for the implementation of Community operations which contribute to the general objective of developing and consolidating democracy and the rule of law and to that of respecting human rights and fundamental freedoms, within the framework of Community development and non-development co-operation policies, respectively (Nos. 975/1999 and 976/1999, OJ 1999 L 120/1 and 8), reflect increasing concern for minority issues in a number of their provisions. The most significant substantive aspects are those associated with the work which is being performed by the EU as part of the general eastward enlargement and rapprochement processes. Furthermore, the EC/EU has played a particular role in the search for, *inter alia*, appropriate minority standards as a response to the crisis in the former Yugoslavia (for example, through an *ad hoc* conference and an arbitration commission). It is important to mention in this context the Stability Pact in Europe, which resulted from a CFSP joint action approved by the EU Council in 1993 and was eventually signed in 1995 by fifty-two representatives of the participating states of the OSCE. The Pact is as such a "political", non-legally binding document, mainly designed to facilitate the solution of frontier and minority problems in eastern Europe, in a way that is consistent with international standards. It incorporates many bilateral treaties and declarations concluded by eastern European countries among themselves, dealing in whole or in part with minority issues. The declaration included in the Pact stresses the linkage between peace, democracy and human rights, including the rights of persons belonging to national minorities.

In line with these developments, the CEI and the Commonwealth of Independent States, two major intergovernmental institutional frameworks comprising respectively central and eastern European countries and all the former Soviet republics except the Baltic states, each produced an instrument on minority rights in 1994.

Contemporary institutional approaches to minority issues reveal a marked preventive content (see *infra*, Chapter X), somewhat developing an important assumption underlying the minorities treaties after the first world war. In 1989, the UN Sub-Commission on Prevention of Discrimination and Protection of Minorities entrusted special rapporteur Asbjørn Eide with the task of carrying out a study on possible ways and means of facilitating the peaceful and constructive solution of problems involving minorities. The final report, submitted in 1993, highlights, *inter alia*, the need for constructive national arrangements for minorities based on international human rights standards, within the framework of a broad conflict-prevention strategy (an update to this study is being prepared following a request from the sub-commission, now renamed "Sub-Commission on the Promotion and Protection of Human Rights"; UN Sub-Commission on Human Rights Resolution 2001/9: paragraph 9). The 1993 report was particularly influential in leading to the establishment in 1995 of the UN Working Group on Minorities. The working group reviews the implementation of the 1992 UN declaration, promotes dialogue between minorities and governments, and recommends measures which may serve to defuse minority tensions. The UN High Commissioner for Human Rights also provides a focus on minority issues in connection with the above purposes, and in the context of multilateral or bilateral programmes of technical assistance and advisory services, while other general UN human rights procedures provide further opportunities for bringing up matters affecting minorities.

The work of both the UN working group and the High Commissioner for Human Rights is inspired by the experience of the OSCE HCNM, acting since 1993 as an institution for "preventive diplomacy". Along comparable lines, the Office of the Commissioner on Democratic Institutions and Human Rights, including the Rights of Persons Belonging to Minorities was established in 1994 by the CBSS (set up as a conference of foreign ministers comprising, among others, the Baltic states and the northern countries). In June 2000, the Council further revised the commissioner's mandate, which still contains, however, a remit to address minority rights issues, and appointed him as "Commissioner on Democratic Development". In May 1999, the Council of Europe established a Commissioner for Human Rights entrusted with mostly promotional (so-called confidence-building) tasks. His broad mandate clearly covers minority rights education as a tool for facilitating the implementation of the pertinent Council of Europe instruments. A variety of measures, including technical assistance and advisory services, are also offered under the umbrella of specific activities of the Council of Europe. The EU, for its part, is devising a range of ways and means of improving minority rights compliance in eastern Europe. In particular, "respect for and protection of minorities" has been made a requirement for EU membership (thereby building upon the Council of Europe's approach to membership requirements), and access to economic benefits (trade, etc.). The cited 1995 Stability Pact in Europe is now complemented by the Stability Pact for South Eastern Europe, launched by the EU, within the CFSP, in May 1999, and adopted a month later by the EU member states, the south-eastern states concerned, as well as other neighbouring countries, interested states and international institutions. It is a specific conflict-prevention initiative which aims to stabilise the region and promote development by facilitating bilateral and multilateral agreements as well as domestic arrangements, covering the whole range of regional crisis factors, with a special emphasis on the protection of human rights in general and minority rights in particular, in accordance with universal and regional standards.

Such new patterns of scrutiny develop to a certain extent the approach to the implementation of minority rights standards. As outlined later, the patterns typically embodied in the main relevant international instruments (ICCPR, etc.), such as considering reports periodically submitted by states parties to the particular treaty on the measures taken to give effect to that treaty and/or deciding cases of alleged violation of the treaty brought in the form of complaints before the supervisory body by individuals, while in urgent need of improving their effectiveness, remain, however, of considerable significance.

Bibliography

Bagley, I.H., *General principles and problems in the protection of minorities*, Imprimeries populaires, Geneva, 1950.

Bengoa, J., "Existence and recognition of minorities", UN Doc. E/CN.4/Sub.2/AC.5/2000/WP.2, 2000, pp. 1-32.

Bokatola, I.O., *L'organisation des Nations Unies et la protection des minorités*, Etablissements Emile Bruylant, Brussels, 1992.

Brandtner, B. and Rosas, A., "Human rights and the external relations of the European Community: an analysis of doctrine and practice", *European Journal of International Law*, 9, 1998, pp. 468-490.

Capotorti, F., "Minorities", in *Encyclopedia of public international law*, Macalister-Smith, P. (ed.), Volume 3, Elsevier Science B.V., Amsterdam, 1997, pp. 410-420.

Capotorti, F., "Study on the rights of persons belonging to ethnic, religious and linguistic minorities", UN Doc. E/CN.4/Sub.2/384/Rev. I, 1979.

Claude, I.L., *National minorities: an international problem*, Harvard University Press, Cambridge, 1955.

De Azcárate, P., *League of Nations and national minorities: an experiment*, Carnegie Endowment for International Peace, New York, 1972.

Eide, A., "The non-inclusion of minority rights: Resolution 217 C (III)", in *The Universal Declaration of Human Rights: a common standard of achievement*, Alfredsson, G. and Eide, A. (eds), Kluwer Law International, The Hague, 1999, pp. 701-723.

Eide, A., "Possible ways and means of facilitating the peaceful and constructive solution of problems involving minorities", UN Doc. E/CN.4/Sub.2/1993/34, 1993.

Ermacora, F., "The protection of minorities before the United Nations", *Collected Courses of the Hague Academy of International Law*, IV, 1983, pp. 257-370.

Hannum, H., "Contemporary developments in the international protection of the rights of minorities", *Notre Dame Law Review*, 66, 1991, pp. 1431-1448.

Hofmann, R., "Minorities Addendum 1995", in *Encyclopedia of public international law*, Macalister-Smith, P. (ed.), 3, Elsevier Science B.V., Amsterdam, 1997, pp. 420-424.

Horn, F., "Recent attempts to elaborate standards on minority rights", in *Current international law issues: Nordic perspectives: essays in honour of Jerzy Sztucki*, Bring, O. and Mahmoudi, S. (eds), Fritzes, Stockholm, 1994, pp. 81-108.

Kunz, J.L., "The present status of the international law for the protection of minorities", *American Journal of International Law*, 48, 1954, pp. 282-287.

Macartney, C.A., *National states and national minorities*, Oxford University Press, London, 1934.

Mandelstam, A.N., "La protection des minorités", *Collected Courses of the Hague Academy of International Law*, I, 1923, pp. 361-519.

Modeen, T., *The international protection of national minorities in Europe*, Åbo Akademi, Åbo, 1969.

Muldoon, J.B., "The development of group rights", in *Minority rights: a comparative analysis*, Sigler, J.A. (ed.), Greenwood Press, Westport, 1983, pp. 31-66.

Musgrave, T.D., *Self-determination and national minorities,* Clarendon Press, Oxford, 1997.

Pollet, K., "Human rights clauses in agreements between the European Union and central and eastern European countries", *Revue Des Affaires Européennes*, 7, 1997, pp. 290-301.

Preece, J.J., *National minorities and the European nation-states system*, Clarendon Press, Oxford, 1998.

Rehman, J., *Weaknesses in the international protection of minority rights*, Kluwer Law International, The Hague, 2000.

Sigler, J.A., *Minority rights: a comparative analysis, Greenwood Press*, Westport, 1983.

Thornberry, P., "Minority rights", *Collected Courses of the Academy of European Law*, VI-2, 1995, pp. 307-390.

Thornberry, P., "International and European standards on minority rights", in *Minority rights in Europe: the scope for a transnational regime*, Miall, H. (ed.), Pinter/Royal Institute of International Affairs, London, 1994, pp. 14-21.

Thornberry, P., *International law and the rights of minorities*, Clarendon Press, Oxford, 1991.

Thornberry, P., "Is there a phoenix in the ashes? International law and minority rights", *Texas International Law Journal*, 15, 1980, pp. 421-458.

United Nations Secretariat, "Study of the legal validity of the undertakings concerning minorities". UN Doc. E/CN.4/367, 1950.

United Nations Secretary General, "Definition and classification of minorities", UN Doc. E/CN.4/Sub.2/85, 1949.

Verhoeven, J., "Les principales étapes de la protection internationale des minorités", *Revue Trimestrielle Des Droits De L'Homme*, 30, 1997, pp. 177-203.

Wippman, D., "The evolution and implementation of minority rights", *Fordham Law Review*, 66, 1997, pp. 597-626.

CHAPTER II

HUMAN RIGHTS, MINORITY RIGHTS, PEOPLES' RIGHTS

1. Rights and human rights: philosophical and legal considerations

In legal philosophy, "rights" are usually understood as legal rights, namely interests protected by law and supported by a legitimate justification (or "just claim"). As a result, the inter-relation between rights and duties is emphasised. For instance, human rights are normally seen as legal rights connected to state duties (see *infra*). Nevertheless, some commentators have observed that defining rights solely through a reference to duties is not entirely satisfactory, given the circularity of the argument (the right of X is indeed described by referring to the duty upon Y) and the fact that there may well exist duties which are not specifically attached to rights. In 1919, Hohfeld, a distinguished legal philosopher, submitted a model for assessing rights theories. He identified four categories or aspects of a right:

– *stricto sensu* right ("claim");

– privilege (no claim against the privilege-holder);

– power (entitlement to change legal positions); and

– immunity (no entitlement to change the legal position of the power-holder).

Nino (1991) has developed the Hohfeldian rights within the context of human rights theory. He characterises rights in five different ways, namely as:

– the absence of prohibitions;

– direct permissions;

– correlates of active and passive duties of others;

– claims; and

– immunities.

Although these propositions, by pointing to the various facets of rights, may lead to different protections, in Nino's view, the very essence of a "right" lies in the enjoyment of some good or the avoidance of some evil, and/or in the exclusion or involvement of actions by a party other than the right-holder depending on whether such a party might cause, respectively, harm or benefit to the right-holder (*idem:* 30-34).

Based on Nino's approach, Spiliopoulou Åkermark (1997: 39-40) maintains that the critical element in the concept of rights is provided by the notion of "goods" or "interests" that such rights are designed to secure. She contends that while legal rights are those particular rights which are established by the institutions having the legal power to do so, and which are conferred upon the status prescribed by the relevant "sources of law", a theory of legal rights should not be limited to the aspect of the formal recognition of rights but should also address the central issue of their justification (namely, what "goods" or "interests" legal rights are meant to protect). Given this understanding of legal rights, she also indicates a distinction between the recognition of rights and the possibilities of enforcing them.

In the light of the above considerations, two questions should now be answered: What are human rights? Why do human rights exist at all? The references contained in the UDHR to "the inherent dignity" and "the equal and inalienable rights of all members of the human family", "fundamental human rights", etc., well illustrate the natural law and natural rights background to the development of international human rights law. Indeed, it was the seventeenth-century English philosopher John Locke who first argued that certain rights such as the rights to life, liberty and property, inherently pertain to individuals as human beings, and the state has been given only the right to secure those natural rights, not the rights themselves, which are "inalienable". This conception was clearly reflected in the Declaration of Independence proclaimed by the thirteen American colonies on 4 July 1776, and in the French Declaration of the Rights of Man and of the Citizen adopted on 26 August 1789. The doctrine of natural law fell into disfavour most notably during the nineteenth and twentieth centuries, as it came under attack as "unreal" law with an absolutist connotation. Although nowadays human rights theories provide a range of policy justifications for protection, based on justice, utility, equality, etc., and "human rights" have thus developed into a fully-fledged distinct category of no transempirical derivation, a certain natural law flavour is clearly discernible not only in the UDHR but also in other human rights texts.

In philosophical terms, international human rights as embodied in major instruments (the UDHR, the 1966 covenants, etc.) have been said to present a number of basic properties. They are:

– universal and inherent (they belong to each and every human being because of the inherent dignity of each and every human being; as inherent, they exist independently of human acts implying their recognition or neglect; they are inalienable; legal rules do not "establish" human rights but only secure them);

– protected on the basis of equality and non-discrimination (dignity and thus human rights are assigned to every human being; discrimination does exist only when there is infringement on human rights; differential treatment has to be based on proper reasons and justifications);

– primarily designed to enable free choices and individual development (still, freedom is not a value independent of other values);

– related to a social environment (as indicated, for instance, in Article 29, paragraph 1, of the UDHR; the individual remains, however, the ultimate beneficiary – society exists for his or her benefit); and

– indivisible and interdependent (all human rights are to be treated globally and with the same emphasis).

Piechowiak defines "human rights" as:

> a complex of relations which is constituted of real relations between individuals who have the duty to act (or refrain from acting) towards each other, and the relations of every human being to certain goods (things, circumstances) securing his or her well-being. (Piechowiak, 1999: 10.)

As regards the question why human rights exist at all, Piechowiak identifies two basic philosophical reasons:

- the very existence of human beings with their development projects; and
- the establishment of relations between individuals who are ends in themselves, and whose well-being depends on the free and rational actions of others.

In strictly legal terms, the issue of international human rights is approached through the question of the "subjects of international law" or through a definition of the bearer and beneficiary of these rights. The latter perspective is the most commonly resorted to – in fact, it is generally accepted that individuals as such lack international legal personality, notwithstanding their special position in a number of fields and their limited procedural capacity before pertinent bodies. Broadly speaking, human rights can be described as legal rights recognised to all human beings to protect their dignity (namely, the "good" or "interest" represented by their well-being).

2. Human rights as legal norms

Drzewicki (1999) has summarised the typical components of a human rights norm as follows:

- subject (individual, group of individuals or NGO), entitled to the right recognised in a legal rule (right-holder) and, within the limits of his/their procedural capacity, to take permissible action to secure the right;
- duty-holder (mostly a state), obliged either to fulfil the subject's demands or to create the conditions which are necessary for their realisation;
- object, revealing the content of any given right and any corresponding duties, as a reflection of the values and needs protected; and
- implementation, namely a range of measures which aim to realise the right in question domestically and to supervise the concomitant process through available domestic or international procedures and institutions.

The identification of the above components taken together is not based on an explicit formulation of each human right norm, but rather stems from the appreciation of the substantive norm in its overall legal context. Such a typology serves the concrete purposes of establishing the right-holder as a possible victim of violations and the actual scope of the norm, as well as determining the modalities for an effective protection of the right (exceptionally, individuals or groups other than the victims or their close representatives may activate an implementation machinery to the benefit of the victims themselves).

For a legal description of human rights norms, their self-executing nature and the type of obligation they impose on states are also important questions. In general, a norm (notably a treaty norm) is self-executing when it is clear, complete and precise for "direct applicability" by domestic authorities, including the judicial bodies, whereas a non-self-executing norm is one requiring legislative or other measures (for example, comprehensive policy action) in order to achieve the objectives set out therein. The obligations of states in the human rights field may indeed generate variations in duties given the scope or normative content of individual human rights norms; in other words, the characterisation of a state duty depends on the interpretation or definition of the norm. A noteworthy traditional distinction is between obligations of result (where the duty consists in the achievement of a specific outcome, for example the outlawing of torture) and obligations of conduct (where what is required is "due diligence" in striving to achieve specific objectives, for example adequate standard of living or the highest attainable standard of physical and mental health in, respectively, Articles 11 and 12 of the 1966 International Covenant on Economic, Social and Cultural Rights). Another established distinction can be made on a different level, between obligations which do not determine the means by which a particular goal (for example, securing education for all) must be achieved (normally in view of different factual situations to which the norm applies), and obligations which require a specific course of conduct instead (for example, the introduction or repeal of a specific piece of legislation: see, for example, Article 10, paragraph 3, of the ICESCR which sets out a duty to make certain types of employment of minors "prohibited and punishable by law"). The latter types of obligations do not compete with, but complement one another, and this explains why, although the first type is perhaps more common in international human rights law, a network of duties of both such types can be found in the context of many human rights instruments.

Nino's construction of rights in relation to abstention from causing harm, or active support, by parties other than the right-holder (see *supra*) usefully highlights an aspect which is increasingly considered in contemporary international human rights law when determining the reach of state duties, namely whether the state is required only not to interfere in the enjoyment of the right or must also take positive action to ensure and support it. Eide (1995b) appears to indirectly embrace such new dimensions by classifying state duties under international human rights norms as duties to respect (right-holders, their freedoms, etc.), to protect (right-holders against other subjects by legislation and provision of effective remedies) and to assist and fulfil (by providing available resources for better infrastructures and by direct provision of basic needs). Whatever the effects of individual state duties, they are of course all equally binding where they have been validly undertaken.

3. The content of international human rights

a. The evolution of protection: basic frameworks and aspects

The stages of development of the international protection of human rights are basically four:

- 1945-48 (with the adoption of the UN Charter and the UDHR, and some basic treaties such as the 1948 Genocide Convention);

- 1949-66 (with the adoption of the ICCPR and ICESCR, and a number of specialised treaties on refugees, women, racial discrimination, etc.);
- 1967-89 (with the adoption of further specific treaties, such as the 1984 Convention against Torture and Other Cruel, Inhuman or Degrading Treatment or Punishment and the 1989 Convention on the Rights of the Child; the emphasis on implementation measures; and the gradual appearance of so-called rights of the "third generation", see *infra*); and
- from 1989 onwards (with a wider supervision in eastern Europe as a result of the demise of East-West confrontation; the development of preventive diplomacy mechanisms; and proposals for further standard-setting activities establishing "new" rights, for example on privacy, and reinforcing or complementing existing standards, for example on the protection of vulnerable groups).

Moreover, along with developments at the universal level, three regional systems of human rights protection have been set up: the European (Council of Europe and ECHR), the American (OAS and the American Convention on Human Rights, 1969), and the African (Organisation of African Unity, now the African Union, and African Charter on Human and Peoples' Rights, 1981).

According to recent classifications, human rights treaties may be roughly divided into general conventions (UN covenants, etc.), specific conventions (on genocide, etc.), conventions addressing the position of certain categories of individuals (refugees, migrant workers, women, etc.) and conventions concerning discrimination (on racial or sexual grounds, discrimination in education, etc.). In addition to that, several declarations, resolutions *et similia*, have been adopted on a wide range of human rights matters at universal and regional level, which complement the treaty achievements and the relevance of which to the law-making process should not be underestimated despite the fact that they are *per se* non-binding, so-called "soft law" instruments (Shelton, 2000: 345-463). Some human rights norms (mostly taken from the non-binding UDHR) have been recognised as part of general international law, frequently endowed with, or suggesting, peremptory (*ius cogens*) character. Without claiming to be exhaustive, the *Restatement of the Foreign Relations Law of the United States (Third)* (1987) (paragraph 702) lists a number of practices as prohibited under international customary law, such as genocide, slavery, torture, systematic racial discrimination and consistent patterns of gross violations of international human rights (see also *infra*, Chapter IV; and, generally, Meron, 1989: 79-135). Importantly, there is nowadays wide support for the notion that international human rights obligations in general are so basic that all of the states belonging to the circle to which those obligations apply have a correlative legal interest in their fulfilment by the other states, and may therefore bring, individually or jointly, permissible actions against the breaching state, even though they are not materially affected (see *infra*, Chapter IV; and, generally, Meron, 1989: 188-201; Simma, 1994: 364-376).

The erosion of "domestic jurisdiction", the coexistence of universal and regional systems, a greater attention on the part of the international community to the indivisibility and interdependence of the recognised rights, to developing conventional and extra-conventional special regimes for, among others, vulnerable groups, as well as streamlining or advancing the methods of supervision and implementation, all reflect major accomplishments or tendencies in the modern evolution of human rights protection. On the other hand, serious shortcomings in the whole system are being pointed out. Although most human rights norms already allow states to limit their effectiveness on broadly construed grounds such as protection of public order, national security, public health or morals, etc., a state may nullify or reduce the operation of a human rights treaty norm by entering a reservation to such a norm upon ratification of that treaty. The ever increasing practice of lodging reservations to human rights conventions is putting the system under considerable pressure, raising deep concerns about the quality of such reservations and their permissibility (Simma, 1998). Another critical dimension is that of human rights treaty supervision, in view of present resource and time constraints, backlog in state reporting and delays in processing reports and communications, etc.; this aspect raises the problematic question as to what reforms can and should be adopted with a view to improving human rights treaty compliance (Alston and Crawford, 2000; Bayefsky, 2000).

b. Categories and their relation to beneficiaries and addressees

International human rights are usually divided into three main general categories:

— civil and political rights;
— economic, social and cultural rights; and
— "third generation" rights, such as the right to peace, the right to development and environmental rights.

CPR are deemed to be the core of human rights, the origins of which can be dated back to the American and French revolutions, or even earlier times. Consistent with standard liberal propositions (see *infra*), CPR are typically said to set limits on state power over individuals (vertical dimension) and to be often judicially enforceable. ESCR are seen as "programmatic" rights requiring positive state action (financial assistance or other services). "Third generation" rights are conceptualised as rights of collectivities linked to notions of international solidarity and premised on structural global problems.

On a closer look, these assumptions do not necessarily reflect developments in human rights theory and practice. A cluster of human rights may be invoked in concrete cases from all of the above categories; certain rights as such cover more than one category (for example, property rights), and the same may apply to human rights instruments as a whole: for instance, the EurCtHR has held that "there is no water-tight division" between the sphere of social and economic rights and the field covered by the ECHR (*Airey v. Ireland*, Judgment of 9 October 1979, Series A, No. 32, 15: paragraph 26); CPR often require positive state action (see, for example, the HRC General Comment No. 3 on Article 2 of the ICCPR, UN Doc. CCPR/C/21/Rev. 1), while ESCR are mostly addressed to individuals and generate various obligations which are of immediate effect (see the General Comment No. 3 (1990) of the Committee on Economic, Social and Cultural Rights, established to supervise the ICESCR, Report of the Committee on Economic, Social and Cultural Rights, Fifth Session, UN Doc. E/199/23; E/C.12/1990/8: 83); "third generation" rights are disputed as true human rights *per se* (see *infra*), but at least may be seen as having an important individual dimension (see, for example, the right to development as understood in the Declaration on the Right to Development adopted by the UN General Assembly in 1986, Resolution 41/128), whereas CPR and ESCR embrace, to a greater or lesser extent, a typical group right (namely, the right to self-determination), and rights with a collective (mainly cultural and social) dimension. Yet, an important distinction can be drawn in respect of presently available international implementation procedures. CPR may often be brought before international bodies in the form of complaints, whereas, with very few exceptions (for example, under the Additional Protocol to the European Social Charter Providing for a System of Collective Complaints, adopted by the Committee of Ministers of the Council of Europe in 1995), reporting systems are the only means of supervision applicable to ESCR.

During the cold war, the debate on human rights became part of the East-West confrontational exercise, and mainly developed in terms of CPR versus ESCR, and then even "third generation" rights. Although discussions have continued in different forms, there has been recognition of the notion, hinted at earlier, that internationally recognised human rights are in fact "universal, indivisible and interdependent and interrelated" (Vienna Declaration and Programme of Action, adopted by the UN World Conference on Human Rights, held in Vienna in 1993).

At the same time, the question of group and/or minority rights, on the one hand (see *infra*), and new issues regarding the role of non-state actors as duty-holders, on the other, pose particular challenges to the classical individualistic paradigm of human rights protection, with its concomitant vertical relation to state duties. In the latter respect, the debate within the EU and other international institutions on the human rights components of their policies is particularly significant. Article 6.2 (ex Article F.2 of the TEU) provides that the EU "shall respect fundamental rights", as guaranteed by the ECHR and as they result from the constitutional traditions common to the member states, "as general principles of Community law". The constituent instruments of international institutions normally do not provide for express human rights obligations on the institutions themselves – though the possibility of establishing such obligations is clearly part of present-day discussions.

Another current issue is that of the responsibility of non-governmental domestic actors in armed conflicts or who are otherwise engaged in violent activities such as terrorism. The applicability of international human rights law to such actors is rather problematic (see, for example, Rosas and Scheinin, 1999: 59-60; Koufa, 2001). The human rights obligations of non-state actors are not specifically addressed in international human rights

45

instruments, although these instruments may entail "horizontal" protection (or *Drittwirkung*), by obliging a state to protect individuals from the conduct of private parties (Clapham, 1993; see also the next chapters, *passim,* in respect of specific instruments). However, no action may be taken against the latter before an international body. On the other hand, a classical body of humanitarian law (as distinct from human rights law) norms apply to all parties to a civil war (Buergental, 1995: 255-257 and 262-265), while international law reaches out to the position of individuals who commit well-defined serious human rights-related violations (for example, genocide) by holding them internationally accountable for such violations as amounting to acts of a criminal nature (for the possible characterisation of terrorism as a crime against humanity, see Cassese, 2001: 994-995). This individual criminal responsibility is not based on the breach of obligations binding on individuals as such, but rather reflects specific situations entailing the above international legal consequences. Nevertheless, the possibility of prosecuting individuals for "crimes under international law" (as it is now the case before the international criminal tribunals which have been established in recent years; see *infra*, Chapter IV), can be seen as an advanced scheme compared to the above limited perspective offered by international human rights law.

c. Individual rights and group interests: the case of minority rights

i. Extra-legal justifications of group protection

As noted, the traditional conception of human rights as legal rights of individuals seems also prima facie difficult to reconcile with an active consideration of the position of groups such as minorities. The question is usually addressed from the point of view of individual versus group (or collective) rights. In general terms, protection for minority groups is being currently discussed in relation to the role of multiculturalism in a liberal social context.

As a political theory, liberalism centres on individuals at the level of political, justificatory and contextual theses (see, generally, McDonald, 1992). The most basic liberal political thesis indeed rests on three major propositions:

– individual (mainly civil and political) rights set limits on the actions of others (individuals and the state);

– the state serves as a guarantor of such rights; and

– both the above combine to create a realm of individual choice.

Arguments based on utility (welfare of individuals) and the primacy of free consent provide the main justifications for this approach. The latter, in turn, assumes (but also requires) a wide functional context where an array of choices and opportunities is made available to a critical mass of responsible choosers.

Among contemporary liberal thinkers, the attitude vis-à-vis active consideration of group protection by states varies, ranging from outright hostility to more sympathetic positions. As for the latter, Kymlicka (1995a), for instance, believes that individual freedom is in fact dependent on the presence of a "societal culture" providing a meaningful "context of choice". In other words, access to one's language and culture is central to the effective enjoyment of freedom. Kymlicka offers a set of "group-differentiated rights" (self-government rights, such as forms of autonomy or territorial jurisdiction, polyethnic rights understood as "group-specific measures", and special representation rights, such as proportional representation or guaranteed seats in legislatures), which are intended to accommodate minority groups within an advanced liberal (individualist) framework. In this connection, there is also support for a conception of group rights, according to which rights are held jointly by a set of individuals (namely, minority members), without granting moral and legal standing to the group as such (Jones, 1999). Other liberal thinkers, such as McDonald (1992), go even further in that they suggest that states should protect minorities *qua* groups whether or not they fit the liberal individualist paradigm.

ii. Individual versus group (or collective) rights

Much of the literature in law, philosophy and political science focused on the issue of individual versus group (or collective) rights seeks in fact to address the question of whether it is the individual or the community to be given priority in terms of rights recognition and protection. Thus, it is possible to classify writers (roughly) as "individualists" or "communitarians". Unlike individualists, communitarians emphasise the social dimension of the individual and describe his or her rights and duties on the basis of their relations to other individuals and groups.

In legal terms, group rights are ascribed, by definition, to a group of people and can only be invoked by the group and its authorised agents. Some commentators reject the notion of group rights because, in their view, it would pose a threat to the territorial integrity of states or to individual rights, whereas others accept it on purely empirical grounds (they contend that national and international law have recognised rights of groups such as peoples and minorities). Moreover, a sceptical view about group rights has been submitted, on the ground that the fundamental issue is whether or not there is a means of enforcing such rights and the groups may make use of it. In fact, these positions (see, generally, Spiliopoulou Åkermark, 1997: 42-46) appear flawed in whole or in part (see also *infra*). The right to self-determination is a widely acknowledged group right (see *infra*, Chapter VIII), as is the right to be protected against genocide (see *infra*, Chapter IV), and collective rights are being increasingly recognised to indigenous peoples (on these rights, see *infra*, Chapters V and VIII). Moreover, all such group rights, including a large part of "third generation" rights or "peoples' rights" (see *infra*), do not, or would not, necessarily constitute a threat to territorial integrity or imply their automatic priority over individual rights. In this latter respect, individual human rights can be seen as limiting the exercise of group rights, on the one hand, and often contributing to defining their actual content, on the other (see, for example, the case of the right to development, *supra; infra*, Chapter VIII; and, generally, Rosas and Scheinin, 1999: 55-56). At the same time, one can hardly deny that rights of collectivities as a general category do not fit well, prima facie, into the individualistic and egalitarian human rights framework. In addition, the argument that links groups rights to the existence of concomitant enforcement procedures within which groups have *locus standi,* might be objected on the grounds that group rights might well be established irrespective of specific possibilities of enforcing them (see *supra*).

iii. Minority rights within the corpus of international human rights

Are minority rights individual or collective? Or both? Are minority rights human rights? There is no doubt that minority rights form an integral part of the international protection of human rights. For instance, Article 27 of the ICCPR situates the issue of minorities within a wider context of human rights entitlements. The Framework Convention for the Protection of National Minorities confirms this by explicitly recognising minority rights as a human rights issue (Article 1). And the same notion is reflected in the pre-amble to the 1992 UN declaration and paragraph 30 of the 1990 OSCE Copenhagen Document.

These considerations also reveal that minority rights and human rights are not identical notions. The concept of human rights is something qualitatively different in that the rights of all individuals are placed under international protection. In terms of rights supervision, the league system somewhat reflected such an approach when distinguishing between internal (constitutional) protection for all inhabitants or citizens of the minority states and international "guarantee" for members of minorities only. Human rights means equal enjoyment of basic rights for everybody, whereas minority rights can be described as special rights recognised to the exclusive benefit of minority groups. Yet, minority rights are not privileges. As early as 1935, the PCIJ, in its advisory opinion in the case concerning *Minority Schools in Albania,* held that minority rights represented some of the implications of the concept of substantive equality, as opposed to formal equality (equality in fact as distinct from equality in law). This point is linked to the more general question, discussed in Chapter IV, of so-called "positive" or "reverse" discrimination and the determination of criteria for justifying difference in treatment.

Thus minority rights are also human rights. Basic rights for all combine with special rights designed to protect minorities: they are complementary and mutually reinforcing. But, as has been mentioned, minority rights raise the issue of their individual or collective nature in international law.

Article 27 of the ICCPR epitomises the approach to minority rights under human rights law. Such a provision refers to "persons belonging to" minorities. Some experts (see, for example, Dinstein, 1976) take the generous view, that Article 27 rights are the expression of group rights in international law (see, generally, *supra*). In fact, the context of the ICCPR, as reflected in the other rights recognised therein, its *travaux préparatoires* and the First Optional Protocol (establishing a procedure which allows communications from individuals), substantiate the widely shared argument that Article 27 provides for individual rights, not rights of minorities *qua* groups. Nevertheless, it appears unquestionable that Article 27 is designed to protect a collective interest, since the rights are to be exercised in community with the group members. As recognised by former UN special rapporteur Capotorti, "[it] is the individual as member of a minority group, and not just any individual, who is destined to benefit from the protection granted by Article 27". (Capotorti, 1979: paragraphs 206-210) In sum, Article 27 recognises individual rights premised on the existence of a distinctive community.

Thornberry notes the difficulty of the contemporary international law of minorities to "grapple with the group dimension within the individualistic framework of human rights work" (Thornberry, 1991: 12), and considers the rights in Article 27 as a "hybrid" between individual and group rights because of the community requirement. According to Capotorti:

> it is conceivable that the individuals forming a group may be entitled to treatment, based on advantages to be ensured to each member of the group. At the same time, this approach has significant repercussions on the status of the group as such ... Article 27 does not refer to minority groups as the formal holders of the rights described in it, but rather stresses the need for a collective exercise of such rights. Therefore it seems justified to conclude that a correct construction of this norm must be based on the idea of its double effect-protection of the group and its individual members. (Capotorti, 1990: 353-354.)

The "collective exercise" of individual rights referred to by Capotorti essentially indicates the enjoyment of such rights by individuals who are similarly affected as members of a group which stands as the indirect beneficiary of protection. That captures quite clearly the collective substance of the protection of minority rights as recognised to minority members. The same line of reasoning is also reflected in the pertinent case law of the HRC under the First Optional Protocol to the ICCPR (see *infra,* Chapter V), and confirmed by the 1992 UN declaration, which recognises rights of "persons belonging to minorities", while at the same time providing for a state duty to protect the existence and identity of a minority as a whole (Article 1). The interaction between the recognition of individual rights and the aim of group protection is indeed a constant theme in international instruments on minority rights.

iv. Multiple justifications of minority rights protection in international law

As shown by a recent scholarly work (Spiliopoulou Åkermark, 1997), the protection of minority rights in international law may be usefully discussed within a broad framework of aims and justificatory grounds.

In fact, the concepts of "peace" and "security" are being expanded so as to embrace societal sources of actual or potential conflict. Human rights/minority rights considerations have gained prominence in the new concept, as illustrated by the linkage between respect for human rights and the maintenance of internal and international stability highlighted by former UN Secretary General Boutros Boutros-Ghali in his 1992 report on an agenda for peace (UN Doc. A/47/277-S/24111: paragraph 18), and reaffirmed, for instance, in the Stability Pact in Europe of 1995 (see also *infra,* Chapter X).

Minority provisions reflect an obvious concern for human dignity. Minority rights guarantee individual dignity and well-being in keeping with the very notion of human rights. As noted earlier, Kymlicka strongly argues for rethinking the liberal tradition in order to accommodate minority rights. Thus, the protection of a minority rectifies unchosen inequalities and pre- serves effective individual freedom. Minority provisions as contained in human rights instruments assume human dignity as their most basic justifi- cation.

At the same time, the protection of minority distinctiveness can and should be viewed as having an intrinsic value in international law, along the lines indicated by the PCIJ in *Minority Schools in Albania*. The PCIJ indeed high- lighted that the core of minority rights protection was to ensure for the minority elements suitable means for the preservation of their traditions and characteristics (PCIJ Series A/B, No. 64, 1935: 17). In its 1994 General Comment No. 23 on Article 27 of the ICCPR (general comments are non- legally binding statements issued under Article 40, paragraph 4, of the covenant, with a view to elaborating on the rights and obligations contained in the treaty), the HRC (the supervisory body under the ICCPR) stated that:

> [t]he protection of [the rights in Article 27] is directed to ensure the survival and continued development of the cultural, religious and social identity of the minori- ties concerned, thus enriching the fabric of society as a whole. Accordingly, the Committee observes that these rights must be protected as such and should not be confused with other personal rights conferred on one and all under the Covenant. (General Comment No. 23: paragraph 9.)

In the final analysis, the "right to identity" captures the essence of minority rights within the corpus of international human rights. On the other hand, the said justifications often overlap in such a manner as to influence the approach to minority issues. For instance, the security-oriented dimension to the protection of minority rights prevails in certain contexts (for example, the OSCE), whereas in other contexts (for example, the HRC acting under the complaints procedure established by the First Optional Protocol to the ICCPR) the protection of the human dignity of individuals stands out encompassing the protection of minority members against the "intolerant" groups to which they belong (see, for example, the issues brought up before the HRC in *Sandra Lovelace v. Canada*, Communication No. 24/1977, Views of 30 July 1981, (1981) Annual Report: 166; (1983) Annual Report: 248: see *infra*, Chapters IV and V).

v. Cultural rights and "peoples' rights" in relation to minorities

Minority rights are sometimes described as cultural rights. The protection of minority groups has been considered also within the framework of so-called "peoples' rights". The characterisation of minority rights as cultural rights emphasises the preservation and development of minority cultures as the rationale for the protection of those rights. Stavenhagen refers to "culture" in the anthropological sense of a coherent self-contained system of values and symbols, namely "the sum total of the material and spiritual activities and products of a given social group which distinguishes it from other similar groups" (Stavenhagen, 1995: 66). He advocates a distinctive approach to minorities and indigenous peoples *qua* groups, conceptualising the rights as culture-specific.

In international law cultural rights are normally seen from the perspective of universal individual rights, as in the context of Article 15 of the ICESCR and Article 27 of the UDHR. The right of everyone "to take part in cultural life" (Article 15, paragraph 1, sub-paragraph a, of the ICESCR) or "to participate in the cultural life of the community" (Article 27 of the UDHR) pose, however, broad questions in human rights theory and practice which do not specifically address the complexities of the minority question, though they are of general relevance to minority members as well. Consequently, the identification of minority rights through the category of cultural rights may turn out to be misleading.

The category of "peoples' rights" (Crawford, 1988; Alston, 2001) is even more problematic from the point of view of minority rights. They can be identified with "third generation" rights (such as the right to peace, the right to development and environmental rights) or with a broader multifaceted cluster of rights concerned with the situation of groups and their members. The right to self-determination, minority rights and/or indigenous rights would feature in the latter framework. The notion of "peoples' rights" has been criticised for being vague and difficult to establish as such in positive international law, namely beyond the individual (and often, equally far from uncontroversial) legal existence of the rights indicated as being covered by this notion. Still, at regional level, this overarching category, including (only) "third generation" rights and the right to self-determination, is embodied in the African Charter on Human and *Peoples' Rights* (author's emphasis), the so-called "Banjul Charter", adopted by the member states of the then Organisation of African Unity in 1981 and entered into force in 1986 (on the problematic issue of minorities and indigenous peoples within the African human rights protection system, see Thio, 2002: pp. 445-467). The primary focus of "peoples' rights" is on rights of collectivities *qua* groups; and yet, as already noted, these rights can relate, in one way or another, to existing individual human rights. Minority rights as described earlier are not rights of collectivities, though they reveal a strong collective dimension. Overall, with their emphasis on equality in fact and the protection of cultural identity, minority rights constitute a separate category. Moreover, it has been argued (Donnelly, 1993) that conceptualising minority rights within the wider context of "peoples' rights", or of a stretched notion of "third generation" rights, may risk undermining the specific protection granted to minorities under existing human rights regimes.

Two caveats should, however, be entered. Firstly, minorities must benefit from a "third generation" right or "peoples' right" (assuming its existence in international law) as long as they are part of the collectivity placed under protection. This is the same logic that applies to minority members as regards the enjoyment of individual human rights recognised to everyone. Secondly, minority rights as such can and should constructively interact with the other rights, including the right to self-determination. The relation between self-determination and the position of minorities, including the preliminary question as to whether there exists a specific entitlement to that right for a minority *qua* group, will be discussed in Chapter VIII.

Bibliography

Addis, A., "Individualism, communitarianism, and the rights of ethnic minorities", *Notre Dame Law Review*, 67, 1992, pp. 615-676.

Alston, P. (ed.), "Peoples' rights", *Collected Courses of the Academy of European Law*, Vol. IX-2, Oxford University Press, Oxford, 2001.

Alston, P. and Crawford, J. (eds), *The future of UN human rights treaty monitoring*, Cambridge University Press, Cambridge, 2000.

Alston, P. and Steiner, H. (eds), *International human rights in context: law, politics and morals*, second edition, Oxford University Press, Oxford, 2000.

Bayefsky, A.F. (ed.), *The UN human rights treaty system in the 21st century*, Kluwer Law International, The Hague, 2000.

Brownlie, I., "The rights of peoples in modern international law", in *The rights of peoples*, Crawford, J. (ed.), Clarendon Press, Oxford, 1988, pp. 1-16.

Buergental, T., *International Human Rights*, St. Paul, Minnesota, West Publishing Co., 1995.

Capotorti, F., "Are minorities entitled to collective international rights?", *Israel Yearbook on Human Rights*, 20, 1990, pp. 351-357.

Capotorti, F., "Study on the rights of persons belonging to ethnic, religious and linguistic minorities", UN Doc. E/CN.4/Sub.2/384/Rev.I, 1979.

Cassese, A., "Terrorism is also disrupting some crucial legal categories of international law", *European Journal of International Law*, 12, 2001, pp. 993-1001.

Clapham, A., *Human rights in the private sphere*, Oxford University Press, Oxford, 1993.

Crawford, J., "The rights of peoples: some conclusions", in *The rights of peoples*, Crawford, J. (ed.), Clarendon Press, Oxford, 1988, pp. 159-175.

Dinstein, Y., "Collective human rights of peoples and minorities", *International and Comparative Law Quarterly*, 25, 1976, pp. 102-120.

Donnelly, J., "Third generation rights", in *Peoples and minorities in international law*, Brölmann, C., Lefeber, R. and Zieck, M. (eds), Martinus Nijhoff Publishers, Dordrecht, 1993, pp. 119-150.

Donnelly, J., *Universal human rights in theory and practice*, Cornell University Press, Ithaca and London, 1989.

Drzewicki, K., "Internationalization of human rights and their juridization", in *An introduction to the international protection of human rights: a textbook*, Hanski, R. and Suksi, M. (eds), Åbo Akademi, Åbo, 1999, pp. 25-47.

Eide, A., "Cultural rights as individual human rights", in *Economic, social and cultural rights: a textbook*, Eide, A., Krause, C. and Rosas, A. (eds), Martinus Nijhoff Publishers, Dordrecht, 1995a, pp. 229-240.

Eide, A., "Economic, social and cultural rights as human rights", in *Economic, social and cultural rights: a textbook*, Eide, A., Krause, C. and Rosas, A. (eds), Martinus Nijhoff Publishers, Dordrecht, 1995b, pp. 21-40.

Hohfeld, W.N., *Fundamental legal conceptions as applied in judicial reasoning*, Yale University Press, Yale, 1919.

Jones, P., "Human rights, group rights, and peoples' rights", *Human Rights Quarterly*, 21, 1999, pp. 80-107.

Kamenka, E., "Human rights, peoples' rights" in *The rights of peoples*, Crawford, J. (ed.), Clarendon Press, Oxford, 1988, pp. 127-139.

Kly, Y.N., *Societal development and minority rights*, Clarity Press, Atlanta, 1997.

Koufa, K.K., "Terrorism and human rights", UN Doc. E/CN.4/Sub.2/2001/31 (progress report), 2001, pp. 1-52.

Kymlicka, W., *Multicultural citizenship: a liberal theory of minority rights*, Clarendon Press, Oxford, 1995a.

Kymlicka, W. (ed.), *The rights of minority cultures*, Oxford University Press, Oxford, 1995b.

Lipkin, J., "Can liberalism justify multiculturalism?", *Buffalo Law Review*, 45, 1997, pp. 1-48.

Mannens, W., "The international status of cultural rights for national minorities", in *Minority rights in the "new" Europe*, Cumper, P. and Wheatley, S. (eds), Kluwer Law International, The Hague, 1999, pp. 185-196.

McDonald, M., "Should communities have rights? Reflections on liberal individualism", in *Human rights in cross-cultural perspectives: a quest for consensus*, Ahmed An-Naim, A. (ed.), University of Pennsylvania Press, Philadelphia, 1992, pp. 133-161.

Meron, T., *Human rights and humanitarian norms as customary law*, Oxford University Press, Oxford, 1989.

Nino, C., *The ethics of human rights*, Oxford University Press, Oxford, 1991.

Oestreich, J.E., "Liberal theory and minority group rights", *Human Rights Quarterly*, 21, 1999, pp. 108-132.

Packer, J., "On the content of minority rights", in *Do we need minority rights? Conceptual issues*, Räikkä, J. (ed.), Martinus Nijhoff Publishers, The Hague, 1996, pp. 121-178.

Piechowiak, M., "What are human rights? The concept of human rights and their extra-legal justification", in *An introduction to the international protection of human rights: a textbook*, Hanski, R. and Suksi, M. (eds), Åbo Akademi, Åbo, 1999, pp. 3-14.

Prott, L.V., "Cultural rights as peoples' rights in international law", in *The rights of peoples*, Crawford, J. (ed.), Clarendon Press, Oxford, 1988, pp. 93-106.

Ramcharan, B.G., "Individual, collective and group rights: history, theory, practice and contemporary evolution", *International Journal on Group Rights*, 1, 1993, pp. 27-43.

Rodley, N.S., "Conceptual problems in the protection of minorities: international legal developments", *Human Rights Quarterly*, 17, 1995, pp. 48-71.

Rosas, A. and Scheinin, M., "Categories and beneficiaries of human rights", in *An introduction to the international protection of human rights: a textbook*, Hanski, R. and Suksi, M. (eds), Åbo Akademi, Åbo, 1999, pp. 49-61.

Shelton, D., *Commitment and compliance: the role of non-binding norms in the international legal system*, Oxford University Press, Oxford, 2000.

Simma, B., "Reservations to human rights treaties: some recent developments", in *Liber Amicorum Professor Seidl-Hohenveldern – In honour of his 80th birthday*, Hafner, G., Loibl, G., Rest, A., Sucharipa-Behrmann, L. and Zemanek, K. (eds), Kluwer Law International, The Hague, 1998, pp. 659-682.

Simma, B., "From bilateralism to community interest in international law", *Collected Courses of the Hague Academy of International Law*, VI, 1994, pp. 221-376.

Spiliopoulou Åkermark, A., *Justifications of minority protection in international law*, Kluwer Law International, The Hague, 1997.

Stavenhagen, R., "Cultural rights and universal human rights", in *Economic, social and cultural rights: a textbook*, Eide, A., Krause, C. and Rosas, A. (eds), Martinus Nijhoff Publishers, Dordrecht, 1995, pp. 63-77.

Thio, L., "Battling Balkanisation: regional approaches toward minority protection beyond Europe", *Harvard International Law Journal*, 43, 2002, pp. 403-468.

Thornberry, P., "Images of autonomy and individual and collective rights in international instruments on the rights of minorities", in *Autonomy: applications and implications*, Suksi, M. (ed.), Kluwer Law International, The Hague, 1998, pp. 97-124.

Thornberry, P., *International Law and the rights of minorities*, Clarendon Press, Oxford, 1991.

Thornberry, P., "Is there a phoenix in the ashes? International law and minority rights", *Texas International Law Journal*, 15, 1980, pp. 421-458.

Triggs, G., "The rights of peoples' and individual rights: conflict or harmony?", in *The rights of peoples*, Crawford, J. (ed.),. Clarendon Press, Oxford, 1988, pp. 141-157.

Van Dyke, V., *Human rights, ethnicity, and discrimination*, Greenwood Press, Westport, 1985.

Weston, B., "Human rights", in *International human rights in context: law, politics and morals*, second edition, Alston, P. and Steiner, H. (eds), Oxford University Press, Oxford, 2000, pp. 324-326.

DEFINITION OF "MINORITY" AND DETERMINATION OF AN INDIVIDUAL'S MINORITY MEMBERSHIP

1. Introduction

The discussion of minority rights, and the position of minorities generally, has always triggered wider considerations about the identification of such groups. Indeed, the issue of the definition of the term "minority" has long been debated within scientific and political circles. From the point of view of international law, it has raised two basic questions:

- is there a definition?

- is it possible to determine its scope of application?

As to the first question, some commentators argue that the absence of a clearly formulated definition at the international level (mainly in the form of a provision contained in a "law-making" treaty) amounts to an absence of a legal definition. This is explained by referring to the difficulty to identify common elements which are able to grasp the plurality of existing relevant communities living within states and observing that the existence of, and coherence within, a minority group are basically context-dependent (namely, factual) matters. Often, this view derives from a scepticism towards the need to have a legal definition, which as such leads us to deal with the problematic character of (or some of) the inherent elements or criteria.

On the other hand, the prevailing view is that it is possible to find some elements of the concept of minority endorsed by international law and therefore to determine the scope of application of the respective rules *ratione personae*. This view appears a great deal more convincing as will be shown by the discussions below. Demands for a legal definition had already been made some decades ago. The PCIJ, in its advisory opinion in the case concerning *Interpretation of the Convention between Greece and Bulgaria Respecting Reciprocal Emigration (Greco-Bulgarian Communities)* (PCIJ Series B, No. 17, 1930) (hereinafter the "*Greco-Bulgarian Communities* case"), sought to clarify the concept of "community", defining it (in paragraph 33) as a:

> group of persons living in a given country or locality having a race, religion, language and tradition in a sentiment of solidarity, with a view to preserving their traditions, maintaining their form of worship, ensuring the instruction and upbringing of their children in accordance with the spirit and traditions of their race and mutually assisting one another.

The numerous initiatives which have been taken over the years at different international forums in order to clarify the (essence of the) concept of minority have confirmed the legal significance of the matter. This has also oriented the doctrinal debate, normally centred on the scope of application of the definition. The latter aspect is in fact crucial: the importance of a definition lies at a practical level, in its capacity to delimit the subject matter to be dealt with and at a theoretical level (while, also in this case, with concrete implications), in the fundamental demand for the clarity and foreseeability of law, removing any possible doubts regarding the beneficiaries of minority rights.

2. The scope of application of the definition of minority

a. Early doctrinal views

Earlier academic commentators occasionally offered definitions of the term "minority". In his *National minorities: an international problem*, Claude advocated a purely subjective definition by observing that:

> a national minority exists when a group of people within a state exhibits the conviction that it constitutes a nation, or a part of a nation, which is distinct from the national body to which the majority of the population belongs, or when the majority element of the population feels it possesses a national character in which minority groups do not and perhaps cannot share. (Claude, 1955: 2)

Besides rejecting objective definitional criteria, Claude included the majority's subjective opinion concerning the existence of a (national) minority, thereby failing to make an important distinction between "minorities by force" (namely, groups which want to assimilate but are prevented from doing so by the majority) and "minorities by will" (namely, self-conscious groups which want actively to preserve their own cultural identity).

Laponce, in his book entitled *The protection of minorities,* submitted a definition which combined objective and subjective factors. He described a minority as:

> a group of people who, because of a common racial, linguistic or national heritage which singles them out from the politically dominant cultural group, fear that they may either be prevented from integrating themselves in the national community of their choice or be obliged to do so at the expense of their identity. (Laponce, 1960: 6)

He saw the subjective criterion given by the group's feelings as a parameter for confirming or rebutting the existence of a minority as an assumption based on objective criteria. Moreover, like Claude, he included both "minorities by force" and "minorities by will" in the definition.

Other earlier scholars, such as Macartney (1934) and Modeen (1969), discussed the concept of national minorities. Just as Laponce, they combined objective and subjective definitional criteria. However, unlike Macartney, Modeen disregarded racial and religious differences as relevant elements. He defined a national minority as "a population which through some external quality – chiefly linguistic or cultural – or on grounds of national sentiment may be distinguished from others independent of formal citizenship" (Modeen, 1969: 122). This minority was further described as a "non-dominant group which wishes to preserve its distinct national characteristics"

(Modeen, 1969: 15): the notion was thus limited in scope, and confined to a "minority by will".

b. The options

From the point of view of clarifying the contemporary international legal concept of "minority", there are essentially two options which are to be considered:

— the first option aims at pointing out the special features of the minority group, such as the stability of its relationship with the state in which it lives within the framework of broadly and clearly stipulated rights and obligations;

— the second option, based on a broad and dynamic approach to group protection in modern societies, accommodates the needs of a variety of groups with different kinds of links with the state.

c. The traditional position

The first option embraces the main international efforts to identify and clarify the essential elements of a minority definition. The first clarification of the concept of minority delivered by the UN Sub-Commission on Prevention of Discrimination and Protection of Minorities in 1950, on the basis of a Memorandum prepared by the Secretary General on the Definition and Classification of Minorities (1949), underlined:

— the stable ethnic, religious or linguistic peculiarities of the groups, as to make them "markedly different" from the rest of the population;

— their non-dominant position as national groups or sub-groups;

— the demand to preserve their own cultural identity; and

— their "loyalty" to the state in which they live and whose members are citizens of that state.

A formally binding definition was never agreed upon, but the conviction that "minority protection is only possible if the notion of minority is clarified" (Ermacora, 1983: 271) remained. Subsequently the issue was dealt with in the same context in two important studies: the first one conducted by Francesco Capotorti (as special rapporteur), concerning the various legal aspects of the minority question; the second one, entrusted to Julius Deschênes, aimed at a further clarification of the concept of minority. According to the definition provided by Capotorti in 1978 (with regard to Article 27 of the ICCPR), the term "minority" refers to:

> a group numerically inferior to the rest of the population of a State, in a non-dominant position, whose members – being nationals of the State – possess ethnic, religious or linguistic characteristics differing from those of the rest of the population and show, if only implicitly, a sense of solidarity, directed towards preserving their cultures, traditions, religion or language. (Capotorti, 1979: paragraph 568).

Objective elements (numerical size, non-dominant position, ethno-cultural distinctive characters, citizenship) are connected with a subjective element (sense of solidarity directed towards preserving one's own cultural identity).

The former express the "visibility" and peculiarity of the group (compared to the rest of the population), as well as its stable ties to the state. The latter concerns the group's active awareness of its own identity independent of any previous "recognition" by the state. The existence of the group is, in turn, premised on individual, freely chosen membership ("a group ... whose members ... show ...", etc.).

The definition suggested by Deschênes in 1985 does not introduce true elements of novelty. A "minority" is:

> [a] group of citizens of a State, constituting a numerical minority and in a non-dominant position in that State, endowed with ethnic, religious or linguistic characteristics which differ from those of the majority of the population, having a sense of solidarity with one another, motivated, if only implicitly, by a collective will to survive and whose aim is to achieve equality with the majority in fact and in law. (UN Doc. E/CN.4/Sub.2/1985/31, paragraph 181)

The element of firm ties of the group to the state is confirmed. The aspect of majority-minority relationship is emphasised by recognising the wish of the minority "to survive" as a group maintaining a specific and different identity, in addition to enjoying equality "in fact and in law".

Such initiatives, in view of the important context in which they have been taken and discussed (especially considering the active involvement of states during the *travaux*), highlight their significance in identifying the basic elements of the definitions that would be embraced by international law. This is confirmed by subsequent practice, mainly at the European level. A number of instruments have been adopted and/or proposed within the Council of Europe and OSCE which evidence continuity of the present approach. The prevailing use of the expression "national minority" provides strong proof to that effect. It appears in Article 14 of the ECHR which, however, does not clarify its meaning. In other texts, the (explicit or implicit) concept of national minority essentially designates "historical" minority groups, namely groups which have long acquired a permanent status within a state and whose members are citizens, and desire to preserve their ethno-cultural traits that make them markedly different from the rest of the population: see, for example, Article 2, paragraph 1, of the Proposal for a European Convention for the Protection of Minorities, adopted on 8 February 1991 by the Venice Commission of the Council of Europe; Article 1 of the draft additional protocol on the rights of minorities to the ECHR, adopted by the Parliamentary Assembly of the Council of Europe in 1993 by Recommendation 1201; Article 1 of the European Charter for Regional or Minority Languages of 1992; the Copenhagen Concluding Document on the Human Dimension adopted in 1990 by the (then) CSCE; and important bilateral and multilateral instruments adopted at a sub-regional level (Pentassuglia, 2000 and *infra*, Chapter XII).

Though occasionally showing slight differences, the definitions elaborated reflect the core conviction that the term "minority" means a group historically rooted in the territory of a state and whose specific ethno-cultural features (with the respective claims of protection) markedly distinguish it from the rest of the population of the state. The effect is also to "orient" the permanent social and political links of its members with the state as manifested by citizenship. The main implication of the reasoning about the institutionalised ties of the group and its members is that some categories are not covered by the definition of minority, notably foreigners, migrant workers, refugees. One of the main concerns is to look at minority regimes from the point of view of internal and international stability. According to the prevailing view, the above core understanding is part of traditional international law, which delimits the legal scope of the term "minority".

d. A new definition of minority? Critical appraisal

Nevertheless, views for adopting a broader concept of minority have recently emerged, raising the issue of whether today a new and more "liberal" concept of this term has actually been embraced by international law. Such views range from supporting the conceptualisation of "minority" as any "group of people who freely associate for an established purpose where their shared desire differs from that expressed by the majority rule" (Packer, 1995: 45), to advocating expansive interpretations of the scope of application of Article 27 of the ICCPR and other specific international instruments (basically, the 1992 UN Declaration on Minorities and the Framework Convention for the Protection of National Minorities). In fact, most of those who support the broad view concede that the distinctive ethno-cultural features of the group must be seen as a crucial assumption underlying the whole system of minority rights protection. The following discusses the key aspects of this perspective.

The broad view fundamentally differs from the one described above by abandoning the requirement of citizenship and easing the necessity of a long stay on the territory of the state. This rests, as noted, on a more dynamic understanding of the minority phenomenon so as to cover categories traditionally excluded, such as foreigners and migrant workers. The demand to protect the cultural identity of (members) of all "minority" groups becomes the primary concern. The HRC has confirmed this approach in the cited General Comment No. 23 on Article 27. A major point made by the HRC is that Article 27 also applies to non-citizens, irrespective of any particular degree of permanency on the state territory (thereby including "migrant workers or even visitors": paragraph 5, sub-paragraph 2). The same, or a comparable, view is reflected in some "concluding comments" issued by the HRC under the covenant's reporting procedure (Article 40) (see, for example, those on Slovenia, UN Doc. CCPR/C/79/Add. 40).

The broad view does not appear entirely persuasive (see in more detail, Pentassuglia, 2000). As regards the interpretation of Article 27 of the ICCPR (but also outside this specific interpretative context), two fundamental aspects have to be considered:

– citizenship; and

– all degree of permanency on the territory of the state of residence.

The broad doctrine insists essentially on the textual interpretation of the terms used ("persons" instead of "citizens") and on the scope of the covenant, which is that of protecting individuals. But implicit in the formulation of the provision in Article 27 is the idea of minority generally accepted since the very beginning of the normative work on international minority rights, namely the Capotorti-type minority. In fact, that was the notion underlying the minorities treaties entered into after the first world war (see, for example, Claude, 1955:17). The Capotorti report was approved by the UN Commission on Human Rights in 1978, that is to say twelve years after the adoption of the ICCPR and two years after its entry into force; the definition contained therein, guided by previously delivered comments by UN member states, was perceived of as the lowest common denominator. Later developments (as it will be partly confirmed by the discussion below) have not really changed this understanding. Thus, the textual argument may be rejected by using it against itself, on the basis of the criterion of "ordinary meaning" in the sense of Article 31 of the 1969 Vienna Convention on the Law of Treaties.

This is reinforced by the fact that the formula used in Article 27 has been endorsed in other international texts, though there is little doubt that within the latter contexts (notably at the European level) by "persons belonging to minorities" is meant, *inter alia*, citizens of the state. In sum, the above formula serves as a linguistic convention. Besides, this approach under the covenant is consistent with the way of interpreting important and interrelated provisions such as those in Article 1, where, it is usually conceded, the "ordinary meaning" of the expression "all peoples" is subject to conceptual qualification (which results, *inter alia*, in excluding minority groups among the holders of the right to self-determination; see, generally, *infra*, Chapter VIII). By contrast, in interpreting the expression "persons belonging ...", etc., in Article 27, the broad view makes the criterion of "ordinary meaning", in relation to the prevailing international legal understanding, be without any significance.

Further justification for a restrictive interpretation of the scope of application of Article 27, *ratione personæ*, can be found through establishing the real intention of states parties (basically, in the sense of Articles 31, paragraph 4, and Article 32 of the cited Vienna convention). Latin American countries, together with Australia and the United States, made it clear that the reach of the provision should be limited to well-defined and long-established groups, while the "old" world was basically against the creation of new minorities. In fact, the prevailing opinion during the *travaux* was that foreigners, including stateless persons and migrant workers, did not fall within the scope of Article 27, confirming what may be plausibly contended on the basis of the "persons belonging" formula alone (Pentassuglia, 2000: 23-24). Although subsequent practice of states parties is relevant to interpreting the ICCPR, under Article 31, paragraph 3, of the Vienna convention, such a practice seems far from reflecting a different widely shared understanding. For instance, in its third periodic report submitted to the HRC under Article 40 of the ICCPR, Italy made it clear that "under a generally accepted legal principle, immigrant workers were not considered as minorities" (UN Doc. CCPR/C/SR.1330: paragraph 6); along the same lines, Germany, in its fourth periodic report, reaffirmed the traditional understanding of "minority" as confined to traditional groups (UN Doc. CCPR/C/84/Add. 5: paragraphs 242-245); other countries have reported on their laws excluding non-citizens from the benefit of minority rights (see, for example, the HRC's concluding comments on Senegal, Slovenia, Lybian Arab Jamahiriya and Austria, UN Doc. CCPR/C/79/Add. 5, 40, 101 and 103). Some such positions may prove unduly restrictive (see *infra*); nevertheless, they manifestly reveal no consensus on the extension of Article 27 rights to non-citizens. It is interesting to note that, the HRC's concluding comments mentioned above, though often critical, do not find a breach of this article because of a failure to adopt the broad concept.

Another argument supporting the application of Article 27 to non-citizens draws attention to the expression used in Article 2, paragraph 1, of the ICCPR to the effect that each State Party is obliged to respect and ensure the rights recognised therein to "all individuals within its territory and subject to its jurisdiction". And yet, Article 2 only sets out fundamental objectives and means of realisation. It does not deal with the question of the personal scope of application of a single norm. Here the possibility remains (exceptionally) to restrict or qualify the group of individuals who are the beneficiaries of protection, as in Article 25 and other articles (Pentassuglia, 2000: 25; see, for example, also the HRC General Comment No. 18 on non-discrimination: paragraph 8). Article 2, paragraph 1, mentions in general "the rights recognised in the present covenant" when providing that each State Party undertakes to secure those rights to "all individuals within its territory and subject to its jurisdiction". The ICCPR provides a set of guarantees from which individuals may profit: while providing for criteria of general value in their context, Article 2, paragraph 1, is not a *sine qua non* for the other articles; on the contrary, it presupposes their applicability.

There are two reasons for dismissing the specific proposition of the HRC, that Article 27 also applies to (foreign) non-permanent residents and short-term "visitors". Firstly, as recalled by Germany in its above-mentioned fourth periodic report under the covenant's reporting procedure, the word "exist" was clarified by the Third Committee of the General Assembly, particularly in response to the point firmly made by Latin American countries that immigrant groups were not minorities for the purposes of this provision (see also *infra*, Chapter V):

> It was agreed that the article should cover only separate or distinct groups, well-defined and long-established on the territory of a State ... [and] should not be applied in such a manner as to encourage the creation of new minorities or to obstruct the process of assimilation. (UN Doc. A/2929, paragraphs 184 and 186)

Secondly, the requirement of citizenship should be valued in connection with close ties to the territory (see, for example, Article 3 of the Polish Minorities Treaty of 1919; Article 1, paragraphs a and b, of the Parliamentary Assembly's 1993 proposed protocol to the ECHR; and paragraph 31 of the explanatory report regarding the 1992 European Charter); it is no coincidence that the citizenship legislation of states "makes general use of ... membership of ethnic groups associated with the state territory, as connecting facto[r]" (Brownlie, 1998: 412). The HRC itself indirectly acknowledges this aspect. It indeed links the circumstance of non-permanent or even occasional residence to the absence of citizenship. Arguably, this confirms that, also for the HRC, the criterion of citizenship cannot be really dissociated from that of a long-established presence on the territory. And yet, by pointing out that "it is not relevant to determine the degree of permanence that the term 'exist' connotes" (HRC General Comment No. 23: paragraph 5, subparagraph 2), the HRC does not provide justifications for equating the "long-established permanency-citizenship" scheme with the "non-permanent or occasional residence-non-citizenship" scheme. In a sense, the HRC goes even beyond most of the commentators who join the broad view, who in effect view "new" groups in the light of progressively establishing permanent ties with the country of residence.

In its General Comment No. 24 on reservations (paragraph 8), the HRC includes the ICCPR minority provision among those which, in its opinion, reflect customary rules of international law. Still, the reference to non-permanent residents and visitors as beneficiaries of Article 27 may lead to jeopardising, rather than reinforcing, the credibility of the provision as an expression of a generally binding minimum standard.

It is difficult to find arguments in other contexts supporting a broader concept of minority. The report by Eide on possible ways and means of facilitating the peaceful and constructive solution of problems involving minorities embraces a flexible notion (including non-citizens and/or recent immigrants) as a practical tool for addressing issues of non-dominant groups, but it is not intended as a legal definition (Eide, 1993: paragraphs 27, 29, 41-42). Eide presented a working paper at the second session of the UN Working Group on Minorities which, as recorded in the respective general report, stressed the complexities of the definitional question and reflected awareness of still existing restrictions in international law (UN Doc. E/CN.4/Sub.2/1996/28: paragraph 155). The draft definitions submitted by a member of the working group were basically in line with already elaborated definitions within the UN, leaving little room for extending the concept. In a revised draft, the requirement of citizenship was used, providing that nothing would prevent the view that a minority is only a group of persons who share traditional features and "who are citizens of the state in question" (UN Doc. E/CN.4/Sub.2/1996/2: paragraph 88). Given the difficulties attached to the matter, the working group seems to be turning to a flexible and "open" approach to group protection, irrespective of what kind (or level) of protection is to be considered from a strictly legal standpoint.

The 1992 UN declaration raises the question of the adjective "national" in connection with the adjective "ethnic" in the title: nationality is not linked to citizenship, thus the notion of minority presupposed by the declaration seems to be broader than the traditional one. In fact, the term "national" has been mostly avoided within the UN context. This term has indeed been seen as susceptible to being included in the term "ethnic" as it alludes to a group's particular conviction that it constitutes a nation or part of a nation (Pentassuglia, 2000: 32). Thus, no wonder that the UN declaration seems to resort to those terms in a way that presupposes their convergence. But the concept of "ethnic (including national), religious or linguistic" minority has traditionally coincided with the notion of "national minority" at the European level. Helgesen aptly notes that:

> the concept 'national' in the Helsinki Final Act [*infra*, Chapter VII] corresponds to the opening words of Article 27 ('in those States in which ethnic, religious or linguistic minorities exist'). According to established interpretation, these words exclude newly settled groups on the territory from the protection under Article 27. (Helgesen, 1992: 163-164.)

Based on this correlation, there is good reason to believe that, in the context of the UN, the "ordinary meaning" of the term "national" is to be found essentially in the element of "ethnicity", without altering, however, the traditional perception of what constitutes a minority. In other words, we witness different uses of terms and not different meanings.

On the other hand, the following should be noticed (see in more detail, Pentassuglia, 2000: 31-36): no consensus emerged in favour of the broad view during the *travaux*; quite the contrary, some states, such as Germany, confirmed the traditional understanding, which was also referred to at a juncture of the specific drafting stage; far from revealing a new approach, the absence of an explicit definition invites the interpreter to refer back to the "classical" notion of minority, as it has come to be applied to Article 27, which also lacks an explicit definition; the preamble of the declaration emphasises the contribution of the text to the political and social stability of the states where minorities live, while its core provisions (namely, Articles 1, 2, 4 and 8) largely meet the needs of long-established groups; and UN member states predominantly report on, or highlight, the situation of minorities as traditionally understood, not "new" groups. Certainly, nothing precludes a state from extending, *uti singulus,* the scope of application of the declaration *ratione personæ*, but the development of a general broad concept under this instrument appears unlikely.

As for the Framework Convention for the Protection of National Minorities (see in more detail, Pentassuglia 2000: 36-42), its Explanatory Memorandum states that 'there was no consensus on the interpretation of the term "national minorities"' (paragraph 4). Yet, the debated interpretative options concerning the term 'national', highlighting, respectively, the elements of citizenship or nationality in the ethnic sense (Benoît-Rohmer 1995: 579-581), do not really conflict with the traditional widely supported notion of minority at the European level. At the same time, the reluctance shown by certain states (e.g. France, Turkey, Bulgaria, and Greece) to recognise the existence of minorities on their territory does not prejudice the question of knowing what the minimum requirements for establishing the existence of a minority are. The advisory committee established pursuant to the Framework Convention's implementation machinery (see *infra*, chapter X), relies on the flexible nature of the Framework Convention to defend an article-by-article approach. As explained in one of its recent opinions:

> In the Advisory Committee's opinion, the Framework Convention is not an instrument which operates on an 'all-or-nothing' basis. Even if a group is covered by the

Framework Convention, it does not necessarily follow that all of the Convention's articles apply to the persons belonging to that minority. Similarly, if a minority is not covered by the majority of the provisions in the Framework Convention, that does not necessarily mean that none of the provisions is relevant to the members of that group. The Advisory Committee believes that a nuanced, article-by-article approach to the 'definition' question is not only fully in line with the text of the Framework Convention but is actually dictated by it. This flexibility in the implementation of the Framework Convention could be made more difficult by including a definition in a legally binding European instrument" [i.e. a minority rights protocol to the ECHR as put forward by the Parliamentary Assembly, see *infra*, chapter VI] (paragraph 17 of the Opinion of the Advisory Committee on the Framework Convention for the Protection of National Minorities adopted on 14 September 2001 on Parliamentary Assembly Recommendation 1492 (2001) on the rights of national minorities).

This line of reasoning appears correct as far as the degrees of protection offered by the Framework Convention are concerned, but begs the question as to what is a national minority with regard to any particular level of treatment applicable in this context. In other words, the substantive protection may well vary depending on the article, but it is by no means certain that this should result in multiple understandings of "national minorities" referred to in the title of the treaty. The variations *ratione materiæ* should not be taken out of context, as if the respective provisions were disconnected from one another *ratione personæ*. For instance, Article 6 deals with inter-cultural dialogue "among all the persons living on the territory"; the undisputed fact that, because of the very nature of the matter, it benefits the whole population should not be a good reason to disregard the fundamental object and purpose of the Convention as a whole, which is to protect national minorities. The same applies to other provisions which are essentially taken from general human rights instruments (e.g. Articles 4, 7 and 8; for an overview of the Convention, see *supra*, ch. VI): while general in scope *ratione materiae*, their function should nevertheless be related to the specific purposes of the Convention *rationæ personæ*. The Committee of Ministers, in its capacity as the supervisory body entrusted with final responsibility in the monitoring of the Framework Convention (see *infra*, ch. X), has not directly addressed the Advisory Committee's approach to the definition. Rather, it has so far generically recommended the States concerned "to take appropriate account" of the "various comments" in the Advisory Committee's opinions, and in some cases (see e.g. paragraph 1 of Resolution CMN (2001) 2 regarding Denmark) it has indicated that the issue of the personal scope of application of the Framework Convention "merits further consideration" by the State party with the people concerned, or has referred without additional explanation to "potential for application of a number of provisions of the [Framework Convention], albeit rather limited" vis-à-vis parties which have declared that there are no national minorities in the sense of the Framework Convention within their own territory (see paragraph 1 of Resolutions CMN (2001) 6, CMN (2001), 7, and CMN (2001) 8, concerning respectively Liechtenstein, Malta and San Marino).

At the same time, the following elements further suggest that the Framework Convention, viewed in the context of other Council of Europe, OSCE, and specific bilateral and multilateral instruments (*loc. cit*), is certainly applicable to those groups which meet the traditionally shared concept (or "ordinary meaning") of national minority:

- the language of the Convention follows an established terminological tradition which refers to the ethnic, linguistic, etc. identity of persons belonging to (national) minorities (see *supra, mutatis mutandis,* the considerations regarding the formulation of Article 27 of the ICCPR and other relevant instruments);

- the lack of any particular definition (i.e. clarification) of "national minority", which already justifies reliance on the traditional notion (Pentassuglia 2000: 39), is coupled with considerations in the Explanatory Memorandum, at paragraphs 26 (excluding extension to the Framework Convention of "any definition of a national minority" which *may* be contained in UN texts) and 43 (emphasising the absence of an automatic link between ethno-cultural differences and the creation of national minorities), which seemingly indicate a restrictive approach; the reference to the UN texts is particularly significant, given the above-mentioned debate about a broad concept of minority under such texts (see also *infra* the comments by Finland);

- despite the flexibility of the Convention, there is no proof for the existence of a general acceptance of a broad notion, while it is unproblematic to establish wide state support for the core criteria attached to the classical concept as the lowest common denominator;

- the content of the provisions which are most genuinely connected to the essential purposes of the protection of minority rights are typically premised on the existence of long-established groups (see e.g. Articles 10 to 14, 15, 18 and 21);

- the 1993 Vienna Summit Declaration of the Heads of State and Government of the member states of the Council of Europe, which endorsed the drafting of the Convention, refers to the need for protecting the national minorities created by the "upheavals of history" (Appendix II), which is also recalled in the fifth preambular paragraph of the Convention; and

- the "interpretative declarations" (as distinct from "reservations"), formulated by various states parties upon signature and/or ratification, directly or indirectly describe the concept of minority in conformity with the traditional understanding (quite a different legal question is whether a 'declaration' in fact results in denying minority status to specific groups which in general qualify for protection under the Convention, and may be viewed as an objectionable reservation under the Vienna Convention's object and purpose test in Article 19, sub-paragraph (c); see also below).

In the final analysis, it is submitted that at this stage, from a strictly legal point of view, the Framework Convention, as in the case of the 1992 UN Declaration, only does not prejudice a *liberty* for a state party to extend the guarantees of the convention to individuals other than those who comprise traditional groups which have normally been considered national minorities. The flexible position taken by some states parties seems prima facie to reflect this approach (e.g. the United Kingdom has adopted a relatively wide notion of "ethnic minorities" based on its anti-discrimination legislation; see also Pentassuglia 2000: 42), obviously with no effect on the views of the other states, whether or not parties to the convention. This is consistent with Article 22 which contains a "principe de faveur" vis-à-vis higher degrees of protection afforded by a state party under its national legislation or other treaty regimes, which may thus not be limited or derogated on the basis of this treaty itself (see also, *mutatis mutandis*, Article 8.1 of the UN Declaration). At the same time, the convention does not preclude a future broader concept where states parties, irrespective of making recourse to such permissible individual solutions, agree, by means of subsequent practice (consistent with standard international law methodology of treaty interpretation, notably pursuant to Article 31.3 of the Vienna Convention on the Law of Treaties), to establish a *specific duty* to conform to such a concept, and therefore to apply the treaty provisions to a wider number of groups. In this respect, the article-by-article approach to the matter, in conjunction with Article 3, taken by the Advisory Committee might well lead to a consistent pattern of state practice involving a systematic reassessment of the notion of "national minority" under this treaty. However, one should wonder how likely this is to happen. Indeed, it should be noted that, for instance, Finland, in its comments on the Opinion delivered by the Advisory Committee regarding the report submitted by this country (the Finnish report and comments on the Advisory Committee's Opinion as well as those prepared by the other states parties, notably in relation to Article 3, are now available on the Council of Europe's website, http://www.humanrights.coe.int/Minorities/), firmly emphasises that when the Framework Convention was prepared and agreed upon, "the purpose was to only cover such minority groups as are deeply rooted in and have strong ties with their country of residence", thereby excluding "recent" groups. In addition, it recalls its decision not to take an exclusive position as to the minorities to be protected in Finland and therefore not to provide an explicit list of minorities upon signature or ratification of the treaty, while mentioning the Government Bill for the acceptance of the Framework Convention which does provide a list of traditional groups, in line with the groups mentioned by this country in other reports submitted pursuant to UN human rights treaties; it goes on to say:

> In this context it must be remembered that minorities do in fact emerge, and the right to self-identification is important for persons constituting a minority. However, the question of whether there are such persons within the territory of a given State to which the Framework Convention is applicable, could also be discussed within the monitoring mechanism of the Convention. The UN definition is wider than the one adopted in Europe, encompassing also so-called new minorities.

The Advisory Committee is pointing out, in connection with Article 3, that it intends "to examine the personal scope given to the implementation of the Framework Convention in order to verify that no arbitrary or unjustified distinctions have been made" (see e.g. the Committee's Opinion on Finland of 22 September 2000: para. 13). For instance, the Advisory Committee has expressed concern at the fact that persons belonging to groups with long historic ties to Denmark other than the German minority in South Jutland, such as Faroese persons and Greenlanders, seem to have been excluded a priori from protection under the Convention (Committee's Opinion on Denmark of 22 September 2000).

e. Concluding observations on the definitional question

What conclusions, therefore, can be drawn thus far? Certainly, the definition of minority, in spite of efforts to play it down, remains a tool for determining the concrete bearing of obligations undertaken by states and achieving clarity and certainty in the regime of minority rights. The existence of a minority as a matter of "fact" and not of "law" (which has been acknowledged at least since the *Greco-Bulgarian Communities* case before the PCIJ: PCIJ Series B, No. 17, 1930: 19, 21-22, 33), does not exclude the need for establishing the legal implications of "minority". To the contrary, the "fact" (or "context") calls for (or presupposes) criteria for it to be "observed". The importance of legal parameters can be illustrated by the question whether individuals belonging to the majority population of the state qualify for minority status where they are in the minority within a region. Does the existence of such individuals give rise to a "fact" relevant to international minority rights law? The notion of a minority at sub-state level has been dismissed by the HRC in its case-law (see *infra*, chapters IV and V), though some positive views have been expressed recently (see the Opinion on Possible Groups of Persons to Which the Framework Convention for the Protection of National Minorities Could Be Applied in Belgium, adopted by the Venice Commission in March 2002, CDL-AD (2002) 1; it should be noted that the Commission states in the introduction that "the conclusions reached in the present document only pertain to Belgium", CDL-AD (2002) 1; in its general part, it refers, *inter alia,* to the favourable position taken by the Advisory Committee on the possible applicability of the Framework Convention for the benefit of the Finnish-speaking population living in the Finnish province of Åland; but see the opposite view reflected in the Finnish comments under the Framework Convention's reporting procedure, *loc. cit,* and *infra,* chapter XI; Recommendation 1201 (1993) of the Parliamentary Assembly of the Council of Europe endorses this notion in Article 1 sub-paragraph d in conjunction with Article 13, although its Explanatory Report refers to objective features for distinguishing a national minority "from the rest of the population", Assembly Doc. 6742 of 19 February 1993, Report of the Committee on Legal Affairs and Human Rights). In effect, a standard assumption has been that majorities do not become "minorities" where they are numerically inferior within a region, just as minorities in a state do not lose their minority status where they constitute numerical majorities within a particular area of that state. Indeed, "oppressed majorities" have been normally said to be entitled only to general human rights protection without any discrimination (for a similar proposition, see e.g. the Declaration and Programme of Action adopted in September 2001 by the UN World Conference against Racism, Racial Discrimination, Xenophobia and Related Intolerance: para. 48 of the Programme of Action).

The irrelevance of state "recognition" under international law (so aptly made clear already by the PCIJ in the above-mentioned *Greco-Bulgarian Communities* case) advances matters but does not tell us what minorities are for legal purposes. It is evident that "self-definition" is not a decisive or absolute criterion (see also *infra*): there indeed appears to be agreement that minority status may not be enjoyed on the basis of purely subjective feelings or perceptions by any group concerned. Thus we get back to the general issue of conceptualising "minority" based on a proper combination of subjective and objective components.

The approach one might call "minimalist" aimed at the concretisation of a widely accepted and sufficiently precise minimum standard as a way of achieving adequate and effective substantive protection, as well as meeting particular concerns for stability, has in recent years been supervened by a broader approach including groups traditionally falling outside the international legal understanding of 'minority'. It pays particular attention to recent forms of transboundary movements of populations, mainly due to socio-economic reasons (as in the case of migratory fluxes from areas in economic distress) or purely political reasons (as in the case of refugees, when economic motives do not prevail). In addition, the ending of the cold war has brought to light the plight of particular population groups affected by changes in territorial sovereignty or discriminatory practices. These new phenomena have induced an expansive approach to the question of "minorities", which seeks to overcome the approach of the past and conceives the minority rights regime as aimed at meeting the particular needs of an increasing number of disadvantaged groups.

In spite of this, there are in fact no decisive arguments (at least not for the time being) supporting the extension of the concept of minority as historically embraced by international law. The dividing line goes between two radically different positions on the issue of defining a minority: the first one shies away from a definition or seeks to delimit its significance in order to make it easier for states to deny the existence of a minority on their own territory and thus eschew the obligations or commitments generated from the respective regime of protection. Upon a closer look, this approach does not necessarily result in rejecting the traditional defining criteria. In fact, the goal is sometimes pursued to restrict their content or practical impact within the state, in line with domestic standards and/or practices.

For instance, France (one of the countries which is most reluctant to implement minority rights protection), during the drafting of the 1992 UN Declaration, strove to restrict the focus to regional groups by referring to the traditional conceptual parameters of Article 27 of the Covenant. Apart from the particular case of France, some states indeed show reluctance to provide adequate protection to old groups which are not identifiable with a specific geographical area within the territory of the state (dispersed minorities) compared with those groups which are (territorial minorities). Moreover, a number of countries (e.g. in eastern Europe) pursue similar (further) restrictive purposes by *de jure* or *de facto* classifying well-established minority groups differently ("nations", "nationalities", "national minorities", "ethnic groups", etc.), for differentiating their treatment according to their own policy views. Hence, such an approach arguably comprises the possibility of excluding *certain* minorities from protection as a result of an individual application of the above criteria, that is to say, as a consequence of an extremely wide discretion leading to *selecting* among *traditional* groups.

The second approach is in favour of extending the concept to a variety of non-dominant groups, in the way described earlier. Neither position enjoys any substantial support. The Capotorti definition (and its progeny) may not be perfect (words, especially those used for legal purposes, are almost never self-contained; see e.g. *infra*, chapter X), but at least reflects a basic convergence of views historically consolidated. It is hard to believe that any change in the general outlook has actually occurred. The absence of a "law-making" treaty codifying an *opinio iuris* on the matter does not preclude the possibility of establishing a basic meaning of "minority" under general international law, based on the relevant "hard" and "soft" law sources running throughout the history of the international protection of minorities (on the general aspect of the role of "hard" and "soft" law in the process of interpretation, see Riedel 1991). The concept of people, in connection with the right to self-determination, is not clarified in any relevant international instrument, yet there exists a core understanding under general international law (see e.g. Thornberry 1989). That does not freeze the concept or self-determination itself, but rather identifies the minimum implications which are unquestionably attached to this term (see *infra*, chapter VIII). As for the concept of minority, a similar pattern may be discerned. The lack of a universal consensus on the Capotorti definition and the ongoing discussion of additional dimensions to the traditional understanding of 'minority' do not prejudice the existence of a general consensus on its core meaning, not as a purely abstract notion singled out for its own sake, but as a concrete fundamental *legal* threshold that all states must meet without any unreasonable distinctions. A certain inevitable margin of action enjoyed by states in identifying the groups to be protected at the domestic level must therefore be exercised in accordance with general principles of international law.

On the other hand, such a core meaning should be interpreted, where appropriate, with a degree of flexibility. For instance, Special Rapporteur Capotorti indicated that when there was no clear majority population in the country, but only various population groups in a non-dominant position willing to preserve their identity, then all such groups should be considered as minorities entitled to international protection. At the same time, he recalled the widely shared view that, although the group as such has to be, *inter alia,* numerically inferior to the rest of the population to enjoy minority status, a specific numerical threshold to identify a minority should be avoided, thereby allowing for pragmatic considerations in this respect, also in connection with the determination of reasonable modalities of substantive protection. In addition, the Capotorti definition importantly includes the notion of "implicit" will to preserve minority identity, so as not to make the subjective requirement too demanding, especially in relation to minorities living under undemocratic regimes.

As a matter of fact, international law provides different responses to the protection of different categories of individuals and/or groups. Both the protection of foreigners, and more specifically, of migrant workers and refugees, rest on premises different from those applying to minorities. The international legal protection of the latter is animated by concerns for maintaining cultural identity rather than for safeguarding equality and non-discrimination, which is simply a starting point for a protective regime (see *infra*, chapter IV). By contrast, when it comes to the international legal protection of the former groups, socio-economic and/or political aspects determine why the prohibition and prevention of discrimination, rather than the safeguarding of cultural identity as such, is the main concern.

This also explains the existence of specific conventions, resolutions, etc., for such groups. These instruments provide minimum (mainly social and economic) guarantees against discrimination. Respect for general cultural rights of "new" groups (e.g. under Article 31 of the 1990 UN Convention on the Protection of the Rights of all Migrant Workers and Members of their Families) only serves as one of the logical implications of this broad approach. Minority rights go beyond such a vision in that they recognise the objective existence of groups whose members need clearly established guarantees because of their ethno-cultural, territorial and personal situation (see *supra*, chapter II, and *infra*, ch. IV).

But might a "new" group become a minority? Yes, it might. Still, this is subject to assessment in the very long term – what was a "new" group would turn into a minority *tout court* (not a "new" minority). A current "new" group normally abandons an active ethno-cultural link with its state of origin; if it does not, the original precariousness remains, constituting an obstacle to establishing the group as a well-defined minority. The general point here is that international law hardly "projects" future minorities: its traditional function is simply to look back into a tangible past to identify the subject of protection and then to assume this reliable, factual result as a basis for its purposes of regulation. Such a clear retrospective logic obviously poses dilemmas when one confronts prospective candidates for minority status.

If a group meets most but not all of the definitional requirements, as in the case of a traditional ethno-cultural group of non-citizens, it is important first to determine if the lack of minority status is a function of domestic provisions which are not in conformity with international law. That may result, for instance, from unreasonable distinctions in determining citizenship in breach of Article 26, if not Article 25 (HRC General Comment No. 25 (57) 1996: para. 3), of the ICCPR (see *infra*, chapter IV), or from ethnically motivated deprivation of citizenship or other measures in this area, in breach of Article 5 or other provisions of the ICERD. In such cases, the related, albeit indirect, purpose or effect of impairing the exercise of minority rights must be viewed as unacceptable from the perspective of international law (the relation of international law and domestic law was usefully addressed by the PCIJ in a number of cases; see generally Brownlie 1998: 34-36; *Acquisition of Polish Nationality* case, Advisory Opinion No. 7, PCIJ Series B, 1923: 13-16). Of course, greater protection for a traditional group would indirectly derive from the establishment of automatic international entitlements of long-term residents to citizenship (Orentlicher 1998), particularly in connection with changes in territorial sovereignty (see e.g. Article 3 of the Polish Minorities Treaty of 1919). In sum, if rights are not respected, then the issue is not one of modifying the status requirements, but one of remedying obstacles to the enjoyment of minority rights.

At the same time, it should be noted that a generous identification of the beneficiaries of protection, while lacking wide support, could not be branded as contrary to international law. In particular, a state may extend rights enjoyed by its minority members to other group members as well, because of the absence of an international rule prohibiting such an extension. To put it another way: the fact that a given concept of minority is widely shared does not imply that certain guarantees may not be extended to members of groups which do not fit, strictly speaking, into that concept. As mentioned earlier, the UN Declaration and the Framework Convention might serve that purpose, though as a matter of a *liberty* for states rather than a specific ('soft' or "hard" law) *duty* upon them (unless, of course, a consensus to this effect can be established by way of subsequent practice). Special domestic and/or treaty-based regimes can be set out to achieve the same goal. Such an extension would be especially needed to accommodate the demands of "new" groups or even newcomers who are somehow linked to old groups, which go beyond the prescriptions of the general and specific human rights instruments applicable to them. Some contemporary bilateral treaties seem to reflect this approach. For instance, the concept of "equivalent group" in the Treaty on Good-Neighbourly Relations and Co-operation between the Federal Republic of Germany and the Republic of Poland of 1991 appears to be a case in point: the Polish group in Germany, made up of relatively more recent arrivals as compared to the traditional "German minority" in Poland, is granted rights addressed to minority members, but not minority status (see *infra*, chapter IX). For purposes of domestic law, even an individual broad concept may be used whether or not in connection with the implementation of existing international minority rights instruments. To balance against these options remains, however, the international law principle endorsing a treatment for persons who do fit the widely shared minority concept which is legitimately different from that accorded persons who do not; by way of corollary, a possible extension of (minority) rights to the latter should not allow for a failure to treat differently persons whose situation is significantly different (see *infra*, chapters IV and VI).

Having said that, a number of reasons stand in the way of an extension *tout court* of the international understanding of minority (and thus minority status) (for a more detailed discussion of the following, see Pentassuglia 2000):

– the key role of majority rule in societal law-making processes and the universalistic philosophy of human rights (accommodating minority rights protection, which prefers the bargaining principle to majority rule, and its relation to general human rights guarantees, have long come under pressure);

- the long-asserted linkage between citizenship and long-established presence on the territory, inspired by socio-political and stability concerns, or a "territorial/civic" model of citizenship (Orentlicher 1998) which arguably affects the vision of minority rights within the larger community (the requirement of "effective link" affirmed by the ICJ in the *Nottebohm* case (Second Phase) [ICJ Reports 1955: 23] may indeed be viewed essentially to underlie, *mutatis mutandis*, the international and domestic conceptualisation of "minorities" in relation to the development of standards for the protection of their members);
- the very existence of separate normative regimes for minorities and "new" groups, with their attendant specific goals (this feeds claims and tendencies to distinctiveness);
- the inherent restrictions to a general legal definition ("umbrella arrangements" or more differentiated, expansive options are either unworkable or unlikely to accommodate all group interests at stake); and
- considerations of legal policy (the numerous international legal instruments protecting the rights of "new" groups contrast with the paradoxical absence of a universal and comprehensive treaty regime for minorities as traditionally understood; the "expansive option" might in fact induce to elaborate weaker minority standards; see also *infra*, chapter XII).

In conclusion, the Capotorti definition still reflects the prevailing general understanding of minority in international law, and consequently mandates minority *status* for the groups fulfilling the respective criteria without any unreasonable distinctions. With regard to possible manipulations of the citizenship requirement by states vis-à-vis traditional non-dominant communities, at least available anti-discrimination clauses should bear their full weight. At the same time, widening the number of beneficiaries of protection is by no means forbidden by international law. In particular, the above minimum concept and the entitlements to protection attached to it do not prejudice a liberty for states to reasonably and proportionately afford *rights* granted to members of minorities to other sets of individuals as well, so as to provide the latter with higher standards of treatment (institutional tools, such as the OSCE High Commissioner on National Minorities, might even facilitate *ad hoc* arrangements at the domestic and/or bilateral level; see *infra*, chapter X). Moreover, where adopted, such generous regimes may not be limited or derogated on the grounds of the scope of general multilateral instruments on minority rights. And yet, as noted, an extension of the very notion of minority, and thus minority status, as a fundamental parameter of international law remains unlikely.

3. Determination of an individual's minority membership

How is an individual's minority membership to be determined? Membership of a group may represent a delicate balance between self-identification and acceptance by the group. The existence of minority members and minorities themselves do not depend on domestic legal acts of recognition (as noted earlier, the "factual" nature of minority existence was already made clear by the PCIJ in the *Greco-Bulgarian Communities* case; it is now reaffirmed in the

HRC's General Comment No. 23 (50): para. 5.2), though such acts may benefit the people concerned. At the same time, individuals may not be forced to embrace membership of a minority by the group, nor may the group benefit from domestic provisions unjustifiably preventing the recognition of such a membership, as clearly indicated by the HRC in *Sandra Lovelace v. Canada* (Communication No. 24/1977, Views of 30 July 1981, [1981] Annual Report: 166; [1983] Annual Report: 248), and at least implicitly confirmed in *Ivan Kitok v. Sweden* (Communication No. 197/1985, Views of 27 July 1988, [1988] Annual Report: 221) (see *infra*, chapters IV and V).

Interestingly, in another case brought before the HRC, *R.L. et al. v. Canada* (Communication No. 358/1989, Views of 5 November 1991, [1992] Annual Report: 358), the applicants, members of an Indian band in Canada, challenged the amendment made to Canada's Indian Act in order to address the issues raised in *Lovelace*, on the ground that this amendment interfered with their freedom of association with others since they could not themselves determine membership in their community. The HRC did not rule on the merits as it declared the communication inadmissible for failure to exhaust local remedies. By applying a general line of reasoning to a specific context, the HRC, in its recent General Comment No. 28 on "Equality of Rights Between Men and Women" under Article 3 of the ICCPR, makes it clear that Article 27 rights do not authorise "any state, group or person" to violate the equal rights of women under the Covenant, and, based on its *Lovelace* decision, calls upon states parties to report on any legislation or administrative practices related to membership in a minority community that might constitute an infringement of those rights (UN Doc. CCPR/C/21/Rev.1/Add. 10: para. 32).

In sum, the fundamental assumption is that, as mentioned above, to belong to a minority is a matter of a *person's individual choice* and no disadvantage may arise from the exercise of such choice (see e.g. the 1990 Copenhagen Document: para. 32).

Self-identification has a prominent role in some recent and earlier instruments, such as Article 74 of the 1922 German-Polish Convention relating to Upper Silesia. In the case concerning *Rights of Minorities in Upper Silesia (Minority Schools)* (PCIJ, Series A, No. 15, 1928: 46-47), the PCIJ held that the question whether a person belonged to a racial, linguistic or religious minority, which was the fundamental criterion to determine admission to the German-speaking schools in Poland, "is subject to no verification, dispute, pressure or hindrance whatever on the part of the authorities". Likewise, the Declarations of Denmark and Germany of 1955 concerning the German group in Denmark and the Danish group in Germany state that profession of each other's minority identity is free and must not be challenged by the authorities. And yet, self-identification should not be viewed as an absolute subjective parameter to the extent that this would imply the extension of minority entitlements to persons with an indeterminate membership.

73

In *Rights of Minorities in Upper Silesia (Minority Schools)* (*loc. cit.*: 33) the PCIJ pointed out that:

> [i]t would not be in conformity with the true construction of the provisions of the Minorities Treaties ... to consider as excluded the extension of the advantages of protection stipulated on behalf of minorities to persons who in fact do not belong to a minority. But, on the other hand, such an extension cannot be presumed.

In general, it indeed upheld the notion, as reflected in the minorities treaties, that the individual declaration of affiliation with a minority group was to reflect a fact, not solely the expression of an intention or a wish (*loc. cit.*: 32).

In fact, neither state recognition nor individual choices which are not substantiated by objective elements are relevant to establishing an individual's minority membership. In this regard, former UN Special Rapporteur Capotorti referred to an active sentiment of identity clearly manifested (if only implicitly) in everyday life as an expression of a firm will of preserving one's minority culture. In *Lovelace*, the HRC stated (*loc. cit.*: para. 14) that:

> [p]ersons who are born and brought up on a reserve, who have kept ties with their community and wish to maintain these ties must normally be considered as belonging to that minority.

In *Kitok*, the HRC expressed its "concern" at "the ignoring of objective ethnic criteria in determining membership of a minority" (*loc. cit.*: para. 9.7), and stressed the retained cultural and territorial links of the complainant with the Sami community.

Facts and intention combine, setting out general membership criteria. The Explanatory Memorandum of the Framework Convention is rather clear on this point; the "choice of belonging" principle in Article 3:

> does not imply a right for an individual to choose arbitrarily to belong to any national minority. The individual's subjective choice is inseparably linked to objective criteria relevant to the person's identity (paragraph 35).

It is submitted that this approach, rooted in the fundamental purposes served by the special international guarantees applicable to persons belonging to minorities (see *infra*, chapter IV), should be considered as embraced by general international law and should be adopted, in particular, when interpreting recent provisions of bilateral treaties which lay emphasis on the self-identification criterion (see e.g. the treaties stipulated by Hungary and Germany, on which generally *infra*, chapter IX), unless a different intention of the parties can be clearly established.

Bibliography

Benoît-Rohmer, F., "La convention-cadre du Conseil de l'Europe pour la protection des minorités nationales", *European Journal of International Law*, 6, 1995, pp. 573-597.

Brownlie, I., *Principles of public international law*, fifth edition, Clarendon Press, Oxford, 1998.

Capotorti, F., "Study on the rights of persons belonging to ethnic, religious and linguistic minorities", UN Doc. E/CN.4/Sub.2/384/Rev. I, 1979.

Claude, I.L., *National minorities: an international problem*, Harvard University Press, Cambridge, 1955.

Eide, A., *Possible ways and means of facilitating the peaceful and constructive solution of problems involving minorities*, UN Doc. E/CN.4/Sub.2/1993/34, 1993.

Ermacora, F., "The protection of minorities before the United Nations", *Collected courses of the Hague Academy of International Law*, IV, 1983, pp. 257-370.

Helgesen, J., "Protecting minorities in the Conference on Security and Co-operation in Europe (CSCE) process", in *The strength of diversity: human rights and pluralistic democracy*, Rosas, A. and Helgesen, J. (eds), Martinus Nijhoff Publishers, Dordrecht, 1992, pp. 159-186.

Laponce, J.A., *The protection of minorities*, University of California Press, Berkeley and Los Angeles, 1960.

Macartney, C.A., *National states and national minorities*, Oxford University Press, London, 1934.

Modeen, T., *The international protection of minorities in Europe*, Åbo Akademi, Åbo, 1969.

Orentlicher, D.F., "Citizenship and national identity" in *International law and ethnic conflict*, Wippman, D. (ed.), Cornell University Press, Ithaca and London, 1998, pp. 296-325.

Packer, J., "Problems in defining minorities", in *Minority and group rights in the new millennium*, Fottrell, D. and Bowring, B. (eds), Kluwer Law International, The Hague, 1999, pp. 223-274.

Packer, J., "On the definition of minorities", in *The protection of ethnic and linguistic minorities in Europe*, Packer, J. and Myntti, K. (eds), Åbo Akademi, Åbo, 1995, pp. 23-65.

Pentassuglia, G., *Defining "minority" in international law: a critical appraisal*, Lapland's University Press, Rovaniemi, 2000.

Preece, J.J., *National minorities and the European nation-states system*, Clarendon Press, Oxford, 1998.

Riedel, E., "Standards and sources. Farewell to the exclusivity of the sources triad in international law?" *European Journal of International Law*, 2, 1991, pp. 58-84.

Secretary General of the United Nations, "Definition and classification of minorities", UN Doc. E/CN.4/Sub.2/85, 1949.

Shaw, M.N., "The definition of minorities in international law", *Israel Yearbook on Human Rights*, 20, 1990, pp. 13-43.

Thornberry, P., "Self-determination, minorities, human rights: a review of international instruments", *International and Comparative Law Quarterly*, 38, 1989, pp. 867-899.

Part B

Substantive entitlements available to minorities: general standards and special regimes

CHAPTER IV

EXISTENCE, EQUALITY AND NON-DISCRIMINATION

1. Physical integrity and group existence

a. Protection against genocide

Whatever the core content of minority rights under contemporary international law, the corpus of international standards which are of relevance to minorities features a fundamental set of prescriptions on the "right to existence" of groups. In this regard, the prohibition of genocide is of primary significance. The jurist Lemkin is credited with having been the first to use and define "genocide". He described it as:

> a co-ordinated plan of different actions aiming at the destruction of essential foundations of the life of national groups, with the aim of annihilating the groups themselves. The objectives of such a plan would be disintegration of the political and social institutions, of culture, language, national feelings, religion, and the economic existence of national groups, and the destruction of the personal security, liberty, health, dignity, and even the lives of the individuals belonging to such groups. Genocide is directed against the national group as an entity, and the actions involved are directed against individuals, not in their individual capacity, but as members of the national group. (Lemkin, 1944: 79.)

Thus, he identified different forms of genocide, taking examples from nazi practice – "political genocide", "social genocide", "cultural genocide", "economic genocide", "biological genocide", "physical genocide", "religious genocide" and "moral genocide". The term "genocide" progressively entered into the specific realm of international law. Article 6, sub-paragraph (c), of the Charter of the International Military Tribunal annexed to the Agreement for the Prosecution and Punishment of the Major War Criminals of the European Axis, signed in August 1945 by the United States, the United Kingdom, France and the Soviet Union, and later on by nineteen other states, did not refer to genocide as such, but the latter could be inferred from the broad category of "crimes against humanity", namely:

> murder, extermination, enslavement, deportation, and other inhumane acts committed against any civilian population before or during the war or persecutions on political, racial or religious grounds in execution of or in connection with any crime within the jurisdiction of the Tribunal, whether or not in violation of the domestic law of the country where perpetrated.

Genocide emerged later on as a separate legal concept. Resolution 96 (I) on the crime of genocide, adopted by the UN General Assembly on 11 December 1946, defined genocide as "a denial of the right of existence of entire human groups, as homicide is the denial of the right to live of individual human beings"; the basic sense of existence referred to was "physical existence" of racial, religious, political and other groups. It affirmed that genocide "is a crime under international law which the civilised world condemns" and that those who commit it "whether private individuals, public officials or statesmen are punishable". The crime outlined in the resolution is independent of crimes against peace or war crimes, whereas Article 6, subparagraph c, of the Nuremberg Charter provided that "crimes against humanity" could only be committed in execution or in connection with any of the above crimes (on crimes under international law, see *infra*). Many points in this resolution were taken up during the drafting stage and in the final version of the 1948 Genocide Convention.

Article II of the Genocide Convention describes genocide through enumerating a number of acts "committed with intent to destroy, in whole or in part, a national, ethnical, racial or religious group, as such". The groups protected were regarded as sharing certain features. In the Sixth Committee of the General Assembly reference was commonly made to the group as "distinct", "permanent", "stable", "sharing a common origin", etc. Political and linguistic groups were excluded; language was most often seen as part of the group's identity defined by ethnicity and the like, under Article II. With the notable exception of linguistic groups, the characterisation of the groups protected under the convention is similar to that provided by other international instruments applicable to minorities.

Under Article II, any of the following acts amounts to genocide:

– killing members of the group;

– causing serious bodily or mental harm to members of the group;

– deliberately inflicting on the group conditions of life calculated to bring about its physical destruction in whole or in part;

– imposing measures intended to prevent births within the group; and

– forcibly transferring children of the group to another group.

The acts mentioned in all five points refer to "physical" genocide (the first three) or "biological" genocide (point 4), or having physical and biological effects (point 5). The case under point 5 seems to include an aspect of "cultural genocide", but the debates in the Sixth Committee indicate that the understanding of "forcibly transferring children of the group to another group" was limited precisely to the above physical and biological dimension. On the other hand, the question of "cultural genocide" was raised in the draft convention prepared by the secretary general (Article I, paragraph 3), and in the draft of the *Ad hoc* Committee on Genocide (Article III), in respect of acts including forcible and systematic exile of individuals representing the culture of the group, the prohibition of the use of the group's language in private intercourse or in schools, and the systematic destruction of the basic manifestations of the group's culture, such as books, monuments, etc. However, the proposals for including cultural genocide were eventually discarded, as the concept was seen as a vague one, open to abuse.

Comments were also made to the effect that cultural genocide represented an extension of the concept of genocide amounting to a reconstitution of the minority regime under the cover of a new term. Thus, genocide was overall narrowed to acts targeting the physical integrity of groups, in contrast to the broader notion submitted by Lemkin in the 1940s. Yet, the "right to existence" in its most basic sense of protection against "physical" and "biological" extermination in the sense of Article II clearly benefits minority groups, though they are not the only beneficiaries of the convention.

Such an instrument contains a prohibition to destroy intentionally the group (the *actus reus* and *mens rea* are thus of key importance), and prescribes for the parties obligations to prevent, prosecute and punish the crime of genocide. The principle of individual criminal responsibility is laid down in Article IV, in relation to acts of genocide under Article II and further related acts listed in Article III. Nevertheless, states themselves may be held accountable for such acts (Article IX). This has been confirmed by the ICJ, in the case concerning *Application of the Convention on the Prevention and Punishment of the Crime of Genocide* (Preliminary Objections) (ICJ Reports 1996). The ICJ has indeed observed that state responsibility under the convention is not confined to cases arising out of the breach of the duties to prevent and repress as envisaged in Articles V, VI and VII, but, as reflected in Article IX and inferable from Article IV, it may extend to acts of genocide directly committed by the state. The ICJ has also noted that, given the object and purpose of the convention, the reach of a party's duty to combat the crime of genocide is not limited to the territory of that party's borders.

Article VI and the cited Article IX deal with, respectively, the courts which are competent to try persons charged with genocide (jurisdiction of the *forum loci delicti commissi* or of an international penal tribunal whose jurisdiction is accepted by the contracting parties), and the jurisdiction of the ICJ as regards disputes between the contracting parties relating to the interpretation, application or fulfilment of the convention, submitted at the request of any of the parties to the dispute. Upon ratification of the convention, a number of states (basically from the Soviet bloc) entered reservations that conceded ICJ jurisdiction only on the basis of an agreement of all parties to a dispute. In the absence of a reservation clause, criteria for determining the admissibility of reservations to the convention were provided by the ICJ in its well-known advisory opinion on *Reservations to the Convention on the Prevention and Punishment of the Crime of Genocide* (ICJ Reports 1951), now embodied in Article 19, sub-paragraph c, of the Vienna Convention on the Law of Treaties. Most of the old reservations to ICJ jurisdiction were removed by ex-Soviet states after 1989, while only a few parties continue to reserve against this jurisdictional undertaking; in general, all parties have a standing to raise a claim under Article IX (see also in a wider sense, *infra*). At the time of writing, in addition to the above-mentioned case concerning the application of the Genocide Convention, further proceedings have been instituted before the ICJ for alleged violations of this treaty (including state responsibility for acts of genocide), based on its Article IX (*Application of the Convention on the Prevention and Punishment of the Crime of Genocide, Croatia v. Yugoslavia*, Application of 2 July 1999). However, these are the

81

only Article IX cases which have been brought so far by states parties, notwithstanding further major instances plausibly falling within the convention's substantive scope, and even affecting minority groups (for example, the Kurds of Iraq).

The already cited Resolution 96 (I) of the General Assembly, adopted unanimously and without debate, "affirmed" that genocide is a crime under international law. Other operative paragraphs invited states to make this crime punishable under their legislation and recommended them to co-operate to facilitate its prompt prevention and punishment. Article I of the Genocide Convention was one of the least contentious articles and was relatively little commented upon during the drafting stage. The contracting parties "confirm" that genocide is a crime under international law which they undertake to prevent and to punish. The *travaux* reveal strong support for the view that genocide was contrary to general international law. In the *Reservations* case, the ICJ (*loc. cit.*: 23) quoted from Resolution 96 (I) (genocide as "'a crime under international law' involving a denial of the right of existence of entire human groups, a denial which shocks the conscience of mankind", etc.), and pointed out that:

> the principles underlying the Convention are principles which are recognised by civilised nations as binding on States, even without any conventional obligation.

In the *Barcelona Traction, Light and Power Company, Limited* case (Second Phase) (ICJ Reports 1970: 32), the court distinguished between "the obligation of a State towards the international community as a whole and those arising vis-à-vis another State in the field of diplomatic protection". It went on to state that:

> [b]y their very nature the former are the concern of all States. In view of the importance of the rights involved, all States can be held to have a legal interest in their protection; they are obligations *erga omnes*.

The court noticed that such obligations *erga omnes* in contemporary international law derived from, *inter alia,* the outlawing of genocide. The predominant scholarly view is that the prohibition of genocide is not only a norm of general international law but also a norm of *jus cogens* in the sense of Articles 53 and 64 of the Vienna Convention on the Law of Treaties, namely a norm of general international law from which no treaty derogation is permitted (on these general aspects, see the literature indicated *supra,* Chapter II). Still, the customary law and peremptory status of such a prohibition is said to reflect the narrow concept endorsed in the Genocide Convention, not a broad notion encompassing "cultural" (or other forms) of genocide. Finally, genocide, because of its prohibition by a peremptory norm of general international law, can entail the international state responsibility which is attached to serious breaches of *jus cogens* norms, under the UN International Law Commission's Draft Articles on Responsibility of States for Internationally Wrongful Acts, adopted in 2001 (Articles 40 and 41) (UN Doc. A/CN.4/L.602/Rev. 1).

In strict terms of standards focused on minorities, Article 1 of the 1992 UN Declaration provides, *inter alia,* that states "shall protect the existence ... of minorities". "Existence" has been conceptualised as including "a basic right to be protected against genocide" (Thornberry, 1995: 40). This may be viewed as an explicit reaffirmation of the protection of minority groups against extermination in the sense of the Genocide Convention under general international law.

b. Protection against violations entailing individual criminal responsibility and affecting group existence

Further protection for the physical integrity of minorities derives, albeit indirectly, from the jurisdiction of the UN international tribunals established to prosecute persons responsible for serious violations of international humanitarian law in the former Yugoslavia (under UN Security Council Resolution 827 of 1993, based on Chapter VII of the UN Charter) and Rwanda (under UN Security Council Resolution 955 of 1994, based on Chapter VII of the UN Charter) and, prospectively, of the permanent UN International Criminal Court, the statute of which was adopted in Rome in 1998 (UN Doc. A/CONF.183/9) (for an overview of major aspects regarding these judicial bodies, see Sands and Klein, 2001: 383-390); the setting up of similar special courts is also being currently considered within the UN.

Such crimes under international law as the crime of genocide, crimes against humanity and war crimes (notably "grave breaches of the Geneva Conventions of 1949"), as falling under the competence over natural persons (as opposed to states and legal persons or organisations) of the two abovementioned UN tribunals (Articles 2 to 5 of the Yugoslav Tribunal Statute and Articles 2 to 4 of the Rwandan Tribunal Statute) and the UN International Criminal Court (Article 5 of the statute), indeed cover numerous practices of which minority groups are often the main victims. As for the crime of genocide, the aforesaid judicial forums may provide jurisdiction in the sense of Article VI of the Genocide Convention, although the tribunals set up under Chapter VII of the UN Charter have a compulsory rather than consensual basis (on these general aspects, see Damrosch, 1998: 277-279); they strengthen reliance on international criminal enforcement to repress this crime. "Ethnic cleansing", that is to say, as explained by the UN Commission on Human Rights (Resolution 1992/S/-1/1), the forcible removal or expulsion of persons from their homes, which is aimed at the dislocation or destruction of national, ethnic, racial or religious groups with a view to obtaining the ethnic homogeneity of the areas where they live (see also *infra*, Chapter VII; or the problematic issue of "ethnic cleansing" in relation to the scope of the Genocide Convention, see Schabas 2000: 189-201) is essentially covered by the Statute of the International Criminal Court, together with other practices seriously affecting the physical integrity of a minority group and its members (see, for example, Article 7, paragraph 1, sub-paragraphs (d), (g) and (h), and paragraph 2, sub-paragraphs (d), (f) and (g).

c. Physical and cultural integrity

The specific provisions on genocide and other serious acts causing injury to physical integrity are complemented by more general prescriptions enshrined in international human rights treaties, which, if fully implemented, may prove somehow conducive to the prevention of such grave acts.

In this respect, Article 20 of the ICCPR and Article 4 of the 1965 ICERD, concerning the prohibition of propaganda for war and incitement to discrimination, hostility or violence based on advocacy of national, racial or religious hatred, are also of particular importance to minorities and their members (see, for example, by analogy, the *L.K. v. Netherlands* case (Communication No. 4/1991, Opinion of 16 March 1993, CERD/C/42/D/4/1991) brought before the CERD, the supervisory body under the ICERD, in relation to its Article 4). This is confirmed by Article 6, paragraph 2, of the 1995 Framework Convention, which echoes those provisions. Equally important is the prohibition of expulsion, by means of either an individual or a collective measure, from the territory of the state of one's citizenship in Article 3, paragraph 1, of Protocol No. 4 to the ECHR (ironically, the minority transfers involving several million people arranged between 1944 and 1946 in eastern Europe were generally not considered contrary to human rights, and minority population transfer had already been sanctioned by international law under the 1923 Convention concerning the Exchange of Greek and Turkish Populations between Greece and Turkey).

But the issue of minorities is premised first and foremost on the existence of distinctive groups through the active awareness of their members, manifested "through language, culture, or religion, a shared sense of history, a common destiny" (Thornberry, 1991: 57). One of the points made in favour of including cultural genocide in the Genocide Convention was that a minority could be deprived of its integrity not only through the mass destruction of its members but also through the destruction of its specific traits, even though no attempt had been made on the life of its members. Although the concept of cultural genocide is not embraced by the Genocide Convention, some of its underlying elements can be found in current international human rights instruments relevant to minorities. The prohibitions of respectively discrimination on any ground such as race, national or ethnic origin, language, religion, etc. (see *infra*), forced assimilation or ethnocide (see, for example, Article 1, paragraph 1, of the 1992 UN declaration), and specific measures such as expropriations, evictions or redrawing of administrative boundaries, which alter the proportion of the population in areas inhabited by persons belonging to minorities and are aimed to restrict the reach of guarantees applicable to them (see, for example, Article 16 of the 1995 Framework Convention), well illustrate some basic internationally recognised preconditions for the preservation of minority traits, with equality and non-discrimination standing out as fundamental parameters.

2. Equality and non-discrimination

a. Historical background

Several proposals were made for the inclusion of provisions on minorities and on religious and racial equality in the League of Nations Covenant, but all were finally discarded. The former concerned the situation of minorities in the newly established states, not in all member states. Japan proposed a clause affording to all alien nationals of member states equal treatment in every respect without any distinction in law or in fact on account of their race or nationality, which in fact built upon the traditional principle of international law imposing on states an obligation to treat foreign nationals in a manner that secured "minimum standards of justice" (Buergental, 1995: 13-17). And yet, even such a proposal was not endorsed.

The debate that followed the adoption of the minorities treaties oscillated between proposals for generalising the league minorities system and views favouring a shift to a general regime of basic and fundamental freedoms to all persons without distinction on the grounds of race, religion, sex or language. In this latter case, the assumption was basically that minority problems arose when minorities were discriminated against in the enjoyment of basic rights. Poland drew upon an assembly resolution of 1922 – that recommended generalisation of the minorities treaties' standards at least on a moral basis – to propose the adoption of a general convention on minorities. Other states, such as Haiti, advocated the said broader approach. A resolution was adopted by the Institut de Droit International in 1929, containing a Declaration of the International Rights of Man (AJIL, 24, 1930: 126-127). It was clearly concerned with the legal equality of individuals generally. Haiti strongly supported the content of this declaration and submitted it to the attention of the League of Nations.

The Haitian position did not gain immediate support from the other delegates, who generally preferred a more cautious approach. McKean observes:

> The history of the League debates shows a gradual disenchantment with the League minorities system, as it stood, and an inexorable movement towards the belief that there should be a universal protection of basic human rights in two steps: (1) the firm establishment of the principle of international legal equality of individuals by the proscription of discrimination on the grounds of race, religion, language, or sex; (2) the compilation of a list of those basic rights which were to be enjoyed by all without discrimination ... [a]lthough the discussions appeared unproductive at the time, they sowed the seeds which were to flourish in the more favourable climate which existed after World War II. (McKean, 1983: 45.)

Although the move away from a special system of minority guarantees to a universal system of human rights protection is an essential historical fact, one should not view the League of Nations minority norms as being in antithesis with human rights as were to mature after 1945. As indicated earlier (see *supra*, Chapter I), those provisions were mostly the harbingers of fundamental prescriptions and assumptions informing the contemporary canon of international human rights, particularly those regarding equality and non-discrimination.

b. General principles and their implications

Equality and non-discrimination are now well-established principles of international human rights law. They are prescribed in the UN Charter (Article 1, paragraph 3, and Article 55, sub-paragraph (c)) and the UDHR

(Article 2). The ICCPR and ICESCR contain general and specific clauses to the same effect. Specialised instruments, too, contain anti-discrimination clauses, including the ICERD (1965), the UN Declaration on the Elimination of All Forms of Intolerance and of Discrimination Based on Religion or Belief (1981), the UN Convention on the Rights of the Child (1989), ILO Convention No. 11 concerning Discrimination in Respect of Employment and Occupation (1958), the Unesco Declaration on Race and Racial Prejudice (1978), and the Unesco Convention against Discrimination in Education (1960). Regional human rights instruments, such as the ECHR (Article 14), include comparable clauses. As noted earlier, the recently adopted Protocol No. 12 to the ECHR embodies a general prohibition of discrimination, which provides a scope of protection broader than that of Article 14 of the ECHR (see, notably, *infra*, Chapter VI).

The principles of equality and non-discrimination are also widely acknowledged, at least in racial matters, as forming part of customary international law binding all states. Support for this view comes from authoritative instruments such as those just cited, authoritative legal institutions such as the UN International Law Commission and the ICJ (*Barcelona Traction* case (Second Phase) (ICJ Reports 1970: 32) and advisory opinion in the case concerning *Legal Consequences for States of the Continued Presence of South Africa in Namibia (South West Africa) notwithstanding Security Council Resolution 276 (1970)* (ICJ Reports 1971: 56-57)), pronouncements by worldwide international conferences, and distinguished academic commentators (see, for example, Brownlie, 1998: 602). It has been argued (see *supra*, Chapter II) that only state "systematic" patterns or "policies" of at least racial discrimination (see, for example, Sub-Commission on Prevention of Discrimination and Protection of Minorities Resolution 1 (XXIV), adopted in 1971) fall within the scope of the prohibition developed under general international law, sometimes in conjunction with the proposition that such a prohibition bears *jus cogens* status.

The HRC, in its General Comment No. 18 on non-discrimination under the ICCPR, stated in 1989 that:

> the term "discrimination" as used in the Covenant should be understood to imply any distinction, exclusion, restriction or preference which is based on any ground such as race, colour, sex, language, religion, political or other opinion, national or social origin, property, birth or other status, and which has the purpose or effect of nullifying or impairing the recognition, enjoyment or exercise by all persons, on an equal footing, of all rights and obligations. (General Comment No. 18: paragraph 7.)

Article 2, paragraph 1, of the covenant obliges each State Party to respect and ensure to all persons within its territory and subject to its jurisdiction the rights recognised in the covenant without distinction of any kind, such as race, colour, sex, language, religion, etc. (see, for example, *Antonina Ignatane v. Latvia*, Communication No. 884/1999, Views of 25 July 2001, CCPR/C/72/D/884/1999). Article 26 not only entitles all persons to equality before the law as well as equal protection of the law but also prohibits any discrimination under the law and guarantees to all persons equal and effective protection against discrimination on any ground such as race, colour, sex, language, religion, etc.

As noted by the HRC in the said general comment (and further reflected in earlier cases brought before the HRC, such as *Broeks v. Netherlands* (Communication No. 172/1984, Views of 9 April 1987, (1987) Annual Report: 139) and *Zwan De Vries v. Netherlands* (Communication No. 182/1984, Views of 9 April 1987, *ibid:* 160)):

> While article 2 limits the scope of the rights protected against discrimination to those provided for in the Covenant, article 26 does not specify such limitations ... article 26 does not merely duplicate the guarantee already provided for in article 2 but provides in itself an autonomous right. It prohibits discrimination in law and in fact in any field regulated and protected by public authorities. (No. 18 (37): paragraph 12)

In fact, Article 26 refers "not only to equality before the courts but also to the general 'egalitarian' concept of 'equal protection of the law' in the sense of non-discrimination" (Ramcharan, 1981: 255). Such areas as social security and citizenship laws have frequently come under HRC scrutiny in the context of the First Optional Protocol, mostly in relation to discrimination against women. Still, Opsahl has queried "whether the HRC is likely to become an effective 'Ombudsman for Equality' in every area covered by legislation of any kind, in every respect, on every criterion" (Opsahl, 1988: 64). Some states have appeared concerned at the implications of a general equality clause. For example, Germany, which has fully consented to Article 26 of the ICCPR, has nonetheless entered a reservation to Article 5, paragraph 2, of the First Optional Protocol, to the effect that the competence of the HRC may not extend to communications claiming a violation of Article 26 of the ICCPR, in so far as the alleged violation refers to rights other than those guaranteed under the covenant. This reservation has been criticised by the HRC (UN Doc. CCPR/C/79/Add. 72).

Importantly, the anti-discrimination clauses enshrined in the ICCPR (especially in Article 2, paragraph 1, and Articles 3 and 26), not only prohibit discrimination by state agencies and laws, they also entail a duty on states parties "to ensure" that individuals are protected against discrimination by private actors (see, for example, the HRC General Comment No. 18: paragraph 9). That is also clearly prescribed by the ICERD under Article 2, paragraph 1, sub-paragraph d.

Thus, minorities are not the only beneficiaries of equality and non-discrimination norms. On the other hand, the wording of the prohibited grounds of distinction, in spite of small variations from one instrument to another, repeatedly includes references to race, national or ethnic origin, language, religion, social origin, birth and other status, covering most if not all minority components. The ECHR specifically mentions "association with a national minority" when spelling out the grounds upon which differentiation is not permitted, as now does the cited Protocol No. 12 (Article 1, paragraph 1).

To abstain from discrimination and the corresponding prevention of discrimination have been described, from a specific or more general angle, as implying the placing of members of minorities "in every respect on a footing of perfect equality with the other nationals of the State"; the prevention of "any action which denies to individuals or groups of people equality of treatment which they may wish"; and "the suppression or prevention of any conduct which denies or restricts a person's right to equality" (Alfredsson, 1990: 5). For instance, in General Comment No. 22 on Article 18 of the ICCPR, the HRC stressed the prohibition of discrimination against religious minorities or non-believers, notably by affording privileges to members of the predominant religious community or by imposing special restrictions upon the former (paragraph 9). Interestingly, in *Waldman v. Canada* under the First Optional Protocol (Communication No. 694/1996, Views of 3 November 1999, CCPR/C/67/D/694/1996), the HRC concluded that the impugned distinction had resulted in discrimination between members of the Roman Catholic minority and members of other religious minorities in the country, contrary to the equality clause in Article 26 of the ICCPR. A breach of such a clause was also found in *J. G. A. Diergaardt et al. v. Namibia* (Communication No. 760/1997, Views of 25 July 2000, CCPR/C/69/D/760/1996) in relation to what, according to the HRC's assessment, was an intentional discrimination on linguistic grounds against the speakers of the minority language in question when dealing with public authorities.

That equality and non-discrimination are essential to minority groups may be further illustrated by the emphasis placed on them by the CERD in its General Recommendation XXIII (51), adopted in 1997, on the rights of indigenous peoples (which indeed often constitute minorities: see *infra*, Chapter V), as well as in regard to other relevant groups, in the context of the ICERD (general recommendations are adopted under Article 9, paragraph 2, of this instrument, and are very similar in scope and status to the general comments issued by the HRC under the ICCPR). The position of various non-dominant groups including ethnic, linguistic or religious minorities is addressed from the anti-discrimination perspective in the 2001 Declaration and Programme of Action adopted by the UN World Conference against Racism, Racial Discrimination, Xenophobia and Related Intolerance (see, for example, paragraphs 39, 59-60 and 66 of the declaration). Moreover, as recently shown by expert analysis (de Varennes, 2000), large-scale violations of the equality and non-discrimination norms committed against minority groups are frequently one of the main underlying causes of contemporary ethnic conflicts.

Does respect for the equality and non-discrimination precepts consist in affording identical treatment in every instance? The question, which is of general importance, is especially relevant to minorities, considering that, as noted earlier, virtually all anti-discrimination clauses encompass minority traits such as ethnic origin, language or religion. In particular, should it be concluded that a less favourable treatment accorded to non-minority individuals as compared to members of ethnic, linguistic or religious minority groups, based on the fact that the former do not belong to the latter, is *per se* discriminatory and thus contrary to international law? In the cited General Comment No. 18 on non-discrimination, the HRC observed that not every differentiation of treatment will constitute discrimination if the aim is to achieve a purpose which is legitimate under the covenant and if the criteria used are reasonable and objective (paragraph 13). In fact, such requirements for a permitted distinction drew upon those already spelled out by the EurCtHR in relation to Article 14 of the ECHR, in the *Case Relating to Certain Aspects of the Laws on the Use of Languages in Education in Belgium* (Merits) (hereinafter the *"Belgian Linguistics* case") (EurCtHR, Judgment of 23 July 1968, Series A, No. 6), and later on in, for example, the *Abdulaziz, Cabales and Balkandali v. United Kingdom* case (EurCtHR, Judgment of 28 May 1985, Series A, No. 94): the distinction must pursue a legitimate aim; the distinction must have an objective justification; and the measures must be proportionate to the aim sought to be realised.

Article 1, paragraph 4, and Article 2, paragraph 2, of the ICERD consider special measures taken "for the sole purpose of securing adequate advancement of certain racial or ethnic groups or individuals" and "guaranteeing them the full and equal enjoyment of human rights and fundamental freedoms" as not constituting an act of discrimination; these measures must be discontinued "after the objectives for which they were taken have been achieved". This principle has been broadly formulated in Protocol No. 12 to the ECHR (third recital of the preamble) and, more importantly, can be found in international texts specifically concerning minorities, in connection with basic equality and non-discrimination clauses (for example, paragraph 31 of the Copenhagen Document; Article 4 of the Framework Convention; and Article 4, paragraph 1, of the UN declaration). Depending on the instrument, the adoption by states of the special measures in question is, or may be, justified, encouraged and/or even framed as a matter of duty.

Therefore, in international human rights law equality and non-discrimination can be said to constitute interlocking, "twin" components of a unitary concept:

– abstention from any kind of differentiation based on arbitrary or unreasonable grounds, which is a negative aspect of equality; and

– differential treatment, or "positive" or "reverse" discrimination, which is intended to achieve positive equality (or equality in fact) in relation to demonstrably unequal situations, in conformity with the above-mentioned requirements.

In *Sandra Lovelace v. Canada*, brought before the HRC under the First Optional Protocol to the ICCPR (Communication No. 24/1977, Views of 30 July 1981, (1981) Annual Report: 166; (1983) Annual Report: 248), the complainant was a Maliseet Indian who had lost, under Canadian legislation, her legal status as an Indian as a result of her marrying a non-Indian. After divorcing her husband, she wanted to go back to the Tobique reserve, the place where she was born and brought up, but that had been precluded by law due to the said change of status. With a focus on Article 27 of the ICCPR, the HRC stated (*loc. cit.:* paragraph 16) that statutory restrictions affecting the right to residence on a reserve must have a "reasonable and objective justification and be consistent with the other provisions of the Covenant, read as a whole". Since it did not find the denial to Sandra Lovelace to live on the reserve as reasonable or necessary in order to preserve the identity of the tribe, the HRC concluded that to prevent her recognition as belonging to the group was an unjustifiable impairment of her rights under Article 27, read in the context of other ICCPR provisions, notably the equality and non-discrimination clauses. In *Ivan Kitok v. Sweden,* examined under the same complaints procedure (Communication No. 197/1985, Views of 27 July 1988, (1988) Annual Report: 221), the HRC dealt with the question of whether Ivan Kitok, a Swedish citizen of Sami origin, had been arbitrarily denied, by virtue of the 1971 Reindeer Husbandry Act, immemorial rights granted to the Sami community, in violation of Article 27. By referring to the *ratio decidendi* underlying *Lovelace,* the HRC concluded (*loc. cit.:* paragraph 9, sub-paragraph 5) that the statutory restrictions upon the rights of Kitok did have a reasonable and objective justification (namely, "to restrict the number of reindeer breeders for economic and ecological reasons and to secure the preservation and well-being of the Sami minority"), and that, as a result, no breach of Article 27 had occurred.

Both cases provide illustration of the classic question whether or not given restrictions amount to discrimination in the enjoyment of recognised human rights. The "reasonable and objective" test indeed applies to each and every article of the ICCPR, including Article 27: for instance, in *Hopu and Bessert v. France,* involving indigenous minority members (Communication No. 549/1993, Views of 29 July 1997, (1997) Annual Report II: 70), the HRC, which could not consider the merits of the case under Article 27 due to a reservation entered into by France to this effect (see *infra,* Chapter V), applied such a test to an interference with the authors' rights to privacy and family in Articles 17 and 23 (*loc. cit.:* paragraph 10, sub-paragraph 3).

At the same time, as indirectly revealed by these cases entailing a conflict between a minority and one of its members, and by further elaborating upon the components of equality and non-discrimination mentioned above, difference in treatment which is reasonable and objective might in principle favour a culturally distinctive minority group over rights of others. In other words, differentiation could arise from the objective of responding to the specific concerns of a minority, as significantly different from those of others, and thus ensuring full equality. This question will be discussed in more detail in Chapter VI, in connection with a brief description of the pertinent case law under the ECHR.

c. The anti-discrimination approach and minority rights

Although minorities benefit from the principles of equality and non-discrimination, an important distinction has to be made between the anti-discrimination approach and minority rights. The UN Sub-Commission on Prevention of Discrimination and Protection of Minorities gave useful indication on the matter by explaining the themes of its mandate:

1. Prevention of Discrimination is the prevention of any action which denies to individuals or groups of people equality of treatment which they may wish.

2. Protection of minorities is the protection of non-dominant groups which, while wishing in general for equality of treatment with the majority, wish for a measure of differential treatment in order to preserve basic characteristics which they

possess and which distinguish them from the majority of the population ... [if] a minority wishes for assimilation and is debarred, the question is one of discrimination. (UN Doc. E/CN.4/52, Section V.)

The protection of members of minorities against discrimination in essence constitutes a statute of prohibited treatment, but does not systematically embrace minority rights. The basic aim of the prevention of discrimination is "the integration of persons by legal means" (Ermacora, 1983: 305). This is, for instance, the objective of the ICERD, which incorporates the notion of special, temporary measures for the purpose of securing full and equal enjoyment of human rights and fundamental freedoms (see *supra,* Article 1, paragraph 4, and Article 2, paragraph 2). Its stress on the elimination of "barriers" between races (see, for example, Article 2, paragraph 1, sub-paragraph e), coupled with the principle of special measures for disadvantaged groups, should not be seen as a substitute for the protection of minority rights, which is a wider notion.

As already noted, such rights are not privileges, but represent some of the implications of the concept of substantive equality as opposed to purely formal or legal equality. They are intended to remedy the structural imbalance between minorities and majorities in areas critical to the preservation of cultural integrity. In *Minority Schools in Albania* (PCIJ Series A/B, No. 64, 1935: 17), the PCIJ insisted on the notion of equality in fact and held that the closing of the minority schools was incompatible with equality of treatment; it indeed pointed out that:

> there would be no true equality between a majority and a minority if the latter were deprived of its own institutions, and were consequently compelled to renounce that which constitutes the very essence of its being a minority.

Because of that, general or specific anti-discrimination clauses may pave the way, to a greater or lesser extent, for this goal to be achieved, by not only outlawing unreasonable distinctions against minorities but also producing, under proper conditions, differential treatment benefiting them. And yet, as stated by the PCIJ in that same case (*loc. cit.:* 17), minority rights fall beyond purely anti-discrimination objectives generated by the purpose of "achieving perfect equality with the other nationals of the State"; they specifically aim at preserving the characteristics which distinguish the minority from the majority, satisfying the ensuing special needs.

Hence, whereas the prevention of discrimination demands in general equality, including special, temporary measures designed to remove not only legal but also social and/or economic obstacles to the enjoyment of rights and freedoms (see, generally, for example, the HRC General Comment No. 18 on non-discrimination: paragraph 10; HRC General Comment No. 28 on equality of rights between men and women: paragraph 29; and the declaration adopted by the UN World Conference against Racism, Racial Discrimination, Xenophobia and Related Intolerance: paragraph 108), the core of the "protection of minorities" lies in special, essentially permanent measures which are intended to safeguard the identity of certain groups. From the angle of the prevention of discrimination, minorities come into play, along with other

91

groups, in terms of the achievement of their full integration into all sectors of society. In the field of the protection of minorities, the focus is on what makes minority groups non-assimilated into, and thus different from, the rest of the population, though clearly rejecting a policy of apartheid (for remarkable insights into this important aspect in the context of equality, differential treatment and minority rights, see Judge Tanaka's dissenting opinion in the *South West Africa* cases (Second Phase) (ICJ Reports 1966: 284-316).

On the other hand, the distinctiveness of minority rights protection in international law is indirectly confirmed by the fact that, whenever adopted, positive measures for the protection of the identity of a minority (see *infra,* Chapter V) must, in turn, respect the principles of equality and non-discrimination, both as regards the treatment between different minorities and the treatment between persons belonging to them and the remaining part of the population (HRC General Comment No. 23: paragraph 6, sub-paragraph 2). Coming close to this issue, in *John Ballantyne, Elizabeth Davidson v. Canada and Gordon McIntyre v. Canada* (hereinafter the *"Ballantyne et al. v. Canada* case"; see *infra*), decided in 1993 under the First Optional Protocol to the ICCPR (Communications Nos. 359/1989 (Ballantyne and Davidson) and 385/1989 (McIntyre), Views of 31 March 1993, (1993) Annual Report II: 91), the HRC observed, *inter alia,* that the Article 27 rights of the francophone minority within Canada did not justify under the ICCPR positive measures entailing restrictions on the authors' right to freedom of expression in private, commercial activities. In *Waldman v. Canada,* the HRC found difference in treatment in favour of a religious minority, defended by Canada also on minority rights grounds, to be in breach of Article 26 of the ICCPR, since it discriminated against other religious minorities. In sum, from this perspective, the anti-discrimination approach, pursued through the "reasonable and objective" test, sets a limit to the permissibility of positive measures for the protection of minority identity, thereby relying on its "negative" dimension to determine the confines of equal protection.

In the light of the foregoing considerations, the more specific distinction between non-discrimination rights and minority rights can be easily grasped. As noted earlier, Articles 2 and 26 of the covenant, like any other general clause of this type, are available to everyone. They may be invoked by women, or by persons who hold particular unpopular views, or persons identified with particular political causes, and others. Persons belonging to minorities often feel discriminated against, and they, too, may invoke the said provisions. And yet, Article 2 and 26 are not reserved to ethnic, religious or linguistic minorities. By contrast, Article 27 provides certain guarantees which are available only to persons belonging to such groups. That is due to the above-mentioned distinctive goals pursued by international minority rights.

In the cited *Ballantyne et al. v. Canada* case, the complainant, an anglophone funeral parlour owner, claimed a violation of the covenant in relation to a Quebec law that prohibited commercial advertising outdoors in a language other than French. He wished to advertise in the English language to his potential anglophone clientele, but was prohibited by law from doing so. The complainant argued that this constituted a violation of his rights, under, *inter alia*, Article 27. The HRC stated first that the case raised no minority rights issue, since English language speakers were not a minority in Canada as a whole, and thus were not protected by Article 27. At the same time, the committee found that there was no violation of Article 26 because the above restriction applied to everybody, not just to English speakers. Nevertheless, the committee upheld an alternative argument based on Article 19, determining that commercial speech was protected by the right to freedom of expression, and entailed the freedom to advertise in the language of choice. It concluded that none of the limitations of such a right set forth by the covenant was relevant to the facts of the case, and that, consequently, Article 19 had been violated. In the *Belgian Linguistics* case, involving French language speakers of Belgium, the EurCtHR did not recognise a right to receive instruction in a special way, or in a special language under the ECHR. Still, it decided in favour of the applicants that access to education based solely on residence generated a discrimination on account of language contrary to Article 2 of the First Protocol (right to education) in conjunction with Article 14 (see *infra*, Chapter VI).

These two cases well illustrate, directly and indirectly, the difference between the right not to be discriminated against and minority rights – they represent complementary but distinct categories. One general implication of this distinction is that the issue of respect for minority rights is independent of whether minority members are treated in a non-discriminatory way. Indeed, even if they are, these persons are still entitled to special rights. Some states argue that they have no minorities, hence no minority rights to protect, as they comply with anti-discrimination clauses (for the "existence" aspect under Article 27 of the ICCPR, see *infra*, Chapter V). This argument is aptly dismissed by the HRC in its 1994 general comment in no uncertain terms:

> The Covenant also distinguishes the rights protected under article 27 from the guarantees under articles 2(1) and 26. [Under these articles non-discrimination rights are conferred on individuals within the jurisdiction of the State Party] irrespective of whether they belong to the minorities specified in article 27 or not. Some states parties who claim that they do not discriminate on grounds of ethnicity, language or religion, wrongly contend, on that basis alone, that they have no minorities. (General Comment No. 23: paragraph 4)

Bibliography

Alfredsson, G., "Equality and non-discrimination: minority rights", Council of Europe Doc. H/Coll (90), 6, 1990, pp. 1-23.

Ben Achour, Y., "Souveraineté étatique et protection international des minorités", *Collected Courses of the Hague Academy of International Law*, I, 1994, pp. 325-461.

Bossuyt, M., "The concept and practice of affirmative action", UN Doc. E/CN.4/Sub.2/2001/15 (progress report), 2001, pp. 1-34.

Bossuyt, M., "The concept and practice of affirmative action", UN Doc. E/CN.4/Sub.2/2000/11 (preliminary report), 2000, pp. 1-29.

Brownlie, I., *Principles of public international law*, fifth edition, Clarendon Press, Oxford, 1998.

Buergental, T., *International human rights*, West Publishing Co., St Paul, Minnesota, 1995.

Cholewinski, R., "The racial discrimination convention and the protection of cultural and linguistic ethnic minorities", *Revue de Droit International*, 3, 1991, pp. 157-236.

Damrosch, L.F., "Genocide and ethnic conflict", in *International law and ethnic conflict*, Wippman, D. (ed.), Cornell University Press, Ithaca and London, 1998, pp. 256-279.

de Varennes, F., "Minority rights and the prevention of ethnic conflicts", UN Doc. E/CN.4/Sub.2/AC.5/2000/CRP.3, 2000, pp. 1-14.

de Varennes, F., *Language, minorities and human rights*, Kluwer Law International, The Hague, 1996.

Ermacora, F., "The protection of minorities before the United Nations", *Collected Courses of the Hague Academy of International Law*, IV, 1983, pp. 257-370.

Higgins, R., "Minority rights: discrepancies and divergences between the International Covenant and the Council of Europe system", in *The dynamics of the protection of human rights in Europe: essays in honour of Henry G. Schermers,* Lawson, R. and de Blois, M. (eds), III, Martinus Nijhoff Publishers, Dordrecht, 1994, pp. 195-210.

Lemkin, R., *Axis rule in occupied Europe*, Carnegie Endowment for International Peace, Washington, 1944.

Lerner, N., *Group rights and discrimination in international law*, Martinus Nijhoff Publishers, Dordrecht, 1991.

McKean, W., *Equality and discrimination under international law*, Clarendon Press, Oxford, 1983.

Morsink, J., "Cultural genocide, the universal declaration, and minority rights", *Human Rights Quarterly*, 21, 1999, pp. 1009-1060.

Opsahl, T., "Equality in human rights law with particular reference to Article 26 of the International Covenant on Civil and Political Rights," in *Progress in the spirit of human rights: Festschrift für Felix Ermacora*, Nowak, M., Steurer, D. and Tretter, H. (eds), N.P. Engel Verlag, Kehl, 1988, pp. 51-65.

Packer, J. "On the content of minority rights", in *Do we need minority rights? Conceptual issues*, Räikkä, J. (ed.), Martinus Nijhoff Publishers, The Hague, 1996, pp. 121-178.

Ramcharan, B.G., "Equality and non-discrimination", in *The international bill of rights: the Covenant on Civil and Political Rights*, Henkin, L. (ed.), Columbia University Press, New York, 1981, pp. 246-269.

Sands, P. and Klein, P., *Bowett's law of international institutions*, fifth edition, Sweet & Maxwell, London, 2001.

Schabas, W.A., *Genocide in international law*, Cambridge University Press, Cambridge, 2000.

Spiliopoulou Åkermark, A., *Justifications of minority protection in international law*, Kluwer Law International, The Hague, 1997.

Thornberry, P., *International law and the rights of minorities*, Clarendon Press, Oxford, 1991.

CHAPTER V

IDENTITY: THE UN FRAMEWORK

It is thus clear that any meaningful exercise of minority rights, although "functionally" supported by physical existence and anti-discrimination standards, poses issues which are separately addressed by international law. In other words, physical existence and anti-discrimination entitlements are not "minority rights" but rather essential starting points to enable their protection. The primary focus of the present and the two following chapters will be precisely on minority rights as an autonomous normative category, namely as a set of universal and regional entitlements which aim to protect culturally distinctive identities.

1. Article 27 of the ICCPR

a. Background

As already noted, the UN General Assembly affirmed in Resolution 217 (III) adopted in 1948, that the United Nations "[could not] remain indifferent to the fate of minorities". It instructed the Commission on Human Rights and its sub-commission (through the ECOSOC) to prepare a detailed study of the problems of minorities as a basis for effective measures of protection. In 1950, during the discussion in the sub-commission about the implementation of the above 1948 resolution, it was agreed that the most effective means of tackling the minority question would be to include an article on the subject in the proposed ICCPR. Issues emerged, however, as to which minorities should be afforded protection and through what rights.

Broadly speaking, the differences were between those, such as the Soviet Union, who sought to limit protection to "nationality groups", and others, such as Yugoslavia, who favoured protection for other ethnic, religious and cultural groups as well (on "national" in the UN context, see *supra*, Chapter III). A question was whether the covenant should guarantee merely the freedom of a group to assert its identity, or also the right to maintain and develop that identity by separate institutions (schools, newspapers, etc.). A critical issue was whether states should be required only to tolerate freedom and institutions, or also to provide financial resources and other comparable support.

The first draft of the minority article of the covenant read as follows:

> Ethnic, religious and linguistic minorities shall not be denied the right to enjoy their own culture, to profess and practice their own religion, or to use their own language. (UN Doc. E/CN.4/Sub.2/112.)

At the initiative of the British expert Monroe, the word "minorities" was replaced with "persons belonging to" minorities, since minorities, it was noted, lacked legal personality. In reality, there were also fears that the recognition of a truly group right could trigger autonomist or even secessionist claims. However, in order to maintain the provision's collective element, she proposed the insertion of the passage "in community with the other members of their group".

The sub-commission adopted the draft with these changes in 1950. In 1953, the Commission on Human Rights approved the sub-commission's proposal with only one amendment, which was intended to meet the concerns of Latin American countries that immigrants to these countries might form separate communities claiming minority rights, thereby threatening national unity and security. In fact, Chile proposed that the introduction be replaced with "in those States in which stable and well defined ethnic, religious or linguistic minorities have long been established" (UN Doc. E/CN.4/L.261). The opening phrase of the article eventually became "in those States in which ethnic, religious or linguistic minorities exist". This linguistic amendment was not, however, meant to change the sense of the motion.

The final text read as follows:

> In those States in which ethnic, religious or linguistic minorities exist, persons belonging to such minorities shall not be denied the right, in community with the other members of the group, to enjoy their own culture, to profess and practice their own religion, or to use their own language.

Beyond the said purpose of restricting the beneficiaries of protection, the opening phrase of Article 27 "almost invites States to declare that they have no minorities on their territory, and some have responded to the 'invitation'" (Thornberry, 1995a: 333). France has indeed entered an "official" statement to such negative effect, declaring that "in the light of Article 2 of the Constitution of the French Republic, Article 27 is not applicable so far as the Republic is concerned" (*Human rights. Status of international instruments,* 1987: 35). In *T.K. v. France* (Communication No. 220/1987, Views of 8 November 1989, (1990) Annual Report II: 118) and *M.K. v. France* (Communication No. 222/1987, Views of 8 November 1989, (1990) Annual Report II: 127), the HRC interpreted the French "declaration" as a reservation, dismissing on this ground a case brought by speakers of Breton claiming to be victims of violations of the covenant because of legal restrictions on using Breton in their contacts with an administrative tribunal. Interestingly, in the more recent *Hopu and Bessert v. France* case (Communication No. 549/1993, Views of 29 July 1997, (1997) Annual Report II: 70), the HRC maintained this stand (though finding France in violation of the authors' rights to privacy and family in Articles 17 and 23 of the ICCPR), but five dissenting members considered the French declaration as inapplicable to overseas territories under French sovereignty.

On the other hand, the HRC rejects the interpretation of the article implying that the existence (and protection) of minorities is somehow predicated on an admission of discrimination, and insists, as confirmed in its General

Comment No. 23, paragraph 5, sub-paragraph 2, on the "factual" nature of existence criteria, not linked to any prior decision by a State Party (see also the separate opinion by Higgins in *T.K. v. France, loc. cit.,* and the HRC concluding comments on France issued in 1997 under the reporting procedure, UN Doc. CCPR/C/79/Add. 80). In *Ballantyne et al. v. Canada* (Communications Nos. 359/1989 (Ballantyne and Davidson) and 385/1989 (McIntyre), Views of 31 March 1993, (1993) Annual Report II: 91), the HRC's majority confined the factual connotation of "minority" to exclude members of the majority in a state who are in the minority within a province or autonomous area.

b. Selected issues

i. Aims pursued

What are the aims pursued by Article 27 Ermacora (1983: 309) refers to the right of persons belonging to minorities in community with others to enjoy their own culture, their own religion and their own language, as a way of creating, undertaking and upholding values which are based on self-consciousness as to group membership. The HRC pointed out in its 1994 General Comment No. 23, paragraph 6, sub-paragraph 2, that Article 27 rights depend "on the ability of the minority group to maintain its culture, language and religion", and identified the protection of the "identity of a minority" as a goal of the article. The HRC concluded that:

> The protection of [Article 27 rights] is directed to ensure the survival and continued development of the cultural, religious and social identity of the minorities concerned, thus enriching the fabric of society as a whole. (General Comment No. 23: paragraph 9)

Thus, Article 27 recognises the "right to identity" even if this right is not explicitly formulated. Thornberry describes such a right as "the claim to distinctiveness and the contribution of a culture on its own terms to the cultural heritage of mankind" (Thornberry, 1995a: 332). In this connection, he aptly notes:

> The elements of that identity can be ethnic, religious or linguistic, or all three. The concept projected is not the 'museumification' of cultures, which are subject to inevitable processes of historical change. Rather, international law seeks to locate the processes of change in the protective framework of human rights, so that members of minorities can play a part in the development of their culture and choose the basis on which it adapts to the world. Forced assimilation would violate this right to identity. *(Ibid)*

In *Bernard Ominayak, Chief of the Lubicon Lake Band v. Canada* (Communication No. 167/1984, Views of 26 March 1990, (1990) Annual Report II: 1), Mr Ando, in an individual opinion, replied to claims that industrial exploitation of resources threatened the band's way of life, by observing that "outright refusal by a group to change its traditional way of life may hamper the economic development of the society as a whole". But, as pointed out by Thornberry, "the whole point of Article 27 is to relate 'development' to genuine choices made by groups and not to permit States the liberty of

destruction in the name of utopian projects of social engineering".
(Thornberry, 1995a: 333)

ii. Individual rights and group protection

As indicated in Chapter II, the rights in Article 27 are for "persons belonging
to" minorities, not minorities *qua* groups. They are not, as such, group rights.
However, as noted, at the initiative of the British expert Monroe the passage
"in community with the other members of their group" was inserted in order
to maintain the idea of a group. Nowak points out that:

> Several years later in the H[uman] R[ights] Comm[ission], this passage was accorded
> a different meaning ... it was to prevent individuals from abusing minority rights for
> 'disruptive tendencies' not desired by the minority in its entirety. (Nowak, 1993:
> 497.)

Whatever specific considerations this passage may have generated, its adoption clearly reveals a collective element. Article 27 rights may be described
as rights of individuals premised on the existence of a community, or as individual rights stressing the aspect of their communal exercise (Thornberry,
1995a: 335; Capotorti, 1990: 353-354). Ermacora describes Article 27 as a
"group protection instrument" (Ermacora 1983: 321-324). In *Lovelace*
(Communication No. 24/1977, Views of 30 July 1981, (1981) Annual Report:
166; (1983) Annual Report: 248; paragraph 14), the HRC observed that:

> The rights under Article 27 of the Covenant have to be secured to 'persons belong-
> ing' to the minority. At present Sandra Lovelace does not qualify as an Indian under
> Canadian legislation ... Persons who are born and brought up on a reserve, who
> have kept ties with their community and wish to maintain these ties must normally
> be considered as belonging to that minority within the meaning of the Covenant.

The enjoyment of individual rights is thus situated within a distinctive
minority community context. The implications of this linkage are manifold.

Self-identification as a member of a minority is not an absolute criterion, due
to its connection to objective factors relevant to establishing the person's
minority identity (see *supra*, Chapter III). In *Kitok* (Communication No.
197/1985, Views of 27 July 1988, (1988) Annual Report 221: paragraph 9,
sub-paragraph 7), the HRC confirmed in principle the crucial significance of
"objective ethnic criteria". Complete "individualisation" of rights by the state
is forbidden – the article presupposes and protects the associative nature of
minority identity (namely, the rights are to be enjoyed in community with
the other minority members). This may include the right to reside in a particular place, though this right is not *per se* recognised in Article 27. In
Lovelace, the interference with the complainant's right to reside on the
Tobique reserve resulted in a continuing violation of Article 27, "because
there is no place outside the Tobique reserve where such a community
exists" (*loc. cit*: paragraph 15) – namely, the minority to which Sandra
Lovelace belonged.

At the same time, the individual nature of the rights is confirmed by the
recognition of the fact that being treated as a member of a minority is a
matter of a person's individual choice. Association with the group may not

be denied because of a previous choice not to invoke minority status. Yet, the HRC has also stated in the context of Article 27, that the individual right to belong to a minority and thus to share in aspects of community life may be restricted if a reasonable and objective justification is provided, notably if legislation pursues the legitimate aim of minority group preservation and well-being, and the restriction is proportionate to that aim. As already noted, in *Lovelace* and *Kitok* the HRC came to different conclusions in this latter regard, in favour of the complainant and the group, respectively. Although an effort has to be made at balancing conflicting interests, the "proportionality" argument used to justify rights restrictions in the second case should not be stretched as far as to ignore the individualistic essence of Article 27. In the recent *Apirana Mahuika et al. v. New Zealand* case (Communication No. 547/1993, Views of 27 October 2000, CCPR/C/70/D/541/1993: paragraph 9, sub-paragraph 9), involving the same type of conflict, the HRC found the measures designed to protect the group compatible with Article 27, while at the same time emphasising that, since Article 27 continues to bind the State Party in relation to the authors' rights to enjoy their own culture, those measures must be carried out in a way that such rights are respected.

Despite the absence of a truly group right in Article 27, the protection of the group does nevertheless fall within the purview of this article. For instance, in *Lubicon Lake Band* (*loc. cit*: paragraph 32, sub-paragraph 2), the HRC made it clear that:

> the rights protected by article 27, include the right of persons, in community with others, to engage in economic and social activities which are part of the culture of the community to which they belong.

It concluded (*loc. cit*: paragraph 33) that:

> [h]istorical inequities, to which the State party refers, and certain more recent developments threaten the way of life and culture of the Lubicon Lake Band, and constitute a violation of article 27 so long as they continue.

In this same context, the HRC made the interesting procedural point (*loc. cit*: paragraph 32, sub-paragraph 1) that there was:

> no objection to a group of individuals, who claim to be similarly affected, collectively to submit a communication about alleged breaches of the Covenant.

Thus, from both a substantive and procedural point of view, the HRC stressed the collective dimension to Article 27 rights. In *Apirana Mahuika*, the HRC applied its jurisprudence on "collective communications" to a group of individuals belonging to some of the tribes comprising the Maori people of New Zealand, and used Article 27 rights to assess not only the authors' claims but also, albeit indirectly, the parallel position of the minority as a whole. The same considerations apply to the approach taken by the HRC in the *Diergaardt* case (Communication No. 760/1997, Views of 25 July 2000, CCPR/C/69/D/760/1996), in which the complainants filed the communication not only on their own behalf but also on behalf of the Baster Community in Namibia to which they belonged. However, the HRC has firmly rejected the standing of communities or legal entities to lodge an individual communication under the First Optional Protocol, and confirmed the notion of group protection in terms of the individual rights of members belonging to the group. *I. Länsman v. Finland* (Communication No. 511/1992, Views of 26 October 1994, (1995) Annual Report II: 66) and *J. Länsman v. Finland* (Communication No. 671/1995, Views of 30 October 1996, (1997) Annual Report II: 191) further illustrate the interaction between individual rights and group protection under Article 27. In both of these cases, the HRC elaborated upon the impact of economic activities by enterprises on traditional ways of livelihood of minorities. In the first *Länsman* case (*loc. cit.:* paragraph 9, sub-paragraph 4), the HRC assumed the individual nature of Article 27 rights and, in order to assess the permissibility of the above impact, indirectly applied the test of "proportionality" developed in earlier cases. It indeed stated:

> Article 27 requires that a member of a minority shall not be denied his right to enjoy his culture. Thus, measures whose impact amount to a denial of the right will not be compatible with the obligations under article 27. However, measures that have a certain limited impact on the way of life of persons belonging to a minority will not necessarily amount to a denial of the right under article 27.

At the same time, in both *Länsman* decisions, the HRC, while not finding a violation of Article 27, warned the State Party of the possibly incremental, and thus cumulatively disproportional, repercussions on the Sami people of future economic activities carried out in traditional Sami areas. In the second *Länsman* case (*loc. cit.:* paragraph 10, sub-paragraph 7), the HRC, reaffirming its concern at large-scale activities affecting the area where the Sami people lived, explained:

> [e]ven though in the present communication the Committee has reached the conclusion that the facts of the case do not reveal a violation of the rights of the authors, the Committee deems it important to point out that the State party must bear in mind when taking steps affecting the rights under article 27, that though different activities in themselves may not constitute a violation of this article, such activities, taken together, may erode the rights of the Sami people to enjoy their own culture.

iii. The indigenous peoples question and the "jurisprudential pull"

It is evident that virtually all of the above cases were concerned with members of indigenous peoples. During the drafting of Article 27, a number of delegates to the Human Rights Commission and the General Assembly took the position that indigenous peoples, such as the Indians of North and Latin America or the aborigines in Australia, were not minorities. This view has been rejected by experts. Tomuschat (1983) describes indigenous peoples as perfect examples of clearly defined and long-established ethnic and usually linguistic and religious minorities as well.

However, indigenous peoples claim to be "more than" minorities, thereby favouring a separate protective regime. In fact, international law has given increased recognition to indigenous peoples as distinctive communities meriting a special regime to be distinguished from that of minorities, notably in view of their historical pre-existence and special attachment to ancestral lands (Anaya, 1996). The 1989 ILO Convention No. 169 concerning Indigenous and Tribal Peoples in Independent Countries, and the UN draft declaration on the rights of indigenous peoples adopted in 1993 by the UN Working Group on Indigenous Populations (Sub-Commission on Prevention of Discrimination and Protection of Minorities Resolution 1994/45), feature among the most important international texts attempting to delineate the content of such a regime. Nevertheless, to the extent that indigenous peoples consist, as is often the case, of ethno-cultural groups numerically inferior to the rest of the population of the states where they live, they may well be considered, *de minimis*, as minorities in the sense of Article 27, and of course, by analogy, as beneficiaries of minority rights instruments generally. In sum, for purposes of international law, "indigenous peoples" and "minorities" represent distinct but partly overlapping categories. This has been confirmed by the HRC which has regarded the protection of indigenous peoples under the ambit of Article 27, in the context of both the reporting procedure (see, for example, the concluding comments on Mexico, Sweden, Brazil, Ecuador and Chile, UN Doc. CCPR/C/79/Add. 32, 58, 66, 92 and 104) and, as noted, the complaints procedure.

In fact, indigenous peoples have been extremely adept in exploiting the possibilities of Article 27 under the First Optional Protocol, prompting the development of a jurisprudence with potentially wide repercussions. For instance, in *Kitok* (*loc. cit.*: paragraph 9, sub-paragraph 2), the HRC embraced a broad interpretation of "culture" falling within the scope of protection, which has been consistently recalled in later cases. It noted that:

> [t]he regulation of an economic activity is normally a matter for the State alone. However, where that activity is an essential element in the culture of an ethnic community, its application to an individual may fall under Article 27.

As also indicated by the *Diergaardt* case (*loc. cit.*: paragraph 3, sub-paragraph 1, and the concurring individual opinion by Mrs Evatt and Mrs Quiroga), the cultural dimension to the economic activity must therefore be clearly established to justify the applicability of Article 27 rights. In the *I. Länsman v. Finland* case (*loc. cit.*: paragraph 9, sub-paragraphs 6 and 8), brought by Sami reindeer herders, the HRC applied the (in principle universal) test of consultation and "proportionality" based on economic sustainability, to development activities conducted by private parties and authorised by the state (the same approach was adopted by the HRC in *J. Länsman v. Finland, loc. cit.*). The aim was to determine whether there had been a failure to protect the complainants' specific indigenous economy against "denial" in Article 27, by eroding its actual capacity to sustain their right to enjoy their own culture. In the same case (*loc. cit.*: paragraph 9, sub-paragraph 3), guided by a contextual approach to the determination of such a right as already hinted at in *Kitok*, the HRC emphasised that members of indigenous minorities (and minorities generally) are allowed to invoke Article 27 even though their way of conducting traditional activities has been adapted to modern technology. The *ratio decidendi* in *I. Länsman* afforded the basis for the *Apirana Mahuika* decision (*loc. cit.*: paragraphs 9, sub-paragraphs 4 and 5). Paragraph 3, sub-paragraph 2, and paragraph 7 of the 1994 general comment summarise

103

and/or inspire the committee's jurisprudence (including *Lubicon Lake Band*), containing observations mainly focused on the protection of the particular way of life of indigenous communities constituting minorities, in association with land and its resources. At the same time, the final sentence in paragraph 7, to the effect that the enjoyment of Article 27 rights: "may require ... measures to ensure the effective participation of members of minority communities in decisions affecting them [namely, those that might impact on their culture]", importantly provides a criterion which lends itself to generalisation. In the *Länsman* cases (*loc. cit.:* paragraph 9, sub-paragraph 5, and paragraph 10, sub-paragraph 4, respectively), the HRC, in order to establish the consultation test, recalled this part of the paragraph and stated that "measures must be taken" to ensure the effective participation. One may wonder whether the criterion of "effective participation" in the context of Article 27 might be emerging as *lex specialis,* narrowing for these purposes the apparently wider margin of discretion allotted to states in respect of the right of political participation in Article 25, sub-paragraph a, as interpreted by the HRC in *Marshall et al. v. Canada* (Communication No. 205/1986, Views of 4 November 1991, (1992) Annual Report: 201; see *infra,* Chapters VIII and IX).

Interestingly, for example, in the cases concerning *Miskito Indians of Nicaragua* (Case No. 7964 (Nicaragua), OAS Docs. OEA/Ser.L/V/II.62, Doc. 10, rev. 3, 1983, and OEA/Ser.L/V/II.62, Doc. 26, 1984) and *Yanomami of Brazil* (Case No. 7615 (Brazil), Resolution No. 12/85, 5 March 1985, OAS Doc. OEA/Ser.L/V/II.66, Doc. 10, rev. 1, 1985), as well as in the report on the situation of human rights in Ecuador (OAS Doc. OEA/Ser.L/V/II.96, Doc. 10, rev. 1, 1997), the Inter-American Commission on Human Rights of the OAS relied on Article 27 of the ICCPR in connection with the protection of ancestral lands of the minority indigenous communities concerned, and thus of their cultural integrity (for a succinct account of these cases, see Anaya, 1996: 100, 168-169; Scheinin, 2000: 180-182).

iv. Nature of state obligations

The state seems, prima facie, to be required only not to interfere in the enjoyment of minority rights (they "shall not be denied"), and not also to take positive action. The *Lovelace* case shows that non-denial of Article 27 rights, read in conjunction with other provisions of the covenant (notably, the equality and non-discrimination clauses), amounts to a basic prohibition of forced assimilation. Moreover, it is important to remember in this context that, in the first *Länsman* case (*loc. cit.:* paragraph 9, sub-paragraph 4), the HRC dismissed the applicability to Article 27 of the "margin of appreciation" doctrine invoked by the State Party (as developed by the EurCtHR under the ECHR; see also *infra,* Chapter VI), in connection with the assessment of the impact of economic activities on the right of minority members to enjoy their own culture. Although the HRC, as confirmed by *Apirana Mahuika* (*loc. cit.:* paragraph 9, sub-paragraph 4), performs a strong supervisory role in relation to domestic measures and activities, it seemingly gives states a certain leeway on these matters before a breach of Article 27 can be actually established.

While abstention from interference is of major significance, it is argued that a mere passive stance by states would not ensure the effective protection of minorities. Thornberry points out that:

> the principle of effectiveness in the interpretation of treaties indicates that articles should bear their full weight, and Article 27 would add little to the provisions on non-discrimination (Article 2), equality (Article 26), freedom of thought, conscience and religion (Article 18), and freedom of opinion and expression (Article 19), if it did not attempt to address the reality of minority disadvantage and implicate positive action by States. (Thornberry, 1995a: 336.)

Positive state duties may be construed at two levels:

– horizontal; and

– vertical.

At the horizontal level, the protection of Article 27 rights must be secured against infringements by private actors. To uphold this approach, Nowak (1993: 502-504) interprets Article 27 in conjunction with Article 2, paragraph 1, which obliges states parties not only "to respect", but also "to ensure" the covenant rights to all individuals. He contends that horizontal effects can be ruled out only when they conflict with the purpose of the right or when it is clear from the historical background that protection is only against state interference; he goes on to observe that the historical background to Article 27 does not reveal that horizontal effects were ruled out. Minority rights can in fact be threatened by the private side too. This also applies to minority indigenous communities, whose cultural integrity has been (or is) severely threatened more by colonial settlers or multinational companies than by the governmental side. These considerations are even relevant to conflicts between a minority and its members. For instance, *Lubicon Lake Band* and the *Länsman* cases, on the one hand, and *Lovelace, Kitok* and *Apirana Mahuika*, on the other, present aspects related to the above situations. In its recent General Comment No. 28 on equality of rights between men and women under Article 3, the HRC interestingly calls upon states parties to report on legislative and administrative practices regarding membership in a minority that might produce an infringement on the equal rights of women under the covenant (including the right to equal protection of the law), and:

> on measures taken to discharge their responsibilities in relation to cultural or religious practices within the minority communities that affect the rights of women. (General Comment No. 28: paragraph 32.)

A positive duty of protection "against the acts of other persons within the State party" has been confirmed in the HRC General Comment No. 23 on Article 27 (paragraph 6, sub-paragraph 1).

But positive state action may also be seen from a classic vertical (state-group members) perspective. Special rapporteur Capotorti argued that the article required "active and sustained measures" on the part of states, including the provision of resources, in order to effectively preserve minority identity (Capotorti, 1979: paragraph 588). Thornberry supports this interpretation, as noted earlier; in his view, "[s]tates should take measures to the extent necessary to ensure that the disadvantages of minority status do not result in the negation of the right" (Thornberry, 1995a: 337). Tomuschat (1983) and Nowak (1993) deny the possibility of inferring from Article 27 direct positive duties to guarantee rights. Nevertheless, they maintain that derivative claims of performance may result from measures affecting Article 27 rights. In Tomuschat's words:

> [o]nly in an indirect way can an obligation to take positive steps arise. If and when a State provides financial support to members of majority groups in respect of activities coming within the scope of Article 27, it is then required by virtue of the principle of non-discrimination to extend analogous treatment to persons belonging to an ethnic, linguistic or religious minority since non-discrimination applies to each and every right enshrined in the CCPR. In fact, to exclude such persons from benefits granted to all other citizens would amount to a denial of those rights which apparently are effective only if their exercise is being subsidized out of public funds. (Tomuschat, 1983: 970).

Nowak extends this approach to positive measures exclusively concerning minority groups (Nowak, 1993: 504). This perspective can be well illustrated by the *Waldman v. Canada* case (Communication No. 694/1996, Views of 3 November 1999, CCPR/C/67/D/694/1996), though the HRC did not rule on Article 27, but on Article 26 only. The case concerned a differential treatment conferred under Canadian law on Roman Catholic minority schools compared to other minority religious schools in Ontario, since only the former were entitled to public funding. Canada defended its own legislation by referring, among other things, to the protection of the vulnerable Roman Catholic minority and its minority rights. The HRC judged in favour of the complainant, by finding a breach of Article 26 on the basis of the "reasonable and objective" test. On a smaller scale, the equality issue addressed in this case indirectly reveals Nowak's and Tomuschat's broader point in relation to Article 27 and the ICCPR as a whole: positive measures may work for the aims of Article 27, yet they do not directly arise from it, but rather from the prohibition of discrimination triggered by the implementation of proactive domestic policies. The reverse aspect of this argument, however, is that the cessation of all relevant measures (for example, in *Waldman*, the funding for Roman Catholic schools, thereby providing funding to none of the minority schools concerned) is well possible as a means of removing discrimination against minorities or some of them, and would not be *per se* objectionable on the grounds of Article 27. Therefore, it is not correct to identify the extension of the personal scope of positive treatment so as to include previously discriminated minorities as the only remedial effect that would be attached to the anti-discrimination clauses.

Although Waldman's claim and the HRC's decision were confined to Article 26, Mr Scheinin, in a separate concurring opinion, observed (*loc. cit.:* paragraph 5) that when implementing the HRC's views the State Party should bear in mind that Article 27 "imposes positive obligations" to promote religious instruction in minority religions, to be fulfilled in a manner that is not discriminatory. The HRC has given some indication on the matter of positive action. In its General Comment No. 23 on Article 27, the HRC has noted not only that "positive measures of protection are ... required ... against the acts of the State party itself", but also that "positive measures by States may also be necessary to protect the identity of a minority and the rights of its members" (similarly, the above-mentioned paragraph 7 affirms that these rights "may require" active measures, with special reference to indigenous minorities), provided that the latter respect the provisions of Article 2, paragraph 1, and Article 26 of the covenant both as regards the treatment between different minorities and the treatment between persons belonging to them and the remaining part of the population (No. 23 (50): paragraph 6, sub-paragraphs 1 and 2). The HRC has in fact appeared increasingly assertive with regard to positive measures, notably to address the situation of minority indigenous groups (as reflected, *inter alia,* by its considerations in both the *Länsman* and *Apirana Mahuika* decisions). However, it is not entirely clear whether, in the HRC's view, critical areas of special protection such as minority education and communication with public authorities (for qualified "negative" entitlements to language use, see by analogy the *Ballantyne* decision, *loc. cit.;* and paragraph 5, sub-paragraph 3 of General Comment No. 23), and effective participation as elaborated upon in the cases mentioned above, should be viewed as systematically subsumed under Article 27 (as for the use of minority languages in administrative or court proceedings, see, for example, the HRC concluding comments on Norway, Sudan and Algeria, UN Doc. CCPR/C/79/Add. 27, 85 and 95, the purely "procedural" approach to Article 27: in *T.K. v. France and M.K. v. France, loc. cit.,* as well as the dissenting individual opinion in *Diergaardt, loc. cit.,* delivered by Mr Bhagwati, Mr Colville and Mr Yalden, with reference to Article 19, paragraph 2, and Article 27, paragraphs 2 and 3), or may be simply justified by it, *ex post facto,* in accordance with the equality and non-discrimination clauses (as for the use of the minority language in court, see also paragraph 5, sub-paragraph 3, of General Comment No. 23, which distinguishes Article 27 from Article 14, paragraph 3, sub-paragraph f, and compare it with the statement made by the HCR in *Dominique Guesdon v. France* (Communication No. 219/1986, Views of 25 July 1990, (1990) Annual Report II: 61), that in respect of the author's claim of a breach of Article 27 because of a denial to use his minority language in court, it was not necessary to address the scope of the French "declaration" concerning Article 27 as the facts of the communication "did not raise issues" under this provision; see also the dissenting individual opinion by Mr Lallah in *Diergaardt,* in relation to the authors' language-based claim to Article 27 rights, *loc. cit.:* paragraph 5; for similar questions under the ECHR, see *infra,* Chapter VI).

It is probably fair to note that, although, on a closer look, the view taken by the HRC on this kind of positive action has seemed to date mostly of a justificatory nature (namely, based on indirect reasoning), such a view should be considered as part of an incremental approach to Article 27 rights, the ramifications of which are in fact a function of the support from states parties. Interestingly, in the *Apirana Mahuika* case, New Zealand, with regard to the authors' claim under Article 27, accepted that it had positive obligations to protect Maori culture as manifested, *inter alia,* in fishing activities. A positive interpretation of Article 27 has been accepted also by the Nordic countries, namely Finland, Sweden, Denmark, Iceland and Norway

(UN Doc. E/CN.4/1992/SR.17: paragraph 69). Other affected countries are following suit: for instance, in the fourth periodic report submitted by Germany to the HRC under the covenant's reporting procedure, members of traditional groups within the meaning of Article 27 are presented as enjoying "essential minority rights" under this article, such as "on certain conditions, the right to use their own language when dealing with the authorities" (UN Doc. CCPR/C/84/Add. 5, paragraphs 242-245), which clearly entail positive state action.

The essential spectrum of positive state obligations which may be construed in connection with Article 27 can be thus summarised as follows:

– direct duties at the horizontal level (obligation, mainly due diligence-based, requiring the state to protect minority members against infringements by private parties); and

– duties at the vertical level, namely:

   (i) performance in fulfilment of an underlying obligation requiring the state not to discriminate as a result of the adoption of domestic measures in favour of majority and/or minority groups; or, more progressively,

   (ii) direct duties to take positive action to protect a minority's identity to the extent necessary, in accordance with the ICCPR as a whole (obligation requiring the state to achieve the above objective through means of its choice, in view of different factual circumstances).

Although the question of positive measures presents controversial aspects, the notion of "active" state duties may be said to have gained considerable ground in scholarly and jurisprudential assessment, and among states concerned.

v. Limitations

Despite the fact that, unlike many other provisions of the ICCPR, Article 27 does not contain a specific limitations clause, the view is occasionally maintained that certain limitations in some such provisions, notably Article 18, paragraph 3, are also applicable to Article 27. The reason for this would be the overlap of Article 27 with other provisions of the ICCPR, as well as various favourable oral interventions on this issue in the Third Committee of the General Assembly.

This view is rejected by Nowak (1993) on the rather convincing ground that the oral contributions do not necessarily evidence the majority opinion in the Third Committee, and that Article 27 represents *lex specialis* in relation to general freedoms of religion, association and assembly found in Articles 18, 19, 21 and 22. In fact, Article 27 pursues specific purposes which do not duplicate those of the above provisions. On the other hand, Nowak himself admits that limitations on minority rights may result from conflicts with other rights recognised in the ICCPR or from general limitations clauses.

For instance, minority rights under Article 27 are limited by the right to equality and non-discrimination in Articles 2 and 26, and under Article 3 in relation to equality between men and women (see, for example, HRC General Comment No. 28: paragraph 32), by the right to life in Article 6, the prohibition to disseminate propaganda for war or advocate racial or religious hatred in Article 20, and the prohibition of abuse in Article 5, paragraph 1. In *Lovelace* (*loc. cit.:* paragraphs 15 and 16), restrictions on freedom of movement and residence provided for in Article 12, paragraph 3, to limit access of members of a minority to residency areas of this minority were admitted so long as such measures had a reasonable and objective justification. Still, this view can be considered incorrect in so far as the limitation clause contained in Article 12, paragraph 3, does not apply to access to minority areas as a means of enjoying minority rights under Article 27. In general, restrictions affecting the enjoyment of Article 27 rights may, however, derive from the already-mentioned "proportionality" argument developed by the HRC in that same case and in *Kitok.*

vi. Relation to other international instruments

As noted earlier, Article 27 is the international global treaty text on minority rights. Most contemporary international instruments on minority rights build, in one way or another, on Article 27 rights as a minimum standard. The 1992 UN declaration expressly refers to Article 27 as its main source of inspiration. The case-law of the HRC under the communications procedure reinforces the value of this article for the international protection of minority rights. Over 140 states are now parties to the ICCPR, thereby strengthening Article 27 as setting forth a provision of a truly "universal" character.

In the present-day interpretative process, pertinent treaties and other instruments tend to interact with each other, as do the provisions of one and the same instrument between themselves. In other words, the reading of a treaty or other instrument as a whole is frequently made in the light of comparable texts. The "context" of a treaty in the sense of Article 31 of the Vienna Convention on the Law of Treaties may thus encompass a number of related documents, including so-called "soft law" texts. References in a preamble to other international texts – or even incorporation of these texts – in a treaty dealing in whole or in part with minority rights constitute a typical case in point in contemporary practice (see also *infra*, Chapter IX). By so doing, an attempt is made at avoiding as much as possible conflicting interpretations at the international level, while at the same time mandating conformity of domestic legislation to applicable international standards.

From this point of view, Article 27 of the ICCPR, as interpreted in the literature and the HRC's case-law, may provide guidance for the interpretation of other texts, though the latter are not necessarily to be linked to the limitations of Article 27 – minimum standards may not indeed prejudice higher levels of protection. Rather, such new instruments as the 1992 UN declaration and other instruments adopted at regional and sub-regional levels may, in turn, call for a more progressive interpretation of Article 27 in appropriate circumstances. For instance, although Article 27 rights and its attendant HRC case-law may have partly influenced the CERD General Recommendation XXIII (51) on the rights of indigenous peoples, in relation to the fundamental premise that the protection of indigenous distinct cultural identity must be ensured under the ICERD (for example, paragraph 4, sub-paragraph a), the same text may, in turn, help further elaborate upon the basic themes of equal treatment, non-forced assimilation and cultural integrity, which are subsumed under the scope of Article 27 of the ICCPR. Another example is offered by the previously mentioned paragraph 7 of HRC General Comment No. 23 on Article 27, which refers to "effective participation" of minority members in decisions affecting them. The theme of participation rights represents an important additional note to contemporary instruments on minority and indigenous rights (see *infra* in this chapter, and Chapters VI, VII and VIII); here again, a cross-fertilisation process seems to be taking place, whereby the interpretation of Article 27 and other international provisions is being advanced by considering and developing one another's relevant precepts or aspects of protection. In sum, as aptly observed by a former distinguished HRC member, the ICCPR "does not exist in isolation and provisions of other instruments can unavoidably intrude upon [the Committee's interpretative function]" (Higgins, 1989: 6).

vii. Relation to international customary law

Does Article 27 reflect a rule of international customary law? According to an assessment by Thornberry from the early 1990s, "Article 27 ... appears to be a right granted by a treaty without wider repercussions in customary law" (Thornberry, 1991: 246). The conclusion was essentially based on the following arguments:

– the *travaux* of the ICCPR do not support a contrary view;

– the considerations of the ICJ in the *Barcelona Traction* case (Second Phase) (see *supra*, Chapter IV) do not specifically address minority rights and, as confirmed by such considerations, it is difficult to establish human rights rules of customary law, except for a few cases; and

– there is no evidence that domestic arrangements concerning particular minorities are made in fulfilment of a general obligation to do so under international law.

In recent years, however, the same author has pointed out that "the concept of an underlying customary law of minority rights should not be lightly dismissed" (Thornberry, 1995a: 385). In fact, some commentators do believe that Article 27 rights have become international customary law. The view was already insinuated, albeit indirectly, by the Inter-American Commission on Human Rights of the OAS, in the cited *Yanomami* case of 1985. On this occasion, the commission invoked Article 27 rights even though Brazil was not a party to the ICCPR. It delineated principles of international law aimed at protecting the cultural identity of ethnic groups. More lately, justifications for customary law status of Article 27 rights include references to the current large number of states bound by the article as parties to the ICCPR, the connection between Article 27 requirements and the general principles of equality and non-discrimination, the reaffirmation of the gist of such requirements in Article 30 of the UN Convention on the Rights of the Child (which has been ratified by virtually all states), and their confirmation in other important texts, adopted unanimously or by consensus, such as the 1990 Copenhagen Document and the 1992 UN Declaration.

Support for the view that Article 27 rights are part of customary law can also be found in the General Comment No. 24 on reservations, adopted by the HRC in 1994. The committee contends that the provisions reflecting customary law may not be the subject of reservations; among such provisions is the one concerning minority rights (paragraph 8) (see also *supra*, Chapter III). Finally, the EC Badinter Commission, set up in the context of the crisis in the former Yugoslavia (see *infra*, Chapter VII), made an innovative statement to the effect that "[peremptory] norms of international law require States to ensure respect for the rights of minorities" (Conference on Yugoslavia, Opinion No. 2 of 11 January 1992, ILM 31, 1992, 1497: paragraph 2). Although the commission did not expressly refer to Article 27, its reference to "the right to recognition of [minority] identity under international law" suggested a close connection with this article, irrespective of the specific question of *jus cogens*.

Basic aspects of protection under Article 27, such as the right to the equal enjoyment of one's culture, and, in particular, to assert and preserve it free of any attempt at assimilation against one's will, enjoy nowadays wide support from the international community, in view of broadly formulated notions of cultural pluralism and repeatedly stated concerns for stability. Although specific contours of Article 27 rights require further clarification and areas of interpretative disagreement persist, at least the above aspects might, arguably, be considered as strong candidates for customary law through state practice and *opinio juris*. Whatever conclusions on the matter, it is clear that contemporary practice reveals broader contexts where the emergence of customary law might be of major significance. In this regard, the 1992 UN declaration must be accounted for.

2. The UN Declaration on the Rights of Persons Belonging to National or Ethnic, Religious and Linguistic Minorities

a. Background

In his Study on the rights of persons belonging to ethnic, religious and linguistic minorities (1979), former UN special rapporteur Capotorti recommended the preparation of a draft declaration on the rights of members of minority groups within the framework of the principles set forth in Article 27. The sub-commission endorsed this proposal and submitted it to the Commission on Human Rights. In 1978, the commission set up an open-ended working group to work on the text of the declaration. A draft was submitted by Yugoslavia. The drafting process passed through several stages where a range of questions were dealt with.

In 1992, the draft declaration was approved by the Commission on Human Rights and the ECOSOC. The latter transmitted it to the General Assembly. Many states with minority populations sponsored the resolution containing the draft in the Third Committee of the General Assembly. The declaration was eventually approved by consensus in Resolution 47/135 of 18 December 1992.

The final stages of the drafting were characterised by a remarkable participation of governments.

b. Preamble and substantive provisions

The text, like Article 27, does not recognise minorities as distinct right-holders – the rights are those of "persons belonging to" minorities, not minorities *qua* groups. The title adds "national" to the minorities listed in Article 27, but this, as discussed in Chapter III, should not constitute a real departure from the traditional approach to the definitional question in the UN context. The preamble reveals some crucial assumptions:

– the declaration builds on existing international human rights standards, while at the same time promoting their realisation – minority rights do not exist in isolation as a sort of esoteric category of rights, but are "normal" human rights pursuing specific non-assimilationist aims;

– the declaration is "inspired by", not "based on", Article 27 – its interpretation is not necessarily to be affected by the limitations of that article;

– the declaration is intended to contribute to the internal stability of states – importantly, respect for minority rights is to be secured "within a democratic framework based on the rule of law";

– the declaration stresses the continuing role of the UN in minority questions, and intergovernmental and non-governmental organisations generally; and

– the declaration is designed to ensure "even more effective" implementation of international human rights instruments of relevance to minorities – this may be taken as an acknowledgement of the interaction of human rights instruments among themselves, and its applicability to minority rights and minority-related standards (as for Article 27 of the ICCPR and other instruments, see *supra*).

The main text is short but of major importance. Some brief points can be made. Article 1, paragraph 1, provides for a state duty to protect the existence and identity of minorities and to encourage conditions for the promotion of that identity. This transcends the tentative language of Article 27. The mandatory language is reflected in the use of the verb "shall". "Existence" includes broad aspects falling beyond a basic prohibition of genocide – policies of forced assimilation, ethnocide, population transfer, etc., would violate Article 1, paragraph 1, in relation to the protection of a minority as a whole. Article 1, paragraph 2, requires states to adopt appropriate legislative and other measures to achieve the objectives of Article 1, paragraph 1.

Article 2, paragraph 1, elaborates on Article 27 but replaces "shall not be denied the right" with the positive "have the right". That makes it clear that the actual enjoyment of the right recognised also requires active measures by the state (notably in conjunction with Articles 1 and 4). The exercise of the right "without interference or any form of discrimination" may be seen as encompassing positive protection against infringements by private parties ("horizontal effects"). Paragraphs 2, 3 and 4 of Article 2 introduce the concept of participation rights, including a specific right of persons belonging to minorities to participate effectively in decisions at national and, where appropriate, local level affecting their minority or the regions in which they live, "in a manner not incompatible with national legislation" (Article 2, paragraph 3). Means of participation are not spelled out but Article 2, paragraph 4, provides for the right to establish and maintain minority associations. As pointed out by Thornberry, "participation may evolve towards levels of greater decentralisation and thus more 'effective' involvement" (Thornberry, 1995a: 342). Article 2, paragraph 5, is concerned with contact rights. Free and peaceful contacts may be established:

– with other members of the group;

– with members of other minorities; and

– across frontiers, with "kin-persons".

They supplement the association rights in Article 2, paragraph 4.

Though not entirely consistent with the language of Article 27 of the ICCPR, paragraph 1 of Article 3 confirms the collective dimension of protection (the rights may be indeed exercised "individually as well as in community with other members of their group"), while paragraph 2 reformulates the principle of individual choice. Article 4 indicates the measures to be taken for the benefit of persons belonging to minorities. Article 4, paragraph 1, refers to measures which states "shall take, where required", to secure effective enjoyment of human rights – "without any discrimination" suggests also protection at the horizontal level. Article 4, paragraph 2, provides that states "shall create favourable conditions" for the expression and development of minority cultures, "except when specific practices are in violation of national law and contrary to international standards". The latter reference is a response to the objection that minority traditions may sometimes be inconsistent with human rights. In line with what is stated in the preamble, the clause reflects a firm linkage of the text with general human rights principles and obviously does not condemn minority cultures as such (in the context of the ICCPR, see, for example, the cited HRC General Comment No. 28: paragraph 32, stating that Article 27 rights, and cultural or religious minority practices generally, may not trump upon the equal rights of women). Conversely, it should be noted that the reference to a "violation of national law" must presuppose conformity of national legislation to international human rights law.

Facilitating the expression and development of minority cultures may be direct or indirect (namely, based on spaces of freedom), but "have adequate opportunities" (to learn the minority language) and "have instruction" (in the minority language) in Article 4, paragraph 3, suggest that economic resources "should" be provided by the state. As noted by Packer, "whenever possible" may be constructively interpreted in the sense of "a right to challenge governmental policy which does not facilitate the possible" (Packer, 1996: 159). Article 4, paragraph 4, deals with measures that states "should" take, "where appropriate", in the field of multicultural and inter-cultural education, and the next paragraph 5 introduces the theme of "participation in economic progress" (in conjunction with Article 2, paragraphs 2, 3 and 4, and Article 5). Such a participation would be clearly facilitated by regularly consulting the groups as to economic and development activities which may affect their identity and/or their full participation in the economic life of their society (see *supra* on Article 27 of the ICCPR, and *infra*, Chapter VIII). On the other hand, Article 4, paragraph 5, only refers to "appropriate measures" which states "should consider" for adoption, and the participation rights under Article 2 do not pre-define the modalities of participation. Therefore, these provisions as such do not provide a specific state "duty to consult" with regard to development programmes affecting minority groups.

Articles 5, 6 and 7 invite states to ensure that minority interests and rights are duly taken into account in national planning and international co-operation. Article 8, paragraph 1, states that the declaration adds to existing instruments and cannot thus justify a failure to perform existing (notably, more favourable) obligations and commitments. Article 8, paragraph 2, reaffirms the general principle that minority rights may not prejudice the human rights and fundamental freedoms of others, though its paragraph 3 clarifies that measures taken under the declaration are, prima facie, compatible with the principle of equality. Paragraph 4 of Article 8 essentially safeguards territorial integrity against claims to secession based on the declaration. Finally, Article 9 points to the contribution by the specialised agencies and other organisations of the UN to the realisation of the rights and principles set forth in the declaration.

c. Nature and role of the commitments

Although the declaration is not legally binding and the qualification of certain provisions contained therein might not exclude their "negative" reading, the overall regime provides a rather solid basis for further developments. The Chairperson of the UN Working Group on Minorities (see *infra*, Chapter X) has usefully produced a commentary to the declaration (Eide, 2001), which will generate increased attention and discussion of the various aspects of protection. As a "soft law" instrument, the declaration might positively influence the interpretation of existing texts or otherwise interact with them (see *supra*), notably Article 27 of the ICCPR, by which it is (only) "inspired", and contributes on its own terms to the creation of legally binding rules. As noted in a memorandum of the UN Office of Legal Affairs from the early 1960s:

> In United Nations practice, a 'declaration' is a formal and solemn instrument, suitable for rare occasions when principles of great and lasting importance are being enunciated ... [a] recommendation is less formal ... in view of the greater solemnity and significance of a 'declaration' it may be considered to impart, on behalf of the organ adopting it, a strong expectation that Members of the international community will abide by it. (E/CN.4/832/Rev. 1, paragraph 105).

The UN declaration was indeed approved by consensus as it enjoyed wide support from states. It may be "hardened" through incorporation in treaties (as in the case of the 1995 Treaty on Good-Neighbourliness and Friendly Co-operation between Slovakia and Hungary: see *infra*, Chapter IX) or, as hinted at earlier, the emergence of corresponding customary rules through state practice and *opinio juris*. Some fundamental principles may be viewed as either implicitly reaffirming customary law (see Article 1, paragraph 1, in relation to aspects affecting the physical existence of minorities) or perhaps as customary law *in statu nascendi* (see, for example, Article 2, paragraph 1). Overall, the "maturing" of the declaration into customary law basically depends on whether, and to what extent, states will respond to the above-mentioned expectation of compliance which the adoption of this type of instrument normally carries with it, bridging a recurrent gap between pro-claimed principles and their actualisation within domestic systems. The role of the UN as a source of encouragement and supervision under Article 9 is thus of primary importance.

Finally, the declaration may also be viewed as a widely shared benchmark for a future convention on minority rights. In this connection, it should be noted that the UN Sub-Commission on the Promotion and Protection of Human Rights has recently recommended the Commission on Human Rights and the High Commissioner for Human Rights to invite, *inter alia*, governments to submit their views on the desirability of drafting a convention on minority rights, including regional standard-setting (UN Sub-Commission on Human Rights Resolution 2000/16, 2000: paragraph 9; and Resolution 2001/9, 2001: paragraph 7).

Bibliography

Alfredsson, G., "Minority rights: a summary of existing practice", in *Universal minority rights*, Phillips, A. and Rosas, A. (eds), Åbo Akademi and Minority Rights Group (International), Turku/Åbo and London, 1995, pp. 77-86.

Alfredsson, G. and de Zayas, A., "Minority rights: protection by the United Nations", *Human Rights Law Journal*, 14, 1993, pp. 1-9.

Anaya, J., *Indigenous peoples in international law*, Oxford University Press, New York and Oxford, 1996.

Capotorti, F., Study on the rights of persons belonging to ethnic, religious and linguistic minorities, UN Doc. E/CN.4/Sub.2/384/Rev. I, 1979.

Capotorti, F., "Are minorities entitled to collective international rights?", in *Israel Yearbook on human rights*, 20, 1990, pp. 351-357.

Capotorti, F., "Minorities", in *Encyclopedia of public international law*, Macalister-Smith, P. (ed.), 3, Elsevier Science B.V., Amsterdam, 1997, pp. 410-420.

Eide, A., "Final text of the Commentary to the Declaration on the Rights of Persons Belonging to National or Ethnic, Religious and Linguistic Minorities", UN Doc. E/CN.4/Sub.2/AC.5/2001/2, 2001, pp. 1-21.

Ermacora, F., "The protection of minorities before the United Nations", *Collected Courses of the Hague Academy of International Law*, IV, 1983, pp. 257-370.

Higgins, R., "The United Nations: still a force for peace", *Modern Law Review*, 52, 1989, pp. 1-21.

Horn, F., "Recent attempts to elaborate standards on minority rights", in *Current international law issues: Nordic perspectives: essays in honour of Jerzy Sztucki*, Bring, O. and Mahmoudi, S. (eds), Fritzes, Stockholm, 1994, pp. 81-108.

Joseph, S., Schultz, J. and Castan, M., *The International Covenant on Civil and Political Rights: cases, materials, and commentary*, Oxford University Press, Oxford, 2000.

Nowak, M., *UN Covenant on Civil and Political Rights: CCPR commentary*, N.P. Engel Verlag, Kehl, 1993.

Packer, J., "On the content of minority rights", in *Do we need minority rights? Conceptuel issues?*, Räikka, J. (ed.), Martinus Nijhoff Publishers, The Hague, 1996, pp. 121-178.

Pentassuglia, G., "L'applicazione alle minoranze del primo Protocollo Facoltativo relativo al Patto internazionale sui diritti civili e politici", *Rivista Internazionale dei Diritti dell'Uomo*, VIII, 1995, pp. 295-313.

Scheinin, M., "The right to enjoy a distinct culture: indigenous and competing uses of land", in *The jurisprudence of human rights law: a comparative interpretative approach*, Orlin, T.S. and Scheinin, M. (eds), Åbo Akademi, Turku/Åbo, 2000, pp. 159-222.

Sohn, L.B., "The rights of minorities" in *The international bill of rights: the Covenant on Civil and Political Rights*, Henkin, L. (ed.), Columbia University Press, New York, 1981, pp. 270-289.

Spiliopoulou Åkermark, A., *Justifications of minority protection in international law*, Kluwer Law International, The Hague, 1997.

Thornberry, J., *International law and the rights of minorities,* Clarendon Press, Oxford, 1991.

Thornberry, P., "Minority Rights", in *Collected Courses of the Academy of European Law,* VI-2, 1995a, pp. 307-390.

Thornberry, P., "The UN Declaration on the Rights of Persons Belonging to National or Ethnic, Religious and Linguistic Minorities: background, analysis, observations, and an update", in *Universal minority rights,* Phillips, A. and Rosas, A. (eds), Åbo Akademi and Minority Rights Group (International), Turku/Åbo and London, 1995b, pp. 13-76.

Tomuschat, C., "Protection of minorities under Article 27 of the International Covenant on Civil and Political Rights", in *Völkerrecht als Rechtsordnung Internationale Gerichtsbarkeit Menschenrechte: Festschrift für Hermann Mosler,* Bernhardt, R., Geck, W.K., Jaenicke, G. and Steinberger, H. (eds), Springer-Verlag, Berlin, 1983, pp. 949-979.

United Nations Centre for Human Rights, "Minority rights", in *United Nations Human Rights Fact Sheets Nos. 1-25, 9,* Raoul Wallenberg Institute of Human Rights and Humanitarian Law (ed.), Raoul Wallenberg Institute of Human Rights and Humanitarian Law, Lund, 1998, pp. 341-361.

CHAPTER VI

IDENTITY: THE REGIONAL FRAMEWORKS (PART I)

Türk (1992) usefully divides the work on the protection of minorities in European institutional forums since 1945 into three basic periods:

— the period of "standstill", between 1945 and 1975, which was characterised by relatively little interest in developing minority standards going beyond the limited effect of general or specific anti-discrimination clauses (for example, in Article 14 of the ECHR), though the *Belgian Linguistics* case led to extensive discussions of the prohibition of discrimination in relation to the specific demands of minority groups (see *infra*);

— the period of "slow progress", between 1975 and 1990, most of which was generated by the CSCE where the issue of minorities was "(re)internationalised" in 1975 (by virtue of Principle VII of the Helsinki Final Act), and approached more constructively in the late 1980s; and

— the period of "intensive search", after 1990, consisting in intensive work on minorities by the Council of Europe, OSCE and EU.

Although such recent work is essentially focused on minority rights as an advance upon general and/or anti-discrimination regimes, the following account will include, where appropriate, a short review of the latter, in order to indirectly highlight the stage of development of minority rights considerations within each particular institutional context.

1. The Council of Europe framework

a. Early efforts at elaborating minority rights standards

In the Statute of the Council human rights feature as one of the means of achieving "greater unity" and democracy (Article 1, paragraph b). In fact, pluralist democracy, respect for human rights and the rule of law are the statutory principles. Respect for human rights and the rule of law are expressly indicated as obligations of member states and conditions for admission of new members (Articles 3 and 4).

Although the post-1990 work has proved remarkable (see *infra*), the Council of Europe's efforts to develop minority rights standards are not new but date back to the first decades of the Organisation's activities. As early as the late 1940s, a proposal was indeed made to include a provision on minorities in the ECHR, but it was eventually discarded. That was basically due to the still unclear relation between the concept of human rights and the concept of minority rights, the preference for provisions to be interpreted (at least at

119

that time) as generating purely "negative" obligations, and the absence of minority provisions in one of the main sources of inspiration of the ECHR, namely the UDHR. Nevertheless, it was agreed to add "association with a national minority" as a prohibited ground of distinction (Article 14 of the ECHR). Efforts continued with a view to elaborating special measures for the preservation of the distinctive culture of minority groups.

A proposal for an article to be included in the Fourth Protocol to the ECHR was submitted by the Parliamentary Assembly in 1961 (Recommendation 285). The text read as follows:

> Persons belonging to a national minority shall not be denied the right, in commu-
> nity with other members of their group, and as far as compatible with public order,
> to enjoy their own culture, to use their own language, to establish their own schools
> and receive teaching in the language of their choice, or to profess and practice their
> own religion.

It was drafted along the lines set by Article 27 of the ICCPR, though some differences may be discerned:

– it referred to "national minorities", reflecting a wide preference for this term in Europe;

– it did not contain the phrase "in those States in which ... minorities exist", which is one of the less fortunate elements of Article 27;

– it required compatibility of minority rights with public order, though the implications of this linkage did not appear entirely clear; and

– it provided for the right of persons belonging to minorities "... to establish their own schools and receive teaching in the language of their choice ...", an element missing in Article 27 of the ICCPR and tentatively expressed (with regard to mother-tongue education) in some contemporary instruments on minority rights.

The Committee of Ministers considered the draft and decided to postpone decision on the matter. At the time, the *Belgian Linguistics* case – concerning the question of the right of parents to choose the language of education of their children – was pending before the Strasbourg bodies. It was felt that it would not be appropriate to draft a new article on minorities before this case was decided. The discussion was resumed by the Committee of Experts on Human Rights in 1973, which concluded that there was no special need to make minority rights the subject of a further protocol to the ECHR, though there was "no overriding obstacle of a legal character" against this (Rights of National Minorities, report of the Committee of Experts on Human Rights to the Committee of Ministers, 1973, DH/Exp (73) 47: paragraph 12).

b. *Substantive provisions and the Article 14 right in the case-law under the ECHR*

The Strasbourg bodies have repeatedly stated that the ECHR contains no specific minority rights provisions. However, cases have been (or are being) dealt with under the enforcement mechanism of the ECHR on expulsion, degrading treatment, freedom of expression, language and religion, family and private life, representation rights, etc., concerning members of minority or other ethno-cultural groups (see, generally, Hillgruber and Jestaedt, 1994).

In the *Isop v. Austria* case (Application No. 808/60, YBECHR 5, 1962: 108), the Commission denied a right to "linguistic freedom" where the applicant claimed the right to use the Slovene language before a civil court; similar cases have affected, for example, speakers of Breton (*Bideaut v. France*, Application No. 11261/84, EurCommHR, Decision of 6 October 1986, DR 48, 1986: 232), Flemish (*X and Y v. Belgium*, Application No. 2332/64, YBECHR 9, 1966: 418) and Frisian (*Fryske Nasjonale Partij and Others v. Netherlands*, Application No. 11100/84, EurCommHR, Decision of 3 October 1985, DR 45, 1986: 240). In *G and E v. Norway* (Applications Nos. 9278/81 and 9415/81, EurCommHR, Decision of 12 December 1985, DR 35, 1994, 35: paragraph 2), the Commission conceded that under Article 8, paragraph 1, "a minority group is, in principle, entitled to claim the right to respect for the particular life style it may lead as being 'private life', 'family life' or 'home'"; the case was, however, declared inadmissible due to the specific aspects of the applications. In *Buckley v. United Kingdom*, a case concerning a Gypsy woman who claimed to be able to park her caravan on her land notwithstanding the absence of planning permission, the Commission (EurCommHR, Report of 11 January 1995, EHRR CD 19,1995, 20: paragraph 64) consistently held that "the traditional lifestyle of a minority may attract the guarantees of Article 8". The Commission found a violation of Article 8, but the Court (EurCtHR, Judgment of 25 September 1996, Reports 1996-IV: 1271) reversed the decision, highlighting solely the applicant's right to a home, not a particular way of life.

In a series of recent similar cases involving Gypsy individuals (*Chapman v. United Kingdom*, Application No. 27238/95, EurCtHR, Judgment of 18 January 2001; *Beard v. United Kingdom*, Application No. 24882/94, EurCtHR, Judgment of 18 January 2001; *Coster v. United Kingdom*, Application No. 24876/94, EurCtHR, Judgment of 18 January 2001; *Lee v. United Kingdom*, Application No. 25154/94, EurCtHR, Judgment of 18 January 2001; *Jane Smith v. United Kingdom*, Application No. 27238/95, EurCtHR, Judgment of 18 January 2001), the new Court (Grand Chamber) established following the reforms introduced by Protocol No. 11, recalled the *Buckley* jurisprudence, particularly in regard to a wide "margin of appreciation" enjoyed in principle by national authorities in the choice and implementation of planning policies, and concluded that the relevant facts did not disclose any violation of Article 8. However, the Court appeared to advance matters, although very cautiously. Joining the Commission's view in *Buckley*, the Court (see, for example, paragraph 73 of the Chapman Judgment, *loc. cit.*) indeed acknowledged that the applicants' traditional lifestyle, as part of their long-standing cultural identity, attracted the protection of private life, family life and home under Article 8, and that the contested measures affecting it constituted an "interference" subject to the parameters set forth in paragraph 2 of this article; moreover, it referred (see, for example, paragraph 93 of the Chapman Judgment, *loc. cit.*) to "an emerging international consensus" within the Council of Europe "recognising the special needs of minorities and an obligation to protect their security, identity and lifestyle" (see *infra*), and identified

121

(see, for example, paragraph 96 of the Chapman Judgment, *loc. cit.*) a positive obligation under Article 8 "to facilitate the Gypsy way of life". By contrast, the Court (see, for example, paragraph 94 of the Chapman Judgment, *loc. cit.*) did not bring the above "emerging consensus" to bear upon the cases, as it saw it as not "sufficiently concrete for it to derive any guidance as to the conduct or standards which contracting states consider desirable in any particular situation", rendering the Court's role a "strictly supervisory one", and dismissed the notion that Article 8 imposed upon the respondent state a duty to make available to the Gypsy community an adequate number of suitably equipped caravan sites. The joint dissent of seven judges stressed the need to give practical effect to the rights guaranteed by the ECHR, especially in the light of current developments in the field of minorities within the Council of Europe. In essence, they argued for a narrower "margin of appreciation" on the part of national authorities on planning matters in the context of the measures interfering with the applicants' lifestyle, which they indeed did not consider as reflecting compelling reasons as to make them "necessary in a democratic society" in the sense of Article 8, paragraph 2, and viewed Article 8 as prescribing a positive duty to ensure that Gypsies be afforded a practical and effective opportunity to enjoy their rights to home, private and family life.

Putting the ECHR into a forward-looking perspective, it would seem that a greater measure of concern for ethno-cultural groups might inform the way relevant ECHR rights are interpreted and applied. As limited as it may be, the above latest jurisprudence adds to pronouncements in earlier cases which appear to indicate that the Strasbourg Court might generate some form of protection for minorities and their members, in relation to general needs and rights affecting their position, with a special focus on way of life and identity (Articles 8 and 10), education (Article 2 of the First Protocol), religious life (Article 9) and effective participation in public life (Articles 10 and 11) (see, for example, the surveys by Gilbert, 1999 and 2000; for references, see also *infra*, Chapter VIII). In this connection, it is noteworthy that, in the recent *Cyprus v. Turkey* case (Application No. 25781/94), both the Commission (Report of 4 June 1999: paragraph 478), and the Court (Grand Chamber, Judgment of 10 May 2001: paragraph 278), without reversing the *Belgian Linguistics* case approach to mother-tongue education under the ECHR (see *infra*), held that the circumstances at issue were such that denial of mother-tongue education at the secondary school level did not meet the "legitimate wish" of Greek Cypriots living in Northern Cyprus to have their children educated in accordance with their ethno-cultural tradition, and in fact amounted to a denial of the substance of the right to education under Article 2 of the First Protocol.

In *X v. Austria* (Application No. 8142/78, EurCommHR, Decision of 10 October 1979, DR 18, 1980, 93: paragraph 1), the Commission stated, with regard to the absence of specific provisions on minorities in the ECHR, that:

> the protection of individual members of [a] minority is limited to the right not to be discriminated in the enjoyment of the Convention rights on the ground of their belonging to the minority. (Article 14 of the Convention.)

Therefore, aside from issues which directly arise (or may arise) under the above-mentioned particular substantive provisions, this statement poses the more general question of the role of Article 14 in connection with minority concerns.

The *Belgian Linguistics* case (EurCtHR, Judgment of 23 July 1968, Series A, No. 6) is still considered to be one of the leading cases regarding discrimination under Article 14 of the ECHR. The applicants were parents of families in Belgium who applied both on their behalf, and on behalf of children under age. As French speakers, they wanted their children to be educated in that language although they lived in a Dutch-speaking region under Belgian law, which thus required that public education be conducted in the official language of the region. The case raised issues, in particular, under Article 2 of the First Protocol (right to education) in conjunction with Article 14 (prohibition of discrimination).

The Commission had found that Belgian language legislation was incompatible with the first sentence of Article 2 of the First Protocol as regards the basic questions brought up by the applicants (namely, withdrawal of subsidies from public schools in the Dutch-speaking region providing education in French; residence-based access to education in communes with a "special status" in the Brussels area; refusal to validate secondary education certificates not in accordance with language requirements as provided by law). The case was referred to the Court by the Commission in 1965. As indicated in Chapter IV, the Court pointed out that Article 14 did not forbid every difference in treatment in the enjoyment of ECHR rights, but only prohibited those differences in treatment which pursued no legitimate aim, had no objective and reasonable justification, and were not proportionate to the aim sought to be realised (in later cases, the Court has acknowledged a certain "margin of appreciation" enjoyed by the contracting states in assessing the differences in otherwise similar situations which led to the distinctions, while reserving its final ruling in this respect: see, for example, *Abdulaziz, Cabales and Balkandali v. United Kingdom*, EurCtHR, Judgment of 28 May 1985, Series A, No. 94, 35-36: paragraph 72).

In particular, the Court observed that Article 14 of the Convention and Article 2 of the First Protocol did not produce the effect of guaranteeing to a child or to his parents the right to obtain instruction in a language of his or their choice. Rather, the scope of the article was to ensure that the right to education be secured by each contracting party to everyone within its jurisdiction without discrimination (by way of comparison, *Cyprus v. Turkey, loc. cit.,* may be indicating a more nuanced approach by the Court to mother-tongue education). The Court found that Belgian language legislation pursued a "legitimate aim" (namely, to achieve linguistic unity within a unilingual region of Belgium), and that some of the questions raised (namely, withdrawal of subsidies and refusal to validate certificates relating to secondary education) did not reveal any arbitrary measures which run counter to the Convention. In particular, the Court noticed that private French-speaking education was not affected by the legislation in question.

123

Still, the Court did find discrimination as regards access to education in the communes surrounding Brussels with a "special status": Dutch-speaking children resident in the French unilingual region had access to Dutch-language schools in these communes, whereas French-speaking children living in the Dutch unilingual region had no access to French-language schools in the same communes. It concluded that in so far as access to education was based solely on residence, that resulted in a discrimination on linguistic grounds contrary to Article 2 of the First Protocol in conjunction with Article 14.

This judgment is often used to illustrate that allegations under Article 14 have to be related to a substantive right in the ECHR or in one of its protocols (the aspect was clarified in *Abdulaziz, Cabales and Balkandali v. United Kingdom, loc. cit.*). This approach may lead to a finding of a breach of both Article 14 and the related substantive provision, yet in such cases as, for instance, *Informationsverein Lentia and Others v. Austria* (EurCtHR, Judgment of 28 November 1993, Series A, No. 276), *Mathieu-Mohin and Clerfayt v. Belgium* (EurCtHR, Judgment of 2 March 1987, Series A, No. 113), and *Cyprus v. Turkey* (*loc. cit.*: paragraph 501 of the Commission's report, and paragraph 199 of the Court's judgment), the Court and/or Commission did not find it necessary to consider Article 14 since a violation of the substantive provision taken alone had been found. The Court in fact believes that the examination of the "Article 14 issue" is generally not required under these circumstances. But in the *Belgian Linguistics* case, the Court (*loc. cit.*, 35-36: paragraph 9) took the view that a substantive provision (for example, Article 2 of the First Protocol) could be violated in conjunction with Article 14 even though no direct breach of this substantive provision was established. As recently reaffirmed in *Thlimmenos v. Greece* (Application No. 34369/97, EurCtHR, Judgment of 6 April 2000: paragraph 40), for Article 14 to become applicable it suffices that the facts of the case fall within the ambit of another substantive provision of the ECHR or its protocols. In addition, just as Article 14 is frequently not considered where a breach of the substantive provision has been determined, so the question whether the substantive provision has been breached is likely not to be examined where a violation of Article 14 taken together with this provision has been found (*loc. cit.*: paragraph 53).

Eide and Opsahl conclude that Article 14 of the ECHR has "an autonomous meaning without independent existence" (Eide and Opsahl, 1990: 14). This is further illustrated by the *Mathieu-Mohin and Clerfayt* case, in which the Court found no violation of Article 3 of the First Protocol (electoral rights) and Article 14 of the ECHR, whereas five dissenting judges (*loc. cit.*: 27-29) maintained that the special system of political representation at regional level under Belgian law in fact discriminated against the French-speaking electorate in question, and was thus incompatible with Article 3 of the First Protocol read in conjunction with Article 14 of the ECHR.

It follows from this reading of Article 14, that when a State Party takes measures going beyond what it is directly obliged to in respect of the ECHR substantive rights and freedoms or those of its protocols, then that state is indirectly forbidden from doing so in a discriminatory way, so long as those measures fall within the ambit of the ECHR or its protocols. As suggested by the *Belgian Linguistics* case, such an approach may in principle prove especially important to removing unreasonable distinctions affecting minority groups which result from the implementation of proactive domestic policies addressing only the language and education needs of the majority. As noted in Chapter V, some experts embrace a comparable line of reasoning by referring in particular to derivative claims of performance arising from positive measures coming within the scope of Article 27 of the ICCPR. From this point of view, it is even more significant that the Court, in *Thlimmenos* (*loc. cit.*: paragraph 44), considered, as an additional dimension to its established case-law, that the right not to be discriminated against in the enjoyment of the ECHR rights, under Article 14, could be violated also where states without an objective and reasonable justification failed to treat differently persons whose situations were significantly different. In the Gypsy cases mentioned above, the Court, quite cautiously, expressed the view that according protection under Article 8 to Gypsy individuals in unlawful residence in a caravan on their land would raise problems under Article 14 in relation to non-Gypsy individuals in a similar situation, whereas the joint dissent pointed to the applicants' specific lifestyle as precisely the additional factor justifying the application of Article 14 as interpreted in *Thlimmenos* (see, for example, paragraph 8, of the joint dissent in *Chapman, loc. cit.*).

Nevertheless, in general the criteria provided by the Court in the *Belgian Linguistics* case for justifying difference in treatment under the ECHR, reinforced by the expansive reading of Article 14 in *Thlimmenos*, might in principle prove to favour a minority group over rights of others or the majority population. In the *Belgian Linguistics* case, the Commission had observed that a "territorially-based linguistic system" was not necessarily to be considered as contrary to the ECHR. Arguably, special linguistic rights for minority members, including a "territorially-based linguistic system" encompassing mother-tongue education and/or mother-tongue communication with public authorities, designed to duly reflect the differences between a minority and the rest of the population, might be considered in line with the prohibition of discrimination as set forth in the ECHR, provided that the above requirements for differential treatment are met.

Based on the *ratio decidendi* in other cases brought before the Commission or the Court, arguments can be found that a state might have to endorse difference in treatment whose reasonable and objective justification is that the resulting measures enable members of a minority group to assert their rights under the ECHR (for example, by analogy with the *Plattform "Artze für das Leben" v. Austria* case, EurCtHR, Judgment of 21 June 1988, Series A, No. 139), or enable to secure, or to improve the effectiveness of, a convention right for their benefit (see, for example, the considerations of the Commission in *Lindsay and Others v. United Kingdom*, Application No. 8364/78, EurCommHR, Decision of 8 March 1979, DR 15, 1979: 247; *The Liberal Party, Mrs R. and Mr P. v. United Kingdom*, Application No. 8765/79, EurCommHR, Decision of 18 December 1980, DR 21, 1981: 211; see also the joint dissent in the Gypsies cases, *loc. cit.*, regarding positive measures benefiting Gypsies). An element common to all of the above aspects of "indirect" protection is that the upholding of a right or treatment granted by the state, though essentially linked to the discriminatory effects that its absence would implicitly entail, may not be claimed on the basis of a corresponding, specific entitlement under the ECHR.

In conclusion, the Strasbourg case-law so far has generally appeared rather hesitant to address minority issues under the substantive provisions of the ECHR and/or to bring the "Article 14 issue" to bear upon the special situation of certain ethno-cultural groups. The criteria of "pluralism, tolerance and broadmindedness" and "fair and proper treatment of minorities" mentioned by the Court in relation to the protection of individuals in a "minority" (namely, non-dominant) position in specific factual contexts (*Young, James and Webster v. United Kingdom*, EurCtHR, Judgment of 13 August 1981, Series A, No. 44) does not seem to have spurred on considerable attention to groups with a culturally distinctive identity. Nevertheless, a far better chance of greater protection is now slowly emerging, and that might be even reinforced by a possible increase in the number of "minority cases" stemming from the adherence of most eastern European countries to the ECHR and its protocols. However, one should be careful with predicting entirely innovative stands by Strasbourg on minority issues under this instruments: the "strictly supervisory" role claimed by the Court in the recent Gypsy cases seems to be a reminder that a great deal of judicial activism (if at all) is unlikely to come, at least until further parallel progress on minority standards will be made within the Council of Europe. After all, it is still tenable the proposition by Gilbert, referred to the ECHR case-law prior to the reforms instituted by Protocol No. 11, that:

> while some decisions of the Commission and the Court have protected minority groups by means of a wide interpretation of discrimination in Article 14 and an expansive view of Article 8, the general trend has been to deny that minorities are protected under the ECHR.

This author goes on to observe that:

> It is timely to enquire whether the deliberative organs of the ECHR should be provided with a mechanism whereby they could directly address the needs of minority groups. (Gilbert, 1999: 61)

c. Protocol No. 12 to the ECHR

This new protocol does not directly address the needs of minority groups. Still, the preamble reaffirms the notion, first elaborated by the Strasbourg Court, that difference in treatment does not amount to discrimination when it has an objective and reasonable justification. The explanatory report clarifies that the protocol does not *per se* enshrine a duty to adopt measures designed to achieve equality in fact (paragraph 16).

Moreover, as noted earlier, the protocol contains in its operative part a general prohibition of discrimination, which goes beyond the scope of application of Article 14 of the ECHR. Article 1 indeed prohibits discrimination on any ground such as "association with a national minority" in the enjoyment of "any right set forth by law", whereas Article 14 of the ECHR only prohibits

discrimination in the enjoyment of the rights and freedoms set forth
ECHR. As indicated in the respective explanatory report, the additio.
scope of protection for individuals mainly, though by no means exclusively
(see *infra*, Chapter X), covers the enjoyment of rights (under paragraph 1)
and/or the exercise of public authority (under paragraph 2) under domestic
law. In this respect, Article 1 of Protocol No. 12 is comparable to Article 26
of the ICCPR as interpreted by the HRC in General Comment No. 18 on non-
discrimination (paragraph 12).

The explanatory report notes that the obligation under Article 1 "to secure"
the enjoyment of any right set forth by law may entail "horizontal effects",
namely between private parties, in the public sphere for which the state has
a certain responsibility. Article 1 of Protocol No. 12 shall not amend or abro-
gate Article 14 of the ECHR, which will continue to apply also to states parties to the protocol, though such provisions partly overlap.

Subject to the above considerations about the overall approach of the ECHR
and the Strasbourg case-law to the issue of minorities, Protocol No. 12 might
.certainly contribute to affording effective protection of, among others,
minority members against discrimination, especially in view of the eastward
extension of ECHR supervision. In addition, the jurisprudential work under
this instrument could well join forces with, and even inspire, that which is
being carried out by the ECRI, an organ created by the 1993 Vienna Summit
of the Heads of State and Government of the Member States of the Council
of Europe to counter racism and intolerance through a range of legal and
policy tools (Hannikainen, 1999; see also *infra*, Chapters X and XII). On the
other hand, Protocol No. 12 (the entry into force of which requires ten ratifications) does not remove the need, as noted by Gilbert, for a mechanism of
protection focused on minorities, although submitted proposals for a protocol to the ECHR on minority rights have so far proved controversial.

d. Recent efforts at elaborating minority rights standards

i. Assembly recommendations

In fact, it was not until recently that the idea of introducing specific legal
standards on minority rights regained support, after the unproductive discussions in the 1950s and 1960s. Developments in eastern Europe brought
to the fore serious minority problems in the region, but also in other parts of
Europe. In October 1990, the Parliamentary Assembly adopted Recommendation 1134 following a "report on the rights of minorities" produced by the
Committee on Legal Affairs, through its rapporteur Brincat.

Recommendation 1134 indicates respect for minority rights "as an essential
factor for peace, justice, stability and democracy"; recommends the
Committee of Ministers to draw up a protocol to the ECHR or a special convention; stresses not only the need for a general (non-accessory) clause on
the prohibition of discrimination in the ECHR and basic guarantees such as
equal access to court, but also the need for special measures for minorities,
including transfrontier contacts rights; lists rights of minorities as such
(namely, group rights) and rights of persons belonging to minorities (namely,

individual rights) – including the right to have one's own institutions, to participate in decision-making and to receive public instruction in the mother tongue – involving positive measures by states; reaffirms the principle of territorial integrity of states and mentions the duties of minority members vis-à-vis the state where they live.

It is interesting to note the reference to the concept of group rights and the effect of minority issues on European security. The Committee of Ministers did not take action in accordance with this recommendation. In February 1992, the Assembly adopted Recommendation 1177 following discussions about a new report prepared by rapporteurs Brincat and Worms. In this recommendation, the Assembly firmly favoured the adoption of an additional protocol to the ECHR and a declaration setting out basic principles relating to the protection of minorities to serve as parameters to assess new applications for Council of Europe membership. The latter proposal was abandoned almost immediately, but in January 1993 the Assembly adopted Recommendation 1201 containing the already cited draft additional protocol on the rights of minorities to the ECHR, as a result of another report on the matter, presented by rapporteur Worms.

In terms of substantive provisions, this recommendation follows the lines set by Recommendation 1134, yet the focus is on individual rights (namely, rights of persons belonging to a national minority) and the rights framework is complemented by a definition of "national minority" (Article 1), and a clause (in Article 14) regarding restrictions on the rights recognised. In particular, the text features not only remarkable provisions on language and education rights (Articles 7 and 8) but also a far-reaching right to autonomy regimes for persons belonging to a national minority which is numerically in the majority within a region (Article 11). Although Recommendation 1201, like the other cited recommendations, is not *per se* legally binding (see also *infra*), it has nonetheless triggered important legal consequences, both as part of "commitments" undertaken by new member states of the Organisation upon accession (Djerić, 2000; and *infra*, Chapter X), thereby embracing a revised version of the above-mentioned earlier proposal, and through its incorporation by reference in important bilateral treaties (see *infra*, Chapter IX). The text has been intensively discussed, considering the above increasingly greater double function, which also prompted the Committee on Legal Affairs and Human Rights of the Assembly to request the Venice Commission to deliver an opinion on the rather controversial Article 11 (CDL-MIN (96) 4). As will be discussed later on (see *infra*, Chapter IX), the question of autonomy under Article 11 emerged as a major cause for concern within the context of the basic treaties between Hungary and, respectively, Slovakia and Romania.

In Recommendation 1255 adopted in 1995, the Assembly, *inter alia*, confirmed the principles listed in its Recommendation 1201 and urged the Committee of Ministers to start work on a protocol to the ECHR in the cultural field guaranteeing individual rights, in particular for persons belonging to national minorities. In recent years, the Assembly has adopted other recommendations on the protection of national minorities. Interestingly, in

Recommendation 1492, adopted in 2001, the Assembly, *inter alia*, reaffirmed the need for an additional protocol to the ECHR on the rights of national minorities, inspired by Recommendation 1201, including its definition of national minority. The most recent discussions on this matter are indeed taking place in the context of the follow up to this recommendation, although it appears unlikely that they will lead to any major developments in the short term. The other Assembly recommendations address procedural matters relating to normative developments, and/or provide an overview of the relevant activities; their description will thus be omitted in this context.

ii. Further attempts at law-making: the work of the Venice Commission

Other submitted texts include the proposal for a European Convention for the Protection of Minorities, adopted by the Venice Commission in 1991 (hereinafter "the Venice Commission's draft convention"), and the draft protocol to the ECHR guaranteeing the protection of ethnic groups, submitted by Austria in that same year. Neither proposal was adopted by the Parliamentary Assembly or the Committee of Ministers.

Nevertheless, both instruments, especially the Venice Commission's draft convention (Malinverni, 1991), offer useful indication of possible overall solutions to the minority question. Although the emphasis is on the individual dimension of protection, some of their provisions reflect a strong collective approach, particularly as regards political participation and contacts with administrative and judicial authorities. Besides defining "minority" in keeping with the Capotorti definition (Article 1) (see *supra*, Chapter III), the Venice Commission's draft convention even enshrines truly group rights, namely the right of minorities to be protected against any activity capable of threatening their existence (which is in effect in line with the physical existence entitlements discussed earlier in Chapter IV), and to the respect, safeguard and development of their identity (which in fact expresses in the stronger language of "rights" what Article 1, paragraph 1, of the 1992 UN declaration construes as a matter of a duty upon states). In addition, this draft appears constructive with regard to the use of the minority language before public authorities and education rights in Articles 8 and 9, although the use of a more cautious language should be noted. The architecture of substantive entitlements is balanced by clauses which set limits on the enjoyment of rights, notably in relation to respect by members of a minority for the rights of members of other minorities and the prevention of discrimination against members of the majority which find themselves in the minority within a region.

Although the Venice Commission has not submitted other minority rights instruments so far, it has remained actively engaged in the clarification and promotion of either minority standards (for example, through examining and advising on draft national legislation concerning the protection of minorities) or provisions impinging upon the situation of minorities, as in the context of the drafting of a general legal reference framework to facilitate the settlement of ethno-political conflicts in Europe (CDL (2000) 70; see also *infra*, Chapters VIII and XI).

iii. The European Charter for Regional or Minority Languages

The European Charter for Regional or Minority Languages was produced in 1992. The charter refers to "minority" languages in the title and operative articles. Although the explanatory report recognises that the state obligations and the respective domestic measures of implementation "will have an obvious effect on the situation of the communities concerned and their individual members" (paragraph 11), this instrument is not *per se* concerned with minority rights. At the same juncture, the explanatory report indeed makes it clear that the charter is not set out to protect linguistic minorities nor does it establish individual or collective rights for the speakers of the languages protected. Rather, the charter provides guarantees for the benefit of the historical regional or minority languages of Europe, with a view to promoting and protecting multilingualism in general. Such a fundamental trait must be kept in mind when appreciating the role of this instrument in the context of the protection of minorities.

The definition of regional or minority languages does not apply to dialects of the official languages of the state or the languages of migrants (Article 1, paragraph a, sub-paragraph ii), even though the charter may extend to less widely official languages under the terms of Article 3. The charter consists of two main parts, a general one setting out fundamental principles and objectives underlying state policies and practices pertaining to regional or minority languages (Part II), and a more specific part laying down undertakings in the fields of education, judicial authorities, administrative authorities and public services, the media, cultural activities and facilities, economic and social life and transfrontier exchanges, which may vary according to the State Party and language (Part III). Indeed, whereas the provisions of Part II apply to all regional or minority languages spoken within the territory of the contracting state, each party is allowed to select a minimum of 35 paragraphs or sub-paragraphs contained in the provisions of Part III, in respect of each language specified upon adherence to the charter (Article 2, paragraph 2, and Article 3, paragraph 1). The assumption behind the choice of a "menu" approach to state duties was that this approach would make it possible to commensurate the scope of protection to the particular context of each language, so as to accommodate the wide diversity in the *de facto* situation of regional or minority languages (see, for example, the explanatory report: paragraph 46). In their declarations, some states (Croatia and Hungary) have undertaken to apply all of the chosen provisions of Part III to all of the regional or minority languages concerned, while others (Finland and Switzerland) have specified a different list for each language. Germany has not only indicated a different list for each language but also varied the protection for one and the same language in various regions according to the federal system and local factors.

The operative provisions are rather elaborate but extremely flexible. For instance, Article 8 addresses education through a lengthy list of measures regarding pre-school education, primary education, secondary education, technical and vocational education, university and other higher education as well as adult and continuing education. It must be emphasised that there is no strict obligation to secure the above types of education in the languages protected and states may limit themselves to providing teaching of these languages, according to the situation of each of them, at primary, secondary and/or technical and vocational education level, to those people who so request or wish in a number "considered sufficient" (see, for example, the obligations undertaken by Croatia). Under Article 2, paragraph 2, a party is not held to agree to be bound by more than three of the paragraphs or subparagraphs chosen from among the provisions of which Article 8 is composed. Another example is offered by Article 9, which enumerates a variety of options regarding the use of regional or minority languages before judicial authorities, while at the same time limiting the alternative options themselves in three different ways. Indeed, it is stated that the undertaking only addresses those judicial districts in which the number of language speakers justifies the measures specified, must be according to the situation of each language and is conditioned on the use of the facilities afforded by the paragraph not being considered by the judge "to hamper the proper administration of justice". A party can avoid the most progressive provisions contained in Article 9, including the obligations that the proceedings be conducted in the language concerned at the request of one of the parties and/or that the accused or litigant be guaranteed the right to use his/her regional or minority language in court, by consenting to be bound by solely one paragraph or sub-paragraph of this article (see Article 2, paragraph 2).

There is reason to believe that the wide range of options offered to states, while positively allowing for accommodation of specific circumstances, in practice precludes a great deal of *ipso facto* protection. The notion that a variety of factual situations can be addressed through a diversity in legal duties rather than the means of implementing a body of common prescriptions appears questionable, raising the issue of whether it might even generate discrimination among similarly affected languages or language speakers. An important point is that the charter, despite its untypical approach, should not be viewed as disconnected from international human rights law principles, as already implied by references to the ICCPR and ECHR in the preamble, to the ECHR in Article 4, paragraph 1, and to the anti-discrimination parameter in Article 7, paragraph 2.

As yet, the charter, which entered into force on 1 March 1998, has attracted fifteen ratifications – less than one might expect of a ten-year-old instrument. It should be noted, however, that the ratifications have doubled over the past two years, and that in general, time may be needed for a state to be able to choose the options for the languages, and/or, as in the case of France (Oellers-Frahm, 1999), to positively address the wider legal and political implications of ratifying the charter. Whatever the merit of the instrument *per se* (namely, in the general context of multilingualism), and the actual impact of inevitable considerations of language users under specific provisions (for example, in Article 7, paragraphs 4 and 5, and Article 14, paragraph a), the role of the charter vis-à-vis minorities must be measured against the above starting-point made clear by the drafters, namely that the charter does not deal with rights of (minority) language speakers, nor with (linguistic) minorities themselves. In the final analysis, the charter constitutes a very important source for developing domestic policies in support of regional or minority languages, but the "obvious effect" on the communities concerned expected to be generated by its implementation, as indicated by the explanatory report, cannot claim any alternative conception of minority rights standards; rather, it amounts to a widely flexible degree of mere indirect protection for minority groups, among other groups, defined by language, which might contribute to ameliorating their situation (see also the explanatory report: paragraph 13; for the implementation procedure established by the charter, which is now fully effective, see *infra*, Chapter X).

iv. The Framework Convention for the Protection of National Minorities

In 1993, the heads of state and government of the member states of the Council of Europe met in Vienna in order to elaborate further guidelines for the Organisation's continued work in the field of human rights. The 1993 Assembly proposal, contained in Recommendation 1201, was not pursued, due basically to a lack of political will. Still, it was decided to draft "with a minimum delay" a framework convention setting out principles for the protection of national minorities, and also to begin work on drafting a protocol to the ECHR concerning individual rights pertaining to the cultural field, including those of persons belonging to national minorities. The work on this protocol was suspended by the Committee of Ministers in 1996, and it is unlikely to be resumed in the near future, due to difficulties experienced regarding, *inter alia,* the precise nature of such rights (see, for example, *supra*, Chapter II) and their relation to the ECHR rights and the case-law of the EurCtHR. At the same time, the Committee of Ministers decided to continue reflection more generally, although this has not led to any specific results so far.

By contrast, the Framework Convention for the Protection of National Minorities was open for signature in 1995, and entered into force on 1 February 1998. At the time of finalising this book, thirty-four states had ratified or acceded to it. The instrument is also open to states which are not members of the Council of Europe, clearly due to a special concern for the situation of minorities in eastern Europe. However, most of the countries from this area have become parties to the convention after being admitted to the Council of Europe as full members. There are currently two non-member states which are parties to the Framework Convention, namely Bosnia and Herzegovina and the FRY.

In this context, the concept of "framework convention" designates a set of principles, the clarification and realisation of which are to be fundamentally achieved at the domestic level. The last paragraph of the preamble to the Framework Convention confirms this approach by stating that states parties are "determined to implement the principles set out in this Framework Convention through national legislation and appropriate governmental policies". As clarified in the explanatory memorandum, the convention contains programme-type provisions setting out objectives which the parties undertake to pursue. Thus, the provisions are not directly applicable (meaning that they are not self-executing, not that they are not of immediate effect), leaving the states concerned a measure of discretion in the implementation of the convention, in consideration of particular factual circumstances.

In line with other recent instruments, the preamble links pluralist democracy to respect for the identity of persons belonging to a national minority and the creation of "appropriate conditions enabling them to express, preserve and develop this identity" (seventh paragraph of the preamble). Moreover, various instruments of the Council of Europe (notably the ECHR), the UN and the OSCE (notably the 1990 Copenhagen Document: see *infra*, Chapter VII) are indicated as sources of inspiration. The text covers a spectrum of guarantees in favour of national minorities. It reformulates some basic standards of individual human rights protection in connection with those recognised in the ECHR (freedom of expression, freedom of association, etc.), and provides for a number of specific guarantees on issues such as preservation and development of cultural identity (Article 5, paragraph 1), intercultural dialogue in society (Article 6), establishment of religious institutions, organisations and associations (Article 8), access to the media (Article 9), use of minority languages and education (Articles 10 to 14), participation in cultural, social, and economic life and in public affairs, particularly in areas of minority concern (Article 15), etc.

Article 1 confirms the placing of minority rights within the human rights framework, while Article 3 restates the principle of freedom of choice and the principle of individual as well as communal exercise of the rights. As already noted, the explanatory memorandum confirms that the "choice of belonging" is inseparably linked to objective criteria relevant to the person's identity. Article 4, paragraph 2, importantly establishes a duty to adopt, "where necessary", special measures designed to achieve "full and effective" equality (see, generally, *supra*, Chapter IV). Strictly speaking, this provision goes further than Protocol No. 12 to the ECHR (see *supra*); however, the latter offers an overall greater protection of the general right not to be discriminated against due to the possibility, unavailable under the Framework Convention (see, generally, *infra*, Chapter X), of appeal to the EurCtHR.

Under Article 5, paragraph 1, the parties undertake to promote the conditions necessary to maintain and develop minority culture, and to preserve the essential elements (namely, religion, language, traditions which are not contrary to national law or international standards, and cultural heritage) of minority identity. If it has to bear its full weight, then the provision must extend to positive action by the parties. On the other hand, Thornberry (1995: 353) critically comments on a possible hiatus (somehow echoing the ambiguities of paragraph 33 of the Copenhagen Document: see *infra*, Chapter VII) between "culture" (the maintenance and development of which are to be promoted through the creation of adequate conditions) and other aspects of identity (which are to be preserved). As regards the latter aspects, he also notes their possible restrictive impact compared to other texts and the more open expression of a "right to identity". It is important to add that the above reference in the explanatory memorandum to "national law" as a limit to the protection of minority "traditions" does not allow for domestic measures which are in breach of international human rights standards (see also *supra*, Chapter V).

Article 5, paragraph 2, prohibits forced assimilation, but does not preclude measures taken by the parties in pursuance of their general integration policy. "Without prejudice" might suggest that greater weight is accorded to the general integrationist policy than the freedom from assimilation against one's will. Thus, the level of protection under Article 5, paragraph 2, appears limited. Other provisions are noteworthy, such as those contained in Article 8 (notably with regard to the right to establish religious institutions, organisations and associations) and Article 9 (access to the media). The latter prohibits discrimination with regard to the creation (including the ownership) and/or use of minority media, but appears weak in relation to the representation of national minority views within the mainstream media.

Articles 10 to 14 address language and education rights. Article 10, paragraph 2, deals with minority language use vis-à-vis administrative authorities in areas inhabited by persons belonging to national minorities traditionally or in substantial numbers. Such clauses as "if those persons so request and the request corresponds to a real need" and "as far as possible" heavily qualify the right. The explanatory memorandum notes that the paragraph does not cover all communications with public authorities; this is in fact suggested by the very notion of "administrative authorities" and indirectly confirmed by Article 10, paragraph 3, concerning language guarantees in case of arrest or any accusation brought against a person belonging to a national minority, which does not afford wider protection than Article 5, paragraph 2, and Article 6, paragraph 3, sub-paragraphs a and e, of the ECHR (by contrast, see Article 7 of the proposed protocol to the ECHR contained in Recommendation 1201 of the Parliamentary Assembly, and Article 8 of the Venice Commission's draft convention). The explanatory memorandum states that the existence of a "real need" under Article 10, paragraph 2, must be assessed by the state on the basis of objective criteria and that "as far as possible" indicates consideration of, *inter alia*, the financial resources of the party concerned.

Given the reference to objective criteria, one may wonder why "need" must be assessed only by the state. "As far as possible" should be interpreted at least to implicitly permit challenging state policies which do not encourage or favour the possible (see *infra*). Article 11 formulates in the first two paragraphs the right to use and have recognised names in a minority language, and to display signs, inscriptions and other information of a private nature visible to the public. As clarified by the explanatory memorandum, Article 11, paragraph 2, does not exclude the requirement to use, in addition, the official language and/or other minority languages.

Article 11, paragraph 3, is no better formulated than Article 10, paragraph 2, as regards the right to display, in areas traditionally inhabited by substantial numbers of persons belonging to national minorities, traditional local names, street names and other topographical indications intended for the public also in the minority language (see also the explanatory memorandum: paragraph 70). The clauses limiting the scope of the provision tend ultimately to obfuscate the substance of protection. Articles 12 and 13 are concerned with general aspects of education rights. Paragraphs 2 and 3 of Article 12 include interesting references to access to textbooks and equal opportunities for access to education at all levels. Article 13, paragraph 1, provides for the right to set up and manage private educational establishments, but the next paragraph clarifies that "the exercise of this right shall not entail any financial obligation for the parties". Yet, the explanatory memorandum specifies that the possibility of a state contribution is not excluded (paragraph 73).

Under Article 14, paragraph 1, the parties "undertake to recognise" the right of every person belonging to a national minority to learn his or her minority language. Still, as explained in the memorandum, paragraph 1 does not imply positive action, notably of a financial nature, by the state. Moreover, as in some of the above provisions, the language of the next paragraph, concerning the teaching of, or instruction in, the minority language in areas inhabited by persons belonging to national minorities traditionally or in substantial numbers, is considerably qualified (for example, "sufficient demand", "shall endeavour to ensure", "as far as possible"; compare the text with the wider Article 8 of the proposed protocol to the ECHR contained in Recommendation 1201 of the Parliamentary Assembly, and Article 9 of the Venice Commission's draft convention). "As far as possible" points to the availability of resources, though, by analogy with "whenever possible" in Article 4, paragraph 3, of the UN declaration, the constructive interpretation might be advanced implicitly establishing "a right to challenge governmental policy which does not facilitate the possible" (Packer, 1996: 159). With regard to the "demand" criterion, Thornberry rightly notes that:

> It is not open to the State to set artificially high levels before a 'demand' is recognised. Principles of good faith, effectiveness in the interpretation of treaties and respect for the facts must be accounted for. (Thornberry, 1995: 358.)

Article 14, paragraph 3, specifies that the preceding paragraph "shall be implemented without prejudice to the learning of the official language or the teaching in this language".

Article 15 provides for a right to participation along the lines of Article 2 of the UN declaration, but without an explicit right to participation in decisions concerning the minority. However, the explanatory memorandum provides a range of advisable modalities of participation to be considered for adoption within the framework of the parties' constitutional systems, ranging from consultation to decentralisation of power, which are not spelled out in Article 2 of the UN declaration. Article 16 importantly forbids the alteration of the proportions of the population in minority areas aimed at restricting the rights and freedoms flowing from the convention's principles (see *supra*, Chapter IV), while the remaining provisions in Section II address crossborder contacts (Article 17, paragraph 1), minority participation in the activities of national and international NGOs (Article 17, paragraph 2), promotion of bilateral agreements and transfrontier co-operation (Article 18), and the linkage with the ECHR concerning relevant restrictions on rights (Article 19). Section III deals with respect by persons belonging to national minorities for the national legislation and the rights of others (Article 20), the abuse of right and territorial integrity (Article 21), the safeguard of higher levels of protection (Article 22), and the conformity with the ECHR in relation to corresponding provisions (Article 23).

Under Article 19, there is, regrettably, no indication of which of the clauses allowing to limit the enjoyment of rights and freedoms, provided for, in particular, in the ECHR, are "relevant to the rights and freedoms flowing from the [Framework Convention's] principles". This should be contrasted with the absence of a limitations clause in Article 27 of the ICCPR and the relatively broad scope (reinforced by the "margin of appreciation" doctrine) of the limitations clauses in the ECHR – which is, however, tempered by a tight control of the EurCtHR and, in any event, does not embrace any specific minority provisions – as well as with the inclusion in the Framework Convention of separate general clauses limiting, directly or indirectly, the enjoyment of the rights and freedoms flowing from the listed principles (notably in Articles 20, 21 and 23).

As noted, the obligations are "softened" in a way that affects both the general structure of the provisions and their specific content. The Parliamentary Assembly has been sharply critical of the convention in Recommendation 1255 (1995). The indication provided by the EurCtHR in the recent Gypsy cases (see, for example, paragraph 84 of the Chapman Judgment, *loc. cit.*), that in particular the Framework Convention did not attest to any "sufficiently concrete" consensus among Council of Europe member states on the protection of minorities for it to derive any guidance on standards, as it simply set out general principles and goals but signatory states "were unable to agree on means or implementation", may be viewed as exceedingly cautious, but does not come as a surprise. Clearly, the key to making the Framework Convention a truly fruitful step as the first multilateral treaty on the protection of national minorities in general lies in a satisfactory supervision of its actual functioning, under the procedure provided for in Articles 24 to 26 (see *infra*, Chapter X).

Bibliography

Aarnio, E.J., "Minority rights in the Council of Europe: current developments", in *Universal minority rights*, Phillips, A. and Rosas, A. (eds), Åbo Akademi and Minority Rights Group (International), Turku/Åbo and London, 1995, pp. 123-133.

Benoît-Rohmer, F., *The minority question in Europe: towards a coherent system of protection for national minorities*, Council of Europe Publishing, Strasbourg, 1996.

Benoît-Rohmer, F., "La convention-cadre du Conseil de l'Europe pour la protection des minorités nationales", *European Journal of International Law*, 6, 1995, pp. 573-597.

De Schutter, O., "Le droit au mode de vie tsigane devant la Cour européenne des droits de l'homme: droits culturels, droit des minorités, discrimination positive", *Revue Trimestrielle des Droits de L'Homme*, 30, 1997, pp. 64-93.

Djerić, V., "Admission to membership of the Council of Europe and legal significance of commitments entered into by new member states", *Heidelberg Journal of International Law*, 60, 2000, pp. 605-629.

Eide, A., and Opsahl, T., *Equality and non-discrimination,* Norwegian Institute of Human Rights, Oslo, 1990.

Fenet, A., "L'Europe et les minorités", in *Le droit et les minorités: analyses et textes*, Fenet, A., Koubi, G., Schulte-Tenckhoff, I. and Ansbach, T. (eds), Etablissements Emile Bruylant, Brussels, 1995, pp. 83-195.

Gilbert, G., "Jurisprudence of the European Court and Commission of Human Rights in 1999 and minority groups", UN Doc. E/CN.4/Sub.2/AC.5/2000/CRP.1, 2000, pp. 1-13.

Gilbert, G., "Minority rights under the Council of Europe", in *Minority rights in the "new" Europe*, Cumper, P. and Wheatley, S. (eds), Kluwer Law International, The Hague, 1999, pp. 53-70.

Gilbert, G., "The Council of Europe and minority rights", *Human Rights Quarterly*, 18, 1996, pp. 160-189.

Gilbert, G., "The legal protection accorded to minority groups in Europe", *Netherlands Yearbook of International Law*, XXIII, 1992, pp. 67-104.

Gjidara, M., "Cadres juridiques et règles applicables aux problèmes européens de minorités", *Annuaire Français de Droit International*, XXXVII, 1991, pp. 349-386.

Hannikainen, L., "The European Commission Against Racism and Intolerance", in *New trends in discrimination law: international perspectives*, Hannikainen, L. and Nykänen, E. (eds), Turku Law School, Turku, 1999, pp. 177-220.

Hillgruber, C. and Jestaedt, M., *The European Convention on Human Rights and the protection of national minorities*, Verlag Wissenschaft und Politik, Cologne, 1994.

Malinverni, G., "The draft convention for the protection of minorities: the proposal of the European Commission for Democracy through Law", *Human Rights Law Journal*, 12, 1991, pp. 265-269.

Oellers-Frahm, K., "Charte européenne des langues régionales ou minoritaires, Decision No. 99-412 DC, French Conseil Constitutionnel, 15 June 1999", *American Journal of International Law*, 93, 1999, pp. 938-942.

Packer, J., "On the content of minority rights", in *Do we need minority rights? Conceptual issues,* Räikkä, J., (ed.), Martinus Nijhoff Publishers, The Hague, 1996, pp. 121-178.

Pierré-Caps, S., "Peut-on parler actuellement d'un droit européen des minorités?", *Annuaire Français de Droit International,* XL, 1994, pp. 72-105.

Poulter, S., "The rights of ethnic, religious and linguistic minorities", *European Human Rights Law Review,* 3, 1997, pp. 254-264.

Preece, J.J., *National minorities and the European nation-states system,* Clarendon Press, Oxford, 1998.

Rosas, A., "The protection of minorities in Europe: a general overview", in *The protection of ethnic and linguistic minorities in Europe,* Packer, J. and Myntti, K. (eds), Åbo Akademi, Åbo, 1995, pp. 9-13.

Spiliopoulou Åkermark, A., *Justifications of minority protection in international law,* Kluwer Law International, The Hague, 1997.

Thornberry, P., "Minority rights", *Collected Courses of the Academy of European Law,* VI-2, 1995, pp. 307-390.

Türk, D., "Protection of minorities in Europe", *Collected Courses of the Academy of European Law,* III-2, 1992, pp. 143-206.

1. The OSCE framework

a. Comprehensive approach to minority issues

The CSCE began with the signing of the Helsinki Final Act in 1975. One of the main characteristics of the "Helsinki process" has been its multidimensional approach to international peace and security. The participating states have indeed considered this issue in the light of its inter-linked – political, military, economic, environmental and humanitarian – dimensions (Bloed, 1997). The protection of minorities, too, has been tackled in connection with paramount concerns for internal and international stability.

Although, as pointed out by Helgesen, "the minority question was not an ideal battleground for an East-West exercise" (Helgesen, 1992: 161), some progress was made in this area during the 1980s, which culminated in major achievements with the collapse of the communist regimes in eastern Europe. Besides its important standard-setting activities in the field of minority rights, the "conference", renamed in 1994 "Organisation for Security and Co-operation in Europe", as a result of an institutional transition opened up by the ending of the cold war, has devoted particular attention to the prevention of ethnic conflicts, and to monitoring the implementation of the relevant international standards. By so doing, the (now) OSCE, as the largest European institution with a membership of more than fifty states, including the United States and Canada, has significantly contributed to making the protection of minorities an essential component of multilateral dialogue and inter-state co-operation in Europe.

b. Nature of OSCE commitments

One general aspect of the OSCE process is the legal characterisation of its concluding documents (see, generally, Bloed, 1993: 22-25). In legal doctrine it is virtually undisputed that the Helsinki Final Act and the other OSCE instruments do not have the nature of treaties – they are "political", non-legally binding, documents. With regard to the final act, this is clearly reflected in an express reference to the text as non-eligible for registration under Article 102 of the UN Charter. Under the latter article, every member of the UN entering into a treaty obligation is indeed obliged to register the treaty with the secretariat.

However, it has been emphasised that the binding force of such documents cannot be questioned either. Van Dijk observes:

> A commitment does not have to be legally binding in order to have binding force; the distinction between legal and non-legal binding force resides in the legal consequences attached to the binding force [not in the binding force as such]. (van Dijk, 1980: 110)

Although non-compliance with a non-legally binding commitment may not *per se* generate international legal responsibility, a violation of "politically" binding agreements is thus as unacceptable as a violation of norms of international law. Further to that, legal implications are discernible in a number of respects. For instance, it may be argued that the rules regarding the interpretation of international treaties are applicable, by analogy, to OSCE instruments as well, and that a signatory state may not invoke the domestic jurisdiction argument in relation to the matters which are considered in the relevant document.

Moreover, the provisions contained in these texts often reflect well-established principles of international law, such as the principle of the territorial integrity of states and that forbidding the use of force, or can be traced to international agreements by which a large number or all of the OSCE states are bound. OSCE provisions may also develop into customary law through state practice and *opinio juris*. From the latter point of view, the Helsinki Final Act and subsequent texts are frequently referred to as "soft law" instruments, which may thus be "hardened" at a later stage.

c. Minority rights standards

i. The Helsinki Final Act (1975)

The first three sections of the Helsinki Final Act are normally referred to as the three "baskets". The most important for present purposes is "Basket I", which begins with a Declaration on Principles Guiding Relations between Participating States. As noted, Principle VII of the so-called "Decalogue" of fundamental principles, concerning respect for human rights and fundamental freedoms, including the freedom of thought, conscience, religion and belief, contains a clause which commits the participating states to respect the rights of persons belonging to national minorities to equality before the law, to afford them the full opportunity for the actual enjoyment of human rights and fundamental freedoms, and to protect their legitimate interests in this sphere (paragraph 4). A number of points can be made in this regard:

- the provision originated from a proposal submitted by Yugoslavia, but such a proposal was in fact intended to establish specific minority rights for individuals and groups as such; seen against this background, the provision basically amounts to a prohibition of discrimination (Helgesen, 1992: 163); at the same time, the reference to "full opportunity" and "actual enjoyment" may be said to imply some form of positive action in order to ensure equality in fact;
- the text uses the term "national minority", but, as already noted, this is due to historical reasons rather than a fundamental conceptual difference

between this term and the expression used, for instance, in Article 27 of the ICCPR;

— the opening phrase "the participating States on whose territory national minorities exist" has the same connotation as that of the opening phrase in Article 27 of the ICCPR; yet, neither of these texts should be interpreted in such a way as to give states a free hand to recognise or not to recognise the existence of a national minority, which is an objective phenomenon; and

— the reference to "legitimate interests" (introduced by virtue of a proposal from Greece) is vague and something of a counterpart to "right"; it should not be interpreted to mean "legal" or "legally recognised", due to the above-mentioned factual nature of minority existence, and thus concerns of minority existence as being at the basis of minority claims; "legitimate" can and should be taken to indicate conformity to international law and OSCE commitments.

In "Basket III", on co-operation in humanitarian and other fields, a short subsection is devoted to the fields of culture and education. The participating states agreed to facilitate the contribution of national minorities in these areas; the significance of the provisions is rather modest compared to the remaining and more precise provisions concerning cultural and educational development generally.

ii. The Madrid (1983) and Vienna (1986) Concluding Documents

Following the adoption of the Helsinki Final Act, it was agreed to convene a series of diplomatic "follow-up meetings" aimed at advancing the "Helsinki process". The Madrid follow-up meeting, held in Madrid between 1980 and 1983, did not produce any progress with regard to minority standards. In the first part of the concluding document, in the section devoted to security in Europe, it only reiterated commitment to the respect for and actual enjoyment of the rights of persons belonging to national minorities as well as the protection of their legitimate interests as provided by the final act. The prevailing position of states was to avoid innovative language on the matter.

The next major gathering, the Vienna follow-up meeting, took place between 1986 and 1989, at a time when the cold war was gradually coming to an end. Some steps forwards were taken in the field of minority rights. In the first section, on questions relating to security in Europe, the text spells out an explicit commitment to adopting all the necessary measures ("legislative, administrative, judicial and other") for the protection of national minorities and to applying the relevant international instruments by which the participating states may be bound. Moreover, it restates the protection of minority members against discrimination and formulates a commitment to protecting and creating conditions for the promotion of the ethnic, cultural, linguistic and religious identity of national minorities on their territory.

Truly "new" provisions can be found in the third section, concerning co-operation in humanitarian and other fields, notably as regards transfrontier contacts, access to – and dissemination of – information in the mother tongue,

141

as well as maintenance, development and transmission of minority culture. The occasional use of "on their territory" does not represent a change of substance compared to "on whose territory national minorities exist"; at the same time, it may be viewed as another way of expressing the traditional approach to "new" groups such as immigrants (Helgesen, 1992: 170). Finally, some useful formulations of the rights of religious believers and communities are also presented in the concluding document.

iii. The Copenhagen Concluding Document on the Human Dimension (1990)

One of the major achievements of the Vienna Concluding Document was the setting up of a series of meetings (called "the conference" or "the human dimension") focused on human rights issues. Deeply influenced by the post-cold war political scenario, the concluding document adopted at the second meeting on the human dimension, held in Copenhagen in 1990, was to prove the most influential elaboration of minority rights standards at the international level. Both the 1992 UN declaration and the Framework Convention have benefited from the Copenhagen text as one of their main sources of inspiration. The Copenhagen provisions have also been incorporated as legal obligations in important bilateral treaties, such as the 1995 basic treaty between Hungary and Slovakia (see *infra*, Chapter IX). At least some of them may have even developed into international customary law (Hofmann, 1997: 420-421).

The text highlights the deep linkage between minority rights and democracy and the role of civil society in the promotion of tolerance, cultural diversity and the resolution of questions relating to national minorities. Moreover, it "reaffirms" that minority rights are part of "universally recognised human rights" (paragraph 30, sub-paragraph 3), and indicates them as a crucial factor for peace and stability. In terms of operative standards, it sets forth the principles of equality and non-discrimination (including equality in fact, "where necessary"), and of free choice of belonging to a national minority with no disadvantage arising from the exercise of such choice, and the right of persons belonging to national minorities to identity, free of any attempts at assimilation against their will.

The text moves on to address the components of the right to identity, namely use of mother tongue in private and in public, association rights, transfrontier contact rights, etc., and affirms that the rights can be exercised individually as well as in community with other members of the group. Under paragraph 33, the participating states will protect minority identity and "create conditions for" the promotion of such identity; the language is rather tentative, suggesting a distinction between direct and indirect forms of state action, while the necessary measures are to be taken after due consultations, including contacts with minority organisations, in accordance with the decision-making procedures of each state. Paragraph 34 refers to "adequate opportunities" for instruction of – or in – the mother tongue, and its use, "wherever possible and necessary", before public authorities, "in conformity with national legislation".

Paragraph 35 introduces the notion of autonomy by referring to the efforts made by some participating states in this regard. Autonomy is "noted" as one possible means of realising the right of persons belonging to national minorities to effective participation in public affairs, in connection with the protection of the identity of such minorities. That raises the question whether – and to what extent – there is support for this way of tackling the minority question (see *infra*, Chapter VIII). Further paragraphs include provisions on the principle forbidding any activities contrary to the UN Charter and territorial integrity, the principle of "minimum standard" (namely, that nothing in the text prejudices existing human rights conventions and other relevant instruments), and the recognition of the "special case" of Roma/Gypsies in the context of efforts to combat racial and ethnic hatred, anti-Semitism, and similar phenomena.

iv. The Charter of Paris for a New Europe (1990) and the report of the expert meeting in Geneva (1991)

In the spring and summer of 1990, many heads of state and government came to admit that Europe had changed so dramatically that the "old" Helsinki Final Act needed to be supplemented by a new "constitution" for Europe. The Charter of Paris for a New Europe, adopted in November 1990, reaffirmed the participating states' commitment to the protection of minorities. Like the Helsinki Final Act, the Charter of Paris firmly places respect for minority rights in the context of human rights protection, as premised on the fundamental equality and non-discrimination precepts.

In addition, it acknowledges that "the rights of persons belonging to national minorities must be fully respected as part of universal human rights", that such persons have "the right freely to express, preserve and develop" their "ethnic, cultural, linguistic and religious identity", and reaffirms that the "identity of national minorities be protected and conditions for the promotion of that identity be created".

This time the overall approach to minorities was more constructive than the one reflected in the 1975 Helsinki Final Act. The heads of state and government decided to convene an expert meeting to be held in Geneva in 1991. The text produced by the expert meeting reaffirmed the Copenhagen principle that persons belonging to national minorities have the right to their identity free of any attempts at assimilation against their will. The meeting emphasised in no uncertain terms the "internationalisation" of minority rights, by asserting that issues concerning national minorities, as well as compliance with the relevant international obligations and commitments, are matters of legitimate international concern and thus do not constitute exclusively an internal affair of the respective state.

In addition, the experts elaborated a "shopping list" of policies on national minorities which had proved successful in a number of states, notably in the area of political participation (see, generally, *infra*, Chapters VIII and XI).

v. Further developments and concluding observations

In accordance with the schedule laid down in the Charter of Paris, further meetings have been held since, dealing with substantive human rights matters. The section devoted to further co-operation in the human dimension, contained in the concluding document adopted at the Helsinki follow-up meeting of 1992, reaffirms "in the strongest terms" the determination of the participating states to implement existing commitments on national minorities, and, among other things, adds a provision condemning "ethnic cleansing". The latter is defined, in paragraph 17, as consisting of "all attempts, by the threat or use of force, to resettle persons with the aim of changing the ethnic composition of areas within their territories". Such a new provision reflected a new political situation, with the Copenhagen and Paris "euphoria" giving way to deep concerns at the unravelling of ethnic conflicts prompted by the dissolution of the Soviet Union and Yugoslavia.

Finally, it is noteworthy a report produced by the HCNM (see, generally, *infra*, Chapter X) in 1999 on the linguistic rights of persons belonging to national minorities in the OSCE area, based on the OSCE and further relevant international instruments. This report analyses responses by OSCE participating states to questions put to them on a range of issues, particularly official languages and languages with special status, mother-tongue education and communication with public authorities, private minority schools and access to public media, and offers general conclusions and specific recommendations.

Overall, the contribution of the OSCE to the development of minority rights standards is considerable. Still, the structural "flexibility" of the OSCE is reflected in "flexible" standards. As pointed out by Thornberry, in relation to the length of many provisions and the "shopping-list" approach, the OSCE narrative on minority rights "can be ponderous, prolix and disorderly ... this is not simply a question of *elegantia juris*, but of consistency" (Thornberry, 1995: 364).

2. The European Union framework

a. Fundamental rights as general principles of Community law and the role of the ECJ

In the *Nold v. Commission* case (Case 4/73, (1974) ECR 491: paragraph 13), the ECJ stated that fundamental rights formed an integral part of the general principles of Community law, the observance of which the court ensured:

> in safeguarding those rights, the Court is bound to draw inspiration from constitutional traditions common to the Member States ... [s]imilarly, international treaties for the protection of human rights on which the Member States have collaborated or of which they are signatories, can supply guidelines which should be followed within the framework of Community law.

The ECJ summarised this doctrine in *Friedrich Kremzow v. Austria* (Case-C/299/95, (1997) ECR I-2405: paragraphs 14-15). The court has progressively developed a case-law on human rights, regarding control over both

Community measures and national measures as falling within the scope of EC law, despite the initial absence of specific human rights references in the EC Treaty. While, as indicated earlier, there is no instrument on minority rights at Community or Union level, the dictum in *Nold* may arguably reach out towards minority rights considerations, in relation to basic international treaty provisions, irrespective of reservations that individual members may have formulated to such provisions, so long as the latter are contained in human rights treaties on which member states have "collaborated" or of which they are "signatories" (see, for example, the French reservation to Article 27 of the ICCPR, though all member states are parties to the ICCPR). A view has been expressed that major "soft law" texts such as the 1992 UN declaration should also provide guidelines to be followed within the framework of Community law (Martín Estébanez, 1995: 160). On the other hand, the ECJ gave human rights a prominent place in Community law at a time (early 1970s) when there was no particular concern for the issue of minorities in the EC context.

It has been argued that in spite of the fundamental rights discourse embraced by the ECJ and even the elevation of such rights to the level of general principles of EC law, it has been the general Community rule or the Community objective which has prevailed against claims as to the violation of such fundamental rights (Coppel and O'Neill, 1992: 683; de Witte, 1999: 878). In the *Nold* case, the ECJ admitted the possibility of justifying restrictions on fundamental rights where necessary for pursuing Community objectives. *A fortiori*, this approach may lead to minimising specific minority rights considerations on the basis of the Community general interest.

In the *Bickel and Franz* case (Case C-274/96, *Criminal Proceedings against Bickel*, (1998) ECR I-7637; see also Pentassuglia, 2001: 32-33), the ECJ upheld the right of Mr Bickel and Mr Franz, two German-speaking persons of, respectively, Austrian and German citizenship, being prosecuted in the Province of Bolzano, to have the criminal proceedings conducted in the German language, on the same basis as the members of the German-speaking minority in the Region of Trentino-Alto Adige. The court importantly acknowledged that the protection of a minority "may constitute a legitimate aim", while insisting on equal treatment of Mr Bickel and Mr Franz under Community law (ex Article 6, now Article 12, of the EC Treaty) notwithstanding the special minority rights regime adopted by Italy for that region and the distinction in scope between minority (language) rights and general (language) fair trial guarantees under international human rights law (for example, under Article 6, paragraph 3, sub-paragraph e, of the ECHR). In spite of the dearth or absence of human rights/minority rights considerations in the judgment, the "legitimate aim" criterion referred to by the court seems implicitly to confirm that, although particular aspects of certain minority regimes may prove incompatible with Community law, the essential principles of such regimes, or other aspects of it, are, or may be, directly or indirectly justified in the Community legal order (see also *Angonese v. Cassa di Risparmio di Bolzano SpA*, Case 281/98, (2000) All ER (EC) 577). Such a protection, however, would not *per se* entail the recognition of minority rights in relation to fundamental rights.

Article 6 paragraph 2 (ex Article F paragraph 2) of the TEU states that the Community shall respect fundamental rights, as guaranteed by the ECHR and as deriving from the constitutional traditions common to the member states, as general principles of EU law. In terms of the hierarchy of EC sources of law, this provision has the effect of placing the general principles referred to on the same footing as that of the provisions of the EC Treaty. By contrast, the other general principles of Community law are normally considered as having a status which is higher than that of the secondary acts of legislation (regulations, etc.), but lower than that of the provisions of the EC Treaty. Under the new wording of Article 46 (ex Article L) of the TEU, introduced by the Amsterdam Treaty (see *infra*), the exercise of the ECJ's powers has been extended to Article 6 paragraph 2 (ex Article F paragraph 2) of that treaty, with regard to actions of the institutions, in so far as the ECJ has jurisdiction under the EC Treaty (and the other founding treaties) and the TEU. The references in Article 6 paragraph 2 (ex Article F paragraph 2) of the TEU to the ECHR (which does not contain specific minority rights provisions) and the common constitutional traditions of the member states (which have never been assessed by the ECJ with regard to the protection of minorities) make, however, the substance of minority rights which may be protected within this context further problematical.

At the very least, the "special significance" of the ECHR repeatedly stated by the ECJ in indicating the substance of fundamental rights as part of general principles of Community law (see *infra*) should be taken seriously and should lead the court to draw, in appropriate circumstances, on the case-law which might be developing under such a convention, in relation to general needs and rights of minorities and their members (see *supra*, Chapter VI). Additional minimum protection could derive from the cited Protocol No. 12 to the ECHR, setting forth a general prohibition of discrimination.

On the one hand, situations where the ECJ might use international minority rights standards, or the Strasbourg anti-discrimination criteria, including the upholding of regimes or individual measures protecting minority groups, in the event of a prima facie (direct or indirect) conflict with a general Community rule or objective, are likely to be limited, if not exceptional (Pentassuglia, 2001: 32-34). On the other hand, as confirmed by the discussion below, a judicial human rights discourse which proved to be essentially confined to the ECHR and its protocols or related instruments, as sophisticated as it may be or become, could not encompass "minority rights" considerations. With this in mind, and in view of the forthcoming EU enlargement (see *infra*), one may perhaps wonder whether in the long term a stronger influence on the ECJ's jurisprudence might be exerted by a protocol to the ECHR focused on minorities, along the lines of the proposal of the Parliamentary Assembly of the Council of Europe. On a more general level, jurisprudential developments in this area appear to be largely a function of the evolving EU human rights/minority rights framework.

b. General provisions of the TEU

In the Maastricht (and post-Maastricht) era, emphasis on human rights issues has increased considerably. In Opinion 2/94 on accession by the Community to the ECHR ((1996) ECR I-1759), the ECJ held that the Community had no competence to accede to the ECHR (notably on the basis of Article 308, ex Article 235, of the EC Treaty). Still, the court (*loc. cit.*: paragraphs 23-36) reaffirmed the above case-law, stressing the "special significance" of the ECHR, and listed a number of sources which established the importance of respect for human rights, thereby pointing to a range of internal and external competencies in the field. In this regard, it referred to various declarations of the member states and institutions, the preamble to the Single European Act, the preamble to, and Article F paragraph 2 (now Article 6 paragraph 2), Article J.1 (now Article 11) and Article K.2 (now Article 30) of the TEU, and Article 130u (now Article 177) of the EC Treaty.

The Amsterdam Treaty has taken further steps forward in the process of strengthening human rights protection within the EU framework. Notably, a new Article 6 paragraph 1 (ex Article F paragraph 1) states that the EU:

> is founded on the principles of liberty, democracy, respect for human rights and fundamental freedoms, and the rule of law, principles which are common to the member States.

Respect for such principles is singled out as an essential admission requirement in the latest version of Article 49 (ex Article O). Restrictive measures relating to membership rights are now permissible under a new Article 7 (ex Article F.1), further amended by the Nice Treaty of 2000 (see *infra*, Chapter X), in the event of a serious and persistent breach of principles mentioned in Article 6 paragraph 1 (ex Article F paragraph 1). It is thus clear that such a mechanism applies to all (namely, "old" and "new") member states on a footing of equality.

As discussed in Chapter II, minority rights are clearly part of the international protection of human rights. This is confirmed by the enlargement process of the EU, based on Article 49 (ex Article O) of the TEU in conjunction with Article 6 paragraph 1 (ex Article F paragraph 1) (see *infra*). Yet, the reluctant attitude of some EU member states vis-à-vis protection of their own minorities (as vividly illustrated by the fact that so far not all of them have ratified the relevant Council of Europe treaties, and that hostility to the adoption of a protocol on minority rights to the ECHR persists) makes it difficult to foresee the actual impact of Articles 6 paragraph 1 (ex Article F paragraph 1) and 7 (ex Article F paragraph 1) of the TEU (and, by implication, of the other general EC/EU human rights instruments or components as well) on minority rights, in terms of the EU's internal dimension (Pentassuglia, 2001; see also *infra*, Chapter X). To date, the only relevant references to "internal" minorities are indirectly made in the Accession Treaties, such as those relating to the status of the Åland Islands in Finland and the position of the Sami in both this country and Sweden, as well as in connection with the EU Special Support Programme for Peace and Reconciliation in Northern Ireland.

Nevertheless, although no international human rights treaty has been entered into by the Community or the Union so far, all EU member states adopted (as OSCE participating states) the 1990 Copenhagen Document, are bound by Article 27 of the ICCPR (with the exception of France), and actively contributed to the drafting and adoption of such a major international text on minority rights as the 1992 UN declaration. The principle of indivisibility and interdependence of all human rights frequently asserted by the EU further strengthens the placing of minority rights within the context of Articles 6 paragraph 1 (ex Article F paragraph 1) and 7 (ex Article F paragraph 1) of the TEU.

c. Article 151 (ex Article 128) and other relevant provisions of the EC Treaty

Specific minority concerns entered, albeit indirectly, the new stage of European integration opened up by the Maastricht Treaty, through the inclusion of Article 151 (ex Article 128) of the EC Treaty – committing the Community to contributing to the flowering of the cultures of the member states, while respecting their national and regional diversity (paragraph 1) – and a number of further education- and culture-related Community competencies (Title XI, ex Title VIII, and Title XII, ex Title IX). Under the latest version of Article 151 (ex Article 128), as amended by the Amsterdam Treaty, it is reaffirmed respect for national and regional diversity alongside efforts at "bringing the common cultural heritage [of the member states] to the fore" (paragraph 1), while at the same time requiring the community to take cultural aspects into account in its actions under other provisions of the treaty, "in particular in order to respect and to promote the diversity of its cultures" (paragraph 4).

Although the protection of the "common European heritage" (defined by the national identities of the member states under Article 6 paragraph 3 of the TEU) remains the dominant theme, measures have been adopted, or recommended by the European Parliament (see, for example, the 1994 resolution on linguistic and cultural minorities in the European Union, A3-0042/94, OJ 1994 C 61/110; also, the parliament unsuccessfully proposed the adoption of an EC charter for ethnic groups in the late 1980s; Pentassuglia, 2001: 34), which safeguard and promote, directly or indirectly, regional and cultural diversity, on the basis of the above provisions. Still, the Community's role has been one of supporting and supplementing the action of the member states in several pre-defined areas (Martín Estébanez, 1995). This in fact reflects a restrictive interpretation of the principle of subsidiarity enshrined in Article 5 (ex Article 3b) of the EC Treaty, as regards educational and cultural policies. At the same time, the principle of subsidiarity seems to call for a broader approach when read in conjunction with Article 1 (ex Article A) of the TEU, which refers to decisions taken "as openly as possible and closely as possible to the citizen". In this respect, the creation of the Committee of the Regions and Local Authorities is noteworthy. According to Thornberry, "while the powers are essentially minor, there is potential to assist in transforming subsidiarity into practice for sub-national groups" (Thornberry, 1995: 331). So far, this has not been the case (Biscoe, 1999; compare with the activities of the Council of Europe's counterpart body, *infra*, Chapter VIII). It has been even argued that European integration has tended to reinforce, rather than limit, the central states in their relation with local administrations (de Witte, 1993).

d. The anti-discrimination approach

i. Article 13 (ex Article 6a) of the EC Treaty

The Amsterdam Treaty has introduced a new Article 13 (ex Article 6a) in the EC Treaty, which enables the council, under certain conditions, to take appropriate action to combat discrimination based on, *inter alia*, racial or ethnic origin, and religion. This marks a progress in comparison with Article 12 (ex Article 6), which confines the prohibited differentiation to nationality grounds. However, unlike Article 12 (ex Article 6), the provision does not contain a directly effective prohibition which the ECJ may use as a standard for reviewing either Community or member state measures. Despite its pro-gramme-type nature and the requirement of unanimity for council measures (though, a new paragraph 2 introduced by the Nice Treaty will provide for variations in procedure and council *quora* in the case indicated therein), it may be seen as a (rather timid) development for future human rights policies.

Important acts have already been adopted based on this provision, such as the Council Directive of 29 June 2000 implementing the principle of equal treatment between persons irrespective of racial or ethnic origin (2000/43/EC, OJ 2000 L 180/22), and the Council Decision of 27 November 2000 estab-lishing a Community action programme to combat discrimination (2001-2006) (2000/750/EC, OJ 2000 L 303/23). These acts essentially aim to provide a comprehensive framework for fighting discrimination in a number of areas (for example, access to employment and working conditions, health care and social security, and education) regarding both the public and private sectors. The action programme established under the Council Decision of 27 November 2000 focuses on the analysis of discrimination and factors lead-ing thereto, the development of the capacity to fight discrimination, and awareness-raising against it. In terms of some of the most crucial aspects of the Council Directive adopted on 29 June 2000, it should be mentioned that discrimination based on racial or ethnic origin is defined in relation to both direct and indirect effects. In addition, those who believe themselves to be victims of this sort of discrimination must have access to appropriate admin-istrative or judicial procedures, enjoy a shift back of the burden of proof on to respondents, and may seek the involvement of associations which have a legitimate interest in the procedure. Harassment related to racial or ethnic origin is also outlawed in the fields covered by this text. Time limits are set for both complying with the directive under domestic law and reporting to the commission. Although there is no good reason why minorities should not stand to benefit from these anti-discrimination measures (notably, as part of efforts to combat such phenomena as racial and ethnic hatred, xenopho-bia, anti-Semitism, etc.), as recently confirmed by activities conducted by the-matic budget lines such as the European Initiative for Democracy and Human Rights, and by the commission itself (COM, 2001, 252 final of 8 May 2001), the ensuing dimension of protection cannot be viewed as a substitute for a policy focused on minority rights (see *supra*, Chapter IV).

ii. The Charter of Fundamental Rights of the EU

As illustrated above, human rights add to the complexities of the internal and external activities of the EU on the road to political integration. As a response to such an evolving framework, the Cologne European Council of 1999 decided the preparation of a Charter of Fundamental Rights of the European Union. The proposed charter passed through a number of drafting stages involving the main EU institutions, and was solemnly proclaimed by the latter on the occasion of the Nice European Council in December 2000.

The text is as such a non-legally binding document. A proposal for its incorporation by reference in Article 6 (ex Article F) of the TEU met with opposition by several member states. However, the Laeken European Council in December 2001, which established a "convention" charged with considering the future of the EU prior to the next Intergovernmental Conference in 2004, adopted a declaration setting out the issues that the convention is expected to consider, including whether the charter should be included in the basic treaty.

In terms of relevant human rights standards, the EU Charter further develops the anti-discrimination approach as it embodies a provision on equality before the law (Article 20) and a general clause prohibiting discrimination (Article 21, paragraph 1) – whose scope of application thus reaches beyond the more limited one of, for instance, Article 14 of the ECHR – addressed to EU institutions and bodies as well as member states only when implementing EU law, in accordance with their respective powers (Article 51).

On a positive reading, such a free-standing clause (listing "membership of a national minority" among the prohibited grounds of distinction) might also allow for differential treatment, along the lines indicated in the HRC General Comment No. 18 on non-discrimination, with regard to, *inter alia*, the comparable clause in Article 26 of the ICCPR (though the latter does not contain an equally explicit reference to a national minority), and further reflected in Protocol No. 12 to the ECHR (which, like Article 14 of the ECHR, refers to "association with a national minority" as an impermissible ground for differentiation instead). In this connection, it should also be remembered that positive action entailing a measure of differential treatment is already permitted under Article 5 of the above-mentioned Council Directive 2000/43 on the principle of equal treatment between persons irrespective of racial or ethnic origin. Despite the importance of these (potential) gains, coupled with references to respect by the EU for cultural diversity in paragraph 3 of the preamble, and Article 22 (in the latter case, combined with respect for religious and linguistic diversity) in conformity with earlier developments (notably under Article 151, ex Article 128, of the EC Treaty), the charter regrettably does not contain any specific minority rights provisions which might be enforced by the ECJ or other competent bodies. The reason why the charter does not reach out to "minority rights" notwithstanding proposals for a minority provision that had been submitted during the drafting stage (see, for example, Liisberg, 2001: 43), mostly lies in the fact that, while steps forward may be noted, the text elaborates to a large extent upon the common constitutional and ECHR *acquis* mentioned in Article 6 paragraph 2 (ex

Article F paragraph 2) of the TEU, with a view to making the respective rights, as stated in the preamble, "more visible in a Charter".

At least, the EU Charter, which is expected to provide important guidance to EU institutions and member states in the field of human rights both internally and externally, may not be used as an excuse to cut down higher levels of protection under the (somewhat confusing) "minimum standard" clause in Article 53 (namely, as deriving from EU law, international law, international treaties to which the Community, the Union or all member states are party, including the ECHR, and the member states' constitutions) (Liisberg, 2001). For instance, broader rights under Article 8 of the ECHR, subsuming aspects of minority identity (see *supra*, Chapter VI), could not be restricted at the EU level by using the corresponding provision in Article 7 of the charter. Besides, an ECHR-based interpretation of this provision could be construed on the basis of a positive reading of Article 52, paragraph 3. By adapting the line of reasoning submitted in specific relation to the ECJ's dictum in *Nold* (*loc. cit.*), it may be argued that provisions contained in agreements adhered to by all member states, such as those in Article 27 of the ICCPR, should be covered by Article 53 irrespective of reservations which individual members may have formulated to such provisions upon accession to the instrument. Given the generic reference to "international law" in Article 53, the "negative" safeguard purpose of the clause calls, it is further submitted, for its extension to "soft law" texts, at least where they enjoy support from the member states and/or are somehow interrelated to "hard law" provisions falling within the scope of this clause.

More importantly, the above-mentioned "minimalist" anti-discrimination approach of the charter may not adversely affect the developing EU minority rights *acquis* in external relations (see *infra*), and should not in general prevent, not least in view of the (current) "soft law" nature of the charter's provisions, a wider and more adequate vision of the issue of minorities from being fully embraced by the TEU under its Article 6 paragraph 1 (ex Article F paragraph 1), in accordance with the relevant OSCE and UN achievements involving EU member states (see *supra*).

e. Substantive profiles of minority rights considerations in external action

i. Some general aspects

In terms of ECJ case-law and treaty and/or treaty-based provisions, the position of minority rights certainly needs to be further clarified. On the other hand, human rights protection may be seen, in recent commentators' words, as a "transverse" objective of the Community (EC/EU pillar), reaching out, with varying degrees of intensity, towards the (non-EC/EU) inter-governmental pillars, notably the CFSP, under Article 11 paragraph 1 (ex Article J paragraph 1, paragraph 2) of the TEU, which includes the objective of developing and consolidating democracy and the rule of law, and respect for human rights and fundamental freedoms. One may even argue that, by virtue of Article 6 paragraph 2 (ex Article F paragraph 2) of the TEU (now falling, subject to certain limits, under the jurisdiction of the ECJ), the EU is bound to respect human rights in internal as well as external relations (see also *supra*, Chapter II).

Aside from the question of the precise delimitation of competencies in the human rights field, the role of minority rights considerations, in a broader, external human rights policy, has been confirmed by the EU practice of the 1990s. Unlike the 1986 Declaration on Human Rights adopted by the EC member states within the EPC, which contained no reference to minority rights, the Declaration on Human Rights adopted by the Luxembourg Summit in June 1991 devoted an entire paragraph to the subject. In fact, the end of the cold war, with the resulting new challenges posed by the dissolution of the Soviet Union and Yugoslavia, were inevitably to bring about change in the perception of the significance of minority rights on the (now) EU agenda. Following this act of political recognition, and in the wake of other major international efforts designed to contain ethnic conflicts in the world, a number of EU initiatives were progressively set in motion, addressing the human rights/minority rights situation in eastern Europe as an essential component of a comprehensive, regional approach (see *infra*).

So far, the EU has generally appeared rather hesitant to develop a broad approach to minority issues, reaching beyond the area of eastern Europe (for a general perspective, see the European Union Annual Report on Human Rights adopted by the council in October 2001; Pentassuglia, 2001: 31). For instance, the CFSP Common Position of 25 May 1998 defined by the council concerning human rights, democratic principles, the rule of law and good governance in Africa (Doc. 98/350/CFSP, OJ 1998 L 158/1) confirms the concept of interrelatedness, indivisibility and interdependence of all human rights but contains no explicit reference to the protection of minorities. At the same time, indigenous peoples matters are being increasingly considered by the EU in the framework of the ACP–EU partnership (African, Caribbean, Pacific countries–EU) on development and other policies. Nevertheless, specific attention to minority rights protection as part of the Community external human rights policy is expected to increase as a result of the cited Council Regulations No. 975/1999 and 976/1999, laying down the requirements for the implementation of Community operations to promote respect for human rights and consolidate democracy and the rule of law, within the framework of development and non-development co-operation policies, respectively. Such regulations, which are meant to provide a coherent legal basis for all financing activities in those contexts, feature significant references to minority and general group issues, namely matters encompassing "minorities, ethnic groups and indigenous peoples" (paragraph 14 of the common preamble, Article 3, paragraph 1, sub-paragraph d, and Article 3, paragraph 3, sub-paragraphs b and c, of Regulation No. 976/1999, as well as Article 2, paragraph 1, sub-paragraph d, and Article 2, paragraph 3, sub-paragraphs b and c, of Regulation No. 975/1999). Interestingly, the second regulation is based, in particular, on Article 308 (ex Article 235) of the EC Treaty: this may be interpreted as an acknowledgement of the possibility to use the above article as a basis for Community external human rights/minority rights activities.

ii. The case of eastern Europe

The EU approach to eastern Europe as developed in the 1990s rests on a variety of mechanisms and initiatives designed to facilitate and/or consolidate transition to market economy and further regional peace and stability. Minority rights considerations are implied within different contexts, principally associated with the EC pillar, but encompassing the CFSP in significant respects (Pentassuglia, 2001). As noted earlier, the new version of Article 49 (ex Article O) of the TEU sets out, *inter alia,* democratic and human rights requirements for admission to EU membership. It is interesting to note that until the Amsterdam Treaty, Article O of the TEU did not contain any particular membership requirement save that the prospective member was to be a European state.

The European Council held in Copenhagen in 1993 broke new ground in this respect. It indeed agreed to a number of economic and political conditions to be met by new candidate countries, notably from eastern Europe. In terms of "political criteria" for accession, the country concerned must have achieved "stability of institutions guaranteeing democracy, the rule of law, human rights and *respect for and protection of minorities*" (author's emphasis). The latter reference reflects a remarkable progress in the approach to EU membership. In assessing applications for accession, the opinion of the commission is of particular – substantive and procedural – significance. On the basis of the "Copenhagen criteria", the commission was asked by the council to give its opinions on ten eastern European candidate countries. The assessment of the commission resulted in an extensive report, delivered in 1997, entitled "Agenda 2000".

In addition to overviews of the functioning of the institutional system (under the separate heading "Democracy and the rule of law") and the situation of civil and political, as well as economic, social and cultural rights, the commission devotes considerable attention to minority issues, through an autonomous chapter on "minority rights and the protection of minorities". The analysis appears rather brief in the case of economic and social rights, and mainly focused on *de jure* (as opposed to *de facto*) developments generally. By contrast, the chapters on minorities reveal a relatively more extensive and critical assessment. The situations of, respectively, the Hungarian minorities in Slovakia and Romania, the Russian-speaking groups in the Baltic states, and the Roma in many of the candidate countries, feature among the major causes for concern. Such issues as the use of minority languages, the subsidisation of minority education and political and social discrimination in public life, are discussed at some length. As a result, a number of countries are singled out for their problematic record, whereas some of the countries praised by the commission also by virtue of their overall human rights/minority rights record are required to secure further improvements in the protection of particular groups. A similar framework of analysis is reflected in the annual regular reports on progress towards accession, issued by the commission as a follow-up to the 1997 report. Some of the respective concerns are also reaffirmed in the accession partnerships which have been adopted within the context of the enhanced pre-accession strategy.

Another vehicle of minority rights considerations in Community relations with east European countries may be offered by a so-called "human rights clause", included in the "second generation" trade agreements stipulated with the prospective members (association, or Europe, agreements), the new states emerged from the collapse of the Soviet Union (partnership and co-operation agreements), and some states from south-east Europe (co-operation agreements). In accordance with the Vienna Convention on the Law of Treaties (Article 60), the basic purpose served by the clause is to make "respect for the democratic principles and human rights as defined in the Helsinki Final Act and Charter of Paris for a New Europe" an essential element of the agreement, thereby enabling a party (and thus the Community), under the terms of a final non-execution provision and a joint interpretative declaration often accompanying this provision, to suspend or terminate such an agreement in connection with a failure of the other party to comply with those standards. As described earlier, both the Helsinki Final Act and the Charter of Paris for a New Europe firmly entrench respect for minority rights in the context of human rights protection, as based on the paramount principles of equality and non-discrimination. Arguably, the protection of minorities forms an integral part of the "essential element" of the agreement consisting in the said broader obligation to respect the human rights mentioned.

This argument is reinforced when considering that, except for the early (association) agreements with Hungary, Poland and Czechoslovakia, the above agreement's preamble contains not only references to relevant CSCE (now OSCE) documents – sometimes including the comprehensive 1990 Copenhagen Document – but also an explicit recognition of the importance of protecting minority rights, in conformity with CSCE (now OSCE) standards. The combination of such references in the preamble and the content of the human rights clause in the operative part of the agreement, suggests that, as a matter of principle, concerns for the minority question inform to a significant extent the scope of the linkage between human rights and economic liberalisation established within this framework. The concrete impact of minority rights considerations on the treaty-based linkage remains, however, to be seen (Pentassuglia, 2001: 23-25).

Economic benefits have been linked to respect for human rights, including minority rights, through an autonomous policy elaborated by the Community vis-à-vis certain countries of south-east Europe, namely Bosnia and Herzegovina, Croatia, FRY, FYROM and Albania. Particularly important for present purposes are the council conclusions on the principle of conditionality governing the development of the EU's relations with these countries, adopted on 29 April 1997 (Bulletin of the European Union 4-1997: point 2.2.1). They condition trade preferences, financial assistance, economic co-operation and contractual relations on, *inter alia*, "respect for and protection of minorities" (as part of a broader commitment to democracy, the rule of law, and human rights, and in line with the obligations assumed by some of these states under the Dayton Peace Agreement; on the latter, see *infra*, Chapter XI).

The 1997 conditionality requirements are now being placed within the wider context of an enhanced approach to south-east Europe, whose main component is indeed constituted of the negotiation and conclusion of so-called "stabilisation and association agreements", subject to the fulfilment of these requirements. General objectives of consolidation of democracy and respect for human rights/minority rights feature among the central purposes that such new agreements will pursue. This has been confirmed in the first two stabilisation and association agreements, concluded on 9 April and 14 May 2001 between the EC and its member states and, respectively, the FYROM and Croatia, in accordance with the existing conditionality criteria.

A further vehicle of minority rights considerations (implied by references to general human rights, or specific minority rights, requirements) has been created which somewhat resembles the above human rights clause in bilateral trade agreements, within the context of related technical (mainly financial) assistance programmes to eastern European countries (notably Phare, for present applicant countries; Tacis, for the Russian Federation, the newly independent states and Mongolia; and Cards, replacing Obnova, for the above-mentioned countries from south-east Europe). Finally, without prejudice to the provisions of Council Regulation No. 975/1999 and Title XX of the EC Treaty on Development Co-operation, Council Regulation No. 976/1999 concerning the financing and administering of Community action to promote respect for human rights and consolidate democracy and the rule of law in non-development co-operation activities, as well as a new Title XXI of the EC Treaty, introduced by the Nice Treaty, on Economic, Financial and Technical Co-operation with Third Countries, could provide a solid legal basis for further Community measures mostly of the sort indicated (including support for "bottom-up" activities), involving human rights/minority rights considerations. The latter are also involved, to a greater or lesser extent, by various thematic budget lines, such as the European Initiative for Democracy and Human Rights indicated earlier.

But what is the underlying concept of minority rights assumed by the EU in this context? With regard to the accession procedure, Article 49 (ex Article O) of the TEU refers back to the principles mentioned in Article 6 paragraph 1 (ex Article F paragraph 1), including "respect for human rights and fundamental freedoms". In contrast with the Copenhagen political criteria, "respect for and protection of minorities" is not explicitly referred to, yet the above-described practice of the enlargement process confirms the specific role of minority requirements precisely by virtue of the Copenhagen political criteria, in addition to their ("implied") significance as part of human rights requirements. When assessing the situation of minorities in the present candidate countries, the commission's opinions contained in Agenda 2000 (which, as noted above, have set the framework for subsequent follow-up assessments) often make reference to the ECHR, the Framework Convention for the Protection of National Minorities, Recommendation 1201 (1993) of the Parliamentary Assembly of the Council of Europe, and, occasionally, to some relevant bilateral treaties (for example, the 1995 and 1996 basic treaties between, respectively, Hungary and Slovakia and Hungary and Romania; see *infra*, Chapter IX). Such international instruments (in conjunction with the relevant national legislation) are intended to give substance to the above conditions for admission. In fact, they appear to be material sources for an overall, pragmatic assessment rather than individual parameters for a strictly legal analysis. This may also explain a certain amount of flexibility on the commission's part when considering group issues which do not necessarily display any strict connections with the traditional framework of international minority rights law (for example, the problematic situation of the Roma communities in many of the countries concerned, on which see also *infra*, Conclusions, and the non-citizens of Russian origin in Latvia and Estonia). Still, the commission does not seem to be demanding a new, broader concept of minority (see *supra*, Chapter III), but rather it is encouraging solutions which can secure internal and international stability (Pentassuglia, 2001: 21).

As noted, respect for the rights of persons belonging to national minorities in accordance with the commitments entered into in the context of the OSCE is frequently referred to in the preamble of the various Europe agreements, as well as in other trade agreements stipulated with eastern European countries. Whereas the 1999 Stability Pact for South Eastern Europe (see *supra*, Chapter I) does not contain any references to specific instruments on minority rights, the earlier Stability Pact from 1995 (see *supra*, Chapter I) singles out the 1990 Copenhagen Document and the 1995 Framework Convention among the instruments relevant to the protection of minorities (the substantive aspects of bilateral regimes generated, or expected to be generated, by these pacts as a result of CFSP action, will be discussed separately in Chapter IX). It should be remembered that the 1990 Copenhagen Document was adopted unanimously by the (then) CSCE participating states, including all current EU member states, and might thus in principle be said (despite the above-mentioned hesitant approaches to minority issues within the EU) also to provide the most comprehensive set of minority rights standards within the framework of Article 6 paragraph 1 (ex Article F paragraph 1) of the TEU.

The 1997 council conclusions on conditionality vis-à-vis certain countries of south-east Europe (*loc. sit.*) mention "generally recognised standards of human and minority rights"; yet, "respect for and protection of minorities" described in the annex to the council conclusions, combine guarantees in traditional areas of concern for minorities (the "right to establish and maintain their own educational, cultural and religious institutions, organisations or associations"; "adequate opportunities for these minorities to use their own language before courts and public authorities"; it appears, however, unlikely that the reference to minority language use in court should be understood as going further than the ECHR or the Framework Convention: see *supra*, Chapter VI), with "adequate protection of refugees and displaced persons returning to areas where they represent an ethnic minority". Such a combination reflects the complexities of the situation in the former Yugoslavia and the interrelatedness of human rights issues as evidenced by the Dayton Agreement of 1995. It is a *sui generis* approach serving the practical need for protecting the rights most endangered on the ground, but the issue of refugees and displaced persons clearly goes beyond the protection of minorities under international law.

In the early 1990s, OSCE commitments (referred to in the EC Declaration on the Guidelines on the Recognition of New States in Eastern Europe and in the Soviet Union, adopted within the EPC in December 1991; ILM 31, 1992: 1486-1487), other international instruments (conference on Yugoslavia's drafts, notably the so-called "Carrington Draft": see *infra*, Chapter XI), and relevant pronouncements (opinions of the Badinter Commission), were indicated as providing the basis for the protection of minority groups in the former Yugoslavia. The Badinter Commission, whose members were drawn from constitutional court judges and experts in public international law, was established by the EC to address legal differences or issues relating to the Yugoslav crisis. In particular, it was entrusted by the 1991 EC Declaration on Yugoslavia (adopted within the EPC; ILM 31, 1992: 1485-86) with advising, *inter alia*, on the fulfilment of the minority rights requirements by the newly emerging states which had applied for recognition. Minority rights as recognised by international law were clearly brought to the fore by the commission in relation to specific issues arising from the situation of the Serbian population in the republic of Bosnia and Herzegovina and in the republic of Croatia. As noted earlier, it made an innovative statement to the effect that "[peremptory] norms of international law require States to ensure respect for the rights of minorities" (Conference on Yugoslavia, Opinion No. 2 of 11 January 1992, ILM 31, 1992, 1497: paragraph 2).

On the other hand, the overall EC (and then EU) approach to the protection of minorities in eastern Europe is basically concerned with facilitating the implementation of internationally recognised minority rights standards irrespective of their specific legal significance, and as part of a pragmatic policy to promote stability in those states in transition towards democracy. In fact, the above activities are not entirely consistent in drawing upon existing international standards (for example, in key documents, there is usually no reference to Article 27 of the ICCPR and the 1992 UN declaration, and the 1990 Copenhagen Document is not always mentioned), and/or reveal deficiencies with regard to clarifying those standards on which to focus for implementation purposes (for example, in the context of the enlargement process and the relevant bilateral trade agreements). Certainly, they do not reflect the general purpose of establishing new norms in the field of the international protection of minorities (Pentassuglia, 2001: 20-23).

Bibliography

Alston, P., Bustelo, M. and Heenan, J. (eds), *The EU and human rights*, Oxford University Press, Oxford, 1999.

Biscoe, A., "The European Union and minority nations", in *Minority rights in the "new" Europe*, Cumper, P. and Wheatley, S. (eds), Kluwer Law International, The Hague, 1999, pp. 89-103.

Bloed, A. (ed.), *The Conference on Security and Co-operation in Europe: analysis and basic documents, 1993-95*, Martinus Nijhoff Publishers, Dordrecht, 1997.

Bloed, A., "The OSCE and the issue of national minorities", in *Universal minority rights*, Phillips, A. and Rosas, A. (eds), Åbo Akademi and Minority Rights Group (International), Turku/Åbo and London, 1995, pp. 113-122.

Bloed, A. (ed.), *The Conference on Security and Co-operation in Europe: analysis and basic documents, 1972-1993*, Martinus Nijhoff Publishers, Dordrecht, 1993.

Coppel, J. and O'Neill, A., "The European Court of Justice: taking rights seriously?", *Common Market Law Review*, 29, 1992, pp. 669-692.

de Witte, B., "Politics versus law in the EU's approach to ethnic minorities", European University Institute Working Paper No. 2000/4, 2000, pp. 1-28.

de Witte, B., "The past and future role of the European Court of Justice in the protection of human rights", in *The EU and human rights*, Alston, P., Bustelo, M. and Heenan, J. (eds), Oxford University Press, Oxford, 1999, pp. 859-897.

de Witte, B., "The European Communities and its minorities", in *Peoples and minorities in international law*, Brölmann, C., Lefeber, R. and Zieck, M. (eds), 1993, pp. 167-185.

Helgesen, J., "Protecting minorities in the Conference on Security and Co-operation in Europe (CSCE) process", in *The strength of diversity: human rights and pluralist democracy*, Rosas, A. and Helgesen, J. (eds), Martinus Nijhoff Publishers, Dordrecht, 1992, pp. 159-186.

Hofmann, R., "Minorities: Addendum 1995" in *Encyclopedia of public international law*, Macalister-Smith, P. (ed.), 3, Elsevier Science B.V., Amsterdam, 1997, pp. 420-424.

Liisberg, J.B., "Does the EU Charter of Fundamental Rights threaten the supremacy of Community law? Article 53 of the charter: a fountain of law or just an inkblot?", Harvard Jean Monnet Working Paper 04/01, 2001, pp. 1-55.

Martín Estébanez, M.A., "Minority protection and the Organisation for Security and Co-operation in Europe" in *Minority rights in the "new" Europe*, Cumper, P. and Wheatley, S. (eds), Kluwer Law International, The Hague, 1999, pp. 31-52.

Martín Estébanez, M.A., "The protection of national or ethnic, religious and linguistic minorities", in *The European Union and human rights*, Neuwahl, N. and Rosas, A. (eds), Martinus Nijhoff Publishers, The Hague, 1995, pp. 133-163.

Pentassuglia, G., "The EU and the protection of minorities: the case of eastern Europe", *European Journal of International Law*, 12, 2001, pp. 3-38.

Thornberry, P., "Minority rights", *Collected Courses of the Academy of European Law*, VI-2, 1995, pp. 307-390.

Van Dijk, P., "The Final Act of Helsinki: basis for a pan-European system?", *Netherlands Yearbook of International Law*, XI, 1980, pp. 97-124.

Wright, J., "The OSCE and the protection of minority rights", *Human Rights Quarterly*, 18, 1996, pp. 190-205.

CHAPTER VIII

STATE SOVEREIGNTY
AND THE SELF-DETERMINATION PUZZLE

Whereas the discussion about standards has so far concentrated on basic preconditions for the enjoyment of minority rights, and core substantive entitlements contained in general instruments addressed to minority members, this chapter will situate the issue of minorities within the larger and problematic context of self-determination and changing visions of sovereignty.

1. "Absolute" and "relative" sovereignty

Seen from a historical perspective, sovereignty is linked to the role of sovereigns, in whose hands "absolute" power rested. In modern discussions of sovereignty, few, if any, would support an absolutist conception of state sovereignty, meaning a power above international law. There is in fact general agreement, that the very concept of the equality of states, solemnly endorsed in Article 2, paragraph 1, of the UN Charter, at least implies that sovereign rights of each state are limited by the equally sovereign rights of others.

Sovereignty is essentially equated with independence, namely the fundamental authority of a state to exercise its powers without being subservient to any outside authority, but international law has increasingly imposed limitations on the permissible scope of the internal and external actions of independent sovereign states (from the basic prohibition of the use of force to a range of constraints deriving from the complexities of present-day international, political and legal, relations). The gradual erosion in the field of human rights of the "domestic jurisdiction" principle, embodied in Article 2, paragraph 7, of the UN Charter, is only a major symptom of a broader process with multiple components. As aptly noted by Anaya:

> Notions of state sovereignty, although still very much alive in international law, are ever more yielding to an overarching normative trend defined by visions of world peace, stability, and human rights. (Anaya, 1996: 42)

The question of self-determination is precisely one of the issues striking at the heart of this "overarching normative trend" and, therefore, of contemporary discussions of sovereignty and its ultimate repositories.

2. Self-determination

a. Historical background

Historically, self-determination has embraced elements of "democracy", associated with popular sovereignty, individual freedom, and representative government, and "nationalism", understood through the vision, mostly generated by the upheavals of the French Revolution, that national and state boundaries should coincide, namely, that the state should consist of a homogeneous ethno-cultural community.

The principle of self-determination championed by US President Wilson in the aftermath of the first world war was designed to accommodate democracy, in the sense of a regime based on the consent of the governed, within a nationalist framework. Lenin supported self-determination as promoting, in his own conception of democracy, the proletarian interests in the class struggle. Self-determination as an entitlement to popular free choice, including a representative government, did not play a major role in the Versailles settlements, nor did it in the years that followed. The League of Nations Covenant required "full self-government" of applicants for admission, but the clause was intended to mean only "full control of its internal affairs and ... foreign relations", rather than "full control of the government by the people of the country" (Robinson et al., 1943: 31).

As in earlier times in history, the ideal of the homogenous nation-state was to conflict with the reality of ethno-cultural heterogeneity. A large number of groups demanding self-determination had to be satisfied with recognition as minorities. Self-determination and minority rights were essentially applied to Europe, with colonial systems outside the reach of the principle. The limited practice of self-determination did not give rise to customary law, as confirmed in 1920 by a League of Nations Commission of Jurists set up to address the position of the Swedish-speaking population in the Åland Islands. In fact, the Commission of Jurists did not consider the relevant practice "as sufficient to put [the principle] upon the same footing as a positive rule of the Law of Nations" (*League of Nations Official Journal*, Special Supplement No. 3, 1920: 5).

b. Self-determination as a legal right: external and internal aspects

"Equal rights and self-determination of peoples" is the formula that appears in Article 1, paragraph 2, and Article 55 of the UN Charter. Higgins (1994b) notes that the context of these articles seems to be the rights of the "peoples" of one state to be protected from interference by other states or governments; the coupling of "equal rights" with "self-determination" was meant, in the intentions of the charter's drafters, to recognise the equal rights of states, not of individuals. There was originally no indication of the right of dependent peoples to be independent, or even to vote. In fact, Chapters XI and XII, concerning dependent territories, do not use the term "self-determination": the former is concerned with non-self-governing territories, and the latter covers the trusteeship system. Chapter XII refers to "self government or independence", but there is still no use of the term "self-determination", and independence was thus not meant to be the only appropriate outcome.

At the same time:

> there was nothing in the Charter which actually *prohibited* the emergence of a norm that required states not only not to interfere with each other but also to provide to dependent peoples the right to determine their own destiny. (Higgins, 1994b: 113.)

This right was increasingly invoked in the 1950s and 1960s in the UN, as Afro-Asian membership expanded. A broader interpretation of the state duties under Article 73, paragraph e, of the charter was accepted, eventually linking the concept of self-determination to the process of decolonisation. Self-determination began to be recognised as a legal right in this context. In most cases, self-determination meant independence for the peoples concerned, but the concept was never restricted to a choice for independence (choices for integration or association with an established state, including the former colonial power, were indicated as equally viable options).

The recognition of self-determination as a legal right in relation to decolonisation was confirmed by important General Assembly resolutions (Resolution 1514 (XV) and Resolution 1541 (XV), both adopted in 1960) and ICJ pronouncements (notably, in the well-known 1971 and 1975 advisory opinions on *Namibia* and *Western Sahara*, respectively, recently recalled by the court in the case concerning *East Timor*. ICJ Reports 1995: 102). At the same time, it came to be further accepted that the right of self-determination was applicable also outside the specific colonial context. Under the UN Declaration of Principles of International Law concerning Friendly Relations and Co-operation among States in accordance with the Charter of the United Nations (hereinafter the "UN Declaration on Friendly Relations"), adopted by the General Assembly in 1970 (Resolution 2625 (XXV)), which has been widely referred to in this regard as embodying principles of general international law notwithstanding it is contained in a non-binding instrument, self-determination applies not only to situations of colonialism, but also to "subjection of peoples to alien subjugation, domination and exploitation".

Of fundamental importance is the recognition of self-determination as a free-standing human right in the UN Covenants on Human Rights of 1966, entailing a duty on the parties to promote and respect this right, formulated as the right of 'all peoples' to freely determine their political status and freely pursue their economic, social and cultural development (common Article 1). Other international texts, too, provide for the right of "all peoples" to self-determination, such as the 1975 Helsinki Final Act (Principle VIII) and the 1981 African Charter on Human Rights and Peoples' Rights (Article 20), focusing on, or reaching out to non-colonial situations. As correctly noted by Higgins in view of the relevant international practice, "self-determination has never simply meant independence. It has meant the free choice of peoples" (Higgins, 1994b: 119). The "internal" dimension to self-determination is concerned with the relationship between a people and "its own" state or government. Rosas (1993) identifies a number of elements reflecting the concept of "internal" self-determination in UN practice. The issue arose mostly in connection with the adoption of common Article 1 of the UN covenants.

For a considerable period of time, there was something of a East-West and North-South divide on the matter. Germany and other Western countries supported a broad interpretation of the right so as to include an entitlement to democratic processes within the state (in conjunction with Article 25 of the ICCPR and Article 21 of the UDHR), whereas other countries such as India firmly opposed this interpretation. India also entered a statement to that effect upon ratification of the ICCPR, which was objected by Western countries. Many new states, largely supported by the old Eastern Europe, regarded self-determination only as a matter between them and their former colonial masters, not as between them and their own population.

And yet, the notion of internal self-determination has been progressively fostered by the HRC, both in its General Comment No. 12 on Article 1 (1984), and when commenting upon the periodic state reports. In these cases, the HRC endorses the existence of the right as a continuing entitlement vis-à-vis one's state or government (with widespread acceptance among the states parties, in spite of India's reservation which needs to be judged objectively) (Higgins, 1994b: 116-117; Cassese, 1995), and the debate is most frequently about the forms that the right can take. In 1996, the CERD delivered a general recommendation on the right to self-determination in which the distinction between "external" self-determination, exemplified by the liberation of peoples from colonialism, and "internal" self-determination in the above-mentioned sense (GR XXI (48) 1996) was explicitly acknowledged. References to – or elements supporting – the right to internal self-determination can also be found in the context of other major international instruments (notably, the UN Declaration on Friendly Relations, penultimate paragraph on the principle of equal rights and self-determination of peoples, the above-mentioned Helsinki Final Act and Banjul Charter, and the UN Vienna Declaration and Programme of Action, Part I.2). With the virtual ending of cold war polarities, a "democratic" order has been increasingly demanded in many regions of the world. As it will be argued below, the contemporary notion of self-determination can be captured by its strong linkage with human rights (in accordance with, for instance, the UN covenants and the UN Declaration on Friendly Relations) and broad processes of democratic change (as emphasised by, for instance, various Council of Europe and OSCE documents, which insist and elaborate upon the triad of "democracy, human rights and the rule of law"; see, for example, the 1990 Charter of Paris for a New Europe). Though not entirely uncontroversial, internal self-determination can be said to have clearly gained ground in international law.

3. Self-determination for minorities?

a. The "self" and the territorial dimension

Minorities often demand self-determination. As noted, self-determination has developed from a parameter originally associated with the right of states to non-interference by other states, into a distinctive right recognised to "all peoples", as opposed to states. Thus a question arises: do minorities constitute "peoples" for self-determination purposes, featuring among the relevant right-holders? Minorities claiming self-determination describe themselves as "peoples". Indeed, the description of a "people" on the basis of certain features such as a common history, culture, ethnic identity, etc., as made in a Unesco report from 1989 produced by an international meeting of experts on further study of the concept of the rights of peoples (SHS-89/CONF.602/7), could be used to identify minorities as well. On the other hand, the relevant international instruments, while not providing an explicit definition of "people", show that this term has traditionally designated all inhabitants of the territory concerned, irrespective of their ethno-cultural traits. In sum, the concept of people has been implicitly described, for legal purposes, by referring to the territorial unit of self-determination.

For instance, "colonial people" has meant the whole people in a non-self-governing territory (see, for example, the assumptions of Article 73 of the UN Charter). Coupled with the principle of *uti possidetis juris*, this understanding served later on to achieve self-determination for colonised entities overseas ("salt-water doctrine") within colonial borders (which was, in turn, confirmed by a chamber of the ICJ in the 1986 *Frontier Dispute* case between Burkina Faso and Mali, ICJ Reports 1986: 566-567). The "whole people" approach is also reflected in the UN Declaration on Friendly Relations (its penultimate paragraph on self-determination refers to a government representing "the whole people belonging to the territory"), and other instruments pointing to internal self-determination (Thornberry, 1989). Whatever the context of application, self-determination has thus worked for the benefit of peoples expressing whole units, not for minorities. This is also confirmed by the distinction made in the ICCPR between self-determination rights (Article 1) and minority rights (Article 27). The view taken by states during the *travaux* was indeed that minority groups should not be seen as "peoples" in the sense of Article 1, but rather as collectivities whose members would be entitled to distinct rights under Article 27. The HRC has made it clear (General Comment No. 23: paragraph 3, sub-paragraph 1), as recently confirmed in *Apirana Mahuika*, that, unlike Article 27 rights, self-determination is not a right cognisable under the First Optional Protocol, which deals with communications from individuals. This procedural point leaves the question of substance (namely, people versus minority) untouched, but the overall committee approach to self-determination (Higgins, 1994b: 118, 120, 124 and 126) seems to largely reflect the above understanding of people. Importantly, as further explained in the General Comment No. 23 on Article 27 with regard to the distinction between Article 1 and Article 27 (paragraph 3, sub-paragraph 2), the enjoyment of the latter does not prejudice the sovereignty and territorial integrity of a State Party.

In fact, the typical territorial connotation of "people" is to be viewed in connection with the doctrine of sovereignty and its fundamental corollaries protective of state boundaries and political unity (against claims by individual groups defined by ethnicity or other element), as confirmed by corresponding standard clauses following almost all international prescriptions on self-determination.

b. Reassessing "people": the Yugoslav *case and the Canadian Supreme Court's Opinion in* Reference re Secession of Quebec

Recent practice invites further reflection. The demise of the Soviet Union and, in particular, Yugoslavia has been described as resulting from a general process of dissolution (Conference on Yugoslavia, Badinter Commission Opinion No. 1 of 29 November 1991, ILM 31, 1992: 1494-1497). Although some commentators prefer to characterise the disintegration of Yugoslavia as a matter of secession rather than dissolution, the key question for present purposes is whether we are in fact witnessing an unprecedented move by the international community towards the recognition of acts of "ethnic self-determination". Indeed, just as "secession" does not necessarily presuppose a specific ethnic profile of the seceding entity, so the "dissolution" of a metropolitan state does not *per se* exclude the concomitant creation of states each identified with a distinctive "self-determining" ethnic group.

Despite the strong ethnic characterisation of the Yugoslav constituent republics and thus its crucial, though often ambiguous, significance in the context of the crisis, the overall approach eventually taken by the international community has appeared conceptually and operationally unchanged with regard to the material identification of the "self". Self-determination has been recognised to whole units (namely, the former constituent republics within the former boundaries now protected by international law through the principle of *uti possidetis juris*), not to minorities or other specific ethnic communities living within those units. As unsatisfactory as it may be to some analysts, this approach has been even reinforced by the establishment of a general conditional linkage (stressed mostly by the EC in its cited 1991 Guidelines on Recognition; ILM 31, 1992: 1486-1487) between the implementation of internal self-determination on a democratic basis, and the international recognition of external self-determination, of the whole people (namely, the entire population living within the boundaries of the new state) (Tierney, 1999).

The question of defining "people" for self-determination purposes was also incidentally addressed by the Canadian Supreme Court in its opinion in *Reference re Secession of Quebec* of 20 August 1998 (Supreme Court Reports (1998), 2, 281: paragraphs 123-125). The proceedings arose from a reference by the Government of Canada in relation to the secession of Quebec. A number of questions were put to the court, including whether there was a right to self-determination under international law that would give Quebec the right to unilateral secession from Canada. With regard to the particular issue of the notion of "people", the court, while tentatively observing that this notion might include a portion of the population of an existing state, significantly declined to argue, *inter alia*, that the francophone community of Quebec, and/or other groups within Quebec, were as such a "people" in the sense of international law.

c. Claim to secession as a result of gross human rights abuses

Having said that, a scholarly view enters two essential caveats against the territorial connotation of "people". One is that indigenous peoples, as distinct ethnic communities, enjoy (or should enjoy) the right to self-determination. The other challenges the proposition, implied by the considerations presented above, that, in particular, minorities have no international right to secession (which is also precluded under minority rights instruments themselves: see, for example, Article 8, paragraph 4, of the 1992 UN declaration), by advancing a legal right of these groups to secede at least as a result of gross human rights abuses committed against them.

Separating out the case of indigenous peoples (see *infra*), the "oppression" argument is not entirely new. Along broadly similar lines, the Commission of Jurists established by the League of Nations with the task of giving an advisory opinion upon the legal aspects of the Åland Islands dispute between Finland and Sweden (*League of Nations Official Journal*, Special Supplement No. 3, 1920: 6) denied that self-determination constituted a legal right and that, more specifically, minorities had a legal right to dismember an existing state, but conceded that secession might be a last resort when the state was unable or unwilling to enact and apply just and effective guarantees for them.

In present-day scholarly debate, Franck (1993) points out that when a minority persistently and egregiously is denied political and social equality and the opportunity to retain its cultural identity, then the repression may be seen as a somewhat stretched definition of colonialism. He mentions the secession of East Pakistan (then established as Bangladesh) in 1973 to support this view. But most of the scholars who advocate such a secessionist claim base their reasoning on the UN Declaration on Friendly Relations, the penultimate paragraph of which on self-determination, by pointing to the safeguard of the territorial integrity of independent states conducting themselves in compliance with the principle of equal rights and self-determination of peoples, seems to implicitly suggest a link between territorial integrity and the existence of a "government representing the whole people belonging to the territory without distinction as to race, creed or colour" in which that compliance is expected to result. It is argued that this clause, reaffirmed in the 1993 Vienna Declaration, would allow so-called "remedial secession" for a minority group which is egregiously discriminated against and thus denied meaningful access to government, causing the latter to lose the entitlement to the protection of its territorial integrity. This was also incidentally mentioned by the Canadian Supreme Court in its opinion in *Reference re Secession of Quebec* (*loc. cit.*, 278 and 285-286: paragraphs 112 and 132-135), when referring to "exceptional circumstances" in which apparently a right of unilateral secession might arise under the international right to self-determination.

The view is not convincing. A narrow reading of the clause is suggested by the "whole people" formula: it is precisely the whole people, not individual groups comprising it, that is entitled to react to oppressive regimes (the same seems to be implied by CERD Recommendation XXI (48) 1996: paragraph 6). Besides, the broad reading appears uncertain on purely empirical grounds, as illustrated by the controversial cases of Bangladesh and Biafra in earlier decades (Musgrave, 1997: 188-199), and even the most recent Kosovo crisis.

165

Indeed, in this instance the international community does not support a claim to independence, and therefore still endorses the territorial integrity of the FRY, notwithstanding massive human rights violations perpetrated against the Kosovar Albanians by the government (see *infra* in the text, and Chapter XI). The Canadian Supreme Court itself, in the above-mentioned opinion (*loc. cit.*, 285-286: paragraphs 132-135), noted that it remained unclear whether the "oppression" argument actually reflected an established international law standard. Cassese (1995: 108-124), who joins the said scholarly view by submitting the particular contention that the above-mentioned "safeguard clause" of the UN Declaration on Friendly Relations (originally inspired by the case of the apartheid regime in South Africa) would enable "racial groups" to secede from a state with a racist government, concludes that this entitlement has not matured into an international rule of customary law, given the paramount importance attached by states to territorial integrity and sovereign rights.

In general, the predominant view is that unilateral secession of any group within the state, attempted on whatever grounds, is neither authorised nor prohibited by international law; the lack of a specific prohibition does not arise in any sense from a sympathy for the breakdown of states, as made abundantly clear by the emphasis put on their territorial integrity and the above concept of people. Rather, the reason for this is that the matter is fundamentally referred to the domestic jurisdiction of the affected state. Agreements may be freely entered into by the parties concerned (in respect of Kosovo and Northern Ireland, see *infra*, Chapter XI); if a minority, and in particular an oppressed group, is able to create a state of its own, then the international community, prompted by a compelling political imperative rather than a pre-existing legal right of secession, will simply recognise new realities on the ground, with no prejudice to the applicable international law norms that the event has brought into play (including those regarding respect for human rights).

d. Internal (democratic) self-determination of the "whole"

The Vienna Declaration and Programme of Action, adopted by consensus on 25 June 1993 by the UN member states within the World Conference on Human Rights, takes up the saving clause of the UN Declaration on Friendly Relations, but this time the reference is to "a Government representing the whole people belonging to the territory without distinction of any kind", instead of "without distinction as to race, creed or colour". The 1970 clause had caused some controversy between Western and Third World countries: the latter stressed the non-racist composition of the government rather than the broader notion of pluralist representative democracy.

The 1993 clause seems to remove this cause of frictions. Seen in the light of other major developments involving the notion of internal self-determination (Council of Europe and OSCE standards, etc.; see also *infra*), and the paramount assumption (or principle) of "free choice" underlying the whole self-determination concept (as aptly emphasised by the ICJ in *Western Sahara*), the 1993 restatement may be arguably said to reflect, not only a continuing right to participate in the political system of the state without discrimination in connection with the contemporary reading of common Article 1 of the UN Covenants on Human Rights (see *supra*), but also a corresponding norm of general international law (in addition to well-established general and, as often stressed, *jus cogens* norms on external self-determination), at least *in statu nascendi* (for the latter view, see Cassese, 1995: 302-312). In any event, the Vienna provision can be considered as the most recent reaffirmation of the traditional understanding of the concept of people (namely, "the whole people") for self-determination purposes.

A crucial point to be made for present purposes is that the emergence of new "post-cold war" perspectives on self-determination impacts upon the position of minorities.

i. "Whole people" = the majority of the population concerned?

To understand the evolving content of self-determination and, by implication, of its relation to minorities, one first should further clarify the meaning conveyed by the term "whole people". In earlier times, notably at the time of decolonisation, the "whole people" formula was not matched with truly inclusive political processes providing responses also to minority groups as segments of "the whole". In practice, it was the majority of the self-determination unit which benefited from the "free choice" principle and related processes rather than the entire population concerned. The idea of nation-state, with its attendant rejection of cultural diversity, was clearly imported by newly independent states from the universe of values of former colonial masters, consolidating the stress on national unity (and sovereignty) already prompted by the concerns for internal and international stability indicated above. This, as a result, led to promoting (not necessarily achieving) the assimilation of culturally distinctive groups into newly established dominant political and social orders. The 1970 UN Declaration on Friendly Relations intimates ethno-cultural heterogeneity in the clause on representative government ("without distinction as to race, creed or colour"), but does not elaborate on the point.

Contemporary concerns for cultural diversity in society, coupled with an increasing awareness of the beneficial impact upon democracy and stability of respect for such a diversity through effective means of participation within the common territory, have resulted in challenging the *de facto* majoritarian actualisation of the "whole people" precept. As pointed out by Pellet in commenting upon the relevant 1992 statements of the cited Badinter Commission set up by the EC, "the notion of 'people' is no longer homogeneous" (Pellet, 1992: 179). In Opinion No. 2 (ILM 31, 1992: 1497-1499), the commission indeed appeared to link the internationally recognised minority right to identity within a state to a broader process of self-determination involving the whole population. Generally speaking, it may be observed that minorities must partake of self-determination by virtue of belonging to "the whole people".

ii. "Whole people" = "all (distinct) peoples"?

One may wonder whether this latter proposition does equate "whole people" with "all peoples" in the sense of individual, distinctive "peoples" forming the "whole". Would this assumption not be in contradiction to the previously mentioned, ethnically and culturally neutral, thus territorially-based, notion of "people" which assumes no right of minorities to self-determination? In *Reference re Secession of Quebec*, the Canadian Supreme Court cautiously hinted at the applicability of self-determination to several peoples within a particular territory, but appeared unclear as to whether that vision should be linked to a regime of multiple self-determination rights (*loc. cit.*, 281 and 284: paragraphs 123-125 and 130). With regard to the UN Declaration on Friendly Relations, a draft by the United States made reference to "all distinct peoples" in the territory of an independent state rather than "the whole people". As noted by Thornberry:

> [t]he non-recognition of distinct peoples apart from the people of the State as a whole must be accounted for in any interpretation of the text. (Thornberry, 1993: 115.)

In conjunction with the said concerns for preserving state sovereignty and its corollaries of territorial integrity and political unity, this approach in fact underlies other international instruments and essentially means that the right-holder is "the whole" instead of its components. As a result, minorities are not *per se* the holders of the right. In *Apirana Mahuika* under the First Optional Protocol, New Zealand, in response to the Maori people's self-deter-mination claims, observed (Communication No. 547/1993, Views of 27 October 2000, CCPR/C/70/D/541/1993: paragraph 7, sub-paragraph 6), that the rights in Article 1 of the ICCPR attach to "peoples" of a state "in their entirety", not to minorities of any kind. Nevertheless, from a truly inclusive (and stability-oriented) perspective, minority groups must benefit from self-determination as part of the whole population concerned. In fact, the focus (and "value added") of such an overarching (internal and external) perspec-tive, as increasingly supported in contemporary international practice and scholarly analyses (see *infra*), is not on the right-holder as a monolithic (*de facto* majoritarian) entity. Rather, it is on the most appropriate means of implementing the right, elaborated on the basis of the fundamental "free choice" requirement, for the practical and effective benefit of all individuals and groups which, in disaggregated terms, make up the "people".

In this context, the question of indigenous peoples is a *sui generis* one. ILO Convention No. 169 on Indigenous and Tribal Peoples provides in Article 1, paragraph 3, that the use of the term "peoples" in the convention shall not be construed as having any implications as regards the rights which may attach to the term under international law. On the other hand, the conven-tion loosely reflects elements of self-determination distinctive to indigenous peoples within the overall societal context. The UN draft declaration on the rights of indigenous peoples explicitly uses the language of "self-determina-tion", but links the right to the establishment of autonomy regimes as a spe-cial way of accommodating the distinctiveness of these communities within the state (Article 31). Indigenous peoples retain the right to participate fully, "if they so choose", in the political, economic, social and cultural life of the state (Article 4), notably in relation to matters of their direct concern (Articles 19 and 20), while no secessionist activity is permitted under the draft declaration (Article 45). Although the precise ramifications of this approach are still being debated at the UN and important areas of disagreement persist, states appear united in the rejection of the option of full independence and relatively more constructive in considering the key objectives of a protective regime within state boundaries. Overall, the term "peoples" associated with "indigenous" serves the general purpose of conceptualising a demand for protection through guarantees appropriate to the unique attributes of the communities concerned.

iii. The human rights substance: participation rights and the "procedural" parameter of "effectiveness"

As a matter of fact, the evolving content of the relationship between self-determination and minority rights should be elaborated on the basis of a dynamic material linkage between self-determination and human rights in the post-cold war era, strongly influenced by notions of cultural pluralism and stability. As regards the democratic substance of self-determination, Thornberry observes:

> It can be argued that self-determination should be understood in terms of the generality of rights, the unity, indivisibility and interrelatedness of which are now constantly underlined ... rights of minorities are a particular barometer of human rights in general. (Thornberry, 1993: 136.)

In fact, self-determination is increasingly understood as a:

> "configurative principle or framework complemented by the more specific human rights norms that in their totality enjoin the governing institutional order". (Anaya, 1996: 77.)

These visions further elaborate on what Franck has broadly identified as an emerging "right to democratic governance" (1992). In sum, a human rights-based understanding of self-determination of the whole people is assumed to inform, by implication, the scope and reach of sovereignty principles as well as the role of the state itself in contemporary international law, thereby promoting democracy and peace within and among societies.

The UN covenants, the UN Declaration on Friendly Relations and other more recent international instruments, such as the 1993 UN Vienna Declaration and Programme of Action, directly or indirectly establish the self-determination/human rights linkage, based on the equality and non-discrimination precepts. The latter aspect is evident in the Declaration on Friendly Relations and 1993 Vienna text, with regard to the crucial notion of representative government. The non-discriminatory enjoyment of such rights as the right to take part in government, freedom of assembly and association, and freedom of speech, are typically referred to when indicating the human rights implications of internal self-determination processes (for example, in its General Comment No. 25 on Article 25 of the ICCPR, paragraph 2, the HRC points out that Article 25 rights are "related" to, while "distinct" from, the

169

right to self-determination under Article 1), but also minority rights and indigenous peoples' rights (see *supra*) can and should be valued in this context.

This has been recently confirmed, for instance, by the already mentioned EC 1991 guidelines (conditioning international recognition of new states on internal self-determination which included respect for the rights of ethnic and national groups and minorities in accordance with OSCE standards; ILM 31, 1992: 1487), and CERD general recommendation of 1996 (explicitly drawing upon minority rights and further standards to elaborate on the content of self-determination of the "whole people", in connection with the anti-discrimination clauses contained in the ICERD; GR XXI (48) 1996: paragraphs 3 to 5). The HRC is taking a similar approach under the Covenant's reporting procedure by increasingly considering participation and other relevant rights affecting minority groups in relation to the implementation of self-determination under Article 1 through broad democratic processes (Anaya, 1996: 157; see also HRC concluding comments regarding Canada, Mexico and Norway, UN Doc. CCPR/C/79/Add. 105, 109 and 112). This approach is reflected, albeit indirectly, in HRC General Comment No. 23 on Article 27 (valuing minority diversity as an essential part of the "fabric" of society as a whole, and relating the enjoyment of minority rights to, *inter alia*, peaceful uses of territory and its resources, with a special emphasis on indigenous minorities; General Comment No. 23: paragraphs 7 and 9), and interestingly endorsed in its latest case-law. Indeed, in *Apirana Mahuika* (*loc. cit.*: paragraph 9, sub-paragraph 2) and *Diergaardt* (Communication No. 760/1997, Views of 25 July 2000, CCPR/C/69/D/760/1996: paragraph 10, sub-paragraph 3), the HRC, while confirming that it had no jurisdiction under the complaints procedure to consider self-determination claims in the sense of Article 1 of the ICCPR, stated that Article 1 could nevertheless be relevant to the interpretation of other rights protected by the ICCPR, in particular Article 27.

On a general level, members of minorities, like everybody else, must enjoy, *inter alia*, the right to political participation recognised in, for instance, Article 25 of the ICCPR, in conjunction with the relevant anti-discrimination clauses (as to citizenship matters see, for example, *supra*, Chapter III). Information and materials about voting should be available in minority languages (HRC General Comment No. 25 on Article 25: paragraph 12). The electoral boundaries and the method of allocating votes should not distort the distribution of voters or discriminate against any group (HRC General Comment No. 25 on Article 25: paragraph 21). A prohibition to alter the proportions of the population in a district, for the purpose of diluting or excluding minority representation ("gerrymandering"), can be based on Article 16 of the Framework Convention. On the other hand, the EurCommHR indirectly indicated that special voting laws aimed at enhancing the election prospects of a religious or ethnic minority could be allowed under the ECHR, in those cases where a minority could never be represented in the legislature "because there was a clear voting pattern along these lines in the majority" (*The Liberal Party, Mrs R. and Mr P. v. United Kingdom*, Application No. 8765/79, EurCommHR, Decision of 18 December 1980, DR 21, 1981: 211).

The aim here is to provide a more accurate representation of the "will of the people" (taken as a whole). Further related general participatory guarantees affecting minorities and their members as part of the larger society, may be directly or indirectly established on the basis of cases recently brought before the EurCtHR (see, for example, *Grande Oriente D'Italia di Palazzo Giustiniani v. Italy*, Application No. 35972/97, EurCtHR, Judgment of 2 August 2001; Decision of 21 October 1999; *Buscarini and Others v. San Marino*, EurCtHR, Judgment of 18 February 1999, Reports 1999-I: 607; *McGuinness v. United Kingdom*, EurCtHR, Decision of 8 June 1999, Reports 1999-IV: 483).

From the perspective of minority rights, particular emphasis is laid on the already mentioned entitlement of minority members to effective participation in affairs affecting them (see, for example, paragraph 35 of the Copenhagen Document, Article 2, paragraph 3, of the 1992 UN declaration and Article 15 of the Framework Convention). A set of measures and techniques are indicated (for example, in the explanatory memorandum of the Framework Convention and Part IV of the Geneva meeting of experts' report), such as consultation, participation in elected bodies, involvement in the preparation of national and regional programmes, etc. Whatever measures are resorted to, states recognise the "procedural" parameter of "effectiveness" as referred to in the relevant provisions. Therefore, they are expected or required to develop appropriate methods of participation for persons belonging to minorities, which can enable these persons to have an actual say in the relevant decision-making process.

As suggested by the HRC's decisions in the *Länsman* and *Apirana Mahuika* cases under Article 27 of the ICCPR (see *supra*, Chapter V), meaningful forms of direct consultation are a minimum way of enabling effective participation suitable to a variety of cases. This jurisprudence may be usefully compared with that reflected in *Marshall et al. v. Canada* (Communication No. 205/1986, Views of 4 November 1991, (1992) Annual Report: 201), concerning the right to directly take part in the conduct of public affairs under Article 25, paragraph a, of the ICCPR. The authors were representatives of an indigenous group who complained of an impairment of that right since they had not been invited to constitutional conferences on aboriginal matters which directly affected their interests and those of the group as a whole. The HRC emphasised the fundamental notion of representative democracy and observed that, although in certain cases the interests of specific groups were directly affected compared to the rest of the population, and consultations or public hearings with such groups were often envisaged as a matter of public policy in the conduct of public affairs, there was no unconditional right for these groups of citizens to choose the modalities of participation under Article 25, paragraph a. It concluded that, in the circumstances of the case and in view of the absence of unreasonable restrictions on the participation in, and representation at the conferences in question, the authors' complaint disclosed no violation of Article 25, paragraph a. In terms of Article 27, it is difficult to envisage at this stage the direct consultation parameter as developed by the HRC in *Länsman* and *Apirana Mahuika* as a matter of an "unconditional right", since the state retains a measure of discretion in choosing the most proper modalities of effective participation that the enjoy-ment of Article 27 rights "may require" (General Comment No. 23: paragraph 7). The review of other instruments in the previous chapters has shown that they normally link minority effective participation to a reference to its con-formity with the "national legislation" (see, for example, Article 2, paragraph 3, of the UN declaration) or the "decision-making procedures" or "policies" (see, for example, paragraphs 33 and 35 of the Copenhagen Document) of each state. Nevertheless, as mentioned earlier, the HRC's jurisprudence is evolving, and may well be incrementally reaching out to an automatic con-sultation right in clearly defined circumstances. Be that as it may, the general criterion of "effective participation" in the context of Article 27 seems to be emerging as *lex specialis* at least in the sense of indirectly placing state action vis-à-vis minority participation under tighter control (see *supra*, Chapter V). That is further suggested by the cited indication provided by the HRC, that Article 1 may affect the interpretation of, *inter alia*, Article 27.

As clearly revealed by the international instruments mentioned above, a deeper aspect is that, beyond minimum forms of participation, more advanced schemes of "effective involvement" may have to be considered, including transfers of power and responsibility.

iv. Effective participation through autonomy?

Minority autonomy regimes essentially consist in systems or subsystems premised on the allocation or devolution of varying degrees of power for the benefit of one or more minority groups. They range from complex govern-mental systems of "power-sharing", to local statutes of territorial autonomy, to regimes of personal law or so-called "cultural autonomy". They have been strongly advocated in scholarly analyses. Lijphart (1977 and 1991) is credited with having been the first expert to argue for a consociational model in deeply divided societies (based on grand coalition, mutual veto, proportion-ality in representation, and segmental autonomy on areas of concerns). In recent years, Wippman has pointed out with regard to the same contexts that:

> consociationalism is not only compatible with self-determination but may be the only way to give effect to self-determination that is consistent with the rights of minorities to effective political participation. (Wippman, 1998: 230.)

Further scholarly input is being provided as part of the discussions on the various facets of autonomy which are being held in the UN Working Group on Minorities, particularly in the light of major regional experiences (see the report of the working group on its seventh session, UN Doc. E/CN.4/Sub.2/2001/22: paragraphs 66-128). And indeed, in one version or another and at different junctures in history, autonomy arrangements have proved a viable option in many countries: Belgium, Estonia, Finland, Hungary, Italy, Spain, Switzerland, etc.; similar regimes have been developed or proposed in specific crisis contexts (Bosnia and Herzegovina, Cyprus, Georgia, Kosovo, Northern Ireland, etc.). Examples of these arrangements and related techniques will be provided in Chapter XI. In his 1993 report on possible ways and means of facilitating the peaceful and constructive solution of problems involving minorities, Eide confirms this state of affairs by referring to autonomy as a practical method for effectively protecting the existence and identity of minorities. Nevertheless, he doubts that the latter have a general right to autonomy under international law (Eide, 1993b: paragraph 88).

Three essential aspects should be considered. In the first place, it must be noted that, although collective – or even autonomy – elements may be said to be indicated, or at least implied, in the area of international minority rights (see, for example, the HRC's case-law and General Comment No. 23 on Article 27 of the ICCPR; Article 2, paragraph 3, of the UN declaration; paragraph 35 of the Copenhagen Document; Part IV of the Geneva meeting of experts' report; Article 14 of the Venice Commission's draft convention; Article 11 of Recommendation 1201 (1993); Articles 10 to 14 of the Framework Convention; and paragraph 80 of the explanatory memorandum of the Framework Convention on Article 15), no distinctive general right to minority autonomy and/or power-sharing can indeed be established in positive international law, whether or not in connection with internal self-determination (Thornberry, 1998). The point was also made clear by the Council of Europe's Venice Commission in its opinion on the interpretation of Article 11 of the draft protocol to the ECHR appended to Recommendation 1201 of the Parliamentary Assembly (CDL-MIN (96) 4: 2) (hereinafter "opinion on Article 11 of Recommendation 1201"); see also *infra*, Chapter IX). In particular, it noted that, having regard to the present state of international law, a general right to autonomy was possible only on the basis of binding international instruments, which was not the case in respect of the Assembly text. As already explained by the commission (*loc. cit.:* 3):

> [s]tates seem in fact to be afraid that the right to have appropriate local or autonomous authorities, combined with the right to transfrontier contacts ... may promote secessionist tendencies ... [e]ven those states which ... have granted a large degree of regional autonomy hesitate to accept binding international instruments on the rights of minorities to a certain autonomy.

Not surprisingly, the lack of a general minority right to autonomy is a reflection of the lack of a right to autonomy for ethno-cultural groups generally. (Christakis, 1999: 544-573).

A second aspect which is equally important is that statutes of autonomy for minorities, while unavailable from the standpoint of a positive general right, may nevertheless be recognised by special treaties. Examples of such treaties can be found in earlier and recent practice, from the Paris Convention concerning the Territory of Memel (1934) to the De Gasperi-Gruber Agreement of 1946 on South Tyrol, to some treaty settlements reached over the last few years in Europe (see *infra*, Chapters IX and XI). If a special treaty does establish an autonomy regime for minorities, then the special legal protection it generates directly stems from the principle *pacta sunt servanda*, not the law of self-determination and human rights as such.

Thirdly, autonomy may be viewed as a way of enhancing protection for minorities under domestic law, in conjunction with international standards.

Indeed, as already said, autonomy, namely one consisting of "appropriate local or autonomous administrations", is "noted" in the unanimously adopted Copenhagen Document among the possible means of securing effective participation of persons belonging to national minorities in the affairs affecting their identity, taking into account "the specific historical and territorial circumstances of such minorities and in accordance with the policies of the State concerned". The provision implicitly refers to the autonomy arrangements elaborated within some of the countries hinted at earlier, which have long proved successful, though not necessarily uncontroversial (see *infra*, Chapter XI). The Venice Commission further elaborates upon this theme in its opinion on Article 11 of Recommendation 1201 (*loc. cit.*: 5), particularly when referring to "special status" schemes which may go as far as to advance on "minimum requirements" to ensure that persons belonging to minorities participate effectively in the relevant decision-making processes, within the confines of national legislation. In addition, in a recent preliminary study by the commission on a general legal framework to facilitate the settlement of ethno-political conflicts (CDL (2000) 70: Part I.D), it is acknowledged that statutes of autonomy provide a way of ensuring the realisation of minority obligations contained in multilateral and bilateral treaties. Along comparable lines, territorial autonomy, local law or special status are the themes of two recommendations adopted by the Congress of Local and Regional Authorities of Europe (representing the entities of local and regional self-government of the member states of the Council of Europe) in 1998 (Recommendation 43 (1998) on territorial autonomy and national minorities) and 1999 (Recommendation 70 (1999) on local law/special status).

In short, while international law does not set out a duty to devolve authority on a territorial (or non-territorial) basis, let alone an entitlement for the minority *qua* group, whether or not in the context of self-determination, international institutions, particularly at the European level, are drawing states' attention to autonomy essentially as a policy option to be considered in certain instances within the framework of participation rights. In the case of indigenous peoples, specific autonomy solutions and/or regimes as well as collective rights, as reflected to a greater or lesser extent in, among others, ILO Convention No. 169 and the UN draft declaration, provide an unprecedented set of parameters, which are different, however, from those for minorities or other ethno-cultural groups.

In terms of legal and policy justifications, Steiner (1991) speaks of "ideals" and "counter-ideals" when discussing autonomy regimes for minorities from a human rights perspective. Alfredsson (1993) contends that self-control by the minority over its own affairs (in its different versions) is probably the most effective means of protecting dignity and cultural identity. Even if one concludes that autonomy regimes are politically desirable, operationally feasible (which is not always the case), and even in line with recommendations contained in international documents, one should not assume that they can be comfortably accommodated within the human rights framework (Wippman, 1998).

In addition to minority rights provisions, respect for diversity may be said to inform many human rights norms (for example, equality and non-discrimination clauses, association freedoms, religious freedoms, etc.). At the same time, autonomy regimes for minorities (or some such regimes) raise problematic questions such as the acceptable level of difference in treatment granted to the group members compared to the rest of the population or other minorities, their compatibility with participation rights for all (see, for example, the clause on access to public service "on general terms of equality", in Article 25 of the ICCPR), possible restrictions on freedom of movement and residence within the autonomous minority area, or even in general on the enjoyment of rights by minority members within the group (see, for example, gender-based distinctions in some religious personal laws), and so forth. A more general issue is whether certain autonomy regimes set obstacles to developing a sense of belonging to an open and larger polity, thereby working against – not for – the inclusive aims pursued by participation rights.

In practice, a broad, but consistent, interpretation of general human rights provisions (notably the equality and non-discrimination clauses in respect of the "positive" protection that they may generate based on difference in treatment which is reasonable and proportionate), viewed against the backdrop of special instruments on minority rights (sometimes embodying references to degrees of autonomy as a tool for furthering the collective dimension to the protection of minorities), may provide arguments justifying autonomy arrangements on a case-by-case basis. It is also of relevance that, though not necessarily uncontested with regard to all their implications, the autonomy schemes which have long been in place in various country contexts have spurred no major human rights objections to their overall permissibility (see also *infra*, Chapter IX). Interestingly, the so-called "Lund Recommendations" on the effective participation of national minorities in public life, adopted in 1999 by a group of internationally recognised independent experts as a result of an initiative of the OSCE HCNM, attempt to delineate the implications of international standards on minority participation rights. This is done somewhat in view of the best domestic practice and even increasingly asserted notions of decentralisation of power as embodied in international instruments of a general nature such as the Council of Europe European Charter of Local Self-Government from 1985. "Self-governance arrangements" are included in order to improve the level of effectiveness of minority participation, with the important caveats that no ethnic criterion is to be used for territorial arrangements and that transfers of responsibility and control, as well as the exercise of the respective powers, must be consistent with human rights. Clearly, the "negative" protection attached to equality and non-discrimination provide the fundamental parameter in determining the legitimacy of such arrangements benefiting minorities, compared to their effects on the rest of the population, other minority groups and individuals within the protected minority. For instance, regimes of personal autonomy based on unreasonable gender-distinctions are discriminatory and thus inconsistent with human rights.

Within these limits, autonomy schemes, though not *per se* legally mandatory, may therefore be compatible with the emerging view of self-determination (notably internal) of "the whole people" (as opposed to the *de facto* simple majority), as an inclusive human rights-based, democratic and pluralistic process, which ultimately provides the materially disaggregated individuals and groups comprising "the whole" with meaningful choices on an occasional and permanent basis (depending, respectively, on its external or internal dimension). The arrangements adopted or proposed in certain recent crisis contexts, such as Bosnia and Herzegovina, Kosovo and Northern Ireland (see *infra*, Chapter XI) at least indirectly appear, to a greater or lesser extent, to bolster such a comprehensive approach, helping reshape the concept and content of sovereignty.

Whereas earlier discussions of sovereignty simply indicated a shift from an "anarchical" to a "regulated" pattern as international law took hold in a variety of fields of international relations, setting an ever higher number of legal constraints, contemporary discussions reveal in fact a progressive qualitative move, from the purely negative concept of sovereignty stressing, in particular, the exclusion of any outside authority within a clearly identified territorial space, to a less absolute and more positive value-laden notion entailing, *inter alia*, the capacity to realise human rights as recognised by the international community. An advanced understanding of self-determination thus assumes the accommodation of individual and group interests to be less a question of "ceding" sovereignty than of responding to sub- and supranational or international constituent pressure and demand. Certainly the human rights implications of autonomy structures (notably, the individual- and group-based equality aspects) must be carefully measured, especially when it comes to truly collective regimes; after all, such structures should be construed as a practical means to an end under particular circumstances, not as an end in themselves. In this respect, pervasive power-sharing systems may be seen as a "least worst" solution in deeply divided societies. For instance, in "Bosnia-like" situations, this approach becomes a meaningful alternative to "ethnic cleansing" or even "voluntary" population exchanges. Steiner (1991) goes as far as to observe that the risks inherent in ignoring the demands of minorities in certain cases may be even greater than those raised by the possibility of frictions or inconsistencies with human rights implied by the prospect of developing autonomy arrangements.

Bibliography

Alfredsson, G., "Minority rights and a new world order", in *Broadening the frontiers of human rights: essays in honour of Asbjørn Eide,* Gomien, D. (ed.), Scandinavian University Press, Oslo, 1993, pp. 55-77.

Anaya, J., *Indigenous peoples in international law,* Oxford University Press, New York and Oxford, 1996.

Cassese, A., *Self-determination of peoples: a legal reappraisal,* Cambridge University Press, Cambridge, 1995.

Christakis, T., *Le droit à l'autodétermination en dehors des situations de décolonisation,* La Documentation française, Paris, 1999.

Crawford, J., "The right of self-determination in international law: its development and future", in *Peoples' rights,* Collected Courses of the Academy of European Law, Alston, P. (ed.), IX-2, Oxford University Press, Oxford, 2001, pp. 7-67.

de Varennes, F., "Towards effective political participation and representation of minorities", UN Doc. E/CN.4/Sub.2/AC5/1998/WP4, 1998, pp. 1-9.

Eide, A., in co-operation with Greni, V. and Lundberg, M., "Cultural autonomy: concept, content, history and role in the world order", in *Autonomy: applications and implications,* Suksi, M. (ed.), Kluwer Law International, The Hague, 1998, pp. 251-276.

Eide, A., "The national society, peoples and ethno-nations: semantic confusions and legal consequences", *Nordic Journal of International Law,* 64, 1995, pp. 353-367.

Eide, A., "In search of constructive alternatives to secession", in *Modern law of self-determination,* Tomuschat, C. (ed.), Martinus Nijhoff Publishers, Dordrecht, 1993a, pp. 139-176.

Eide, A., "Possible ways and means of facilitating the peaceful and constructive solution of problems involving minorities", UN Doc. E/CN.4/Sub.2/1993/34, 1993b.

Franck, T.M., "Post-modern tribalism and the right to secession", in *Peoples and minorities in international law,* Brölmann, C., Lefeber, R. and Zieck, M. (eds), Martinus Nijhoff Publishers, Dordrecht, 1993, pp. 3-27.

Franck, T.M., "The emerging right to democratic governance", *American Journal of International Law,* 86, 1992, pp. 46-91.

Gilbert, G., "Jurisprudence of the European Court and Commission of Human Rights in 1999 and minority groups", UN Doc. E/CN.4/Sub.2/AC.5/2000/CRP.1, 2000, pp. 1-13.

Hannikainen, L., "Self-determination and autonomy in international law", in *Autonomy: applications and implications,* Suksi, M. (ed.), Kluwer Law International, The Hague, 1998, pp. 79-95.

Hannum, H., *Autonomy, sovereignty, and self-determination: the accommodation of conflicting rights,* revised edition, University of Pennsylvania Press, Philadelphia, 1996.

Hannum, H., "Rethinking self-determination", *Virginia Journal of International Law,* 34, 1993, pp. 1-69.

177

Henrard, K., *Devising an adequate system of minority protection: individual human rights, minority rights and the right to self-determination*, Kluwer Law International, The Hague, 2000.

Higgins, R., "Minority rights: discrepancies and divergences between the International Covenant and the Council of Europe system", in *The dynamics of the protection of human rights in Europe: essays in honour of Henry G. Schermers*, III, Lawson, R. and de Blois, M. (eds), Martinus Nijhoff Publishers, Dordrecht, 1994a, pp. 195-210.

Higgins, R., *Problems and process: international law and how we use it*, Clarendon Press, Oxford, 1994b.

Higgins, R., "Comments", in *Peoples and minorities in international Law*, Brölmann, C., Lefeber, R. and Zieck, M. (eds), Martinus Nijhoff Publishers, Dordrecht, 1993, pp. 29-35.

Koskenniemi, M., "National self-determination today: problems of legal theory and practice", *International and Comparative Law Quarterly*, 43, 1994, pp. 241-269.

Lapidoth, R., *Autonomy: flexible solutions to ethnic conflicts*, US Institute of Peace Press, Washington DC, 1997.

Lapidoth, R., "Autonomy: potential and limitations", *International Journal on Group Rights*, 1, 1994, pp. 269-290.

Lijphart, A., *Democracy in plural societies: a comparative exploration,* Yale University Press, New Haven, 1977.

Lijphart, A., "Self-determination versus pre-determination of ethnic minorities in power-sharing systems", in *The rights of minority cultures*, Kymlicka, W. (ed.), Oxford University Press, Oxford, 1991, pp. 275-287.

Müllerson, R., *International law, rights and politics: developments in eastern Europe and the CIS*, Routledge, London, 1994.

Musgrave, T.D., *Self-determination and national minorities*, Clarendon Press, Oxford, 1997.

Myntti, K., "National minorities, indigenous peoples and various modes of political participation", in *Minorities and their right of political participation*, Horn, F. (ed.), Lapland's University Press, Rovaniemi, 1996, pp. 1-26.

Nowak, M., "The right of self-determination and protection of minorities in central and eastern Europe in light of the case-law of the Human Rights Committee", *International Journal on Group Rights*, 1, 1993, pp. 7-16.

Pellet, A., "The opinions of the Badinter Arbitration Committee: a second breath for the self-determination of peoples", *European Journal of International Law,* 3, 1992, pp. 178-185.

Pentassuglia, G., "Protezione delle minoranze e diritto all'autodeterminazione", *La Nuova Frontiera: International Human Rights and Security Review*, II, 1995, pp. 31-40.

Rehman, J., "The concept of autonomy and minority rights in Europe", in *Minority rights in the "new" Europe*, Cumper, P. and Wheatley, S. (eds), Kluwer Law International, The Hague, 1999, pp. 217-231.

Robinson, J., Karbach, O., Laserson, M., Robinson, N. and Vichniak, M., *Were the minorities treaties a failure?*, Institute of Jewish Affairs, New York, 1943.

Rosas, A., "Internal self-determination", in *Modern law of self-determination*, Tomuschat, C. (ed.), Martinus Nijhoff Publishers, Dordrecht, 1993, pp. 225-252.

Steiner, H.J., "Ideals and counter-ideals in the struggle over autonomy regimes for minorities", *Notre Dame Law Review*, 66, 1991, pp. 1539-1560.

Thornberry, P., "Images of autonomy and individual and collective rights in international instruments on the rights of minorities", in *Autonomy: applications and implications*, Suksi, M. (ed.), Kluwer Law International, The Hague, 1998, pp. 97-124.

Thornberry, P., "Minorities, indigenous peoples, participation: an assessment of international standards", in *Minorities and their right of political participation*, Horn, F. (ed.), Lapland's University Press, Rovaniemi, 1996, pp. 27-50.

Thornberry, P., "The democratic or internal aspect of self-determination with some remarks on federalism", in *Modern law of self-determination*, Tomuschat, C. (ed.), Martinus Nijhoff Publishers, Dordrecht, 1993, pp. 101-138.

Thornberry, P., *International law and the rights of minorities*, Clarendon Press, Oxford, 1991.

Thornberry, P., "Self-determination, minorities, human rights: a review of international instruments", *International and Comparative Law Quarterly*, 38, 1989, pp. 867-889.

Tierney, S., "In a state of flux: self-determination and the collapse of Yugoslavia", *International Journal on Minority and Group Rights*, 6, 1999, pp. 197-233.

Tomuschat, C., "Self-determination in a post-colonial world", in *Modern law of self-determination*, Tomuschat, C. (ed.), Martinus Nijhoff Publishers, Dordrecht, 1993, pp. 1-20.

Trifunovska, S., "One theme in two variations: self-determination for minorities and indigenous peoples", *International Journal on Minority and Group Rights*, 5, 1997, pp. 175-196.

Wheatley, S., "Minority rights, power sharing and the modern democratic state", in *Minority rights in the "new" Europe*, Cumper, P. and Wheatley, S. (eds), Kluwer Law International, The Hague, 1999, pp. 199-216.

Wippman, D., "Hearing voices within the state: internal conflicts and the claims of ethno-national groups", *New York University Journal of International Law and Politics*, 27, 1995, pp. 585-609.

Wippman, D., "Practical and legal constraints on internal power sharing", in *International law and ethnic conflict*, Wippman, D. (ed.), Cornell University Press, Ithaca and London, 1998, pp. 211-241.

CHAPTER IX

ROLE OF SPECIAL TREATIES IN MODERN PRACTICE

As revealed by the previous chapters, contemporary international law is seeking to establish or consolidate general multilateral standards which can provide a framework for comprehensive solutions to the question of minorities. At the same time, efforts are being made to produce *ad hoc* conventional regimes whose essential feature is to address the situation of specific minority groups living within the territory of the contracting parties. Most such regimes are of a bilateral nature, but occasionally special treaties have been entered into on a multilateral level as well. In addition, multilateral arrangements have been reached to put an end to such violent conflicts as those that occurred in Bosnia and Herzegovina and Northern Ireland, that in effect generate a complex combination of domestic and truly international undertakings; given their *sui generis* character, they will be outlined separately, in Chapter XI.

An important starting point is that the treaty approach in this context is no new hat but dates back to centuries ago, showing varying degrees of effectiveness over time.

1. The treaty approach until the cold war era: changing perspectives

a. From the treaties of Westphalia to the treaties of Vienna

The minority treaties from Westphalia to Vienna generally protected only religious minorities through the recognition of freedom of conscience and worship. All major treaties of the seventeenth and eighteenth centuries contain clauses to that effect (Laponce, 1960).

They range from the vague guarantees of the Treaty of Utrecht (1731) – by which France gave Hudson Bay and Acadia to England, and the people concerned were allowed to exercise the Roman Catholic religion "insofar as the laws of England permit it" – to the far more precise guarantees of the Treaty of Nijmegen (1678), between France and Holland – granting freedom of religion as well as the possession and use of property not only to the churches but also to the individuals professing the Catholic religion in Holland – and the Treaty of Kutchuk-Kainardji (1774), between Turkey and Russia, which gave the Russian ambassador also the right of remonstrance, and extended protection to all Christians, Catholic or not. As already indicated, the minority provisions, except for those involving Turkey, did not apply to the whole of a country but only to those parts gained from a transfer of territory.

b. From the treaties of Vienna to the Treaty of Versailles

This second period was characterised by the extension of protection to the whole of the countries concerned, and to ethno-cultural groups other than religious minorities, though the latter remained the type of minority most often concerned. As noted in Chapter I, the 1815 Congress of Vienna recognised the existence of, among others, a Polish national group resulting from the partition of Poland among Austria, Prussia and Russia. Still, Article 1 of the General Treaty between Great Britain, Austria, France, Portugal, Prussia, Russia, Spain and Sweden only provided that the Poles, as subjects of Austria, Prussia and Russia, were to obtain "a representation and national institutions, regulated according to the degree of political consideration" that the government of each of those countries would judge "expedient and proper" to grant them.

Some relevant pre-first world war treaties were concerned with the Ottoman Empire and/or the countries created from it. Notably, the General Treaty of Peace between Great Britain, Austria, France, Prussia, Russia, Sardinia and Turkey, signed at Paris in 1856, committed the sultan to ameliorating the conditions of his subjects "without distinction of religion or race". Showing a pattern similar to that already reflected in the London Protocols of 1830, establishing Greek independence from the Ottoman Empire, the 1878 Congress of Berlin set out conditions for the international recognition of new states and/or territorial orders arisen in eastern Europe. In particular, the Treaty between Great Britain, Austria-Hungary, France, Germany, Italy, Russia and Turkey for the Settlement of Affairs in the East provided for requirements to which the independence of Montenegro, Serbia and Romania, and the establishment of Bulgaria as a principality under the sovereignty of the Sublime Porte, were made subject. They included respect for civil and political liberties, religious freedom, and a prohibition of discrimination in public affairs, from which the minorities concerned were to profit as part of the larger polity.

Along with the trend towards addressing the issue of minorities by treaty, there was a definite tendency, especially in the late nineteenth and early twentieth centuries, to restrict the use of treaty guarantees to the area of eastern Europe.

c. Post-first world war treaties

As explained earlier, the various treaties stipulated after the first world war, comprising specific entitlements for members of cohesive racial, religious or linguistic groups, constituted the building-block of the first true system of minority rights protection (see *supra*, Chapter I). As also noted, the system was placed under the League of Nations guarantee internally and externally, and it was not intended for general application. It indeed only applied to certain countries, mostly in the east, as a result of the post-war border revision.

d. Post-second world war treaties

Unlike the post-first world war treaties, the peace treaties of 1947, between the allied and associated powers and Bulgaria, Finland, Italy, Hungary and Romania contained no specific clause on the protection of minorities. The treaties only provided for respect for individual human rights, without distinction as to race, sex, language or religion, or in the case of the Hungarian and Romanian treaties, forbade discrimination among citizens, including language-based discrimination. In the peace treaty with Italy, the obligation to guarantee enjoyment of human rights was imposed even on states to which Italian territories had been ceded.

Although Hungary's efforts at the Paris Peace Conference of 1946 to secure a general treaty regime for the protection of minorities proved unsuccessful (unsurprisingly, given the mistrust generated by the pro-nazi Hungarian government's annexations between 1938 and 1940, see *infra*, and the initial claims of Hungary in 1946 for readjustment, based on ethnic criteria, of its borders with Czechoslovakia and Romania as defined by the Trianon Treaty of 1920), minority issues continued to feature on a bilateral and multilateral level. The Austrian and Italian governments signed on 5 September 1946 an agreement (annexed to the peace treaty of 1947), under which "German-speaking inhabitants" of the Province of Bolzano and of neighbouring bilingual townships of the Province of Trento were granted a number of rights, notably the right to receive primary and secondary teaching in the mother tongue, parity of the German and Italian languages in public offices and official documents, as well as in bilingual topographic names, the right to re-establish German family names which had been "Italianised" under the fascist regime and equality of rights in relation to access to public posts, with a view to reaching an appropriate proportion of employment between the two ethnic groups. Moreover, a special statute of autonomy, including legislative and administrative powers, was provided for the (overwhelmingly German-speaking) populations of the above-mentioned zones, the frame of which was to be drafted in consultation with local representatives of the German-speaking element (Article 2).

The Special Statute contained in the Memorandum of Understanding between the Governments of Italy, the United Kingdom, the United States and Yugoslavia regarding the Free Territory of Trieste, initialled in London on 5 October 1954, laid down provisions concerning the rights and treatment to be enjoyed by the Yugoslav ethnic group living in Zone A (under Italian administration) and the Italian ethnic group living in Zone B (under Yugoslav administration). Of particular importance were linguistic rights in educational matters and contacts with administrative and judicial authorities. The 1975 Treaty of Osimo between Italy and Yugoslavia, which endorsed the partition of the above territory and recognised the sovereignty of the two countries over the respective zones previously administered by them, repealed the special statute (Article 8) but guaranteed to the ethnic groups referred to in the memorandum an equivalent level of protection, including the maintenance of the favourable measures already adopted.

The Austrian State Treaty for the Re-establishment of an Independent and Democratic Austria, signed on 15 May 1955 by the Soviet Union, United Kingdom, United States, France and Austria, granted Austrian nationals of the "Slovene and Croat minorities" in Carinthia, Burgenland and Styria the same rights on equal terms as all other Austrian nationals. In particular, they were entitled to primary instruction in the Slovene or Croat language and to a proportional number of their own secondary schools. The treaty also provided that the activity of organisations whose aim was to deprive the Croat or Slovenian population of their "minority character or rights" would be prohibited. Other post-1945 special regimes include the one agreed to by Germany and Denmark in 1955, based on identical unilateral declarations made by each government before its parliament, as regards their respective minorities living in the border region of Schleswig, and the 1959 Memorandum for the Final Settlement of the Problem of Cyprus, signed by the United Kingdom, Greece and Turkey, containing detailed provisions relating to the rights of the Turkish community in the Republic of Cyprus.

2. Can minority treaties work? Preliminary assessment

With regard to all such treaties viewed in historical perspective, Laponce (1960: 41-42) usefully draws a distinction between guarantees of minority rights which, to a greater or lesser extent, were "imposed" by major powers and those guarantees which were "agreed to" by the parties acting on full and effective terms of equality and independence. Indeed, provisions concerning the Ottoman Empire and/or the countries created from it, contained in key nineteenth-century treaties, and those provided for in the post-first world war minority treaties, offer examples of the former pattern. Aside from their substantive legal quality, there is reason to believe that the validity of at least some of them (notably the nineteenth-century treaties) could have been challenged if they had been adopted in the context of contemporary international law, in view of the principles of the Vienna Convention on the Law of Treaties based on free consent and sovereign equality. At the same time, guarantees "agreed to" can be found in most of the treaties up to the Congress of Vienna and, later on, in the Austrian-Italian agreement of 1946, the 1954 memorandum, etc. In seventeenth- and eighteenth-century treaties, minority clauses were consented to by the victorious party. Similarly, the De Gasperi-Gruber Agreement and the London special statute were concluded after discussions by the states concerned on a footing of full equality.

The use of treaties for the protection of minorities cannot be accepted or dismissed without qualification. A study of each particular treaty would be necessary in order to determine whether or not it advanced the situation of the minority which enjoyed protection. And yet, discussion of a minority's situation without a treaty would be purely hypothetical, thereby making it difficult to establish the comparative advantage deriving from the adoption of a treaty. It has been argued that the post-first world war treaty regimes failed to provide lasting protection to the groups concerned because of political factors rather than some conceptual or technical defects inherent in those regimes (Bilder, 1990). In fact, an immediate distinction can be made between such treaties and the post-second world war peace treaties, which lacked not only minority standards but also supervisory procedures (Musgrave, 1997: 134-135). At the same time, some major (and recognised nowadays as largely successful) post-1945 treaties, such as the Austrian-Italian agreement of 1946 and the Austrian treaty of 1955, have been far from uncontroversial, with regard to, respectively, the determination of the actual nature and degree of autonomy to be enjoyed by the German-speaking minority under Article 2 (see also *infra*, Chapter XI), and the interpretation of key minority clauses in Article 7 (Modeen, 1969: 84-85 and 88-89), and do not contain any procedures of supervision. In 1971, Austria and Italy entered into an agreement establishing the competence of the ICJ as regards disputes arising out of the 1946 Paris Agreement, but it was not until 1992 that both parties ratified it. Although the 1954 Memorandum on Trieste established a mixed committee to deal with pertinent minority issues and before which also individual complaints could be heard, this body did not exercise judicial or quasi-judicial functions, but only facilitated dialogue between the two states and national groups.

In his UN study, Capotorti (1979) identified some advantages in the post-1945 treaty approach. He pointed out that special treaties:

- might fill the vacuum caused by either the lack of international instruments of a "universal" character providing for the protection of minorities or the fact that the parties were not also bound by the latter;
- stated clearly the responsibilities of the states to which the minorities belonged; and
- tended to be more comprehensive than the corresponding provisions of the 1919 or 1920 treaties (notably as regards the use of the minority language, education and cultural institutions).

By the same token, he noted that such agreements:

- were relatively few; and
- very often reflected specific territorial and political circumstances.

This latter element might perhaps explain, *inter alia*, why in some of the post-1945 agreements there seems to be more consideration of minorities *qua* groups (Modeen, 1969: 94). Although some of the points made by Capotorti may appear less convincing than others (see, for example, the "clarity" or "greater specificity" argument, in the face of controversies surrounding the interpretation and application of unclear, if not ambiguous, provisions contained in some of the above treaties), these elements cover to a large extent the fundamental aspects relating to the role of special agreements for the protection of minorities. While a progressive decline in interest in the treaty approach may be discerned in the cold war era, it has been recently suggested we appreciate the positive effects which may arise from it. Bilder (1990) has advocated a wider use of special treaties which may attract the support of minority states, minorities, as well as interested third states and international organisations, for solutions which fit particular situations. Defeis (1999) urges in particular close exploration of the potential of the bilateral approach, by presenting the De Gasperi-Gruber Agreement on South Tyrol as a model for future bilateral accords.

3. The treaty approach in the post-cold war era: bilateral agreements in eastern Europe

a. Overview

In the post-cold war era, the significant progress made at the bilateral level consists in the conclusion of several bilateral agreements that are typically called agreements "on co-operation, friendship and good-neighbourliness". Although most of these agreements are in force between former socialist states (at the time of writing, the latest treaty of this kind was between Romania and Moldova, signed in 2000), some such agreements have also been stipulated between these states and some Western countries, notably Germany. While covering bilateral co-operation between the contracting parties generally, these bilateral agreements often embody provisions which address the situation of their own minorities. The common aim of these agreements (together with other non-legally binding texts adopted in the same context) is to further stability in the region concerned. The minority clauses frequently resulted from difficult negotiations, due to political considerations.

Apart from the right to fully enjoy human rights without any discrimination, the right to identity in general, and language, education, religion, association and participation rights in particular, are recognised. Occasionally, references can be found to group rights (for example, in the 1992 minority rights treaty between Hungary and Slovenia), and even autonomy (for example, in the 1995 minority rights treaty between Hungary and Croatia).

Overall, these provisions constitute an important development in the area of minority rights. Although the bilateral pattern, as evidenced by the above-mentioned earlier practice, is not new in the history of the international protection of minorities, its current re-emergence is different in scale from the limited number of post-1945 agreements. To date, the "new" bilateral treaties have been entered into basically by "kin-states" and states where "kin-minorities" live. The treaty approach enjoys increasing support at the political level and is expressly encouraged by a number of relevant international instruments (see, for example, Article 18, paragraph 1, of the Framework Convention). In the 1993 report by Eide on possible ways and means of facilitating the peaceful and constructive solution of problems involving minorities, a similar approach is urged. Still, Eide notes and recommends that bilateral treaties or other arrangements should be based on the principles of the UN Charter and on international human rights law, and that they should contain an additional provision ensuring that minorities not mentioned in the treaty shall enjoy the same level of protection of their identity (Eide, 1993: 27-28).

As hinted at earlier in the book, the resolve to encourage the conclusion of bilateral treaties dealing in whole or in part with minority issues as a means of "preventive" and "quiet" diplomacy led to the adoption of the EU-sponsored Pact on Stability in Europe, and reflects one of the primary objectives of the EU-sponsored Stability Pact for South Eastern Europe. In the latter context, a new wave of bilateral agreements of this sort is being sought in close association with the implementation of the Framework Convention (see *infra*, Chapter X). Although the 1995 Pact as such did not produce a large-scale process of negotiation of minority rights agreements, it facilitated the conclusion of the Treaty on Good-Neighbourliness and Friendly Co-operation between Slovakia and Hungary (1995), which was then incorporated in the Pact, and spurred on the signing in 1996 of the Treaty on Understanding, Co-operation and Good-Neighbourliness between Hungary and Romania.

b. Some Hungarian and German bilateral treaties

The Hungarian-Slovakian and Hungarian-Romanian basic treaties, both of which entered into force in 1996, treat the minority question as part of a broader political settlement between the respective countries. After the first world war, Hungary ceded Slovakia, Ruthenia and Transylvania to the newly established Czechoslovakia and to Romania. As a result, many ethnic Hungarians found themselves outside the borders of their "kin-state". The pro-nazi Hungarian Government regained control over the above territories in 1938-40, but the inter-war boundaries were restored after 1945. This explains why such bilateral treaties firmly proclaim the immutability of the post-war borders.

Interestingly, they provide for the protection of national minorities on the basis of multiple legal regimes. Certain entitlements are applicable to all national minorities living in the contracting states (see, for example, Article 15, paragraph 2, sub-paragraph c, of the Hungarian-Slovakian treaty and Article 15, paragraph 7, of the Hungarian-Romanian treaty). At the same time, various rights and entitlements are recognised solely to respectively the Hungarian minorities in Slovakia and Romania and to the Slovakian and Romanian minorities in Hungary. In the latter case, listed international "soft law" texts are to be applied as "legal obligation". Article 15, paragraph 4, sub-paragraph b of the Hungarian-Slovakian treaty incorporates by reference the 1990 Copenhagen Document, the 1992 UN declaration and Recommendation 1201 (1993) of the Parliamentary Assembly of the Council of Europe (the international texts are identical in the Hungarian-Romanian treaty). And yet, the content of those supplementary rights is not elaborated upon, and no specific criterion is provided in order to resolve real or potential inconsistencies among the various texts.

A question arose in connection with Article 11 of Recommendation 1201 providing for the right to appropriate local or autonomous authorities or to have a special status, in the regions where the persons belonging to a national minority are in a majority, "matching the specific historical and territorial situation and in accordance with the domestic legislation of the state". Slovakia has publicly stated that it did not agree under the treaty to the principle of collective rights allowing for the creation of ethnically-based autonomous structures. Romania has made the same objection, which is contained, unlike the case of Slovakia, in the agreed annex to the treaty. Such reactions typically mirror strong reluctance on the part of states to endorse the principle of autonomy in legally binding international instruments. As noted, this was stressed in the opinion on Article 11 of Recommendation 1201, delivered by the Council of Europe's Venice Commission at the request of the Committee on Legal Affairs and Human Rights of the Parliamentary Assembly, essentially as a response to the polemics surrounding the interpretation of this article (see *supra,* Chapter VIII). With regard to the Hungarian-Romanian treaty, Kovács (2000) correctly notes that forms of cultural autonomy or non-ethnically-based territorial autonomy are not, prima facie, prohibited by its agreed supplement. Such an interpretation appears in line with the above Venice Commission's opinion. Besides indicating that Article 11 cannot be understood as requiring measures which would fundamentally affect the structure of the state, this opinion indeed refers to the European Charter of Local Self-Government, the general aims of Article 11 and the main domestic patterns within the Council of Europe member states, to determine the most suitable substance of "appropriate local or autonomous authorities" and "special status" (not precluding personal autonomy) which would enable the discharge of obligations arising under the provision in question. This is reinforced by "in accordance with the domestic legislation of the state" in Article 11, meaning, according to the commission, that it is for the state to prescribe the legal framework for exercising the right, which is also, however, a guarantee that such a framework will exist (CDL-MIN (1996) 4: 4-5).

Unlike the said three international texts, the Framework Convention has been incorporated in both the Hungarian-Slovakian and Hungarian-Romanian basic treaties as major part of the entitlements benefiting all national minorities living in the countries concerned. Nevertheless, the concrete impact of this treaty (already ratified by the parties in 1995) might prove limited due to its structural deficiencies (flexible wordings and implementation procedure: see *infra,* Chapter X), its recognition of, *inter alia,* general principles which are already affirmed in the treaty or in other human rights treaties, such as the ECHR, applicable to the parties, or a lower level of treatment that it may provide for compared to the one available under the treaty for the designated minorities.

The technique of incorporating "soft law" texts as "legal obligation" under the treaty has been frequently resorted to in the agreements concluded by Germany with a number of eastern European countries. For instance, Article 20, paragraph 2, of the Treaty on Good-Neighbourly Relations and Co-operation between the Federal Republic of Germany and the Republic of Poland (1991), provides that:

> [t]he Contracting Parties shall give effect to rights and obligations of the international standard applicable to minorities, especially in accordance with ... the Document of the Copenhagen Meeting on the Human Dimension of the CSCE of 29 June 1990 and the Charter of Paris for a New Europe of 21 November 1990.

Besides mentioning minorities in general, the treaty protects persons belonging to the German "minority" in Poland, and persons belonging to the "equivalent" Polish group in Germany, identified through a general reference to "persons of German nationality in the Federal Republic of Germany who are of Polish extraction or profess affiliation with the Polish language, culture or traditions" (they are relatively more recent arrivals; on the definitional aspect, see *supra*, Chapter III). Fears were expressed on the Polish side that those international texts might be applied solely to the German minority in Poland. In fact, the protection of the equivalent Polish group is strengthened, rather than undermined, by Article 20, paragraph 2, which requires protection to be "in accordance with international standards applicable to minorities". The remaining provisions essentially restate, with minor variations, the substance of the international standards referred to, for the benefit of persons belonging to both these groups.

Other agreements concluded in this context by Germany that incorporate OSCE documents include the Treaty with Romania on Friendly Relations and Partnership in Europe (1992, Article 15), the Treaty with Czechoslovakia on Good-Neighbourly and Friendly Relations (1992, Article 20), and the Treaty with Hungary on Friendly Co-operation and Partnership in Europe (1992, Article 19). In the latter treaty, reference is also made to unspecified "other CSCE documents on the protection of national minorities", which might allow for the interpretation that future texts could automatically be incorporated as well (Heintze, 1999). It is often argued that the elevation of relevant "soft law" texts to the level of "hard law" through the said bilateral treaties strongly contributes to the development of customary law norms on the protection of national minorities, at least within the European context (see also *supra*, Chapter VII).

c. Advantages and disadvantages

Subject to a closer case-by-case assessment, the advantages and disadvantages of the contemporary bilateral pattern are being considered in legal doctrine. Some of the advantages frequently mentioned in scholarly debate, such as a greater specificity of rights and obligations compared to general instruments and thus the possibility of elaborating higher standards of protection, somehow echo those already stressed by Capotorti in his UN study with regard to the post-1945 agreements. In view of current international standards on minority rights, and the need for preventing or containing ethnic tensions or open conflicts, the "value added" of the contemporary pattern is said in principle to consist essentially in:

— the recognition of a genuine bilateral dimension to the minority problems;

— the recognition of legal force to non-legally binding documents and their prescriptions; and

— the enhancing of confidence of national minorities (Pogany, 1999).

The possible disadvantages are equally highlighted within the overall present-day framework of international law and relations (Alfredsson, 1999; Thornberry, 1995 and 1999). They would include, *inter alia*:

— the lowering of the level of protection compared to multilateral standards;

— the use of legal techniques to perpetuate the political approach to minority issues;

— technical deficiencies due to hasty drafting;

- the unequal position of the parties involved (namely, lack of minority representation);
- discrimination between different groups within a contracting state;
- destabilising effects between minority states and "kin-states", particularly by giving the latter a "conflict-creating" role; and
- the effect of minority rights being "traded" for other gains, and made subject to time limits.

Both the advantages and disadvantages must be carefully accounted for. In most cases, such points deconstruct each other, confirming the need for assessing their relative significance within the context of the treaty at issue. The "specificity argument" may be challenged in relation to the Hungarian-Slovakian and Hungarian-Romanian treaties, though certain provisions appear in fact more responsive to local circumstances (see, for example, Article 12, paragraphs 6 and 7, of the Hungarian-Slovakian treaty, on the support of each other's languages and culture). Nowadays, bilateralism and multilateralism are being viewed as, prima facie, mutually reinforcing, whereas for a considerable period of time the post-1945 treaties came in practice to substitute for general international minority rights instruments. Nevertheless, there is a genuine danger of reduced standards at the bilateral level. Hence, the need for clauses which safeguard pre-existing (and higher) levels of protection.

The "prescriptive force" of *per se* non-legally binding provisions is in principle a welcome development, but does not provide any meaningful responses to interpretative aspects or possible controversies surrounding the incorporated documents and their relation to one another (for instance, minority language and education rights under Recommendation 1201 are far more strongly worded than is the case under the UN declaration). As will be argued later on, the treaties as such provide weak or no means of implementation, reproducing a shortcoming generally discernible in the post-1945 agreements, but not in their post-first world war predecessors. In this respect, there can be little or no assistance from within the treaty regime in identifying a proper understanding of the relevant provisions. The "Recommendation 1201 question" arisen under the Hungarian-Slovakian and Hungarian-Romanian treaties is only one example of inter-state impasse. The "lesson" to be drawn from the case of South Tyrol's autonomy under the De Gasperi-Gruber Agreement, is that disputes do arise in respect of the interpretation of ambitious treaties (which may also include autonomy solutions), and if there is no effective procedure of dispute settlement enshrined in the treaty, matters may even drag on unresolved for several years.

From a wider angle, the actual impact of a simple reaffirmation of existing international standards on the development of (at least regional) customary norms may prove more problematic than might be believed (except perhaps for very few widely shared starting points). On the other hand, if the treaty standards are distinctive to a given context, then their role in the identification of a body of common norms under general international law appears, at best, less evident than in the case where general standards are incorporated by reference to the respective international instruments. In fact, there might even be treaties which openly encroach on the "universalisation" or "generalisation" of minority rights norms as legally-binding parameters.

As aptly noted by Eide (1993) and recently reaffirmed by Alfredsson (1999), certain treaty-based distinctions between minority groups within the contracting countries may amount to discrimination, contrary to the relevant provisions of the UN Charter and international human rights instruments. And yet, the following aspects should be considered. One might first raise the question as to whether the minority treaty can be deemed void on the grounds that it deviates from the anti-discrimination standard as a norm of *jus cogens* (Article 53 of the Vienna Convention on the Law of Treaties). Without prejudice to international state responsibility which may be established as a result of a breach of distinct agreements or general norms, the legal validity of the treaty cannot be comfortably challenged on the above grounds so long as the view is correct that the prohibition of discrimination is a peremptory norm of general international law, namely a general norm from which no treaty derogation is permitted, only to the extent that systematic patterns of racial discrimination are at issue (see *supra*, Chapter IV). Beyond that, a practical point is that inter-minority discrimination, though it may well be detected under domestic law on the basis of the "reasonable and objective" test, may be more difficult to prove in the context of a treaty where such a treaty assumes, in view of sociological data, that the groups concerned do have distinctive demands and historical backgrounds, and even singles out provisions applicable to all minorities living in the State Party. In short, the issue is the difficult one of determining whether the assumptions underlying the preferences accorded to the designated minorities are based on genuine differences between such groups and other minorities and thus meet the requirements for differential treatment under the applicable anti-discrimination instruments, including that of proportionality. It is also important to remember in this context that virtually all the cited post-1945 agreements were designed to deal with the special situation of certain groups, and that they have gone largely unchallenged with regard to inter-minority discrimination (Hailbronner, 1990). Retrospectively, there is reason to believe that a case for the "most-favoured-minority clause" (Eide, 1993; Alfredsson, 1999), that is to say an automatic extension of the benefits conferred on the "kin-group" to all minorities within the country, would have led to claims questioning the very purpose of those agreements, if not using the equality argument against itself by pointing to what distinguishes the "kin-group" from other minorities.

At the same time, a major focus on "kin-minorities" should also be measured against a distinct possible advantage offered by the development of reasonable and proportionate bilateral regimes, namely to expand the range of beneficiaries so as to encompass, where appropriate, groups with no international minority status. Certain contemporary bilateral treaties, such as the above-mentioned German-Polish treaty from 1991, appear to reflect this pattern. As for the role of "kin-states", it may be viewed from different perspectives, whether or not in specific connection with the conclusion of a bilateral treaty. On a general level, the current cases concerning *Application of the*

Convention on the Prevention and Punishment of the Crime of Genocide, separately brought before the ICJ by Bosnia and Herzegovina (Preliminary
Objections, ICJ Reports 1996) and Croatia (ICJ, Application of 2 July 1999) for
alleged genocidal responsibility of the FRY in the context of its direct
involvement in "kin-group" activities on the territory of the plaintiff states,
indirectly highlight the actual or potential risks of escalation of violence
resulting from "kin-state" engagement. With regard to inter-state bilateral
relations, it is thus essential that states respect general international law principles of non-intervention and non-use of force, encompassing, as usefully
indicated in the 1993 report by Eide, direct or indirect participation in violent group conflicts in other states. Apart from these extreme cases, and in
terms of a specific connection with a bilateral treaty, "kin-states" may play a
negative or positive role: they may push the home-states of their "kin-
minorities" into a vaguely worded accord, causing tension and highlighting
the political approach (see, for example, the earlier Russian attitude towards
its neighbours), or may take a constructive stand, thereby contributing to the
solving of problems in the minority state and thus to furthering stability in
the region. From this point of view, it is of particular legal importance to
ensure that the "kin-state" fully respects the principle *pacta sunt servanda*
and that of friendly neighbourly relations on which the treaty is grounded or
from which it draws. It follows, *inter alia*, that this state may not resort to
unilateral measures on the preferential treatment of its "kin-minority" in
areas which, by virtue of general or specific provisions, are clearly pre-
empted by the treaty and the consultation framework it has established,
without the express or implicit (but unambiguous) consent of the home-
state, or, in the event of objections from the latter based on the treaty, before
all means of dispute settlement, if any, have proved ineffective (see the report
on the preferential treatment of national minorities by their kin-state,
recently adopted by the Council of Europe's Venice Commission: CDL-INF
(2001) 19, paragraph D, sub-paragraphs b and c).

Minority participation in the negotiation of the treaty may certainly serve
conflict prevention and confidence-building purposes. New thinking in international and regional organisations or institutions favours dialogue between
governments and minorities. As noted earlier, recent instruments emphasise
the right of persons belonging to minorities to effective participation in
public affairs, notably those directly affecting them. Measured against the
jurisprudence in *Marshall et al. v. Canada* on direct participation in the conduct of public affairs under Article 25, paragraph a, of the ICCPR, the HRC's
jurisprudence under Article 27 is placing state action vis-à-vis minority participation under tighter control (see *supra*, Chapters V and VIII).
Nevertheless, the state generally retains a measure of discretion in determining the forms of "effective involvement", so that a legal right of minority
members to effective participation cannot *per se* be associated with an
"unconditional right" to participate in the negotiation of a treaty. All the
more so that the treaty-making power constitutes a long-established government prerogative in international law and diplomacy, and that "reasonable and objective" restrictions on such a participation might arguably be
permitted.

A point widely shared is that minorities treaties, whatever the quality of their content, can work if states want them to work, if they are animated by a genuine will to co-operate with one another and fully implement the treaties at the domestic level through adequate legislative and administrative measures as well as judicial remedies. Even where facilitated by strong external leverage (EU action, etc.), minorities treaties alone cannot solve the problems. That is especially true as regards the contemporary bilateral treaties; Kovács observes:

> *Les clauses des traités bilatéraux des pays de l'Europe centrale et orientale ont une nature souvent similaire à celle des clauses élastique et programmatoire des instruments multilatéraux. Si elles rencontrent la volonté des gouvernments successifs, les revendications des minorités seront entendues. Le clauses de ces traités n'étant pas d'applicabilité directe aucun automatisme juridique ne peut venir contrebalancer devant les tribunaux ou les administrations si la volonté défaillante d'un gouvernement. Les traités bilatéraux sont donc les éléments d'un réseau complexe qui présente des déjà-vues c'est à dire non seulement des clauses similaires, mais aussi bien les mêmes lacunes et les mêmes problèmes que les instruments multilatéraux. Il y en a qui semblent être plus perfectionnés et d'autres, plus faibles. Bref, ils sont comme tout traité interétatique: efficaces, si le gouvernements veulent les exécuter, inefficaces, si ceux-ci ne les veulent pas.* (Kovács, 2000: 168)

A possible lack of domestic enforcement at judicial or administrative level may stem from theoretical or political assumptions rather than an absolute normative necessity arising from the treaty (see *infra*, Chapter X). Overall, the contemporary bilateral treaties should be described as one component of a broader dynamic law-making and political process, designed to improve bilateral co-operation, help defuse or prevent minority tensions, and possibly generate some sort of international action within multilateral forums (see, for example, the Venice Commission's legal opinions mentioned above and compare them with the resolutions of the UN General Assembly on the South Tyrol case, *supra*, Chapter I). Consequently, they should not be considered as definite and self-contained regimes, namely agreements meant to substitute for the protection of minorities within a wider international law framework. It is interesting to note in this connection that most of the treaties are expressly intended to endure for a span of years (five, ten, etc.), though they often include the possibility of extension for further limited periods unless one of the parties denounces the treaty under the terms provided. Multilateral instruments on human rights do not necessarily reflect this logic. The ICCPR is not expressly subject to denunciation, and the HRC has made it clear (General Comment No. 26 (1997)) that a right of denunciation cannot be established by way of either an implicit intention of the parties or the nature of the ICCPR (under Article 56, paragraph 1, of the Vienna Convention on the Law of Treaties). In the case of the contemporary bilateral treaties, the protection of minorities can be often viewed as part of a wider politically contingent "package", designed to balance out particular interests, which appears to confirm, rather than substantially intrude upon, the contracting governments' jurisdiction. Even in the absence of provisions regarding termination, denunciation or withdrawal, a bilateral treaty adopted under these circumstances, despite the greater international legal protection it, prima facie, affords, might be exposed to denunciation under Article 56, paragraph 1, if not Article 62 (*rebus sic stantibus*), of the Vienna Convention.

Bibliography

Alfredsson, G., "Identifying possible disadvantages of bilateral agreements and advancing the 'most-favoured-minority clause'", in *Protection of minority rights through bilateral treaties: the case of central and eastern Europe*, Bloed, A. and van Dijk, P. (eds), Kluwer Law International, The Hague, 1999, pp. 165-175.

Benoît-Rohmer, F., *The minority question in Europe: towards a coherent system of protection for national minorities*, Council of Europe Publishing, Strasbourg, 1996.

Bilder, R., "Can minorities treaties work?", *Israel Yearbook on Human Rights*, 20, 1990, pp. 71-92.

Bloed, A. and van Dijk, P. (eds), *Protection of minority rights through bilateral treaties: the case of central and eastern Europe*, Kluwer Law International, The Hague, 1999.

Capotorti, F., "Study on the rights of persons belonging to ethnic, religious and linguistic minorities", UN Doc. E/CN.4/Sub.2/384/Rev. I, 1979.

Defeis, E.F., "Minority protection and bilateral agreements: an effective mechanism", *Hastings International Law and Comparative Law Review*, 22, 1999, pp. 291-321.

de Varennes, F., *Language, minorities and human rights*, Martinus Nijhoff Publishers, The Hague, 1996.

Driessen, B., "A new turn in Hungarian-Slovak relations? An overview of the basic treaty", *International Journal on Minority and Group Rights*, 4, 1997, pp. 1-40.

Eide, A., "Possible ways and means of facilitating the peaceful and constructive solution of problems involving minorities", UN Doc. E/CN.4/Sub.2/1993/34/Add. 4, 1993.

Gál, K., "The role of bilateral treaties in the protection of national minorities in central and eastern Europe", UN Doc. E/CN.4/Sub.2/AC.5/1998/CRP.2, 1998, pp. 1-14.

Hailbronner, K., "The legal status of population groups in a multinational state under public international law", *Israel Yearbook on Human Rights*, 20, 1990, pp. 135-140.

Heintze, H.J., "The international law dimension of the German minorities policy", *Nordic Journal of International Law*, 68, 1999, pp. 117-130.

Kovács, P., *Le droit international pour les minorités face a l'état-nation*, Miskolci Egyetemi Kiadó, Miskolc, 2000.

Jeszenszky, G., "Hungary's bilateral treaties with the neighbours and the issue of minorities", *Ethnos-Nation*, 4, 1996, pp. 123-128.

Laponce, J.A., *The protection of minorities*, University of California Press, Berkeley and Los Angeles, 1960.

Marko, J., Lantschner, E. and Medda-Windischer, R., "Protection of national minorities through bilateral agreements in South-eastern Europe" *European Yearbook on minority issues,* 1, 2001/2002, forthcoming.

McKean, W., *Equality and discrimination under international law*, Clarendon Press, Oxford, 1983.

Modeen, T., *The international protection of national minorities in Europe*, Åbo Akademi, Åbo, 1969.

195

Musgrave, T.D., *Self-determination and national minorities*, Clarendon Press, Oxford, 1997.

Oakes, A., and Mowat, R.B. (eds), *The great European treaties of the nineteenth century*, Oxford University Press, Oxford, 1921.

Pentassuglia, G., "The Treaty between Italy and Croatia concerning Minority Rights: an appraisal", *East European Human Rights Review*, 5, 1999, pp. 49-80.

Pogany, I., "Bilateralism versus regionalism in the resolution of minorities problems in central and eastern Europe and in the post-Soviet states", in *Minority rights in the "new" Europe*, Cumper, P. and Wheatley, S. (eds), Kluwer Law International, The Hague, 1999, pp. 105-126.

Thornberry, P., "Hungarian bilateral treaties and declarations", in *Protection of minority rights through bilateral treaties: the case of central and eastern Europe*, Bloed, A. and van Dijk, P. (eds), Kluwer Law International, The Hague, 1999, pp. 127-161.

Thornberry, P., "Minority rights". *Collected Courses of the Academy of European Law*, VI-2, 1995, pp. 307-390.

Vogel, S., "A comparison of the Hungarian-Slovak and the Hungarian-Romanian Basic Treaty", *Ethnos-Nation*, 4, 1996, pp. 113-121.

Part C

Realising protection: international supervision and domestic dimensions

CHAPTER X

PROCEDURES, PREVENTION AND FURTHER ACTION

1. A short overview of some general techniques of supervision

A gamut of international procedures and institutions concerned with supervision are directly or indirectly intended to secure the implementation of most (if not all) of the standards which are contained in the instruments described thus far.

Within the UN context, the Commission on Human Rights and its Sub-Commission on the Promotion and Protection of Human Rights, essentially employ the well-known "ECOSOC 1503 complaints procedure", set up to identify situations amounting to consistent patterns of gross human rights violations, as well as procedures based on the appointment of special rapporteurs or working groups with country-oriented mandates (namely, authorising to investigate certain human rights violations within a particular state) or thematic mandates (namely, authorising to investigate in general certain human rights matters, such as religious intolerance). Both special rapporteurs and working groups report annually to the Commission on Human Rights, and their reports are made public.

Minorities are frequently victims of a vast range of human rights violations, beyond the specific area of minority rights, whose investigation comes under the scope of many of those procedures. Consequently, pertinent issues, which by and large affect the physical integrity of minority groups and/or the enjoyment by their members of basic human rights on a footing of equality (see *supra*, Chapter IV), have been, or may be brought up by making use of the monitoring opportunities provided by the above procedures, ranging from investigative and/or fact-finding activities to public debate with NGOs. In principle, they might even generate background input leading to a claim under a particular human rights treaty (for example, under Article IX of the Genocide Convention, *supra*, Chapter IV).

Other UN mechanisms are meant to generate a greater focus on minority rights scrutiny. The UN Working Group on Minorities, established within the (then) Sub-Commission on Prevention of Discrimination and Protection of Minorities under ECOSOC Resolution 1995/31, and partially the High Commissioner for Human Rights, review the implementation of the 1992 UN declaration, and consider several related questions affecting the maintenance of peace. The UN working group, whose role will be further addressed later on, held seven annual sessions, between 1995 and 2001, in which a wide range of relevant subjects were reviewed. Although this body has been established more as a framework for discussion than as a strict control mechanism, it nevertheless performs *de facto* an important supervisory work by regularly inviting not only independent experts but also governments, international agencies and minority representatives to offer their perspectives on minority issues. Where NGOs or minority associations make an oral statement or otherwise submit information about the situation of minorities in a specific country, this country is given an opportunity to respond or provide additional information.

Independent expert committees established to monitor compliance with human rights treaties of a "universal" character, such as the CERD and HRC, constitute an important resource to raise the profile of supervision, generally by considering reports which parties are required to submit periodically on the implementation of the obligations of the relevant treaty. In particular, the HRC is increasingly effective not only in questioning government representatives about the situation of minority rights on their own territory, in connection with Article 27, under the reporting procedure, but also, as dealt with at length in the book, in providing specific redress for minority rights violations and improving this understanding of Article 27 rights under the complaints procedure established by the First Optional Protocol.

At the regional level, the OSCE procedures, notably the Vienna mechanism of 1989 and the Moscow mechanism of 1991, consist in an inter-state monitoring process (initially based on exchange of information between the states concerned, and, ultimately, entailing consideration by all the participating states), directed at ensuring the implementation of the human rights commitments, including those concerning minorities, undertaken within the framework of the human dimension. The Moscow mechanism supplements the Vienna mechanism, in that, under certain procedural conditions (notably in case of support from five or nine participating states other than the requesting one, depending on the case), it allows the appointment and dispatch of rapporteur missions even without the consent of the country concerned. Other types of in-country missions, recently developed within the OSCE and called "missions of long duration", operate under target-specific mandates (somewhat permitting minority rights supervision), and are normally a tool of the political process. The possibility for them to continue to work "on the spot" depends on the continuing consent of the government concerned. Admittedly, the need for state initiative to activate or support these procedures is often an obstacle to their substantial use in practice. Notably, the use of the Vienna and Moscow mechanisms to raise human rights issues in general, and minority rights issues in particular, has decreased considerably in recent years, paralleled by an expansion of the functions of the ODIHR established in 1990 by the Charter of Paris for a New Europe (originally named "Office for Free Elections"), with regard to the review of the implementation of human rights/minority rights commitments by the participating states (Schlager, 2000).

Perhaps the most interesting development of the OSCE monitoring system has been the creation of the Office of the HCNM, under the Helsinki

Concluding Document of 1992, which will be briefly discussed later in this chapter.

Within the Council of Europe, the individual-centred enforcement procedure under the ECHR and, prospectively, its Protocol No. 12 might enable some form of protection for minorities and their members, in relation to their general needs and rights (see *supra,* Chapter VI). In principle, the "enjoyment of any right set forth by law" under Article 1 of Protocol No. 12 might even relate to a case affecting rights distinctive to minority members. As indicated in the explanatory report, "the word 'law' [in Article 1] may also cover international law" (paragraph 29), although the jurisdiction of the EurCtHR is limited to those questions that are framed in terms of a specific violation of the protocol.

As for the 1995 Framework Convention, the Committee of Ministers is entrusted with the task of monitoring its implementation by the states parties (Article 24, paragraph 1). To this end, it is assisted by an advisory committee, whose members have recognised expertise in the field of the protection of national minorities (Article 26, paragraph 1). On 17 September 1997, the Committee of Ministers adopted a resolution concerning the rules on the monitoring arrangements under Articles 24 to 26 of the Framework Convention (Resolution (97) 10). Consistent with Article 26, it determines the role of the advisory committee, which is established as a body of experts who are elected by the Committee of Ministers but serve in their individual capacity, and therefore its relation with the latter. The convention provides neither an inter-state nor individual complaints procedures. Rather, the supervision is based (primarily) on periodic state reporting (after initial transmission of full information under Article 25, paragraph 1), in order to evaluate "the adequacy of the measures taken"; it is basically aimed at encouraging states parties to implement the Framework Convention properly, rather than at "sanctioning" those states which breach it. In late 1998, the Committee of Ministers adopted an "outline for reports" to be submitted pursuant to Article 25, paragraph 1, of the convention, regarding their legal, policy and factual components (the outline will be reviewed in the light of the results generated by the first monitoring cycle).

At the time of finalising this book, the advisory committee had adopted "opinions" on the implementation of the Framework Convention in respect of seventeen states parties, while the Committee of Ministers, to which all the advisory committee's opinions have to be submitted for final deliberations, had adopted resolutions containing "conclusions" and "recommendations" in respect of nine of the above parties. No binding decision can be adopted by the monitoring body. The non-judicial character of the procedure, as further discussed in Section 3, reflects the little stringency of the treaty as a whole, and is clearly an off-shoot from states' reluctance to secure supervision based on adjudication and redress.

With regard to the 1992 European Charter for Regional or Minority Languages, the selected provisions of Part III, coupled with the set of general provisions of Part II, determine the scope of application of the implementation machinery established by this treaty. states parties have to submit periodically reports to be examined by the committee of experts set up in accordance with Article 17. Bodies or associations legally established in the party whose report is under review may provide the committee with further information on matters relating to the undertakings entered into by that party. After consulting the latter, the committee may take account of this information in the preparation of its report (Article 16, paragraph 2). In addition, those bodies or associations may submit statements regarding the policy pursued by the party. While the charter does not endorse a complaints procedure (not surprisingly, given that no subjective rights are recognised), the above provisions enable individuals to get partly involved in the monitoring process. The committee eventually draws up a report for the Committee of Ministers, containing proposals for recommendations of the latter body to one or more of the parties as may be required (Article 16, paragraph 4).

The initial periodical reports have been received from all present states parties, and made public by the respective governments. The committee of experts has often requested supplementary information in order to clarify matters insufficiently elaborated upon in the report, and in most cases additional input has been provided by the independent sources mentioned in Article 16. Importantly, the committee of experts has developed the practice of organising "on-the-spot visits" in each State Party as a way of complementing the written procedure and thus obtaining a complete overview of the situation in the party. During these visits, the committee meets NGOs, local and regional authorities and national authorities involved in the protection of regional or minority languages. Such a developing process is enabling the committee of experts to produce impartial and quite accurate assessments, the first of which were delivered in early 2001 and forwarded to the Committee of Ministers. At the time of writing, the committee of experts had adopted reports on Croatia, Finland, Germany, Hungary, Liechtenstein, Norway, the Netherlands and Switzerland, while the Committee of Ministers had addressed recommendations to those same countries except Germany. Such recommendations typically call on the state concerned to take account of all the committee's observations and address matters of priority (the adopted reports and recommendations by the Committee of Ministers can be consulted at http://local.coe.int). In accordance with Article 16, paragraph 5, of the charter, the Secretary General of the Council of Europe presented his first two-yearly report on the application of this instrument to the Parliamentary Assembly in October 2000.

Finally, techniques of supervision, or other devices triggering supervisory activities, have also been embedded, to a greater or lesser extent, in *ad hoc* regimes, mainly bilateral treaties between "kin-states" and states where "kin-minorities" live, agreements under international supervision (see *infra*, Chaper XI), or other case-specific or context-specific instruments, at universal, regional (for the role of the Inter-American Commission of Human Rights, see *supra*, Chapter V; as to the EU context, see *supra*, Chapter VII) and sub-regional level, some of which will be considered in the general forward-looking review offered in Section 3.

2. Basic elements of the supervision process

There are, of course, many ways of classifying minority rights and minority-related procedures and mechanisms of enforcement, depending on the formal or material criteria used for describing them. When viewing the relevant techniques from the perspective of an evolving multi-layered supervision process, a number of critical elements may be noted:

— judicial review is scarce, if at all. Although judicial avenues leading to a binding judgment, available for cases of alleged infringements on human rights, including gross abuses (for example, under the ECHR and, prospectively, its Protocol No. 12, and the jurisdictional clause in Article IX of the Genocide Convention), as well as individual criminal responsibility (under the UN tribunals for the former Yugoslavia and Rwanda, and, prospectively, the UN International Criminal Court, and possibly other special courts of this sort which are currently being considered), can, if consistently used, make an important contribution to ameliorating the situation of minorities and their members, their exhaustion does not secure the enforcement of any "minority rights". Quasi-judicial review is being increasingly used with regard to minority standards but the exercise is fundamentally confined to the individual complaints procedure under the First Optional Protocol to the ICCPR. As a result, the control over minority rights compliance largely consists of varying degrees of resolution- and treaty-based non-judicial supervision, ranging from intense political pressure to independent expert scrutiny to a spectrum of "mixed" options;

— the availability of pertinent information is central to all of those procedures and mechanisms (Pentassuglia, 1999a):

 • *Information through in-country fact-finding.* The sending of missions to examine the situation on the spot may be the best way of gathering first-hand information on minority problems. So far, this option has been drawn upon mostly in the UN and OSCE contexts, but the practice of undertaking fact-finding missions is now being developed also as part of the monitoring work performed under the relevant Council of Europe treaties (on the Framework Convention, see *infra*). Unless exceptions are provided, the consent of the state concerned is required to let the mission carry out its tasks. Good offices or mediation and advisory assistance are often combined with discreet fact-finding, with a view to promoting co-operation between the parties;

 • *Information through the reporting practice.* In addition to state reports under multilateral treaties, specialised agency, rapporteur, working group or research reports, a trend is emerging which values information about minorities from NGOs (including similar non-profit bodies) and/or minorities themselves (including their organisations). For instance, the OSCE HCNM (see *infra*) and a number of UN bodies dealing with minority issues are relying on this kind of information to a large extent. The monitoring bodies under the Framework Convention (see *infra*) and the European Charter for Regional or Minority Languages are moving in the same direction, and the commissioner established by the CBSS, offers further opportunities in this regard under the terms of his mandate. Such outside information is increasingly being considered as a fundamental tool for improving the effectiveness of supervision, in that it contributes to a comprehensive and realistic (as opposed to uncritical) perspective on the human rights/minority rights situation in the country concerned; and

- *Information through participation.* In connection with this trend, there has been an increase in the number of opportunities offered to NGOs and minority groups to provide information also through their direct access to the relevant bodies. Where available, complaints procedures create a forum for members of minorities to articulate their grievances by submitting pertinent factual elements. Hearings of minorities are available under specific procedural umbrellas, as a means of fostering co-operation with the groups while at the same time increasing institutional pressure on the target states. In short, NGOs and/or minority organisations have been given *locus standi* within important organs where the issue of minorities is addressed (including the UN Working Group on Minorities, the UN Commission on Human Rights and its sub-commission and a variety of regional bodies). More importantly, the participatory approach is constantly referred to in relation to the most proper ways of dealing with such issues at the domestic level;

– most of the measures which may be adopted as a result of existing techniques of supervision are not legally binding. This clearly flows from the basic components of the supervision process, as described earlier, and holds particularly true with regard to those methods which go beyond the traditional procedural paradigm of state reporting. Their additional dialogue, mediation, reconciliation, advisory and/or confidence-building purposes call for a comprehensive and flexible approach to the minority problems in the country concerned, so that a range of recommendatory rather than strictly binding measures are perceived to be more suitable. When it comes to other, case-specific means of control such as quasi-judicial review, however, the non-binding nature of the respective decisions reveals itself as a weakness. On the other hand, a number of institutional measures aimed at countering insufficient respect for, *inter alia*, minority rights (denial of membership, financial assistance or economic co-operation, suspension of a treaty, etc.), as recently made available in the context of some intergovernmental contexts such as the EU and partly the Council of Europe as well (see *infra*), amount to "sanctions" the recourse to which rests on political as well as legal grounds.

3. Towards enhancing compliance: problems and prospects

a. On the nature of supervision

Since the early 1990s the "model" of supervising the protection of minorities, basically in relation to "judicial-like" (namely, judicial and/or quasi-judicial) or non-judicial implementation options, has been intensively discussed, notably in Europe. The issue clearly surfaced in the Council of Europe following the adoption of Assembly Recommendation 1201, which made the proposed minority regime subject to the enforcement mechanism of the

ECHR. As said earlier, the member states gathered in Vienna in 1993 took a more cautious approach and instructed the Committee of Ministers to draft a framework convention open also to non-member states, instead of a protocol to the ECHR. As a result of this move, the Framework Convention was eventually adopted, containing a non-judicial implementation procedure based on a "mixed", political and independent expert, review.

At least three aspects should be considered in a broad perspective.

First, to provide for a non-judicial procedure inspired by the programme-type content of the instrument, the implementation of which is at issue, is one thing; to shape its functioning in such a way as to create real or potential obstacles to a satisfactory monitoring is quite another. This has little to do with the ("judicial-like" or non-judicial) character of the procedure, but rather with the fact that such a procedure is a "good" or "bad" one. The Framework Convention's implementation machinery appears to have functioned relatively well so far (see *infra*), in spite of the fact that it is very young and thus, understandably, still finding its feet. And yet, there are structural limitations implied by the interplay of political and independent expert review which cannot be ignored, raising the question of how far this machinery can actually go in terms of the legal quality of its output (Pentassuglia, 1999b).

Second, with special reference to the European context, stressing the need for precise minority standards as an important precondition for turning to a "judicial-like" model of supervision is certainly appropriate but the issue should not be overestimated. Programme-type elements and/or flexible wordings can be found in a large number of human rights instruments, including the ECHR. The case-law under the ECHR plays an essential expounding role, so as to make the respective guarantees "practical and effective" (*McCann and Others v. United Kingdom*, EurCtHR, Judgment of 27 September 1995, Series A, No. 324: paragraph 146) rather than "theoretical and illusory" (*Artico v. Italy*, EurCtHR, Judgment of 13 May 1980, Series A, No. 37: paragraph 33). As noted, there is also a ECHR jurisprudence which might be developing to address general needs and rights of minorities and their members, and Protocol No. 12 might supplement this. The HRC's quasi-judicial review of Article 27 rights confirms that "justiciability" is not necessarily precluded by weakly (or tentatively) worded provisions. Moreover, the OSCE International Court of Conciliation and Arbitration may provide, *inter alia*, judicial (in the broad sense of arbitral) review of the often-flexible international minority rights standards in the context of disputes submitted by the states parties to the 1992 Stockholm Convention on Conciliation and Arbitration within the (then) CSCE, which establishes such a court and its procedures, concerning the interpretation and application of their bilateral treaties incorporating those standards and which was made an integral part of the 1995 Stability Pact in Europe (paragraph 16 of the respective declaration).

In fact, the "juridical language" argument often reflects the theoretical assumption that only classic civil and political rights, or some of them, can be enforced in judicial and/or quasi-judicial proceedings. It is argued that minority rights, or minority issues generally, would be essentially unfit for this kind of review because of their particular nature. Freedom of expression would be "clear" (and yet, it was not until 1993, for instance, that the HRC stated in *Ballantyne* that Article 19, paragraph 2, of the ICCPR included linguistic preferences in private, commercial activities; Communications Nos. 359/1989 (*Ballantyne and Davidson*) and 385/1989 (*McIntyre*), Views of 31 March 1993, (1993) Annual Report II: 91), whereas a "right to identity" would not, even where tentatively framed in the context of very general provisions (for example, Article 8 of the ECHR). Although there is no denying that standard civil and political rights are "justiciable" to a greater extent than other rights, one need not look back to the early example of judicial review by the PCIJ to substantiate the proposition that there are neither logical nor legal obstacles to international norms of relevance to minorities being (or becoming) applicable before pertinent judicial and/or quasi-judicial bodies. The negotiations with the state authorities, which the issue of minorities often carries with it, affect overall policies but do not necessarily preclude enforceability as long as individual rights are recognised, though premised on broader community interests. In particular, there is no "eternal normative necessity" (Scheinin, 1994: 80) compelling a clear-cut divide between the non-justiciable (and always "obscure") minority rights and the justiciable (and always "clear and precise") general rights. For instance, the non-discrimination rights under the ECHR and its Protocol No. 12 are not necessarily more evident than the minority right not to be denied access to one's culture; the right to use, and to official recognition of, one's minority name(s) and surname is not necessarily less evident than the right to respect for private and family life under Article 8 of the ECHR; the right to education under the First Protocol to the ECHR (Article 2) is not necessarily more evident than a right to minority education is or would be, nor would a right of persons belonging to minorities to use their mother tongue in court be necessarily less evident than the fair trial right of all persons to use the language they understand through the free assistance of an interpreter under Article 6, paragraph 3, sub-paragraph e, of the ECHR, or Article 14, paragraph 3, sub-paragraph f, of the ICCPR; and again, the guarantee of free elections "under conditions which will ensure the free expression of the opinion of the people in the choice of the legislature", in Article 3 of the First Protocol to the ECHR, is not necessarily more evident than the right of minority members to "effective participation" in decisions affecting them, especially in connection with minimum forms of consultation. This list of examples could be extended. A different question is whether the formulation of the standard, or a particular factual or legal context, affects the way in which that standard is interpreted and applied. Here, the crucial point is that, although the elaboration of more precise norms clearly contributes to their justiciability, other variables are equally important. For instance, a treaty may provide the normative context for enforcing minority rights even though minority rights are not themselves provided for by the treaty (for example, pursuant to Protocol No. 12 to the ECHR, or Article 14, paragraph 1, and Article 26 of the ICCPR in relation to rights going beyond Article 27; see also the HRC's Views in *Apirana Mahuika*, Communication No. 547/1993, Views of 27 October 2000, CCPR/C/70/D/541/1993: paragraph 6, sub-paragraph 4, and paragraph 9, sub-paragraph 11, and the individual, partly dissenting, opinion by Mr Scheinin).

More importantly, and on a more specific level, a detailed jurisprudential scrutiny greatly facilitates a clearer and more nuanced understanding of the implications of international minority rights norms (see also *infra*, Conclusions). The experience of the HRC under Article 27 of the ICCPR shows that the justiciability of minority rights (and probably of any right) is not based on a mere textual datum, but depends on whether and to what extent particular factual situations impinge upon the understanding of those rights and their degree of applicability. In sum, as often stated by the HRC, the rights cannot be determined *in abstracto* but have to be placed in context. It is precisely such a contextual expounding approach which is giving substance to Article 27 rights, contributing to their nuanced enforceability at the domestic level. Here lies another crucial aspect: as long as close jurisprudential scrutiny is absent at the international level, one can hardly expect such a scrutiny to come from domestic enforcement bodies. And yet, such instruments as the UN declaration, the Copenhagen Document, the Charter of Paris and the ICCPR remind us of the internal benefits of the "rule of law approach" to minority rights and the principle of ("national or international", under the Charter of Paris) effective remedies. To come closer to a "justiciability perspective", apparently echoing the PCIJ experience, the Parliamentary Assembly of the Council of Europe has proposed reinforcing the supervision process of the Framework Convention by way of an additional protocol which gives advisory jurisdiction to the EurCtHR or other judicial authority of the Council of Europe (Recommendation 1492 (2001): paragraph 12, sub-paragraph x). This proposal is worth exploring, but one should note that previous Council of Europe proposals offer a more systematic jurisprudential supervision. That is the case of both the key Assembly proposal for a protocol to the ECHR with its attendant enforcement mechanism, and the Venice Commission's Draft Convention. This latter instrument attaches a balanced set of entitlements to, *inter alia*, an optional quasi-judicial means of control based on state and individual petitions (Articles 25 to 29). It is submitted that the comparative strength of such solutions should not be lightly dismissed, without prejudice to improvements which can be made in their respective substantive architecture (especially in relation to the 1993 text contained in Recommendation 1201). This is also suggested by the increasing integration of eastern European states into the Council of Europe, which is likely to be paralleled by the decreasing significance of a less stringent instrument such as the Framework Convention.

Thirdly, and apart from the "juridical language" argument, it is noted that since minority rights, and minority issues generally, are traditionally viewed as highly sensitive from the perspective of governments, "judicial-like" supervision would result in rulings improperly tainted by policy considerations. In the context of current instruments, judicial or quasi-judicial determination of whether "adequate" or "appropriate" opportunities are provided to receive mother-tongue education, and/or whether they are compatible with the education system of the state, would provide a typical case in point.

In fact, as long as minority rights are a matter of international law, the relevant legal issues could and should be addressed as much as possible through judicial and/or quasi-judicial means. Moreover, many human rights questions present controversial aspects ("hate speech", abortion, euthanasia, etc.), or call for specific activities going beyond constitutional/legislative enactment (see, for example, HRC General Comment No. 3 on Article 2 of the ICCPR, UN Doc. CCPR/C/21/Rev. 1), and most of them are, or may be, subject to policy considerations, including a balancing act with other rights or interests, by enforcement bodies (Meron, 1984). For instance, such notions as "legitimate aim", "reasonable and objective justification", "necessary in a democratic society" (especially in connection with a "pressing social need": see, for example, the point as discussed in the recent Gypsy cases brought under the ECHR, *supra*, Chapter VI), "proportionality", "margin of appreciation", and so forth, as elaborated upon to a large extent by the EurCtHR and/or the HRC when determining the areas of protection within the overall frame of their respective treaties, already entail, or at least permit, policy considerations. In sum, a contextual interpretation of the rights at issue is tantamount to assuming that such rights do not stand in isolation in respect of other rights, nor in a socio-political vacuum, and this is clearly reflected in the jurisprudence of the above-mentioned bodies. The real problem with "judicial-like" review is not to be found in a "juridical language" or "policy considerations" obstacle to their use, but rather in the fact that, as experience shows, the typical or primary model of supervision based on adjudication and redress, while of great importance to strengthening the rule of law by providing responses to limited grievances, making the guarantees operative as well as seeking consistency of the respective regime of rights and duties, is likely to be relatively ineffective in handling claims which are tied up with long-standing group disputes deeply rooted in social and political problems. To put it another way: the minutiae of a "judicial-like" case-by-case approach can be less effective in inducing the kind of policy change which is necessary to respond to those systemic problems that group accommodation may raise. In this respect, the commendable procedural point made by the HRC in *Lubicon Lake Band* (Communication No. 167/1984, Views of 26 March 1990, (1990) Annual Report II: 1: paragraph 32, sub-paragraph 1), and further applied in *Apirana Mahuika* (*loc. cit.*: paragraph 9, sub-paragraph 2) and *Diergaardt* (Communication No. 760/1997, Views of 25 July 2000, CCPR/C/69/D/760/1996: paragraph 10, sub-paragraph 3), on the admissibility of "collective communications" under the First Optional Protocol, does not permit transcending limitations implied by the nature and reach of the procedure. There is in fact a need for complementary approaches, aimed to provide, on the basis of common principles, appropriate protection and supervision for multiple situations.

b. A bilateral approach?

As noted (see *supra*, Chapter IX), bilateral treaties have in recent years turned out to be a frequently resorted to means of protecting minority rights, mostly in eastern Europe. What is the contribution of the contemporary bilateral approach to the control over respect for minority standards? Whatever view on the substantive quality of the "new" bilateral regimes one may take, it is quite clear that their role is far limited as regards the elaboration of adequate means of implementation. As it has been pointed out with regard to such treaties, a common feature lies in "the lack of an effective legal protection mechanism" (Gál, 1998: 8).

As a way of complementing the minority obligations undertaken by the parties, the treaties generally provide for co-operation and consultation duties with a view to addressing matters concerning their implementation; "special significance" is accorded to contacts between the legislative and administrative bodies. Some treaties set up joint intergovernmental committees entrusted with the task of monitoring the implementation of the provisions. However, the composition and/or precise mandate of these political bodies have proved controversial. To be sure, important progress has been made recently, and at least the joint committees set up under the Hungarian-Slovakian and Hungarian-Romanian basic treaties have started their work, resulting in recommendations to the respective governments. A number of bilateral treaties do not provide any control procedures. In general, the use of internal judicial remedies remains problematic, since domestic applicability of international standards may be limited by, *inter alia*, their actual or perceived non-self-executing nature.

In this respect, the contemporary bilateral treaties thus show deficiencies which are generally similar to those reflected in the essentially Western post-1945 pattern. It should nevertheless be noted that the settlement reached on the South Tyrol issue in conjunction with the 1946 De Gasperi-Gruber agreement (see *infra*, Chapter XI) nowadays also lies in the acceptance as compulsory of the jurisdiction of the ICJ in any dispute the parties, notably Austria, want to submit to it concerning the implementation of the above agreement. This aspect may provide useful guidance for future treaty-making activities in the context of bilateral co-operation.

On balance, the "new" bilateral treaties compare unfavourably with the post-first world war ones, with their firmly entrenched enforcement mechanism under the aegis of the League of Nations. On the other hand, unlike the post-1945 treaty approach, the current bilateral pattern is not being seen as foreign to multilateral scrutiny with a remote "post-1919 flavour". Apart from those treaties which embody provisions of the Framework Convention, indirectly falling under the supervisory scope of the implementation machinery established by this treaty, most of the treaties come within the reach of OSCE work, as they have been incorporated in the 1995 Stability Pact. Indeed, the OSCE has been entrusted with monitoring the implementation of the Pact, encompassing "the implementation of the agreements and arrangements" included in it. To this end, the instruments and procedures of the OSCE, "including those concerning conflict prevention, peaceful settlement of disputes and the human dimension" (paragraph 15 of the respective declaration), may be resorted to where the observance of OSCE principles and commitments is involved. To date, the 1996 Vienna Review Conference has been the only meeting where OSCE participating states have gathered in order to review implementation of the Stability Pact. As already mentioned, a dispute between the contracting parties regarding the application of the treaty may be referred to the International Court of Conciliation and Arbitration so long as they are parties to the convention setting up such a court, and the latter's competence to deal with the dispute has been established in accordance with the procedures defined in the said convention (one notable element is that conciliation is accepted as compulsory by becoming a party to the convention): no cases have as yet arisen enabling recourse to this court.

Therefore, the overall actual impact of OSCE supervision should not be overstated, although the indication is provided that the implementation of the bilateral regimes is an important component of a broader initiative of preventive diplomacy mainly directed at integrating eastern European countries into the human rights and institutional framework of the larger Europe. A largely comparable role has been assigned to the OSCE within the context of the implementation of the 1999 Pact on Stability for South Eastern Europe, in connection with bilateral treaties and other arrangements which are expected to be adopted by the states concerned.

c. Streamlining some "traditional" implementation patterns

A problem to be faced is how to enhance the effectiveness of certain long-established or typical techniques of supervision relevant to minorities. Some of them are clearly underused or their role is difficult to assess due to the fact that their functioning is basically under state control.

For instance, the gist of the "ECOSOC 1503 complaints procedure", established in 1970 and revised in 2000 (ECOSOC Resolution E/RES/2000/3), is confidential and its results decided by the Commission on Human Rights, a political body, are extremely flexible, ranging from discontinuing the examination of the case, to keeping the situation under review (with the possible appointment of independent experts), to raising the case in public under the procedure governed by ECOSOC Resolution 1235 (XLII). Obviously, each of these options is open to a number of extra-legal considerations. The focus on "patterns of gross and reliably attested" violations instead of individual cases or the situation of human rights generally, suggests the need for streamlining co-ordination with other relevant procedures, in an attempt to preclude an elusive recourse to the *litispendentia* argument (see ECOSOC Resolution 1503 (XLVIII): paragraph 6, sub-paragraph b.ii) (Pentassuglia, 1999a: 147). On the other hand, a communication may be submitted against any state irrespective of human rights treaty ratifications, and not necessarily by the victims themselves, while the admissibility condition of prior exhaustion of domestic remedies appears relatively less stringent than in other procedural contexts.

A more consistent and widespread coverage of minority concerns is probably needed when it comes to the role of UN special rapporteurs and working groups with specific mandates. Although issues affecting minorities are being examined within the context of thematic monitoring activities regarding, for instance, racial discrimination, religious intolerance and freedom of expression, as well as country scrutiny regarding, for instance, Iraq (Alfredsson and Ferrer, 1998: 21-26), overall the impact of such activities remains limited. Certain political and procedural constraints tend indeed to reduce the effectiveness of this work (Huber and Zaagman, 1994: 61). Nevertheless, ways of getting special rapporteurs and working groups more actively committed to a broad strategy of ethnic conflict prevention and management (see *infra*) should be explored, and perhaps consideration should also be given to the possible appointment of a special rapporteur on minority issues, as recently recommended by the Sub-Commission on the Promotion and Protection of Human Rights (Resolution 2001/91, 2001: paragraph 5).

The achievements of UN human rights treaty bodies have been considerable so far, although the competencies of such bodies still fall short of legally binding powers nor may they lead to restrictive measures against non-co-operative governments. As we have seen, the HRC crucially supervises the implementation of minority rights, within the framework of Article 27. Here again, there is much room for improvement. Some points can be made in this regard:

— the bodies supervising the relevant treaties should consider whether or not the reporting guidelines fully meet the need for dealing with minority issues within the scope of application of the treaty. That is especially important as most such regimes do not contain specific minority rights guarantees but their implementation nevertheless affects the treatment of minority groups. A significant step down this route is offered by the CERD which is increasingly taking up issues involving minorities, including aspects which are critical to the preservation of their cultural integrity, in its considerations and recommendations;

— in order to seriously counter inadequate state reports, the trend highlighting the importance of information from minorities and involved NGOs must be consolidated by establishing a new pattern of scrutiny based on the systematic availability and consideration of non-state sources. Note that, in contrast to the practice of the Committee on Economic, Social and Cultural Rights and the Committee on the Rights of the Child, concerned NGOs may not officially participate in the reporting procedure of other UN treaty bodies;

— as regards the optional treaty-based complaints procedures (for example, before the HRC and CERD), it is crucial to disseminate knowledge about their possible use by minority members, after all available domestic remedies have been exhausted. The case-law of the HRC is of great importance but it is currently confined to a scatter of leading cases (almost invariably involving members of indigenous peoples, whose standard claim, as noted, is to be treated as "more than" minorities), while important areas of protection such as language, education and religious rights, remain unexplored or await further clarification. The other complaints procedures are under-utilised, if at all; and

— finally, the UN Working Group on Minorities should act as a source of advice and inspiration for the treaty bodies to bring about developments in the said direction. It can foster co-ordination and stronger "minority awareness" among them, as suggested, for instance, by general

211

recommendations increasingly addressed by the working group to, among others, the UN treaty bodies for further action (see, for example, the report of the working group on its seventh session, UN Doc. E/CN.4/Sub.2/2001/22: paragraph 158).

At the regional (European) level, the role of the advisory committee in the implementation machinery of the Framework Convention for the Protection of National Minorities is of crucial importance (Pentassuglia, 1999b). The effectiveness of its work depends at least on the:

- mechanisms of selection and election of committee members (governments should abstain from negatively influencing the composition of the advisory committee and exerting pressure on its members, notably on "their" experts, during the process of monitoring);
- access to non-state sources of information (the Committee of Ministers should normally avoid restricting access of the advisory committee to the non-state sources of information under the pertinent rules of Resolution (97) 10);
- support from the Committee of Ministers for the body's conclusions (conflicting assessments should be avoided when the Committee of Ministers adopts its own conclusions and recommendations);
- involvement in the follow-up process (the *ad hoc* involvement provided by Rule 36 of Resolution (97) 10 should give way in practice to a regular follow-up by the advisory committee, because of the expertise needed to evaluate the progress made by a State Party in implementing the convention); and
- support from the Organisation as well as relation with other competent bodies for exchange of information and technical assistance (Resolution (97) 10 contains no explicit undertaking to provide the advisory committee with the necessary financial and technical resources to carry out its work).

At the time of writing, the advisory committee had produced two activity reports, covering the period from June 1998 to October 2000. Although it is too early to assess its impact upon the efficiency of the monitoring procedure, it should be noted that the committee has appeared remarkably active with regard to meetings with representatives of states parties and contacts with non-state (namely, independent) sources. The Ministers' Deputies have authorised the advisory committee to hold meetings with NGOs and other independent institutions for the entire initial monitoring cycle (although in the context of the visits it pays at the invitation of the states parties concerned), making requests for individual mandates, as otherwise implied by Rule 32 of Resolution 97 (10), unnecessary. In terms of the use of non-state sources of information in general, the advisory committee has actively sought the input of international organisations, national institutions and various sectors of civil society, notably NGOs and minority organisations (especially through shadow reports), after notifying the Committee of Ministers of its intention to do so (Rule 31 of Resolution 97 (10)). As indicated earlier, the advisory committee has adopted its first opinions in respect of a number of states parties; they contain specific proposals (Part V of the opinions) on an article-by-article basis. The Committee of Ministers has decided that the advisory committee may be invited to be represented at meetings held for the purpose of monitoring the Framework Convention, in order to introduce the opinions and if necessary answer questions concerning them. At the same time, states parties have been allowed by the Committee of Ministers, as part of the monitoring procedure, to submit within a fixed time-limit written comments on the advisory committee's opinion regarding them, before it delivers its conclusions and recommendations. Arguably, such written comments, besides extending the timeframe of the procedure along with the publication of the advisory committee's opinions (which is already conditioned as a rule on the issuing of the Committee of Ministers' deliberations, unless the individual parties concerned wish to publish them earlier together with their written comments; to date, most of these opinions have been made publicly available several months following their adoption), may be viewed as a kind of *de facto* reply to the written "pleas" of the advisory committee for a better protection, with the Committee of Ministers acting as a political intermediary.

The conclusions and recommendations which have been adopted by the Committee of Ministers to date, essentially recall both the advisory committee's opinion and the comments of the state concerned, and even comments by other governments, highlight major problem areas regarding the implementation of the Framework Convention, and recommend that the party "take appropriate account" of its conclusions and the various comments in the advisory committee's opinion. Further to that, they importantly involve the latter in the follow-up process by inviting the party to continue the dialogue in progress with the advisory committee and to keep the committee regularly informed of the measures taken in response to the conclusions and recommendations set out in the resolution.

Finally, it should be noted that delays in the submission of state reports have emerged, while the increase in the number of states parties has prompted the advisory committee to highlight the key question of resource and staffing constraints.

d. The preventive approach: evolving set of institutional responses

As noted, a marked preventive content characterises some contemporary approaches to minority issues, in view of the recognition of a linkage between respect for human rights/minority rights, and the maintenance of peace and both international and internal stability. This connection was explicitly made by former UN Secretary General Boutros Boutros-Ghali in his well-known 1992 report on an agenda for peace (UN Doc. A/47/277-S/24111: paragraph 18), and confirmed in the cited 1993 report by Asbjørn Eide on possible ways and means of facilitating the peaceful and constructive solution of problems involving minorities, especially in connection with the UN declaration. In effect, a recent study (de Varennes, 2000) shows that the most common underlying sources of conflicts in general, and ethnic conflicts in particular, are found in large-scale discrimination in such key areas as employment and economic development, and lack of compliance with minority rights, notably in the fields of language and education.

Although preventive assumptions are clearly discernible in recent treaty regimes such as the Framework Convention and the eastern European bilateral treaties mentioned above, the preventive content gains full strength at the more general level of the various techniques adopted by international institutions acting in their own right.

i. Role of high commissioners and other institutions

The OSCE HCNM has clearly taken the lead in promoting a comprehensive approach to security. The commissioner works as an institution for conflict prevention, by providing "early warning" and, where appropriate, "early action", so as to prevent tension from escalating into violence and spreading across national borders. He may collect and receive information from any source (save information from people or organisations involved in terrorism or violence), conduct fact-finding missions in the form of visits subject to the consent of the state concerned, and suggest solutions with a view to fostering dialogue between governments and national minorities.

The flexibility of the high commissioner's mandate, coupled with a number of operational tools he has developed over time, are at the basis of a constructive way of tackling situations of potential inter-state conflict involving minorities (Ratner, 2000). To date, the high commissioner has been actively involved in minority problems in numerous OSCE countries, obtaining productive and widely praised results. This is illustrated by such relevant cases as those concerning the Russian-speaking groups in the Baltic states and Ukraine and the Hungarian minorities in Romania and Slovakia. The high commissioner's conclusions with regard to possible solutions of minority problems are not legally binding. Thus, their effectiveness ultimately rests with the willingness of the parties involved to co-operate. Furthermore, the high commissioner is one "on", not "for", national minorities (namely, he is not an ombudsman to whom to appeal) and his activities are based – at least to some extent – on a classic principle of diplomacy, namely confidentiality.

At the global level, the UN High Commissioner for Human Rights and the UN Working Group on Minorities are basically inspired by the methods of the OSCE high commissioner, which might also become a model for the UN promotion of possible further regional institutions for conflict prevention and resolution (see Sub-Commission on Human Rights Resolution 2001/9: paragraph 7). The UN High Commissioner for Human Rights has been entrusted, *inter alia*, with co-ordinating an early warning mechanism aimed at preventing racial, ethnic or religious tensions from spilling over into open conflicts. As hinted at earlier, the work of special rapporteurs and working groups can and should amount to yet another way of addressing minority concerns, especially for the sake of conflict prevention. As noted, in 1994 a CBSS commissioner came along with developments in the OSCE and UN contexts, at sub-regional level, with his mandate then revised in 1997 and 2000. All of the techniques of supervision used by such institutions entail consideration of the relevant international instruments. For instance, the

OSCE high commissioner has occasionally reviewed pertinent standards, as in the 1999 report on the linguistic rights of persons belonging to national minorities in the OSCE area, or requested the drafting of special texts, such as the Hague, Oslo and Lund recommendations on, respectively, the education, linguistic and participation rights of persons belonging to national minorities, adopted between 1996 and 1999, by independent experts in support of his efforts under the auspices of the Foundation on Inter-Ethnic Relations, based in the Hague. It is worth observing, however, that, while the OSCE high commissioner's basic strategy remains one based on pragmatism and "quiet diplomacy", resulting in recommendations for brokered solutions which fit the case at issue, the UN and CBSS mechanisms mostly aim at ensuring a progressive, general implementation of existing commitments and/or obligations. For instance, the preventive functions of the UN working group and the UN high commissioner are being channelled into a normative discourse based on the implementation of the UN 1992 declaration and other relevant international instruments. The UN working group has indeed tackled the issue of conflict prevention from the perspective of how best to improve the protection of minority rights in general; to this end, it has tried, *inter alia*, to identify ways of implementing internationally recognised minority rights, particularly in the area of participation (see, for example, Eide, 2001). The future role of the UN working group has recently come under review, but there is little doubt that standard-implementation will continue to be a major focus. The goal of securing the observance of existing standards is evident under the CBSS commissioner's mandate. Although this commissioner operates along the lines of the OSCE High Commissioner on National Minorities, he has received a specific "ombudsman-mandate" which enables him to receive complaints from, among others, both members of minorities and minorities themselves (including involved organisations). That comes closer to a sort of quasi-judicial approach to conflict prevention.

ii. Minority rights conditionality

The Council of Europe and the EU are stepping up the level of minority rights "preventive" supervision in connection with their own human rights admission requirements and/or within the context of a coherent strategy based on the principle of conditionality.

As for the Council of Europe, it is indeed conditioning admission to the Organisation on compliance, not only with human rights in general, but also with minority rights in particular, especially those foreseen in the proposed protocol to the ECHR contained in Recommendation 1201 of the Parliamentary Assembly. As noted, respect for the principles endorsed by this recommendation has been included as a "commitment" in Assembly opinions on the admission of new member states. The key question is whether the competent body will really "make scrupulously sure" that these rights are respected by the applicant states (Order No. 484 (1993), paragraph 2, subparagraph ii), and will not be content with "paper commitments". On the other hand, as referred to below, follow-up mechanisms have been set up that might help keep the minority rights record of member states under review.

As indicated in Chapter VII, the EU is conditioning EU membership and – as part of a special strategy with certain countries of south-east Europe – trade preferences, financial aid, economic co-operation and contractual relations, on, *inter alia*, "respect for and protection of minorities", and is drawing extensively upon a so-called "human rights clause" (and similar instruments), frequently coupled with minority rights references, in agreements with (and autonomous programmes for) third countries.

Generally speaking, the supervision of the implementation of, *inter alia*, minority rights standards, is being carried out on the basis of internal reporting, supplemented by available sources from other international organisations or bodies. Depending on the initiative pursued, a number of "sanctions" are provided for as a last resort against non-compliant states, ranging from suspension or termination of the relevant agreement to other "appropriate steps", including suspension of financial assistance and/or trade preferences, to denial of membership. In principle, they show a complementary, reactive approach to implementation by providing the competent bodies with a degree of (direct or indirect) coercive power over the states concerned. The EU employs strong political and economic leverage to induce compliance with human rights/minority rights, in line with overall international tendencies to use the financial lever for this aim, which is brought to bear, to a greater or lesser extent, on the prevention of ethnic conflicts (see, for example, Chayes and Chayes, 1998: 191-201). "Anticipatory effects" capture the essence of the outcome expected of this approach: the EU institutions may decline to take certain steps favourable to the country on the basis of a lack of respect for, *inter alia*, minority rights (basically Council of Europe and OSCE standards: see *supra*, Chapter VII). This is clearly illustrated by the already cited 1997 council conclusions on conditionality, where, for instance, the opening of negotiations for contractual relations is expressly subject to a "credible commitment ... to comply with the generally recognized standards of ... minority rights" (Bulletin of the European Union, 1987: point 2.2.1). Such an approach tends to prompt the country which is interested in the benefits deriving from those steps, including the obtaining of EU membership, to demonstrate effective compliance (Pentassuglia, 2001). Political, economic, and legal considerations have thus been brought to the fore in a comprehensive effort to consolidate peace, democracy and human rights. Though *per se* not based on strictly conditional linkages, the 1995 and 1999 EU-sponsored Stability Pacts well illustrate this overarching approach, as they are essentially meant to help the states concerned to meet the above conditionality requirements.

Significant improvements of the minority rights record are actually being made by a number of countries from eastern Europe (new constitutional and legislative provisions, *ad hoc* mechanisms or institutions, etc.). For instance, EU action has been particularly influential in obtaining the passing of significant minority laws on language and education (notably concerning the right to receive instruction of, and in, the mother tongue, and the right to use the minority language in contacts with public authorities in those areas where the group represents a substantial proportion of the local population), as well as further developments, in Slovakia, Romania, and more recently, Croatia and the FYROM. Indeed, the minority rights component of this preventive pattern is being highlighted essentially in relation to the dynamics of integration or rapprochement into European structures by eastern European countries (especially in connection with the process of EU enlargement). While probably necessary in the short term, such a limitation in scope may, however, turn out to be insufficient in the long term, prompting complaints of double-standard treatment (remember, for instance, that not all of the "old" European countries have ratified the Framework Convention, nor are any active or systematic efforts being made to (re-)assess these countries' minority rights record in view of the human rights implications attached to their own Council of Europe or EU membership), and eventually undermining the credibility of supervision. We should learn from the shortcomings of the League of Nations machinery. Moreover, the effectiveness of such procedures may be achieved on the condition of minimising political considerations (or *realpolitik*, as distinct from human rights law) when dealing with the granting of membership or the concession or suspension of financial and/or economic benefits. In general, a lack of permanent, independent human rights monitoring bodies should be noted in this context. Responsibility for action rests with political bodies, which does not necessarily result in consistent patterns (Pentassuglia, 2001: 27-29). Judicial control (if at all) is rather limited, and there is no judicially enforceable "obligation to act" upon those bodies (Pentassuglia, 2001: 22-23 and 37).

With regard to follow-up activities, the mechanism set up by Recommendation 1115 (1997) of the Parliamentary Assembly of the Council of Europe can constitute an additional resource to monitor the implementation of (Council of Europe) minority standards by member states. It is based on reports of a monitoring committee, leading up to restrictive measures of the Assembly (and, ultimately, of the Committee of Ministers) in case of a member state persistently failing to comply with the obligations assumed under Council of Europe treaties and/or the commitments undertaken upon accession to the Organisation. The procedure involves member states generally, but it is clear that special attention is paid to the situation of new members in connection with human rights obligations flowing from admission under Article 3 of the statute. Although of a non-judicial nature, the mechanism is likely to prove more successful than the intergovernmental one established by the Committee of Ministers in 1994 (and further revised in 1998), based on constructive dialogue with the member states concerning appropriate measures to be considered for adoption, which is of a far more marked political nature (this is well illustrated, *inter alia*, by the fact that the procedure consists in delivering entirely confidential assessments) (see, generally, Benoît-Rohmer, 2000).

As noted, within the EU context, restrictive measures relating to membership rights are now permissible under Article 7 of the TEU, in the event of a serious and persistent breach of the principles mentioned in Article 6.1 (including respect for human rights). Although the mechanism is intended for general application, thereby involving all member states on an equal footing, recent commentators have stressed its conflict prevention nature as primarily addressed to prospective EU members (Pollet, 1997). The preventive

content will be further strengthened by the amendments to Article 7 introduced by the Nice Treaty, enabling the EU to adopt recommendations
addressed to the state concerned before any serious infringement of rights
actually occurs. Still, it remains to be seen how significant such a mechanism
will be in EU practice, and to what extent it may involve minority rights considerations. The crucial substantive determinations are not subject to ECJ
review, which under the Nice Treaty will be made available only for "purely
procedural stipulations" (new Article 46(f) of the TEU). The text of Article 7
as revised at Nice only provides that the Council may decide to involve on
an *ad hoc* basis independent persons to report on the situation at a very early
stage of the procedure.

iii. Confidence-building measures

An implementation-oriented pattern of prevention is shown by the recent
use of multilateral and bilateral programmes of technical co-operation and
advisory services. In the context of the UN, such programmes are being
carried out by the office of the UN high commissioner, upon request from
the countries concerned. The basic aims are to assist states in the process of
drafting and reviewing their constitutions and/or pieces of legislation in view
of the relevant international human rights standards, as well as supporting
the setting up of adequate national institutions responsible for implementation. This approach calls for a co-ordinated effort among the various UN
agencies and organisations in conformity with Article 9 of the 1992 UN declaration, as far as the implementation of the latter is concerned.

At the European level, similar issues have been tackled through a broad
spectrum of means, operating between primary implementation concerns,
essentially in relation to Council of Europe and OSCE minority standards,
and the recognition of the need for developing dialogue involving governments, minority representatives and civil society, in an attempt to identify,
and ultimately eradicate, the deep-seated factors that impede compliance.
For present purposes, it is sufficient to limit the following references to institutional action to a few examples of major efforts that are being made within
the Council of Europe.

The action plan adopted by the 1997 Strasbourg Summit of the Heads of
State and Government of the Member States of the Council of Europe
stresses the need for complementing the standard-setting achievements in
the field of minorities "through practical activities, such as confidence-building measures, and enhanced co-operation, involving both governments and
civil society" (Part I, paragraph 6). The post of Commissioner for Human
Rights established by the Committee of Ministers in 1999 (Resolution (99) 50),
largely reflects these objectives, while within a wider human rights framework, notably in relation to educational, advisory and technical assistance
tasks (Article 2 of Resolution 99 (50)). Interestingly, in Recommendation
1492 (2001), the Parliamentary Assembly urges the Committee of Ministers
to attach to the commissioner a person with special responsibility for issues
concerning the protection of minority rights. On the other hand, existing
specialised bodies are contributing significantly to monitoring the situation

of minorities and their rights. The work of ECRI (see *supra*, Chapter VI) encompasses to some extent the protection of minorities (for example, in respect of education) when reporting on country situations, formulating recommendations on general themes and developing co-operation with NGOs. In particular, the Venice Commission (see *infra*, Chapter XI) and the advisory committee under the Framework Convention, are offering their technical services to facilitate the adoption of appropriate domestic measures on the protection of minorities.

The latter body is indeed providing appropriate assistance designed to make the convention better known especially in those states parties from eastern Europe which are undergoing deep constitutional and legislative change. In fact, the Framework Convention is being used in regard to the preparation of draft laws on minority rights, and in general is generating interest at the domestic level in the issue of minorities. In this context, it may be useful to note that the Secretariat of the Framework Convention is currently responsible for the implementation of three projects in the framework of the Stability Pact for South Eastern Europe, consisting respectively in assessing the conformity of domestic practices with equality and non-discrimination standards and developing special measures to ensure full equality, facilitating the acceptance and implementation of existing multilateral standards in the field of minority rights, as well as reinforcing or encouraging bilateral co-operation in this field in accordance with those standards, particularly those of the Framework Convention. A great number of the countries concerned have agreed to participate in these projects, which involve representatives of civil society to a large extent, in addition to national authorities and independent experts.

At the intergovernmental level, a new source of information about, *inter alia*, "policies and good practices for the protection of national minorities at the domestic level and in the context of international instruments", is offered by the Committee of Experts Relating to the Protection of National Minorities (DH-MIN), set up as a permanent body by the Committee of Ministers of the Council of Europe in December 1997 (Resolution (97) 105). At the time of writing, the activities of this body are, however, suspended, due to resource constraints and the decision to prioritise the activities regarding the Framework Convention.

It has been mentioned that minority groups and involved NGOs are being increasingly given access to human rights forums with a view to supplementing the information about the situation of minorities as provided by state sources. From a prevention-oriented perspective, minority participation is obviously crucial, especially when it comes to encouraging states to comply with minority standards. In this respect, the involvement of minorities in the monitoring work of the joint intergovernmental committees set up by some of the relevant contemporary bilateral treaties, as it is now the case under the Hungarian-Slovakian and Hungarian-Romanian treaties (although minority representatives have no veto power over deliberations), is noteworthy and should be consistently pursued. It indeed helps foster a climate of dialogue at the domestic level by providing a measure of minority participation which was lacking at the time of the negotiation of the treaty (see *supra*, Chapter IX).

e. Aspects of ethnic conflict management

The supervision of minority rights standards is more problematic when real or potential violations fall beyond the reach of limited mechanisms and the short-term priority is to stop and/or impede violence on the ground. The level of response may vary depending on the gravity of the situation. However, one major expected effect is to contain, or even remove, the causes that obstruct the process of compliance.

i. UN peace-keeping operations

In terms of UN peace-keeping operations, human rights/minority rights considerations have not yet been channelled into a coherent pattern for dealing with situations of ethnic tension. The deployment of UN monitoring personnel in the FYROM authorised by the Security Council in 1992 as a presence of Unprofor designed to defuse minority tensions in the border areas with Albania and the FRY is no doubt noteworthy (Ramcharan, 1993b). As part of their visiting programme, such observers, *inter alia*, received complaints from members of minority groups about alleged discriminations by the authorities. Where appropriate, complaints were submitted to the internal and/or international competent bodies for consideration. In 1995, the Security Council, by Resolution 983, replaced Unprofor with the UN Preventive Deployment Force (UNPREDEP), which is the first UN peace-keeping operation with an exclusively preventive mandate.

ii. UN Security Council patterns

Under Article 24 of the UN Charter, the Security Council has primary responsibility for the maintenance of international peace and security, in accordance with the principles and purposes of the charter. In recent years, the concept of "threat to the peace", under the terms of Article 39, is being increasingly associated with non-military sources of conflicts, basically amounting to internal situations where a range of human rights issues are at stake (Ramcharan, 1992). In a number of cases involving minorities, the Security Council has acted under Chapter VII (for example, Iraq, former Yugoslavia, region of Kosovo). Depending on the case, it has, *inter alia*, condemned gross violations of human rights (with particular reference to the policy of "ethnic cleansing"), demanded a ceasefire and a peaceful solution ensuring protection for the groups involved, appealed to all states and humanitarian organisations to contribute to relief efforts, called for the establishment of in-country missions and/or security/civil presence under its auspices, decided various measures not involving the use of armed force under Article 41 (including the establishment of international criminal tribunals, *supra*, Chapter IV), and/or authorised coercive (military) actions. At present, it is not possible to establish a truly coherent Security Council approach to ethnic conflicts. Rather, an ever greater "dialogue" with special rapporteurs and the secretary general for fact-finding purposes can be noticed. For instance, the special rapporteurs on Iraq and former Yugoslavia were invited to discuss their reports before the council. Moreover, the latter has supported and/or requested fact-finding (including good offices) initiatives of the secretary general as a means of coping with serious minority problems (in Bulgaria, in the region of Nagorno-Karabakh, etc.). This is essentially a reflection of an increasing recognition of the need for strengthening conflict prevention activities in the UN system (see, for example, generally, Kanninen, 2001).

It would be desirable not only to further consolidate these tendencies, but also to build on them by involving the UN Working Group on Minorities and/or the UN High Commissioner for Human Rights in regular consultations with the council when addressing pertinent situations. By so doing, concerns for the implementation of human rights (at least in cases of gross abuses) may be more firmly embedded in the peace-enforcement functions of the Security Council. A more proactive "advisory" role of such human rights bodies may also trigger further initiatives from member states, the General Assembly, regional arrangements or agencies, or the secretary general, in conformity with the charter (notably under Articles 10, 11, 14, 33, 35, 52, 53 and 99).

iii. Is it permissible to use (or threaten to use) armed force in order to protect an oppressed minority?

A large-scale and systematic mistreatment of minority groups raises the question whether, as a last resort, namely after all permissible techniques or means of pressure have proved unsuccessful, the targeted groups may be relieved, and the respective enforcement of human rights/minority rights may be secured, by military action. Legal grounds have been occasionally invoked for the unilateral use of force designed to protect an oppressed people and/or minority, based on the right of collective self-defence (see, for example, the Indian position to justify forcible action in East Pakistan in 1971) or an alleged right to humanitarian intervention (for example, in relation to the plight of Iraqi Kurds, as singled out in Security Council Resolution 688 adopted in April 1991, and the subsequent military operation "Provide Comfort").

The classic scholarly and jurisprudential view is that, under general international law the threat or use of force by states *uti singuli* is prohibited, as reflected in Article 2, paragraph 4, of the UN Charter. A state may lawfully employ force only as a matter of individual or collective self-defence under Article 51 of the charter (for latest developments, see Cassese, 2001), or when military action has been decided by the Security Council to address threats to, or breaches of, international peace and security or acts of aggression, under Chapter VII of the UN Charter. The ICJ, in the case concerning *Military and Paramilitary Activities in and against Nicaragua* (Merits) (ICJ Reports 1986), discarded any kind of unilateral humanitarian intervention as justifying the use of force.

The 1999 Nato intervention in Kosovo was prompted by the deep disturbance of the international community at the massive abuses committed by the Serb authorities against the Kosovar Albanians, and was taken after attempts to reach a peaceful settlement had failed. The Nato action has posed, *inter alia*, the question whether, in contrast to well-established interpretation, unilateral resort to force aside from self-defence (namely, resort to force without any authorisation of the Security Council, as in this instance) should be seen as permissible where designed to protect populations, including minority groups, which are victims of large-scale and systematic human rights violations. An essential point in legal doctrine is that the Nato action was in breach of the UN Charter and general international law (Simma, 1999). While concurring with this view from a *lex lata* perspective, Cassese (1999a) situates the Nato action within a broad framework of contemporary achievements and tendencies in international law and relations generated by human rights concerns. He contends that a new customary rule might gradually emerge permitting unilateral forcible action for the strictly limited purpose of putting an end to large-scale atrocities constituting a threat to the peace, given, in particular, the (at least temporary) inability of the Security Council to endorse any coercive action, and the lack of any alternative avenues short of force. At present, he sees a mounting favourable *opinio necessitatis* on "Kosovo-like" action, although he acknowledges (Cassese, 1999b) that the evidence which might serve to establish its (prospective) legitimacy under international law, even under tightly defined conditions, remains limited. The much debated matter of "pro-human rights" military intervention is likely to be reviewed by the ICJ if it finds its jurisdiction to adjudicate in the case concerning *Legality of Use of Force* instituted by the FRY against a number of western countries which took part in the Nato military action in Kosovo.

4. Concluding observations

The overview presented above reveals a variety of procedures and institutions concerned with, or relevant to, the implementation of minority rights and minority-related standards. It is well-known that the ultimate responsibility for standard-implementation rests with states at the domestic level as a result of their particular undertakings. However, major international institutions are gradually expanding the range of ways and means of committing states to effective protection.

In principle, they do not prejudice strictly unilateral (individual or joint) state action, so long as *ad hoc* mechanisms are not (or are no longer) available and the specific requirements for permissible unilateral measures established by general international law are met (for a general perspective, see Lattanzi, 1983; the literature cit. *supra*, Chapter II; Crawford, Peel and Olleson, 2001). Still, one can hardly expect direct inter-state confrontation on human rights/minority rights issues, even from within a special regime: this is vividly illustrated by the fact that no inter-state complaint has ever been brought under any of the relevant UN human rights treaty procedures. In fact, the scene of inter-state enforceability of human rights, far from indicating an excessive human rights "vigilantism", has in most cases shown a remarkable lack of willingness on the part of states to pick up on human rights violations committed by other states.

There is no single approach to implementation, but rather a spectrum of differentiated methods of supervision, revealing a mix of legal and "policy-driven" elements. In addition to the traditional, procedural paradigm of state reporting, other paths are emerging or being strengthened. Some of them amount to new institutional techniques basically serving conflict-prevention purposes. They constitute flexible models which envisage minority issues and minority rights compliance from a predominantly pragmatic context-specific perspective. At the European level, such a process is a major part of an overall strategy designed to promote stability in those countries in the east which are in transition towards democracy. The complex of means of control should be viewed in terms of complementarity, in an attempt to compensate for each other's limitations. It is desirable that "judicial-like" models of supervision gain a prominent role over time with regard to norm-interpretation and dispute settlement, thereby improving the coherence of the minority rights regime. However, their impact may prove limited in the face of systemic problems the treatment of certain groups may raise. Comprehensive "policy-driven" responses are being provided, yet, among other things, they typically do not carry with them enforcement possibilities for victims and their representatives, and are often exposed to double standard or *realpolitik* considerations. Moreover, if there is no alternative to such responses, the issue of minorities and minority rights compliance may have to face difficulties in attracting international attention unless it is visibly linked to a potential or actual danger of inter- or intra-state conflict (Schlager, 2000: 369-370; Ratner, 2000: 697).

The co-ordination of the various procedures and mechanisms suggests that varying degrees of overlap are likely to be unavoidable. In fact, "horizontal complementarity", namely that involving the bodies entrusted with monitoring functions of the same (or comparable) kind, may lead to establishing patterns of constructive competition, providing a strong pull towards improving the effectiveness of such functions. Possible divergent approaches arising in this context should be kept to such a level as to represent a sign of the flexibility and enrichment rather than fragmentation of the protective regime and/or enforcement process. Overall, the challenge is to achieve or maximise "vertical" co-ordination (focusing on the nature of minority issues), while at the same time preserving the dynamic and evolutionary substance and structure of the entire supervision system.

Beyond the positive effects expected to flow from most needed general reforms of the human rights monitoring system, particularly in the UN context, which has increasingly become a major subject in scholarly and political debate (see *supra*, Chapters II and Conclusions), the short- and medium-term prospects for improving state compliance with minority rights (and/or other relevant standards) demand at least the relatively modest steps listed below in no strict sequential order:

– increasing access to, and dissemination of, pertinent information in general and seeking equal standing of state and non-state sources of information in particular;

- increasing the use, and thus the efficiency, of existing resolution- and treaty-based procedures, with a special emphasis on those which remain underutilised to date;
- increasing consistency and follow-up capabilities, especially when employing preventive patterns of supervision, in full accordance with international human rights law, and in particular, with a special focus on the EU:
  - clarifying the standards on which to concentrate for purposes of scrutiny (see *supra*, Chapter VII);
  - setting up permanent, independent human rights bodies (which, by building upon inter-institutional activities currently in place in the context of the enlargement process and south-east Europe, should closely co-operate with other pertinent international bodies) to assess periodically the minority rights situation in the countries concerned; and
  - subjecting minority rights conditionality to objective, legal criteria for determining when and what measures are to be adopted in response to reported minority rights issues;
- extending the range of possibilities for "judicial-like" review as a fundamental way of enhancing the understanding of norms and contributing to dispute settlement as well as the coherence of the minority rights regime; and
- increasing the effectiveness of the normative and operational framework of, notably UN, conflict management functions.

Bibliography

Alfredsson, G., "Encouraging and monitoring compliance with minority rights", UN Doc. E/CN.4/Sub.2/AC.5/1997/WP.8, 1997, pp. 1-13.

Alfredsson, G. and de Zayas, A., "Minority rights: protection by the United Nations", *Human Rights Law Journal*, 14, 1993, pp. 1-9.

Alfredsson, G. and Ferrer, E., *Minority rights: a guide to United Nations procedures and institutions*, Minority Rights Group (International), London, 1999.

Alfredsson, G. and Türk, D., "International mechanisms for the monitoring and protection of minority rights: their advantages, disadvantages and interrelationships", in *Monitoring human rights in Europe: comparing international procedures and mechanisms*, Bloed, A., Leicht, L., Nowak M. and Rosas, A. (eds), Martinus Nijhoff Publishers, Dordrecht, 1993, pp. 169-186.

Baka, A.B., "The European Convention on Human Rights and the protection of minorities under international law", *Connecticut Journal of International Law*, 8, 1993, pp. 227-242.

Benoît-Rohmer, F., "Mécanismes de supervision des engagements des Etats membres et l'autorité du Conseil de l'Europe", in *Law in greater Europe: towards a common legal area – Studies in honour of Heinrich Klebes*, Haller, B., Krüger, H.C. and Petzold, H. (eds), Kluwer Law International, The Hague, 2000, pp. 80-101.

Bothe, M., "The legitimacy of the use of force to protect peoples and minorities", in *Peoples and minorities in international law*, Brölmann, C., Lefeber, R. and Zieck, M. (eds), Martinus Nijhoff Publishers, Dordrecht, 1993, pp. 289-299.

Brandtner, B. and Rosas, A., "Trade preferences and human rights", in *The EU and human rights*, Alston, P. (ed.), Oxford University Press, Oxford, 1999, pp. 699-722.

Brandtner, B. and Rosas, A., "Human rights and the external relations of the European Community: an analysis of doctrine and practice", *European Journal of International Law*, 9, 1998, pp. 468-490.

Cassese, A., "Terrorism is also disrupting some crucial legal categories of international law", *European Journal of International Law*, 12, 2001, pp. 993-1001.

Cassese, A., "*Ex iniuria ius oritur:* are we moving towards international legitimation of forcible humanitarian countermeasures in the world community?", *European Journal of International Law*, 10, 1999a, pp. 23-30.

Cassese, A., "A follow-up: forcible humanitarian countermeasures and *opinio necessitatis*", *European Journal of International Law*, 10, 1999b, pp. 791-799.

Chayes, A.H. and Chayes, A., "Mobilizing international and regional organizations for managing ethnic conflict", in *International law and ethnic conflict*, Wippman, D. (ed.), Cornell University Press, Ithaca and London, 1998, pp. 178-210.

Crawford, J., Peel, J. and Olleson, S., "The ILC's articles on responsibility of states for internationally wrongful acts: completion of the second reading", *European Journal of International Law*, 12, 2001, pp. 943-962.

de Varennes, F., "Minority rights and the prevention of ethnic conflicts", UN Doc. E/CN.4/Sub.2/AC.5/2000/CRP.3, 2000, pp. 1-14.

225

de Zayas, A., "The international judicial protection of peoples and minorities", in *Peoples and minorities in international law*, Brölmann, C., Lefeber, R. and Zieck, M. (eds), Martinus Nijhoff Publishers, Dordrecht, 1993, pp. 253-287.

Eide, A., "The role of the Sub-Commission on Promotion and Protection of Human Rights and its working groups in the prevention of conflicts", *International Journal on Minority and Group Rights*, 8, 2001, pp. 25-29.

Eide, A., "Possible ways and means of facilitating the peaceful and constructive solution of problems involving minorities", UN Doc. E/CN.4/Sub.2/1993/34, 1993.

Estébanez, M.A. and Gál, K., *Implementing the Framework Convention for the Protection of National Minorities*, European Centre for Minority Issues, Flensburg, 1999.

Gál, K., "The role of bilateral treaties in the protection of national minorities in central and eastern Europe", UN Doc. E/CN.4/Sub.2/AC.5/1998/CRP.2, 1998, pp. 1-14.

Huber, K. and Zaagman, R., "Peace, human rights, and minorities: multilateral responses and the CSCE High Commissioner on National Minorities", *International Journal on Group Rights*, 2, 1994, pp. 55-67.

Kanninen, T., "Recent initiatives by the Secretary General and the UN system in strengthening conflict prevention activities", *International Journal on Minority and Group Rights*, 8, 2001, pp. 39-43.

Lattanzi, F., *Garanzie dei diritti dell'uomo nel diritto internazionale generale*, Giuffrè, Milan, 1993.

Martín Estébanez, M.A., "The High Commissioner on National Minorities: development of the mandate", in *The OSCE in the maintenance of peace and security: conflict prevention, crisis management and peaceful settlement of disputes*, Bothe, M., Ronzitti, N. and Rosas, A. (eds), Kluwer Law International, The Hague, 1997, pp. 123-165.

Martín Estébanez, M.A., *International organizations and minority protection in Europe*, Åbo Akademi, Turku/Åbo, 1996.

Martín Estébanez, M.A., "The protection of national or ethnic, religious and linguistic minorities", in *The European Union and human rights*, Neuwahl, N. and Rosas, A. (eds), Martinus Nijhoff Publishers, The Hague, 1995, pp. 133-163.

Meron, T. (ed.), *Human rights in international law: legal and policy issues*, Clarendon Press, Oxford, 1984.

Mikkelsen, N., "Position and function of the Commissioner of the Council of Baltic Sea States (CBSS) for Democratic Institutions and Human Rights including the Rights of Persons belonging to Minorities", in *The institution of a commissioner for human rights and minorities and the prevention of human rights violations*, Klein, E. (ed.), Berlin Verlag, Berlin, 1995, pp. 37-42.

Nowak, M., "Human rights 'conditionality' in relation to entry to, and full participation in, the EU", in *The EU and human rights*, Alston, P. (ed.), Oxford University Press, Oxford, 1999, pp. 687-698.

Pentassuglia, G., "The EU and the protection of minorities: the case of eastern Europe", *European Journal of International Law*, 12, 2001, pp. 3-38.

Pentassuglia, G., "Minority protection in international law: from standard-setting to implementation", *Nordic Journal of International Law*, 68, 1999a, pp. 131-160.

Pentassuglia, G., "Monitoring minority rights in Europe: the implementation machinery of the Framework Convention for the Protection of National Minorities – with special reference to the role of the advisory committee", *International Journal on Minority and Group Rights*, 6, 1999b, pp. 417-461.

Pollet, K., "Human rights clauses in agreements between the European Union and central and eastern European countries", *Revue des Affairs Européennes*, 7, 1997, pp. 290-301.

Ramcharan, B.G., "Fact-finding into the problems of minorities", in *Peoples and minorities in international law,* Brölmann, C., Lefeber, R. and Zieck, M. (eds), Martinus Nijhoff Publishers, Dordrecht, 1993a, pp. 239-251.

Ramcharan, B.G., "New models of human rights protection: preventive peacekeeping", *International Commission of Jurists Review*, 50, 1993b, pp. 101-105.

Ramcharan, B.G., "Security Council patterns for dealing with ethnic conflicts and minority problems", in *Broadening the frontiers of human rights: essays in honour of Asbjørn Eide*, Gomien, D. (ed.), Scandinavian University Press, Oslo, 1993c, pp. 27-40.

Ramcharan, B.G., "The Security Council: maturing of international protection of human rights", *International Commission of Jurists Review*, 48, 1992, pp. 24-37.

Ratner, S.R., "Does international law matter in preventing ethnic conflict?", *New York University Journal of International Law and Politics*, 32, 2000, pp. 591-698.

Riedel, E. and Will, M., "Human rights clauses in external agreements of the EC", in *The EU and human rights*, Alston, P. (ed.), Oxford University Press, Oxford, 1999, pp. 723-754.

Scheinin, M., "Direct applicability of economic, social and cultural rights: a critique of the doctrine of self-executing treaties", in *Social rights as human rights: a European challenge*, Drzewicki, K., Krause, C. and Rosas, A. (eds), Åbo Akademi, Åbo, 1994, pp. 73-87.

Schlager, E.B., "A hard look at compliance with 'soft law': the case of the OSCE", in *Commitment and compliance: the role of non-binding norms in the international legal system*, Shelton, D. (ed.), Oxford, Oxford University Press, 2000, pp. 346-372.

Simma, B., "Nato, the UN and the use of force: legal aspects", *European Journal of International Law*, 10, 1999, pp. 1-22.

Wippman, D., "The evolution and implementation of minority rights", *Fordham Law Review*, 66, 1997, pp. 612-626.

CHAPTER XI

EUROPE IN COUNTRY PERSPECTIVE: MODELS, DEVICES AND PROBLEMATIC SITUATIONS

It goes without saying that the international protection of minorities pursues the fundamental aim of generating adequate minority rights regimes at the domestic level. Indeed, the achievement of the objectives set out by international instruments could hardly be secured if those objectives were seen as disconnected from major efforts to enhance protection within specific country contexts. This chapter provides a short account of domestic and international practice affecting the position of certain minority groups and/or regarding certain patterns of protection for minorities in the European space.

1. In search of appropriate arrangements within domestic legal systems

The legal orders of European states largely conceive of "fundamental rights" as rights of an individual nature. Still, there are countries (for example, Hungary, Poland and Slovenia) that, while adhering to this conception in relation to "traditional" fundamental rights, recognise the "mixed" character of minority rights as combining individual rights and group protection aspects. Moreover, some countries have developed specific solutions concerning the protection of their own minorities, including the establishment of territorial and/or personal autonomy regimes within a federal or regional framework (Hofmann, 1997; Frowein and Bank, 2001).

In recent years, constructive national arrangements for minorities have been recommended in order to strengthen, where appropriate, the collective dimension of protection and to prevent ethnic conflicts. To this end, UN special rapporteur Eide, in his 1993 report on possible ways and means of facilitating the peaceful and constructive solution of problems involving minorities, indicates a set of measures that should be taken at the domestic and international levels in accordance with the relevant international standards. He stresses, *inter alia*, the need for arrangements enabling minorities to enjoy effective participation in the decision-making process of the state, particularly with regard to those matters which are crucial to the preservation of their own identity. In the same vein, a seminar on case studies on national minorities issues, organised by the ODIHR of the (then) CSCE in 1993, as directed by the concluding document adopted at the Helsinki follow-up meeting of 1992, highlighted a range of ways to ensure participation and representation of minorities in national institutions. Such ways ranged from securing representation in the legislature (for example, reserved seats and proportional electoral systems), to representation at the administrative level (for example, contact or advisory bodies and ombudsmen), to forms of personal or territorial autonomy.

The Council of Europe's Venice Commission has also addressed these questions, including the position of minorities under electoral laws, in the cited opinion on Article 11 of Recommendation 1201, thematic studies, opinions on specific domestic measures (see *infra*), and general surveys of the protection of minorities in federal and regional states (see, for example, the reports on electoral law and national minorities, CDL (2000) 4, and on participation of members of minorities in public life, CDL-MIN (1998) 1 rev; and generally Science and technique of democracy 1994 and 1997). Further elaboration is provided by the cited 1999 Lund Recommendations on the effective participation of national minorities in public life.

Most of the recommended measures draw upon positive examples of group accommodation in a number of European countries. As noted, some of these countries have adopted special regimes for accommodating their own minorities. Although such regimes typically result from specific political and/or territorial circumstances, they have long proved (relatively) successful within their own context, and, for that reason, are often referred to as possible "models" for other countries under comparable conditions.

2. Examples of long-established regimes in western Europe

a. The Swedish-speaking group and the Åland Islands in Finland

The Swedish-speaking population of Finland (amounting to six per cent of the total population) is not considered as a minority. Both languages, Finnish and Swedish, are national languages of Finland and enjoy equal legal standing (Article 14 of the Constitution Act). In practice, however, Swedish is a minority language. The Swedish-speaking population thus constitutes a "*de facto* minority" in Finland (this is also the way in which Finland describes this group in the report submitted under the Framework Convention in 1999, when indicating the beneficiaries of this treaty (ACFC/SR (99) 3)).

The Finnish approach to the question of the protection of the Swedish minority language reflects a compromise between personal and territorial elements. Whereas every Finnish citizen always has the right to use his own language – Finnish or Swedish – before the courts and the administrative authorities, the right of a Finnish citizen to receive service in his own language in other matters depends to a large extent on the linguistic character (monolingual or bilingual) of the district where he resides. Special provisions regulate the fields of access to public service and education, notably at primary and secondary levels.

Far-reaching autonomy is granted to the Åland Islands, the Swedish-speaking province of Finland (Hannikainen and Horn, 1997). Although the international legal foundation of the Åland Islands' autonomy is still the subject of discussion (some experts refer to the arrangement between Sweden and Finland on the preservation of Finnish-Swedish traditions in the Åland Islands, approved by a resolution of the Council of the League of Nations in June 1921, as amounting to a genuine agreement between these countries, whereas others contend that a rule of international customary law has developed over time in respect of the islands), the respective domestic regime is well-settled and largely uncontested. A new Autonomy Act, approved in 1991, has been in force since 1 January 1993. Swedish is the official language of the province and thus the official language of instruction. The provincial parliament and government are the main institutions representing the population. The parliament may pass provincial laws in a number of pre-defined areas, including education and culture. Where the parliament is believed to have exceeded its legislative competence or interfered in matters pertaining to the exclusive domain of the state, the President of the republic may refuse to enact a provincial act. The Autonomy Act can only be amended following the procedure laid down for constitutional amendments, further requiring the consent of the Åland Provincial Parliament. The Åland Islands have the right to collect income and property taxes, but the province receives an appropriation from the state to cover the costs of autonomy. Under the Autonomy Act, a regional Åland citizenship, called "right of domicile", may be acquired under the terms provided, as a prerequisite for the right to vote and stand for election in the Åland Islands' regional and municipal elections (Hannikainen, 1993 and 1996).

b. Other systems of minority and group protection in Scandinavia

Other relevant special provisions applied in Scandinavian countries include those concerning the Sami population in Norway, Sweden and Finland, and the population from the Faroe Islands and Greenland in Denmark. For instance, the Norwegian Constitution contains a specific provision for the protection of the Sami (Section 110(a)). In Finland, recent constitutional amendments recognise the Sami as indigenous people and afford them not only the right to enjoy their own culture but also autonomy as prescribed by parliament. In Norway and Sweden only ethnic Sami have the right to own and graze reindeer, whereas in Finland reindeer are owned by non-Sami as well. In these countries, the Sami also enjoy varying degrees of language rights – and sometimes also land rights – protection.

Interestingly, as reported by Finland under the Framework Convention in 1999 (ACFC/SR (99) 3), the Finnish Act on the Use of the Sami Language before Authorities makes it possible to use the language in the Sami homeland and before authorities and agencies referred to in law. The Sami people have the right to use the Sami language before authorities both orally and in writing and to receive a reply in the same language. And yet, a working group has been set up by the Ministry of Justice for improving the language rights of the Sami people, given that in practice the implementation of the above act (and other relevant legislation) is often related only to interpretation and translation services.

In recent years, Sami bodies of elected representatives have been established. The "Sami Parliament" (*Sameting*) has the task of asserting and protecting the interests and rights of the Sami. This advisory body constitutes a positive example of participation essentially based on the personal approach (it indeed does not presuppose a territorial concentration of the group).

Although the "Sami Parliament" has typically had only consultative authority, the Norwegian *Sameting* may now also monitor compliance with the administrative measures which promote Sami culture.

The Faroe Islands and Greenland are geographically separated from Denmark, though they are under its sovereignty. Both territories – inhabited mainly by the native people – have wide-ranging self-government with their own parliaments and executive governments, the Faroe Islands since 1948 and Greenland since 1978. The self-government for the benefit of the Inuit of Greenland is widely considered a model for the world's indigenous peoples. In this connection, however, it should be noted that, in terms of specific minority rights protection, as mentioned in Chapter III, concerns have been recently expressed by the advisory committee under the Framework Convention at what appears to be an exclusion of Faroese persons and Greenlanders from the scope of application of this treaty in Denmark.

c. The German-speaking minority in Italy

As already noted, the Austrian-Italian agreement of 5 September 1946 set out a special regime for the German-speaking element of South Tyrol, including the granting of a special statute of autonomy for the populations of the Province of Bolzano and of neighbouring bilingual townships of the Province of Trento (Article 2). That indeed resulted from negotiations undertaken in the aftermath of the second world war, in order to remedy the negative effects of aggressive assimilationist policies targeting the German-speaking population living in the South Tyrol, carried out by the Mussolini regime in the years following the cession of South Tyrol to Italy under the Treaty of Saint-Germain-en-Laye of 1919. However, the specific content of the said statute of autonomy was not spelled out in the agreement, notably in relation to its ethnic or territorial basis, and became the subject of serious dispute between the parties in connection with the incorporation of the relevant areas in the wider (and predominantly populated by native Italians) Region of Trentino-Alto Adige established by the Autonomy Act of 1948. Austria brought up the issue before the UN General Assembly in 1959 alleging a breach of Article 2 of the De Gasperi-Gruber Agreement; the General Assembly recommended the parties to resume negotiations to give effect to the agreement. In 1969, a so-called "package" was adopted by Italy concerning a large set of administrative and legislative measures designed to improve and expand South Tyrolean autonomy.

In partial implementation of the "package", Italy enacted in 1972 a new Autonomy Act for the Region of Trentino-Alto Adige. The legislative powers of the Provinces of Bolzano and Trieste were significantly expanded at the expense of both the region and the central government. Among the most significant provincial powers are those concerned with education (there are linguistically separate school systems), language ("equal standing" of German and Italian in the region), and proportional representation in the civil service. Although the autonomy arrangements for South Tyrol are not considered as entirely satisfactory, the system as a whole enjoys general acceptance and has proved workable in practice. In 1992, Austria officially stated that Italy had fully implemented the 1969 "package". Italy has admitted that the "package" may be used to interpret unclear provisions of the 1946 agreement, but it has never accepted the notion that the "package" constitutes *tout court* the object of an international obligation undertaken by Italy vis-à-vis Austria. Importantly, possible disputes regarding the interpretation and application of the 1946 agreement may now be referred to the ICJ, under the terms of an agreement signed by the parties in 1971 to that effect (modifying the scope of application *ratione temporis* of the 1957 European Convention for the Peaceful Settlement of Disputes), but ratified by them only in 1992.

d. The German minority in Denmark and the Danish minority in Germany

Schleswig is a German-Danish border region characterised by a mixed German-Danish population. A referendum in north and central Schleswig took place at the end of the first world war that endorsed the division of Schleswig between Denmark and Germany, putting an end to political controversies about the status of Schleswig arisen at the beginning of the nineteenth century (Lagler, 1980). A clear line of division between the two national groups was impossible to achieve, resulting in the creation of two minorities on both sides of the border.

The 1955 parallel declarations issued by the Government of the Federal Republic of Germany and the Government of Denmark, on the position of the Danish minority in the German *Land* of Schleswig-Holstein and the German minority on the other side of Schleswig under Danish sovereignty, provided a framework of protection which has proved quite effective so far. One of the most important provisions of the Bonn declaration is the exemption of the Danish minority from the five per cent exclusion clause in relation to parliamentary representation in Schleswig-Holstein. In 1958, the Danish group regained its representation in Kiel. The Copenhagen declaration re-established the right to maintain private secondary schools for the German minority. Consultative bodies have been set up on both sides of the border in order to discuss the matters concerning the respective groups. In Denmark, a "Liaison Committee" ensures contacts between the German minority and the Danish Government and Parliament, to negotiate domestic measures of relevance to the minority, as well as to discuss developments in the field of minorities at the international level.

e. Systems of minority and group protection in Spain and Belgium

Spain and Belgium have developed articulated systems based on the principle of autonomy (Juberías, 1998; Aguiar de Luque, 1994; Scholsem, 1994). The Spanish Constitution recognises and guarantees the right to autonomy to nationalities and regions of which Spain is composed. Of special interest is the recognition of a right of provinces with a specific historic regional status to acquire self-government in the form of autonomous communities. The Basques and the Catalans have formed their own special autonomous communities. Although the precise parameters of the regional powers have been the subject of considerable controversy and serious conflicts remain to be solved, overall the autonomy arrangements in Spain have led to a resurgence of regional identity, culture and language within ethnic communities. Moreover, the systems have proved sufficiently flexible to allow for adjustment and refinement.

The Belgian constitutional system is based on the recognition of three linguistic communities (Dutch, French and German) and three regions based on economic criteria, namely the Wallon Region, the Flemish Region and the Brussels Region. Such regions, in turn, include four linguistic regions, namely the French- and the German-speaking Region in relation to the Wallon Region, the Dutch-speaking Region in relation to the Flemish Region, and the bilingual Region of Brussels-Capital in relation to the Brussels Region. The cultural communities have mainly competencies regarding language and cultural matters, whereas the regions have territorial competence. Power-sharing schemes are in place as regards, for instance, the parliamentary activities (veto right) and the composition of the central government (proportional representation). The Belgian system has certainly secured peaceful co-existence among the major linguistic groups, notwithstanding the complexities generated by its functioning, as well illustrated by the already cited *Belgian Linguistics* and *Mothieu-Mohin and Clerfayt* cases, brought before the Strasbourg bodies in the late 1960s and 1980s respectively (see *supra*, Chapter VI), and further examined in the recent Venice Commission's Opinion on Possible Groups of Persons to which the Framework Convention for the Protection of National Minorities could be applied in Belgium (CDL-AD (2002) 1).

3. The eastern Europe context

a. Legal devices and their use at the domestic level: a brief overview

A range of legal devices for addressing the situation of minorities have been adopted or proposed within the more problematic context of eastern Europe (Brunner, 1996). Although group rights-based approaches enjoy little support from the countries concerned, a variety of measures have been taken or submitted for adoption which impinge upon the collective dimension of (the individual rights-based) minority rights protection. For instance, the constitutions of a number of countries explicitly protect minority education (for example, Croatia and Hungary); moreover, special constitutional and legislative provisions are provided concerning political representation (for example, Slovenia, Romania and Poland). Territorial and/or personal autonomy is occasionally granted or proposed as a suitable solution.

Although important examples of personal law regimes can be found in history, such as the well-known Millet system under Ottoman law, the Estonian Law on Cultural Autonomy of 1925 is often indicated as one of the most pertinent historical precedents for present-day purposes, based on the personal approach. It allowed the minority groups which so wished to establish their "cultural self-government" in order to run pre-defined affairs of special relevance to the protection of their cultural identity (education, culture, etc.). The "cultural council" was the highest decisive and legislative organ of the self-government, while the "cultural government" was the executive organ.

"Cultural curatoria" were local bodies entrusted with attending to the local affairs of the minority (Eide et al., 1998).

As nationalism grew in the 1930s, the application of the Estonian law of 1925 was progressively impaired. And yet, unlike a similar but less advanced system in Latvia, the Estonian personal regime survived until it was abolished under the Soviet occupation. The dissolution of the Soviet Union and former Yugoslavia has led to the introduction (or re-introduction) of legislation on cultural autonomy in several countries, including Latvia (1991), Slovenia (1991), Estonia (1993) and the Russian Federation (1996). In such countries as Latvia and Estonia (whose current legislation is inspired by the 1925 law) the effectiveness of these laws is limited due to restrictions primarily affecting the substantial group of non-citizens of Russian origin residing in these countries.

Various draft laws of a constitutional or an ordinary nature on the protection of minorities in specific eastern European countries are now being assessed by the Council of Europe, with a view to advising on how best to entrench minority rights in the context of the draft law in question and on its relation to existing legislation and regulations. In particular, the Venice Commission is contributing to the review of techniques of protection by, *inter alia*, delivering opinions on such draft laws, as for instance the opinion on the new draft constitutional law on the rights of national minorities in Croatia, adopted in July 2001 (CDL-INF (2001) 14) (for updated information in this regard, see http://www.venice.coe.int). The opinion devotes special attention to the provisions on electoral rights and minority self-government, which is being construed as a system of personal autonomy combined with some territorial aspects, and highlights remaining problem areas. Some pieces of minority domestic legislation in eastern Europe have proved controversial. One recent example is the act on Hungarians living in neighbouring countries, adopted by the Hungarian Parliament in June 2001, which confers special benefits on persons belonging to "kin-Hungarian minorities" residing in one of its neighbouring countries. In late 2001, the Venice Commission issued a report on the preferential treatment of national minorities by their kin-state (CDL-INF (2001) 19), in which this law is discussed at great length. For present purposes, it may be useful to note that the report importantly indicates the relevant principles of international law against which domestic legislation of this sort must be assessed, including the principles of the territorial integrity of states (in relation to the extraterritorial effects of the domestic law), *pacta sunt servanda* and friendly relations among states (both as a result of the entering into bilateral treaties which may address the matters covered by the domestic law), and respect for human rights and fundamental freedoms, notably the prohibition of discrimination (in respect of individuals, including members of other minorities, living in either the "kin"- or home-state).

b. The Hungarian approach

The Hungarian Minority Law of 1993 (No. LXXVII/1993) provides for a *sui generis* combination of territorial and personal autonomy elements.

235

Depending on the seats obtained by representatives of a national or ethnic minority in general local elections, "minority local governments" (in case of more than fifty per cent of seats won) or indirectly formed "local minority self-governments" (in case of less than fifty per cent, but at least thirty per cent, of seats won) may be established. In general, "local minority self-governments" are established through separate direct election, which takes place at the same time as the general local elections. Minority self-governments have extensive consent and consultation rights in matters concerning the cultural identity of the minorities concerned. Where set up, "minority local governments" are granted several additional competencies. These are neither strictly personal nor strictly territorially-based solutions: minority representatives may be elected by all citizens of the municipality, and thus, especially "local minority self-governments" may change or disappear in the next elections, and even where created, they do not hold distinct powers of public authorities.

On the other hand, "national minority self-governments" are elected by the minority representatives of the local governments and the minority self-governments, and mostly express their view on draft legislation which may affect critical areas of concern to the group. In spite of proposals for improving its effectiveness, overall the Hungarian system constitutes one of the most advanced domestic patterns of minority rights protection currently available in eastern Europe, and is apparently inspiring provision in other countries as well (see, for example, the above-mentioned Croatian draft constitutional law in respect of minority self-government).

4. Problematic situations in the larger Europe: some recent developments

As incidentally mentioned in Chapter IX, some multilateral arrangements address particularly serious situations generated by violent ethnic conflicts, such as those adopted or proposed in respect of Bosnia and Herzegovina, Kosovo and Northern Ireland. These are complex settlements involving domestic and international actors on the basis of a variety of legal undertakings. The following briefly outlines some aspects relating to the protection of minorities and other ethno-cultural groups.

a. The former Yugoslavia: the Carrington Draft and the Dayton Peace Agreement

In 1991, a document was prepared at the International Conference on the Former Yugoslavia, entitled "Treaty Provisions for the Convention" (so-called "Carrington Draft"), which contained a commitment to the protection of persons belonging to a "national or ethnic group", in accordance with UN, (then) CSCE, and Council of Europe standards. Notably, three sets of special provisions were provided benefiting:

- persons belonging to a national or ethnic group not forming a majority in the area where they lived (in connection with basic cultural guarantees);
- persons belonging to a national or ethnic group which constituted a substantial proportion in the area where they lived (in connection with

additional rights of participation in the decision-making process affecting them); and

– persons belonging to a national or ethnic group which constituted a regional majority (in connection with additional special status, including autonomous legislative, administrative and judicial bodies).

The Dayton Peace Agreement (signed by the Presidents of Bosnia and Herzegovina, Croatia and the FRY), which consists of the General Framework Agreement for Peace in Bosnia and Herzegovina (signed by the said presidents), and eleven annexes thereto, was initialled on 21 November 1995 and officially signed in Paris in 1996. It provides for a complex four-level power-sharing structure, comprising the state of Bosnia and Herzegovina with a few common institutions, the two "Entities" (namely, the Federation of Bosnia and Herzegovina and the Republika Srpska), cantons in the federation, and municipalities in both the federation and the Republika Srpska. In terms of human rights/minority rights standards, the Dayton Peace Agreement does not endorse the 1991 Carrington text, but the Constitution for Bosnia and Herzegovina set out in Annex 4 to the agreement provides for, *inter alia*, the equal enjoyment of rights and freedoms contained in several international agreements listed in Annex 1 to the constitution, including the 1992 European Charter for Regional or Minority Languages (but see on the latter, *supra* Chapter VI) and the 1995 Framework Convention (Article II.4 of the constitution).

Although the legal status of the relevant international agreements has been the subject of discussion, the view appears quite convincing that Article II.4 of the constitution does not contain a mere prohibition of discrimination, but that it actually incorporates by reference the agreements mentioned and explicitly gives the respective rights and freedoms (including minority rights) a constitutional rank (Nowak, 2000: 180-181). The protection of these rights and freedoms may not be abolished or diminished by constitutional amendment (Article X.2 of the constitution). On the other hand, under Article II, paragraphs 2 and 6, of the constitution, only the rights and freedoms set forth in the ECHR shall apply directly in Bosnia and Herzegovina, and shall prevail over all other law.

Annex 6 to the Dayton Peace Agreement contains an extensive "Agreement on Human Rights", which was signed by the three Bosnian parties, namely the former Republic of Bosnia-Herzegovina, the Federation of Bosnia and Herzegovina, and the Republika Srpska. Under Article 1 of this annex, the same instruments indicated above are incorporated by reference through a separate appendix, committing the parties to securing at the highest level the recognised human rights and fundamental freedoms. The annex provides for the establishment of a Commission on Human Rights consisting of the Office of the Ombudsman and the Human Rights Chamber. Within the limits of their different (non-judicial and judicial) competence, both of them may consider cases of violations of any of the human rights protected. Although the commission has to date suffered from budgetary, procedural and other constraints, including a lack of substantial political support from the parties involved, such a *sui generis* domestic supervisory institution (in fact, the composition and functions of the commission reveal the primary purpose of carrying out "external" supervision with the support of the main international institutions) might in principle contribute to the realisation of, among others, minority rights standards. In addition, Article 8 of Annex 6 enables (further) extensive international supervision, which covers the activities of the bodies established to monitor compliance with the international agreements listed in the appendix (for example, the HRC under the ICCPR or the advisory committee under the Framework Convention). There remains a fundamental problem of co-ordinating and streamlining the internal human rights institutions, and better clarifying their relation to the international bodies concerned.

b. The Rambouillet Draft Agreement on Kosovo

With regard to the crisis of Kosovo (a region of the FRY that is predominantly populated by ethnic Albanians, who are, however, a national minority in the whole FRY), the "Interim Agreement for Peace and Self-Government in Kosovo", submitted on 23 February 1999 in the context of the "Rambouillet talks" promoted by the Contact Group for the Former Yugoslavia, does not reveal support for the independence option. Instead, it provides for a substantial autonomy for the region coupled with a set of human rights guarantees to be applied within and outside Kosovo. Unlike the Dayton Peace Agreement, no list of human rights instruments is provided. Rather, similarly to the 1995 accord, it is indicated that the ECHR and its protocols shall apply directly in Kosovo and shall have priority over all other law.

Additional rights are granted to "national communities" within Kosovo, basically designed to preserve their cultural identity, "in accordance with international standards and the Helsinki Final Act" (Article VII, paragraph 1, of the Framework Convention). More controversially, each national community could elect and establish its own institutions, which it was feared might favour the establishment of a parallel state structure within Kosovo. Also controversial is the possibility for the national communities represented in the assembly to submit so-called "vital interest motions", amounting to an attempted veto of legislation (Weller, 1999). The case of Kosovo well illustrates the complexities arising out of the existence of more than one population group in the same area, though the all-embracing concept of "national communities" suggests, in line with the traditional understanding of minority (see *supra*, Chapter III) that, for instance, the Serb group is not perceived of as a true minority, due to the fact that its members belong to the majority population (similar considerations arise, *mutatis mutandis,* as to the relatively broader concept of "national or ethnic group" in the context of the cited 1991 Carrington Draft).

The civilian component of the implementation process provided for in the Rambouillet Draft Agreement (primarily falling under the responsibility of the OSCE) consists, *inter alia,* of an ombudsman who may consider alleged or apparent violations of the applicable human rights and fundamental freedoms in Kosovo and the rights of members of national communities spelled out in the text. The lack of judicial human rights bodies compares unfavourably with the control mechanism established by the Dayton Peace Agreement for the protection of human rights.

Under UN Security Council Resolution 1244 (*1999*) on Kosovo, the "Rambouillet accords" must be taken fully into account, notably in relation to the establishment of substantial autonomy and self-government in Kosovo, "pending a final settlement" (paragraph 11, sub-paragraph a). This latter reference in fact confines independence, as a residual option, to an agreement freely entered into by the parties. The responsibilities of the international civil presence in Kosovo authorised under that resolution include the promotion and protection of human rights (paragraph 11, sub-paragraph j). On 15 May 2001, the Head of the United Nations Interim Administration in Kosovo (UNMIK), based on Security Council Resolution 1244 (*1999*), adopted Regulation 2001/9 establishing a Constitutional Framework for Provisional Self-Government in Kosovo. This document builds upon not only the Rambouillet Draft Agreement but also the example of the Dayton Peace Agreement (for an overview of this Regulation, including relevant human rights issues, in the light of existing instruments, see Stahn 2001).

c. The Northern Ireland Peace Agreement

The Northern Ireland Peace Agreement, which was reached by the British and Irish governments and other participants in the multi-party talks on Good Friday, 10 April 1998, and then annexed to a separate agreement between the two governments entered into on that same day, illustrates yet another recent attempt at group accommodation in a "troubling spot", this time in western Europe. The agreement sets out a framework for a constructive approach to the complex situation in Northern Ireland. Although Northern Ireland is part of the United Kingdom, the situation reveals a particular, *de facto*, double minority question: the Catholic community is a minority in Northern Ireland and the UK as a whole, whereas the Protestant-Unionist population is in the minority in the island of Ireland, and would become a minority under a united Ireland.

A specific section of the agreement on rights, safeguards and equality of opportunity contains provisions committing the signatories to, *inter alia*, religious freedom and linguistic diversity, as well as "mutual respect" and "parity of esteem" between the communities concerned. The United Kingdom is to consider ratifying the 1992 European Charter for Regional or Minority Languages (at the time of writing, the United Kingdom had only signed it), and undertakes to take action in order to protect and promote the Irish language. Although there is no undertaking to entrench the rights listed in paragraph 1 (human rights) in a legal form at the domestic level, there are specific obligations on the British Government to incorporate the ECHR fully into Northern Irish law (which includes, unlike the 1998 Human Rights Act, the power for courts to invalidate parliamentary, in this case Northern Ireland Assembly, legislation for its inconsistency with ECHR rights), to secure statutory protection against discrimination in a number of fields, including religion (this commitment has now gained legislative force under the 1998 Northern Ireland Act), and to consider recommendations concerning a Bill of Rights specific to Northern Ireland. The latter would go beyond not only the said guarantees but also those contained in the above-mentioned 1998 Human Rights Act introduced for the whole of the United Kingdom. Interestingly, paragraph 4 of the part of the above section entitled "human rights", indicates that the additional rights should reflect "the principles of mutual respect for the identity and ethos of both communities and parity of esteem". It is clear that issues relating to language, education and cultural identity generally will feature prominently in this context. On the Irish side, there is an obligation to improve the protection of human rights in relation to an equivalent level of protection as afforded in Northern Ireland, by, *inter alia*, ratifying the 1995 Framework Convention (which the Irish government did in 1999).

Besides, the agreement sets up a power-sharing ("consociational") government for Northern Ireland elected by proportional representation. Cross-community support (parallel consent or weighed majority) is required in critical decisions. More controversially, the assembly members are held to declare their identity – Nationalist, Unionist or other. Gilbert (1998) notes that self-declaration is open to abuse, and may work for making the respective communities monolithic and static, and that those who declare themselves as "other" will have no direct influence on cross-community matters. At present, political efforts are under way to make the devolved government fully effective.

Importantly, a new independent Northern Ireland Human Rights Commission is entrusted with keeping laws and practices under review, making recommendations to government, promoting information and awareness about human rights, considering draft legislation referred to by the new assembly, and where appropriate, bringing, or assisting in the bringing of, court cases. In addition, it is expected to advise the British Government on the above-mentioned Bill of Rights for Northern Ireland "drawing as appropriate on international instruments and experience". A similar independent body is set up in the Republic of Ireland, while representatives from both commissions are appointed to a joint committee dealing with human rights matters in the entire island. However, the lack of a distinct "minority rights ombudsman" seems to be a shortcoming. Two other bodies are specific to Irish questions, the North/South Ministerial Council, set up to deal with issues of concern to Belfast and Dublin and the British-Irish Intergovernmental Conference, within which the Irish Government may submit views and proposals in view of its special interest in Northern Ireland. In terms of minority rights protection, the latter body gives the "kin-state" a far-reaching role in suggesting solutions for the "kin-minority". Finally, the secession of Northern Ireland and concomitant creation of a sovereign united Ireland are not excluded but, as provided for in the separate agreement between the British and Irish governments, must be agreed to by a majority of the people of Northern Ireland (while acknowledging that at this stage such a majority wants Northern Ireland to remain part of the United Kingdom), as part of the people of the island of Ireland's right to self-determination. In this respect, Bell and Cavanaugh (1999) have spoken of "constructive ambiguity", the rationale of which would lie in an attempt at advancing the peace process by avoiding deadlocks on this rather controversial aspect.

5. Concluding observations

To a greater or lesser degree, the situations sketched out above provide models and/or techniques which in appropriate circumstances may be considered in other contexts as well, in accordance with international instruments. In fact, international standards and domestic regimes generally influence and shape each other, and at least some of the latter may be viewed as early signals of what was to be elaborated upon at a later stage within multilateral forums (Defeis, 1999). On the other hand, as the general international human rights/minority rights corpus remains silent or less advanced compared to the articulated and context-specific details or ramifications of each special regime, it nevertheless sets out the fundamental principles to which domestic measures must conform. The recent case of the 2001 Hungarian law on "kin-minorities" abroad provides a useful illustration of this latter point.

At the same time, most recent (adopted or proposed) arrangements generated by conflict situations, such as the ones embodied in the Dayton Peace Agreement, the Rambouillet Draft Agreement and the Good Friday Agreement, reflect contemporary, forward-looking tendencies in international law and diplomacy. Minority issues are being dealt with in an overall context of "increased interdependence, accelerated regionalisation and marked development of the international legal systems" (Mertus, 1999: 278). As emphasised earlier (see *supra*, Chapter X), political (including security), economic and legal considerations have been brought to the fore in a comprehensive effort to consolidate peace, democracy and human rights. The activities of international and regional actors such as financial institutions, security arrangements, etc., are being supplemented by those of transnational social forces (NGOs, etc.). International law principles of internal self-determination, equality and non-discrimination, protection of cultural identity through, *inter alia*, effective political participation and peaceful cross-border contacts, viewed in terms of interrelation and indivisibility, further pierce "the veil of sovereignty" and set the framework for constructive approaches to the accommodation of minorities and other groups, as well as, ultimately, the population at large. As clearly illustrated by the above-mentioned problematic country contexts, such responses are impinging upon not only the substance but also the "shape" of sovereignty, causing a shift of responsibility for supervision and enforcement to multiple entities acting below or above the level of central state governance. For instance, the cross-border forums of the Belfast Agreement typically tap into "federalising" trends combining greater integration "at the centre" with an expansion of authority "at the periphery" through "regional" structures penetrating national borders and thus watering down absolute assumptions of territorial sovereignty. As Wedgwood notes, "[t]he state has lost its opacity" (Wedgwood, 1998: 242). In fact, the organisation of existing states is being redefined accordingly, as explained by Slaughter in relation to those countries torn by ethnic conflict:

States traditionally were conceived of as billiard balls and black boxes – organized in any fashion their rulers wished. Human rights law introduced standards for the way in which these rulers treated their subjects. The array of international legal responses to ethnic conflict reflects a further step toward the imposition of formal requirements concerning the way in which states are themselves constituted. (Slaughter, 1998: 144)

The general legal reference framework to facilitate the settlement of ethno-political conflicts in Europe, which is being drafted by the Venice Commission (see *supra,* Chapters VI and VIII), largely relates to such efforts, in search of wider legal patterns which situate the protection of minorities within the context of a constructive interaction between constitutional forms of multi-layered distribution of powers (federalism, regionalism, etc.) and international guarantees (see also Recommendation 43 (1998) on territorial autonomy and national minorities, and Recommendation 70 (1999) on local law/special status, adopted by the Congress of Local and Regional Authorities of Europe).

The human rights components of such complex approaches are outlined in, for example, the cited 1993 Eide report and the 1999 Lund Recommendations, in conformity with international law in general, and international human rights law in particular. Still, one should caution that provisions of the leading instruments may provide arguments that the functioning of certain group accommodation arrangements, such as autonomy schemes, or aspects of them, are (or may prove) inconsistent with human rights. Hence, once again the crucial role of the principles of international human rights law, not only as starting points for developing a protective regime, but first and foremost as yardsticks for closely assessing its permissibility.

Bibliography

Aguiar de Luque, L., "Les minorités et l'Etat des autonomies en Espagne", CDL-MIN (1994) 002.

Bell, C. and Cavanaugh, K., "'Constructive ambiguity' or internal self-determination? Self-determination, group accommodation, and the Belfast Agreement", *Fordham International Law Journal*, 22, 1999, pp. 1345-1371.

Bell, C., "Minority rights and conflict resolution in Northern Ireland", in *Minority rights in the "new" Europe*, Cumper, P. and Wheatley, S. (eds), Kluwer Law International, The Hague, 1999, pp. 305-323.

Brunner, G., *Nationality problems and minority conflicts in eastern Europe: strategies for Europe*, revised edition, Bertelsmann Foundation Publishers, Gütersloh, 1996.

De Rossanet, B., "Protecting the rights of ethnic and national communities and minorities: the experience of the International Conference on the Former Yugoslavia", *International Journal on Group Rights*, 2, 1994, pp. 79-89.

Defeis, E.F., "Minority protection and bilateral agreements: an effective mechanism", *Hastings International Law and Comparative Law Review*, 22, 1999, pp. 291-321.

Dinstein, Y. and Tabory, M. (eds), *The protection of minorities and human rights*, Martinus Nijhoff Publishers, Dordrecht, 1992.

Edwards, G.E., "Hungarian national minorities: recent developments and perspectives", *International Journal on Minority and Group Rights*, 5, 1998, pp. 345-367.

Eide, A., in co-operation with Greni, V. and Lundberg, M., "Cultural autonomy: concept, content, history and role in the world order", in *Autonomy: applications and implications*, Suksi, M. (ed.), Kluwer Law International, The Hague, 1998, pp. 251-272.

Frowein, J.A. and Bank, R., "The participation of minorities in decision-making processes", *Heidelberg Journal of International Law*, 61, 2001, pp. 1-28.

Geroe, M.R. and Gump, T.K., "Hungary and a new paradigm for the protection of ethnic minorities in central and eastern Europe", *Columbia Journal of Transnational Law*, 32, 1995, pp. 673-705.

Gilbert, G., "The Northern Ireland Peace Agreement, minority rights and self-determination", *International and Comparative Law Quarterly*, 47, 1998, pp. 943-950.

Hanneman, A.J., "Independence and group rights in the Baltics: a double minority problem", *Virginia Journal of International Law*, 35, 1995, pp. 485-527.

Hannikainen, L., "The status of minorities, indigenous peoples and immigrant and refugee groups in four Nordic states", *Nordic Journal of International Law*, 65, 1996, pp. 1-71.

Hannikainen, L., *Cultural, linguistic and educational rights in the Åland Islands: an analysis in international law*, Publications of the Advisory Board for International Human Rights Affairs, Helsinki, 1993.

Hannikainen, L. and Horn, F. (eds), *Autonomy and demilitarisation in international law: the Åland Islands in a changing Europe*, Kluwer Law International, The Hague, 1997.

Hannum, H. (ed.), *Documents on autonomy and minority rights*, Martinus Nijhoff Publishers, Dordrecht, 1993.

Hofmann, R., "Minority rights: individual or group rights? A comparative view on European legal systems", *German Yearbook of International Law*, 40, 1997, pp. 356-382.

Juberías, C.F., "Regionalization and autonomy in Spain: the making of the 'Estado de las Autonomías'", in *Autonomy: applications and implications*, Suksi, M. (ed.), Kluwer Law International, The Hague, 1998, pp. 97-124.

Lagler, W., "The Danish minority in West Germany and the German minority in Denmark", in *World minorities in the eighties: a third volume in the series*, Ashworth, G. (ed.), Quartermaine House Ltd, Sunbury, 1980, pp. 32-37.

McGoldrick, D., "From Yugoslavia to Bosnia: accommodating national identity in national and international law", *International Journal on Minority and Group Rights*, 6, 1999, pp. 1-63.

Mertus, J., "The Dayton Peace Accords: lessons from the past and for the future", in *Minority rights in the "new" Europe*, Cumper, P. and Wheatley, S. (eds), Kluwer Law International, The Hague, 1999, pp. 261-283.

Minority Rights Group (ed.), *World directory of minorities*, Minority Rights Group International, London, 1997.

Müllerson, R., *International law, rights and politics: developments in eastern Europe and the CIS*, Routledge, London, 1994.

Myntti, K., *Minority rights, human rights: legal protection of minorities in the Baltic region*, Uppsala University, Uppsala, 1995.

Nowak, M., "Lessons for the international human rights regime from the Yugoslav experience", *Collected Courses of the Academy of European Law*, VIII-2, 2000, pp. 141-208.

Packer, J. and Myntti, K. (eds), *The protection of ethnic and linguistic minorities in Europe*, Åbo Akademi, Åbo, 1995.

Scholsem, J.-C., "Fédéralisme et protection des minorités en Belgique", CDL-MIN (1994) 003.

Science and technique of democracy, *Local self-government, territorial integrity and protection of minorities*, Collection No. 16, Council of Europe Publishing, Strasbourg, 1997.

Science and technique of democracy, *The protection of minorities: collected texts of the European Commission for Democracy through Law*, Collection No. 9, Council of Europe Publishing, Strasbourg, 1994.

Slaughter, A., "Pushing the limits of the liberal peace", in *International law and ethnic conflict*, Wippman, D. (ed.), Cornell University Press, Ithaca and London, 1998, pp. 128-144.

Stahn, C., "Constitution Without a State? Kosovo Under the United Nations Constitutional Framework for Self-Government". *Leiden Journal of International Law*, 14, 2001, pp. 531-561.

Türk, D., "National minorities in Austria, Italy and in the successor states of the former Yugoslavia", in *Volksgruppen im Spannungsfeld von Recht und Souveränität in Mittel- und Osteuropa*, Ermacora, F., Tretter, H. and Pelzl, A. (eds), Braumüller, Vienna, 1993, pp. 39-54 and 118-120.

Wedgwood, R., "Limiting the use of force in civil disputes", in *International law and ethnic conflict*, Wippman, D. (ed.), Cornell University Press, Ithaca and London, 1998, pp. 242-255.

Weller, M., *The crisis in Kosovo 1989-1999: international documents and analysis*, 1, Cambridge University Press, Cambridge, 1999.

Yacoub, J., *Les minorités dans le monde: faits et analyses*, Desclée De Brouwer, Paris, 1998.

CONCLUSIONS

REINFORCING THE PILLARS
FOR A COHERENT ARCHITECTURE

If anything, the range of questions touched upon in the previous chapters reveal that the specific architecture of international minority rights is still in the making. The description of such rights as a very contemporary *problématique* in international law and relations, the origins of which lie in the collapse of communism in the former Soviet bloc, would amount to a historical misperception.

Looking back to earlier times, there is indeed ample evidence that the question of the protection of minorities has most often appeared on the international agenda, attesting to the unrealistic (to say the least) nature of the nation-state project, according to which political and cultural boundaries should coincide. Consequently, although the outcomes generated by the minority question throughout history have been remarkably different depending on the legal and political setting, it would be equally incorrect to characterise minority rights in terms of their *sic et simpliciter* return to the international stage. After 1945, they fell into the strict leash of cold-war dynamics, remained somehow obscured or unresolved, but never faded away. Rather, the post-cold-war upsurge of minority problems in numerous countries, coupled with social tension and even violence, has prompted the international community to tackle the issue of minorities more constructively than in the past, thereby giving renewed emphasis to the principle that such issue is a matter of legitimate international concern and does not constitute exclusively an internal affair of the respective state. It is thus accurate to view the present efforts as an attempt to avoid past failures and to appropriately advance upon past achievements. However, despite the importance of certain gains, much more remains to be done. Some central aspects should be sketched out, suggesting a few concluding thoughts.

The prospects for enhancing the level of protection for minorities are likely to remain linked to a "minimalist" definition of "minority" for purposes of international law, as reflected in the Capotorti definition, which mandates minority status for the groups fulfilling the respective criteria. From a *de jure condito* perspective, a broad concept is still unproven. From a legal policy perspective, it is especially noteworthy that the magnitude of problems of traditional groups all over the world (Minority Rights Group, 1997) still awaits a comprehensive universal treaty response, and many of them still struggle for recognition and appropriate protection at home. In the latter respect, there is reason to believe that taking the limits of "minority" further would encroach on "unfinished business", and a paradox would result:

minority rights regimes would be most effective in relation to entitlements which are least needed, blurring the distinction between such regimes and general human rights (including the particular instruments elaborating upon them). With regard to the ICCPR, the HRC's jurisprudence under Article 27 is remarkably evolving, but given that the provision is part of a universal human rights treaty to which a variety of states with different cultures and legal systems have adhered, one may wonder whether the promoted expansive reading of its scope of application *ratione personæ*, even if it was accepted at some point in time by a large majority of such states (which, at best, does not seem to be forthcoming), would inhibit major rights-enhancing developments by reducing the standards to the level of the least rights-protective parties. A similar effect would be even less satisfactory under the expanded European system, comprising states with largely concordant values and systems, committed to the rule of law and with a comparatively higher sensitivity to the protection of minorities.

On the other hand, as noted earlier, whereas available human rights provisions may be used to detect abuse of power by states in relation to the citizenship criterion vis-à-vis traditional groups, an appropriate expansion of the range of beneficiaries of protection (notably through the special granting of rights afforded to minority members rather than minority status) is far from contrary to international law. In fact, it is particularly suitable to groups or individuals whose situation stands in a sort of "grey area". Such groups as Roma/Gypsies raise even more specific problems, since they can be only partly accommodated through the classic canon of international minority rights. Although in a number of cases they fully qualify for minority status (see, for example, the Finnish or Hungarian Roma), or may simply benefit from provisions focused on minorities, this group generally calls for *ad hoc* anti-discrimination efforts. A fundamental aspect is to improve the social and economic condition of its members and to respond to their long-standing travelling lifestyle, even though, as also acknowledged by the EurCtHR in the recent cases concerning Gypsy individuals (see *supra*, Chapter VI), many Gypsies no longer live a wholly nomadic existence.

At the universal level, steps in this direction are being taken. For instance, the CERD held in August 2000 a thematic session on a wide range of Roma issues within the context of the ICERD, and delivered General Recommendation XXVII (57) on discrimination against Roma. This text highlights the necessary steps, including special measures, that should be taken by states parties to the ICERD for the benefit of Roma communities especially in regard to racial violence, education and living conditions, and indicate additional concerns of a general nature, such as discrimination against Roma in legislation regarding citizenship and naturalisation. This recommendation is also recalled in the declaration and programme of action adopted by the UN World Conference against Racism, Racial Discrimination, Xenophobia and Related Intolerance, which calls upon states to adopt specific measures for the benefit of Roma, stressing the need for consulting these people in order to identify their concerns and design adequate policies aimed at combating racism and related phenomena (paragraphs 39-44 of the programme of action). Interestingly, this text does not equate the Roma issue with the general question of ethnic, religious or linguistic minorities, but rather recognises this issue after emphasising that members of "certain groups" face barriers arising from a complex interplay of factors (paragraph 67 of the declaration). Along the same lines, a preliminary study on the subject has been submitted to the UN Working Group on Minorities following a request from the Sub-Commission on the Promotion and Protection of Human Rights (Yeung Sik Yuen, 2000).

At the European level, the ECHR provisions, including the prohibition of discrimination in Article 14, and prospectively the general equality clause in Protocol No. 12, apply to Roma members whether or not they are specifically identified as being in "association with a national minority", given the non-exhaustive nature of the prohibited grounds for distinction in both such provisions and their additional reference to race, language and religion. Recommendation 1203, adopted by the Parliamentary Assembly of the Council of Europe in February 1993, indicates that Gypsies are "a true European minority, but one that does not fit in the definitions of national or linguistic minorities". This *sui generis* position has been acknowledged in the 1994 Instrument for the Protection of Minority Rights adopted by CEI member states. Although this instrument applies to typical long-established groups forming an integral part of the society of the states where they live, as defined in Article 1, in Article 7 states recognise the "particular problems" of Roma and undertake not only to preserve and promote their identity, but also to facilitate their social integration and eliminate all forms of intolerance against them.

In fact, the Council of Europe, the EU and the OSCE are developing a "Roma discourse" irrespective of the intensity of its link to "minorities" and "minority rights" (see also *supra*, Chapter VII). As emphasised in the *amicus* brief by the European Roma Rights Centre in the Gypsy cases recently brought before the EurCtHR, there is indeed an ever greater resolve among international institutions to tackle the position of Roma through specific measures, particularly with regard to accommodation and general living conditions. Apart from Recommendation 1203 (1993) of the Parliamentary Assembly of the Council of Europe, which singles out Gypsies for "special protection", ECRI adopted in 1998 Recommendation No. 3 on combating racism and intolerance against Roma/Gypsies (Council of Europe Doc. CRI (98) 29), in which special attention is drawn to prejudices and specific discriminatory practices of which Roma persons continue to be victims, in such fields as employment, housing, education, administration of justice and participation in the decision-making process (see also Hernesniemi and Hannikainen, 2000). Roma matters are attracting considerable attention from the EU as well. In 1994, the European Parliament adopted a resolution on Gypsies urging member states and EU institutions to do everything in their power to assist in the improvement of the social situation of Gypsies and travelling people in Europe. A compendium of EU action in specific support of Roma communities in eastern Europe is provided by a report published by the European Commission in December 1999 (see http://www.europa.eu.int). Especially important are the Guiding Principles for Improving the Situation of the Roma adopted in November 1999 by the EU regarding the situation of Gypsies in the candidate countries, based on pertinent recommendations from the Council of Europe and the OSCE HCNM. The OSCE set up a contact point for Roma and Sinti issues at the Budapest Summit of 1994 (see the Budapest Document: paragraph 23), following a report on Roma produced by the HCNM in 1993 and a thematic seminar held by the ODIHR in co-operation with the high commissioner and the Council of Europe. In April 2000, as a result of an earlier special human dimension meeting on Roma and Sinti issues, the high commissioner delivered the report on the situation of Roma and Sinti in the OSCE region, offering country assessments and general recommendations. This report draws particular attention to, *inter alia*, the past policies of forced "sedentarisation" and the issue of providing nomadic or semi-nomadic Gypsies with suitable parking sites.

In the light of this impressive amount of *ad hoc* action, it would appear that, similarly to the situation of indigenous peoples, the unique position of Roma (and, by analogy, of "Roma-like" groups) might be more effectively addressed by separate instruments which attempt to develop a comprehensive legal framework elaborating upon relevant human rights standards, without prejudice to a partial overlap with the protection of minorities.

Based on fundamental equality and non-forced assimilation or cultural integrity precepts, the "right to identity", going beyond minimum physical existence and anti-discrimination entitlements, stands out as the overarching guarantee informing the whole notion of minority rights. The purely "hands off approach" originally endorsed in Article 27 of the ICCPR has given way to an intensive search for more adequate prescriptions. The precise ramifications of this right are still the subject of discussion, but at least education, language and participation can be identified as key areas of "positive" protection. Religion is likely to become one more test area for action of some kind (Gilbert, 1997). Viewed against the background of general human rights, on the one hand, and special rights or categories of rights, such as the right to self-determination and indigenous peoples' rights, on the other, it is fair to assume that those areas are unlikely to produce group rights in the near future. The "model" of indigenous rights, whatever one's view of it, appears unavailable for a minority rights discourse. In fact, the basic challenge to international law and decision makers is to further clarify and reinforce the aspects of individual protection which are critical to the preservation of the cultural identity of minorities *qua* collectivities. In essence, as already suggested by the post-first world war treaty experiment, this would have to be a function of appropriate additional elaboration upon distinctions between general or minimum rights and their proactive minority counterparts. For instance, mother-tongue education and communication with public authorities, and effective participation in pertinent decision-making processes, place international law before the task of better defining their specific rights-protective contours, against the backdrop of general or minimum entitlements in the field of education, language and political participation as recognised by international human rights instruments and jurisprudence (for example, under Article 2 of the First Protocol to the ECHR and Articles 19 and 25 of the ICCPR).

Many present and earlier sources are of important guidance in this respect, but some such sources may prove more useful than others. An example is offered by minority education rights as recognised in Article 9 of the 1919 Polish Minorities Treaty, Article 8 of the proposed protocol to the ECHR contained in Recommendation 1201 of the Parliamentary Assembly of the Council of Europe, and Article 9 of the Venice Commission's draft convention. All of them limit these special rights to members of quite "visible", as it were, minority population groups, as Article 14 of the Framework Convention does; for purposes of contemporary law-making, an important question is to clarify "considerable proportion", "substantial percentage" and so forth, and strike a proper balance between those parameters that benefit primarily, if not only, territorial minorities and those which take proper account also of the needs of individuals belonging to minorities which are dispersed in smaller or greater numbers throughout the country. All of those texts cover a straightforward entitlement of minority members to learn their own language in the public primary schools (Recommendation 1201 does not specify the type of schooling), while the additional right to receive instruction in the mother tongue in state schools is either fully recognised at the primary school level (Article 9 of the 1919 Polish treaty) or not excluded at any schooling level (Article 8, paragraph 1, of the proposed protocol to the ECHR contained in Recommendation 1201) or (cautiously) recognised in relation to all or part of the obligatory schooling (Article 9 of the Venice Commission's draft convention). Importantly, Article 9 of the Polish Minorities Treaty guaranteed an "equitable share" of public funds under the state, municipal or other budget, for the benefit of, *inter alia*, minority educational purposes. As indicated in Chapter I, a reference to an "equitable proportion" of public funds for the purpose of establishing and maintaining minority schools and cultural institutions also appeared in an earlier draft minority article to be included in the proposed UDHR, but was eventually dropped, along with the eventual rejection of the entire revised draft article. It is perhaps time to reconsider these provisions in the context of present-day discussions of "effective" minority rights protection.

International law neither authorises nor forbids the secession of minorities from the state where they live; secession as such is, *au fond*, referred to the domestic jurisdiction of the state concerned. At the same time, participation rights for the benefit of minority members within the state, as well as minority rights generally, suggest a linkage to a materially-human rights-based process of internal self-determination benefiting the whole population of the state. Viewed from this perspective, firmly entrenched minority political rights, going beyond minimum participation requirements and reaching out, where appropriate, to arrangements based on decentralisation of power in their manifold variants, are increasingly being indicated as meaningful ways of responding to the "free choice" demand attached to self-determination of all segments of society. International law does not enjoin specific outcomes in this regard; it provides for framework principles and the "procedural" parameter of the "effectiveness" of minority participation in affairs affecting them as a tool for developing and assessing constructive arrangements, in conformity with international human rights law. One may wonder, however, whether greater direct protection should be provided, particularly in the form of a specific consultation right under clearly defined circumstances. As for autonomy arrangements, some states have adopted them with positive results within their own territories, and are supporting the same approach in various crisis contexts, while there is a growing level of attention to the constitutional implications of this issue from international bodies. Here lies another important area of scholarly analysis and institutional action for the years ahead, ultimately tied up with changing conceptions of sovereignty premised on a close relation of human rights responses to the organisation of existing states rather than the creation of new ones.

Irrespective of the narrower or wider legal perspective implied by the various components of the "right to identity", the search for more adequate and effective protection for minorities brings two key "structural" dimensions and their respective weaknesses to the fore. One is the quality and legal status of current minority rights standards. Although instruments on minority rights are proliferating, their reach is limited, substantively and/or geographically. For instance, the UN 1992 declaration is universally applicable, but *per se* non-legally binding, whereas the 1995 Framework Convention, as a legally binding regime, only applies to the European context and its provisions are couched in a rather vague language, leaving it to states parties a considerable measure of discretion as to the measures to be adopted in order to implement them properly. Generally speaking, the language of "state undertakings" is preferred to the language of "rights", further compounding the difficulties generated by the specific enforceability of standards. As noted, the incorporation of these instruments in some of the recent bilateral treaties dealing in whole or in part with minority issues can hardly avoid reproducing the same drawback when it comes to identifying the actual level of protection to which minority members are entitled. The shift to a truly "legal" approach, be it on a multilateral or bilateral level, calls for rationalisation and strengthening of minority rights standards through clearly and broadly stated rights and obligations. In particular, multilateral treaties and customary law should gain a more prominent role in the field of minority rights, though "soft law" texts should help shape the content of these rights. The point here is that if minority rights are to be seriously treated as part and parcel of the contemporary canon of international human rights, if they are thus expected not to be dominated by "balkanisation" (namely, conflict-dependent and context-specific) perspectives, but viewed as much as possible as "normal law" consisting of "normal" rights addressed to individuals belonging to particular groups, then a better understanding of their implications cannot be left to a more or less concealed political approach, or confined to a predominantly "narrative" exercise (as in the OSCE context), but must show a tangible legal connotation. The use of non-binding instruments is invaluable to the extent that it is reasonably expected to begin or facilitate the process of consensus by adding more clarity and detail to the substance of protection and/or to help enhance the effectiveness of existing "hard law" provisions, rather than perpetuate disagreement over the content of the norm or norms in question. More importantly, non-binding measures, or the "shopping-list" approach, cannot be viewed as a substitute for legal duties to the extent that they exist or can be established. In this respect, the discussion about positive duties under Article 27 of the ICCPR and the Framework Convention is somehow indicative: here interpretation becomes a sophisticated matter of shifting boundaries between what is required and what is justified, or inspired, by the norm.

With this in mind, "effective implementation" stands out as the other problematic "structural" dimension. The critical questions raised by the varying degrees of legal significance attached to minority rights standards are indeed only part of the picture, though an important one. In fact, beyond the language of "hard" or "soft" law in the mould of which minority rights norms have been, or may be, cast, lies the deeper aspect that compliance seems most directly linked to the existence of effective and independent scrutiny (Shelton, 2000: 462). The "doctrine of effectiveness" developed by the EurCtHR provides quite a telling example in a much celebrated context of human rights protection: the ECHR would remain largely "theoretical or illusory" unless its provisions are interpreted and applied by the Court in such a manner as to make them "practical and effective", for the benefit of individuals. *A fortiori*, this vision can be extended to the field of minority rights, in which independent supervision is needed not only to investigate possible abuses or redress violations, but also, and most importantly, to resolve questions relating to the content of the relevant provisions and the way they should be applied in practice (on declaratory and compensatory aspects of international judicial decisions, see Shelton, 1999: 199-279). In sum, "effective implementation" largely strikes at the substantive core of minority rights protection. The PCIJ's review, even though less far-reaching than it could have been, provides an early example of this expounding perspective, when applying the principle of effective interpretation in landmark cases involving minority clauses (see, for example, *Minority Schools in Albania*, PCIJ Series A/B, No. 64, 1935: 18-19). The present-day experience of the HRC, with its contextual incremental approach to Article 27 rights, in fact confirms that third-party supervision is essential to making textual data meaningful and operative. It goes without saying that independent control, far from being a mere international exercise, is meant to induce enforcement at the domestic level.

Not surprisingly, the implementation of human rights norms is now becoming one of the major preoccupations of different international institutions, demanding serious technical and financial involvement. In the area of minority rights, effective means of control are even more necessary, due to the manifest interrelation of the protection of minorities and internal as well as international stability. Although the growing emphasis on "positive" protection of minority groups is being paralleled by efforts at "positive" supervision in an attempt to assist states in bringing their laws and practices into line with international standards, the enforcement system remains largely inadequate, obviously in connection with the shortcomings of the entire minority rights architecture. Rather than playing off "judicial-like" and "policy-driven" models of supervision against one another, it would be advisable to better appreciate their respective advantages and disadvantages in a way that both of them can appropriately serve the fundamental aim of securing effective minority rights protection.

At least in the long term, judicial review may prove relatively more practical at the European level, where a system of states and highly integrated institutions with largely concordant views of democracy, human rights and the rule of law, appears in principle suitable to building upon one of its adjudicative products, the EurCtHR, to establish international judicial supervision of minority rights. A judicial body would indeed be empowered to interpret and apply limited, as precisely worded as possible, yet "living" (namely, potentially open-ended), minority rights provisions, especially in the context of litigation involving private parties. Perhaps, the emerging trend, at domestic and international level, towards expanding the judicial approach to human rights and/or humanitarian law (see, for example, McCrudden, 2000; Helfer and Slaughter, 1997; Shelton, 1999; Blokker and Schermers, 2001) might progressively turn out to be further conducive to such a regional development (interestingly, the Council of Europe is currently looking at the judicial approach to secure a uniform interpretation of its conventions: see the opinion on the establishment of a general judicial authority, adopted by the Venice Commission in December 2000, CDL-INF (2001) 5). As an alternative to a fully-fledged judicial supervision, a solution might lie in recourse to the advisory competence of a judicial body. However, in the context of the Framework Convention (see, for example, the Assembly proposal in Recommendation 1492 (2001): paragraph 12, sub-paragraph x) this approach would risk duplicating *de facto* the role of the advisory committee (though this body is not of a judicial nature), while under a possible new Council of Europe instrument this solution would *per se* risk duplicating *de facto* the advisory role of the Venice Commission (under Article 2, paragraph 2, of the Statute of the Venice Commission). A more effective pattern might be to combine such an advisory competence with distinct means of control, but even so the question arises as to who would be competent to refer cases for opinion: provision for referral only by states or political bodies would be likely to remain underused (see, for example, the Venice Commission's opinion on the establishment of a general judicial authority, *loc. cit.:* 5).

Quasi-judicial control is another fundamental option to be explored. It may be useful to note that, viewed retrospectively, the 1991 Venice Commission's draft convention, by establishing state reports, optional state petitions and optional individual petitions (Articles 24 to 29), in addition to the right of minority members to have an effective remedy before a national authority (Article 11), appears to steer a half-way course between the flexibility of the Framework Convention's model and the stringency of the judicial control proposed in Recommendation 1201 (1993) of the Parliamentary Assembly. In terms of individual petitions, the review includes complaints from allegedly directly affected groups of individuals and NGOs representatives of minorities as well, the latter as an advance upon the complaints procedure under the First Optional Protocol to the ICCPR. On a global scale, quasi-judicial review, duly adapted to the new challenges and needs of the universal human rights treaty system (Steiner, 2000; Byrnes, 2000), should be carefully considered, particularly in connection with the possible future drafting of a

UN convention on minority rights, in the wake of the undisputed (though, admittedly, limited) successes of the HRC under the First Optional Protocol to the ICCPR, in relation to its Article 27. In fact, more ambitious regimes and control procedures are likely to appear increasingly desirable as the UN continues its work in the field of minority rights (see Sub-Commission on Human Rights Resolution 2001/9). Whether on a universal or regional level, judicial and/or quasi-judicial general supervision, set out in a way which is appropriately commensurate with the reach of the rights protected, would build up a body of jurisprudence over time as a fundamental frame of reference for a largely coherent (as opposed to dispersed) minority rights regime. In other words, they would favour a degree of consistency of the overall system of protection which the current – and in principle welcome – proliferation of minority rights instruments (with often weak or no *ad hoc* enforcement procedures) can hardly secure, no matter how impressive the record of presently available supervisory bodies is or may become.

Various techniques of non-judicial supervision are likely to cover nevertheless a substantial part of the complex of activities concerned with implementation. In this regard, the increasing involvement of NGOs and international institutions, including those with strong political and economic clout, reflects wider dynamics affecting the traditional constitutional structure of the international system, based on the role of state actors. In addition to "low-key" non-coercive forms of human rights/minority rights monitoring, varying degrees of supervision "with teeth" are being put in place, such as those based on "conditionality" in the EU context. Most of the relevant methods should be streamlined and co-ordinated with one another, as indicated in Chapter X. It is clear that the eventual impact of, for instance, the UN declaration and the Framework Convention, also in relation to further standard-setting activities, is clearly connected to the extent to which the UN Working Group on Minorities and the advisory committee, respectively, will assist in their interpretation.

A major question is how to channel the great potential of the new dimensions of supervision resulting from strong political and economic institutional leverage into a coherent pattern which works for the objective and effective protection of human rights as embraced by international law. At least in the context of present EU activities entailing minority rights considerations, the setting up of permanent independent bodies is probably one of the most important minimum steps to secure patterns of scrutiny protected from political (or *realpolitik*) interference. Modelled on existing expert bodies under international human rights treaties, they should be entrusted with assessing periodically human rights/minority rights compliance in the relevant countries on the basis of state and non-state sources of information, and closely co-operating with other pertinent international forums. In this context, third-party assessment is especially needed to create an autonomous realm of human rights jurisprudence, which takes into due account the jurisprudence of existing organs and affords the basis for promoting effective compliance through the set of institutional responses opened up by conditionality strategies. Admittedly, as commentators often remind us, law and politics mutually construct and shape each other: just as more "political" approaches do not entail the wholesale abdication of legal considerations (on the contrary, human rights protection constitutes an important component of those solutions beyond their general legal basis), so legal approaches cannot be fostered in a socio-political vacuum. Nevertheless, third-party work creates a measure of autonomy for supervising human rights/minority rights compliance which constrains the discretion of the political process by avoiding self-serving or uncritical views of the relevant standards and country contexts. Therefore, although the limits of law must be acknowledged, the institutional actors of the supervision process should never forget that standard-implementation cannot be structurally subjected to political visions or short-term political concessions. In a sense, we should learn the following from the logic underlying the twin-pillar-system established under the auspices of the League of Nations: as with judicial, and, by analogy, quasi-judicial, or simply independent expert, supervision, more "political" scrutiny is fit to confront with certain minority situations, but not necessarily with all of them. In a post-cold war context of extensive inter-governmental and non-governmental agencies striving to put a brake on ethnic conflicts, such a scrutiny should be viewed as one functional layer of an emerging, pervasive human rights- and stability-friendly architecture, and should not thus become a substitute for legal responses (whatever they are) to enforcing minority rights as a matter of "normal" human rights law.

In terms of a specific comparison with "judicial-like" review, one should not lose sight of the fact that non-judicial responses to implementation (of an institutional nature or based on an autonomous treaty), as impartial and effective in advancing the process of standard-interpretation as they may be, typically do not carry with them enforcement possibilities for victims and their representatives. Admittedly, judicial review fares no better when it is confined to classic international (namely, inter-state) jurisdiction, as in the relevant cases of the PCIJ and the OSCE Court of Conciliation and Arbitration, though the conception endorsed in the post-first world war minorities treaties, for example, in Article 12, paragraph 3, of the Polish Minorities Treaty, of allowing non-materially affected states to lodge an application with the PCIJ was of a great legal value (for contemporary developments, see *supra*, Chapters II and IV). Nevertheless, whereas "judicial-like" review is increasingly of a supra-national nature (namely, involving private parties), the procedural position of individual victims seeking redress for violations before non-judicial bodies remains, and is likely to remain, far limited. From the perspective of international organisations, the League of Nations petition system constitutes a remarkable exception, but even that system did not provide individuals with *locus standi* before the Council (save, within certain limits, under the German-Polish Convention relating to Upper Silesia), or the minority committees for oral hearings, nor did it flow from general membership obligations with regard to minorities. Precisely because of their systemic nature, non-judicial responses tend to address compliance issues in a comprehensive manner, if not only, as in the case of the OSCE HCNM, in relation to a visible link to a potential or actual danger of conflict. Such aspects reflect advantages and disadvantages depending on the purposes that the method of supervision is supposed to serve. In sum, the repeatedly invoked complementarity among the supervisory mechanisms is and should continue to be, by definition, a two-way street, which is thus to be brought to bear on the role and interrelation of "judicial-like" and non-judicial means of enforcement (for a general analytical framework, see, for example, Pentassuglia, 2001/2002).

Bibliography

Blokker, N.M. and Schermers, H.G., *Proliferation of international organizations: legal issues*, Kluwer Law International, The Hague, 2001.

Byrnes, A., "An effective complaints procedure in the context of international human rights law", in *The UN human rights treaty system in the 21st century*, Bayefsky, A.F. (ed.), Kluwer Law International, The Hague, 2000, pp. 139-167.

Gilbert, G., "Religious minorities and their rights: a problem of approach", *International Journal on Minority and Group Rights*, 5, 1997, pp. 97-134.

Helfer, L.R. and Slaughter, A., "Towards a theory of effective supranational adjudication", *The Yale Law Journal*, 107, 1997, pp. 282-391.

Hernesniemi, P. and Hannikainen, L., *Roma minorities in the Nordic and Baltic countries*, Lapland's University Press, Rovaniemi, 2000.

McCrudden, C., "A common law of human rights? Transnational judicial conversations on constitutional rights", in *Human rights and legal history: essays in honour of Brian Simpson*, O'Donovan, K. and Rubin, R.G., Oxford University Press, Oxford, 2000, pp. 29-65.

Minority Rights Group (ed.), *World directory of minorities*, Minority Rights Group International, London, 1997.

Pentassuglia, G., "On the models of minority rights supervision in Europe and how they affect a changing concept of sovereignty", *European Yearbook of Minority Issues*, 1, 2001/2002.

Pogany, I., "Accommodating an emergent national identity: the Roma of central and eastern Europe", *International Journal on Minority and Group Rights*, 6, 1999, pp. 149-167.

Shelton, D., "Commentary and conclusions", in *Commitment and compliance: the role of non-binding norms in the international legal system*, Shelton, D. (ed.), Oxford University Press, Oxford, 2000, pp. 449-463.

Shelton, D., *Remedies in international human rights law*, Oxford University Press, Oxford, 1999.

Steiner, H.J., "Individuals claims in a world of massive violations: what role for the Human Rights Committee?", in *The future of UN human rights treaty monitoring*, Alston, P. and Crawford, J. (eds), Cambridge University Press, Cambridge, 2000, pp. 15-53.

Yeung Sik Yuen, "The human rights problems and protections of the Roma", UN Doc. E/CN.4/Sub.2/2000/28, 2000, pp. 1-10.

SELECTED DOCUMENTS
AT THE UNIVERSAL AND REGIONAL LEVEL

List of instruments

1. Excerpts from the International Covenant on Civil and Political Rights (1966), adopted and opened for signature, ratification and accession by UN General Assembly Resolution 2200 A (XXI), 16 December 1966.

2. Declaration on the Rights of Persons Belonging to National or Ethnic, Religious and Linguistic Minorities, adopted by UN General Assembly Resolution 47/135, 18 December 1992.

3. Excerpts from the European Convention for the Protection of Human Rights and Fundamental Freedoms (1950), Council of Europe, 4 November 1950.

4. Excerpts from Protocol No. 12 to the European Convention for the Protection of Human Rights and Fundamental Freedoms (2000), Council of Europe, 26 June 2000.

5. Excerpts from Protocol No. 11 to the European Convention for the Protection of Human Rights and Fundamental Freedoms, restructuring the control machinery established thereby (1994), Council of Europe, 11 May 1994.

6. Excerpts from the Document of the Copenhagen Meeting of the Conference on the Human Dimension of the CSCE, 29 June 1990.

7. Excerpts from the Proposal for a European Convention for the Protection of Minorities, adopted by the European Commission for Democracy through Law of the Council of Europe, 8 February 1991.

8. European Charter for Regional or Minority Languages.

9. Recommendation 1201 (1993) on an additional protocol on the rights of national minorities to the European Convention on Human Rights, adopted by the Parliamentary Assembly of the Council of Europe, 1 February 1993.

10. Framework Convention for the Protection of National Minorities (1995), opened for signature 1 February 1995.

11. Central European Initiative Instrument for the Protection of Minority Rights, adopted by CEI member states, 19 November 1994.

1. Excerpts from the International Covenant on Civil and Political Rights (1966), adopted and opened for signature, ratification and accession by UN General Assembly Resolution 2200 A (XXI), 16 December 1966

Entry into force: 23 May 1976

Article 2

1. Each State Party to the present Covenant undertakes to respect and to ensure to all individuals within its territory and subject to its jurisdiction the rights recognised in the present Covenant, without discrimination of any kind, such as race, colour and sex, language, religion, political or other opinion, national or social origin, property, birth or other status.

Article 26

All persons are equal before the law and are entitled without discrimination to the equal protection of the law. In this respect, the law shall prohibit any discrimination and guarantee to all persons equal and effective protection against discrimination on any ground such as race, colour, sex, language, religion, political or other opinion, national or social origin, property, birth or other status.

Article 27

In those States in which ethnic, religious or linguistic minorities exist, persons belonging to such minorities shall not be denied the right, in community with the other members of their group, to enjoy their own culture, to profess and practice their own religion, or to use their own language.

2. Declaration on the Rights of Persons Belonging to National or Ethnic, Religious and Linguistic Minorities, adopted by UN General Assembly Resolution 47/135, 18 December 1992

The General Assembly,

Reaffirming that one of the basic aims of the United Nations, as proclaimed in the Charter, is to promote and encourage respect for human rights and for fundamental freedoms for all, without distinction as to race, sex, language or religion,

Reaffirming faith in fundamental human rights, in the dignity and worth of the human person, in the equal rights of men and women and of nations large and small,

Desiring to promote the realisation of the principles contained in the Charter, the Universal Declaration of Human Rights, the Convention on the Prevention and Punishment of the Crime of Genocide, the International Convention on the Elimination of All Forms of Racial Discrimination, the International Covenant on Civil and Political Rights, the International Covenant on Economic, Social and Cultural Rights, the Declaration on the Elimination of All Forms of Intolerance and of Discrimination Based on Religion or Belief, and the Convention on the Rights of the Child, as well as other relevant international instruments that have been adopted at the universal or regional level and those concluded between individual States Members of the United Nations,

Inspired by the provisions of article 27 of the International Covenant on Civil and Political Rights concerning the rights of persons belonging to ethnic, religious or linguistic minorities,

Considering that the promotion and the protection of the rights of persons belonging to national or ethnic, religious and linguistic minorities contribute to the political and social stability of States in which they live,

Emphasising that the constant promotion and realisation of the rights of persons belonging to national or ethnic, religious and linguistic minorities, as an integral part of the development of society as a whole and within a democratic framework, based on the rule of law, would contribute to the strengthening of friendship and among peoples and States,

Considering that the United Nations has an important role to play regarding the protection of minorities,

Bearing in mind the work done so far within the United Nations system, in particular by the Commission on Human Rights, the Sub-Commission on Prevention of Discrimination and Protection of Minorities and the bodies established pursuant to the International Covenants on Human Rights and other relevant international human rights instruments in promoting and protecting the rights of persons belonging to national or ethnic, religious and linguistic minorities,

Taking into account the important work which is done by intergovernmental and non-governmental organisations in protecting minorities and in promoting and protecting the rights of persons belonging to national or ethnic, religious and linguistic minorities,

Recognising the need to ensure even more effective implementation of international human rights instruments with regard to the rights of persons belonging to national or ethnic, religious and linguistic minorities,

Proclaims this Declaration on the Rights of Persons Belonging to National or Ethnic, Religious and Linguistic Minorities:

Article 1

1. States shall protect the existence and the national or ethnic, cultural, religious and linguistic identity of minorities within their respective territories and shall encourage conditions for the promotion of that identity.

2. States shall adopt appropriate legislative and other measures to achieve those ends.

Article 2

1. Persons belonging to national or ethnic, religious and linguistic minorities (hereinafter referred to as persons belonging to minorities) have the right to

enjoy their own culture, to profess and practise their own religion, and to use their own language, in private and in public, freely and without interference or any form of discrimination.

2. Persons belonging to minorities have the right to participate effectively in cultural, religious, social, economic and public life.

3. Persons belonging to minorities have the right to participate effectively in decisions on the national and, where appropriate, regional level concerning the minority to which they belong or the regions in which they live, in a manner not incompatible with national legislation.

4. Persons belonging to minorities have the right to establish and maintain their own associations.

5. Persons belonging to minorities have the right to establish and maintain, without any discrimination, free and peaceful contacts with other members of their group and with persons belonging to other minorities, as well as contacts across frontiers with citizens of other States to whom they are related by national or ethnic, religious or linguistic ties.

Article 3

1. Persons belonging to minorities may exercise their rights, including those set forth in the present Declaration, individually as well as in community with other members of their group, without any discrimination.

2. No disadvantage shall result for any person belonging to a minority as the consequence of the exercise or non-exercise of the rights set forth in the present Declaration.

Article 4

1. States shall take measures where required to ensure that persons belonging to minorities may exercise fully and effectively all their human rights and fundamental freedoms without any discrimination and in full equality before the law.

2. States shall take measures to create favourable conditions to enable persons belonging to minorities to express their characteristics and to develop their culture, language, religion, traditions and customs, except where specific practices are in violation of national law and contrary to international standards.

3. States should take appropriate measures so that, wherever possible, persons belonging to minorities may have adequate opportunities to learn their mother tongue or to have instruction in their mother tongue.

4. States should, where appropriate, take measures in the field of education, in order to encourage knowledge of the history, traditions, language and culture of the minorities existing within their territory. Persons belonging to minorities should have adequate opportunities to gain knowledge of the society as a whole.

5. States should consider appropriate measures so that persons belonging to minorities may participate fully in the economic progress and development in their country.

Article 5

1. National policies and programmes shall be planned and implemented with due regard for the legitimate interests of persons belonging to minorities.

2. Programmes of co-operation and assistance among States should be planned and implemented with due regard for the legitimate interests of persons belonging to minorities.

Article 6

States should co-operate on questions relating to persons belonging to minorities, *inter alia,* exchanging information and experiences, in order to promote mutual understanding and confidence.

Article 7

1. States should co-operate in order to promote respect for the rights set forth in the present Declaration.

Article 8

1. Nothing in the present Declaration shall prevent the fulfilment of international obligations of States in relation to persons belonging to minorities. In particular, States shall fulfil in good faith the obligations and commitments they have assumed under international treaties and agreements to which they are parties.

2. The exercise of the rights set forth in the present Declaration shall not prejudice the enjoyment by all persons of universally recognised human rights and fundamental freedoms.

3. Measures taken by States to ensure the effective enjoyment of the rights set forth in the present Declaration shall not prima facie be considered contrary to the principle of equality contained in the Universal Declaration of Human Rights.

4. Nothing in the present Declaration may be construed as permitting any activity contrary to the purposes and principles of the United Nations, including sovereign equality, territorial integrity and political independence of States.

Article 9

The specialised agencies and other organisations of the United Nations system shall contribute to the full realisation of the rights and principles set forth in the present Declaration, within their respective fields of competence.

3. Excerpts from the European Convention for the Protection of Human Rights and Fundamental Freedoms (1950), Council of Europe, 4 November 1950

Entry into force: 3 September 1953

Article 8

1. Everyone has the right to respect for his private and family life, his home and his correspondence.

Article 14

The enjoyment of the rights and freedoms set forth in this Convention shall be secured without discrimination on any ground such as sex, race, colour, language, religion, political or other opinion, national or social origin, association with a national minority, property, birth or other status.

4. Excerpts from Protocol No. 12 to the European Convention for the Protection of Human Rights and Fundamental Freedoms (2000), Council of Europe, 26 June 2000

Opened for signature: 20 November 2000

Preamble

The member states of the Council of Europe signatory hereto, …

Reaffirming that the principle of non-discrimination does not prevent states parties from taking measures in order to promote full and effective equality, provided that there is an objective and reasonable justification for those measures,

Have agreed as follows:

Article 1

General Prohibition of Discrimination

1. The enjoyment of any right set forth by law shall be secured without discrimination on any ground such as sex, race, colour, language, religion, political or other opinion, national or social origin, association with a national minority, property, birth or other status.

2. No one shall be discriminated against by any public authority on any ground such as those mentioned in paragraph 1.

Article 3

Relationship to the Convention

As between the states parties, the provisions of Articles 1 and 2 of this Protocol shall be regarded as additional articles to the Convention, and all the provisions of the Convention shall apply accordingly.

5. Excerpts from Protocol No. 11 to the European Convention for the Protection of Human Rights and Fundamental Freedoms (1994), restructuring the control machinery established thereby, Council of Europe, 11 May 1994

Entry into force: 1 November 1998

Article 34

Individual Applications

The Court may receive applications from any person, non-governmental organisation or group of individuals claiming to be the victim of a violation by one of the High Contracting Parties of the rights set forth in the Convention or the protocols thereto. The High Contracting Parties undertake not to hinder in any way the effective exercise of this right.

6. Excerpts from the Document of the Copenhagen Meeting of the Conference on the Human Dimension of the CSCE, 29 June 1990

(30) The participating States recognise that the questions relating to national minorities can only be satisfactorily resolved in a democratic political framework based on the rule of law, with a functioning independent judiciary. This framework guarantees full respect for human rights and fundamental freedoms, equal rights and status for all citizens, the free expression of all their legitimate interests and aspirations, political pluralism, social tolerance and the implementation of legal rules that place effective restraints on the abuse of governmental power.

They also recognise the important role of non-governmental organisations, including political parties, trade unions, human rights organisations and religious groups, in the promotion of tolerance, cultural diversity and the resolution of questions relating to national minorities.

They further reaffirm that respect for the rights of persons belonging to national minorities as part of universally recognised human rights is an essential factor for peace, justice, stability and democracy in the participating States.

(31) Persons belonging to national minorities have the right to exercise fully and effectively their human rights and fundamental freedoms without any discrimination and in full equality before the law.

The participating States will adopt, where necessary, special measures for the purpose of ensuring to persons belonging to national minorities full equality with the other citizens in the exercise and enjoyment of human rights and fundamental freedoms.

(32) To belong to a national minority is a matter of a person's individual choice and no disadvantage may arise from the exercise of such choice.

Persons belonging to national minorities have the right freely to express, preserve and develop their ethnic, cultural, linguistic or religious identity and to maintain and develop their culture in all its aspects, free of any attempts at assimilation against their will. In particular, they have the right

(32.1) to use freely their mother tongue in private as well as in public;

(32.2) to establish and maintain their own educational, cultural and religious institutions, organisations or associations, which can seek voluntary financial and other contributions as well as public assistance, in conformity with national legislation;

(32.3) to profess and practise their religion, including the acquisition, possession and use of religious materials, and to conduct religious educational activities in their mother tongue;

(32.4) to establish and maintain unimpeded contacts among themselves within their country as well as contacts across frontiers with citizens of other States with whom they share a common ethnic or national origin, cultural heritage or religious beliefs;

(32.5) to disseminate, have access to and exchange information in their mother tongue;

(32.6) to establish and maintain organisations or associations within their country and to participate in international non-governmental organisations.

People belonging to national minorities can exercise and enjoy their rights individually as well as in community with other members of their group. No disadvantage may arise for a person belonging to a national minority on account of the exercise or non-exercise of any such rights.

(33) The participating States will protect the ethnic, cultural, linguistic and religious identity of national minorities on their territory and create conditions for the promotion of that identity. They will take the necessary measures to that effect after due consultations, including contacts with organisations or associations of such minorities, in accordance with the decision-making procedures of each State.

Any such measures will be in conformity with the principles of equality and non-discrimination with respect to the other citizens of the participating State concerned.

(34) The participating States will endeavour to ensure that persons belonging to national minorities, notwithstanding the need to learn the official language or languages of the State concerned, have adequate opportunities for instruction of their mother tongue or in their mother tongue, as well as, wherever possible and necessary, for its use before public authorities, in conformity with applicable national legislation.

In the context of the teaching of history and culture in educational establishments, they will also take account of the history and culture of national minorities.

(35) The participating States will respect the rights of persons belonging to national minorities to effective participation in public affairs, including par-

ticipation in the affairs relating to the protection and promotion of the identity of such minorities.

The participating States note the efforts undertaken to protect and create conditions for the promotion of the ethnic, cultural, linguistic and religious identity of certain national minorities by establishing, as one of the possible means to achieve these aims, appropriate local or autonomous administrations corresponding to the specific historical and territorial circumstances of such minorities and in accordance with the policies of the State concerned.

(36) The participating States recognise the particular importance of increasing constructive co-operation among themselves on questions relating to national minorities. Such co-operation seeks to promote mutual understanding and confidence, friendly and good-neighbourly relations, international peace, security and justice.

Every participating State will promote a climate of mutual respect, understanding, co-operation and solidarity among all persons living on its territory, without distinction as to ethnic or national origin or religion, and will encourage the solution of problems through dialogue based on the principles of the rule of law.

(37) None of these commitments may be interpreted as implying any right to engage in any activity or perform any action in contravention of the purposes and principles of the Charter of the United Nations, other obligations under international law or the provisions of the Final Act, including the principle of territorial integrity of States.

(38) The participating States, in their efforts to protect and promote the rights of persons belonging to national minorities, will fully respect their undertakings under existing human rights conventions and other relevant international instruments and consider adhering to the relevant conventions, if they have not yet done so, including those providing for a right of complaint by individuals.

(39) The participating States will co-operate closely in the competent international organisations to which they belong, including the United Nations and, as appropriate, the Council of Europe, bearing in mind their on-going work with respect to questions relating to national minorities.

They will consider convening a meeting of experts for a thorough discussion of the issue of national minorities.

(40) The participating States clearly and unequivocally condemn totalitarianism, racial and ethnic hatred, anti-Semitism, xenophobia and discrimination against anyone as well as persecution on religious and ideological grounds. In this context, they also recognise the particular problems of Roma (Gypsies).

They declare their firm intention to intensify the efforts to combat these phenomena in all their forms and therefore will

(40.1) take effective measures, including the adoption, in conformity with their constitutional systems and their international obligations, of such laws as may be necessary, to provide protection against any acts that constitute incitement to violence against persons or groups based on national, racial, ethnic or religious discrimination, hostility or hatred, including anti-Semitism;

(40.2) commit themselves to take appropriate and proportionate measures to protect persons or groups who may be subject to threats or acts of discrimination, hostility or violence as a result of their racial, ethnic, cultural, linguistic or religious identity, and to protect their property;

(40.3) take effective measures, in conformity with their constitutional systems, at the national, regional and local levels to promote understanding and tolerance, particularly in the fields of education, culture and information;

(40.4) endeavour to ensure that the objectives of education include special attention to the problem of racial prejudice and hatred and to the development of respect for different civilisations and cultures;

(40.5) recognise the right of individuals to effective remedies and endeavour to recognise, in conformity with national legislation, the right of interested persons and groups to initiate and support complaints against acts of discrimination, including racist and xenophobic acts;

(40.6) consider adhering, if they have not yet done so, to the international instruments which address the problem of discrimination and ensure full compliance with the obligations therein, including those relating to the submission of periodic reports;

(40.7) consider, also, accepting those international mechanisms which allow States and individuals to bring communications relating to discrimination before international bodies.

7. Excerpts from the Proposal for a European Convention for the Protection of Minorities, adopted by the European Commission for Democracy through Law of the Council of Europe, 8 February 1991

Chapter I – General Principles

Article 2

1. For the purposes of this Convention, the term "minority" shall mean a group which is smaller in number than the rest of the population of a State, whose members, who are nationals of that State, have ethnical, religious or linguistic features different from those of the rest of the population, and are guided by the will to safeguard their culture, traditions, religion or language.

2. Any group coming within the terms of this definition shall be treated as an ethnic, religious or linguistic minority.

3. To belong to a national minority shall be a matter of individual choice and no disadvantage may arise from the exercise of such choice.

Chapter II – Rights and Obligations

Article 3

1. Minorities shall have the right to be protected against any activity capable of threatening their existence.

2. They shall have the right to the respect, safeguard and development of their ethnical, religious, or linguistic identity.

Article 8

Whenever a minority reaches a substantial percentage of the population of a region or of the total population, its members shall have the right, as far as possible, to speak and write in their own language to the political, administrative and judicial authorities of this region or, where appropriate, of the State. These authorities shall have a corresponding obligation.

Article 9

Whenever the conditions of Article 8 are fulfilled, in State schools, obligatory schooling shall include, for pupils belonging to the minority, study of their mother tongue. As far as possible, all or part of the schooling shall be given in the mother tongue of pupils belonging to the minority. However, should the State not be in a position to provide such schooling, it must permit children who so wish to attend private schools. In such a case, the State shall have the right to prescribe that the official language or languages also be taught in such schools.

Article 11

Any person belonging to a minority whose rights set forth in the present Convention are violated shall have an effective remedy before a national authority.

Article 14

1. States shall favour the effective participation of minorities in public affairs, in particular in decisions affecting the regions where they live or in the matters affecting them.

2. As far as possible, States shall take minorities into account when dividing the national territory into political and administrative sub-divisions, as well as into constituencies.

Article 16

States shall take the necessary measures with a view to ensuring that, in any region where those who belong to a minority represent the majority of the population, those who do not belong to this minority shall not suffer from any discrimination.

Chapter III – Control Machinery

Article 18

To ensure the observance of the undertakings by the Parties in the present Convention, there shall be set up a European Committee for the Protection of Minorities (hereinafter referred to as "the Committee").

Article 24

1. The Parties shall submit to the Committee, through the Secretary General of the Council of Europe, reports on the measures they have adopted to give effect to their undertakings under this Convention, within one year of the entry into force of the Convention for the Party concerned. The Parties shall submit supplementary reports at three yearly intervals concerning any new measure adopted, as well as any other report requested by the Committee.

2. Those reports shall be examined by the Committee who will forward them to the Committee of Ministers of the Council of Europe with its observations.

3. By a majority of two-thirds of the members entitled to sit on the Committee, the Committee may make any necessary recommendations to a Party.

Article 25

1. Provided that a Party has, by declaration addressed to the Secretary General of the Council of Europe, recognised the competence of the Committee to receive a State's request, the Committee may receive petitions from any Party which considers that another party does not respect the provisions of this Convention.

2. The declarations provided for in paragraph 1 may be made for a specific period. In this case, they shall be renewed automatically for the same period, unless withdrawn by previous notice of one year before the expiration of the period of validity.

3. The Committee shall only exercise the powers provided for in this Article when at least five Parties are bound by declarations made in accordance with paragraph 1.

Article 26

1. Provided that a Party has, by declaration addressed to the Secretary General of the Council of Europe, recognised the competence of the Committee to receive individual petitions, it may receive such petitions from any person, group of individuals or any international non-governmental organisation representative of minorities, claiming to be the victim of a violation by this Party of the rights set forth in this Convention.

2. The declarations provided for in paragraph 1 may be made for a specific period. In this case, they shall be renewed automatically for the same period,

unless withdrawn by previous notice of one year before the expiration of the period of validity.

3. The Parties who have made the declarations provided for in paragraph 1 undertake not to hinder in any way the effective exercise of the right of individual petition.

4. The Committee shall only exercise the powers provided for in this Article when at least five Parties are bound by declarations made in accordance with paragraph 1.

Article 27

1. The Committee may only deal with the matter referred to it under Article 26 after all domestic remedies have been exhausted, according to the generally recognised rules of international law.

2. The Committee shall declare inadmissible petitions submitted under Article 26 which:

a. are anonymous;

b. are substantially the same as a matter which has already been examined by the Committee;

c. have already been submitted to another international body and do not contain any relevant new information;

d. are incompatible with the provisions of the Convention, manifestly ill-founded or, an abuse of the right of petition;

e. are submitted to the Committee more than six months from the final internal decision.

Article 28

In the event of the Committee accepting a petition referred to it:

a. it shall, with a view to ascertaining the facts, undertake together with the representatives of the parties an examination of the petition and, if need be, an investigation;

b. it endeavours to reach a friendly settlement of the matter on the basis of respect of this Convention. If it succeeds it shall draw up a report which shall contain a statement of the facts and of the solution reached and be sent to the State or States concerned.

Article 29

1. If no friendly settlement has been reached, the Committee shall draw up a report as to whether the facts found disclose a breach by the State concerned of its obligation under this Convention and make such proposals as it thinks are necessary.

2. The report shall be transmitted to the Committee of Ministers, to the State or States concerned and to the Secretary General of the Council of Europe.

3. The Committee of Ministers may take any follow-up action it thinks fit in order to ensure respect for the Convention.

Article 30

This Convention shall not be construed as limiting or derogating from the competence of the organs of the European Convention on Human Rights or from the obligations assumed by the Parties under that Convention.

8. European Charter for Regional or Minority Languages

Preamble

The member States of the Council of Europe signatory hereto,

Considering that the aim of the Council of Europe is to achieve a greater unity between its members, particularly for the purpose of safeguarding and realising the ideals and principles which are their common heritage;

Considering that the protection of the historical regional or minority languages of Europe, some of which are in danger of eventual extinction, contributes to the maintenance and development of Europe's cultural wealth and traditions;

Considering that the right to use a regional or minority language in private and public life is an inalienable right conforming to the principles embodied in the United Nations International Covenant on Civil and Political Rights, and according to the spirit of the Council of Europe Convention for the Protection of Human Rights and Fundamental Freedoms;

Having regard to the work carried out within the CSCE and in particular to the Helsinki Final Act of 1975 and the document of the Copenhagen Meeting of 1990;

Stressing the value of interculturalism and multilingualism and considering that the protection and encouragement of regional or minority languages should not be to the detriment of the official languages and the need to learn them;

Realising that the protection and promotion of regional or minority languages in the different countries and regions of Europe represent an important contribution to the building of a Europe based on the principles of democracy and cultural diversity within the framework of national sovereignty and territorial integrity;

Taking into consideration the specific conditions and historical traditions in the different regions of the European States,

Have agreed as follows:

Part I – General provisions

Article 1 – Definitions

For the purposes of this Charter:

a. "regional or minority languages" means languages that are:

    i. traditionally used within a given territory of a State by nationals of that State who form a group numerically smaller than the rest of the State's population; and

    ii. different from the official language(s) of that State;

    it does not include either dialects of the official language(s) of the State or the languages of migrants;

b. "territory in which the regional or minority language is used" means the geographical area in which the said language is the mode of expression of a number of people justifying the adoption of the various protective and promotional measures provided for in this Charter;

c. "non-territorial languages" means languages used by nationals of the State which differ from the language or languages used by the rest of the State's population but which, although traditionally used within the territory of the State, cannot be identified with a particular area thereof.

Article 2 – Undertakings

1. Each Party undertakes to apply the provisions of Part II to all the regional or minority languages spoken within its territory and which comply with the definition in Article 1.

2. In respect of each language specified at the time of ratification, acceptance or approval, in accordance with Article 3, each Party undertakes to apply a minimum of thirty-five paragraphs or sub-paragraphs chosen from among the provisions of Part III of the Charter, including at least three chosen from each of the Articles 8 and 12 and one from each of the Articles 9, 10, 11 and 13.

Article 3 – Practical arrangements

1. Each Contracting State shall specify in its instrument of ratification, acceptance or approval, each regional or minority language, or official language which is less widely used on the whole or part of its territory, to which the paragraphs chosen in accordance with Article 2, paragraph 2, shall apply.

2. Any Party may, at any subsequent time, notify the Secretary General that it accepts the obligations arising out of the provisions of any other paragraph of the Charter not already specified in its instrument of ratification, acceptance or approval, or that it will apply paragraph 1 of the present article to other regional or minority languages, or to other official languages which are less widely used on the whole or part of its territory.

3. The undertakings referred to in the foregoing paragraph shall be deemed to form an integral part of the ratification, acceptance or approval and will have the same effect as from their date of notification.

Article 4 – Existing regimes of protection

1. Nothing in this Charter shall be construed as limiting or derogating from any of the rights guaranteed by the European Convention on Human Rights.

2. The provisions of this Charter shall not affect any more favourable provisions concerning the status of regional or minority languages, or the legal regime of persons belonging to minorities which may exist in a Party or are provided for by relevant bilateral or multilateral international agreements.

Article 5 – Existing obligations

Nothing in this Charter may be interpreted as implying any right to engage in any activity or perform any action in contravention of the purposes of the Charter of the United Nations or other obligations under international law, including the principle of the sovereignty and territorial integrity of States.

Article 6 – Information

The Parties undertake to see to it that the authorities, organisations and persons concerned are informed of the rights and duties established by this Charter.

Part II – Objectives and principles pursued in accordance with Article 2, paragraph 1

Article 7 – Objectives and principles

1. In respect of regional or minority languages, within the territories in which such languages are used and according to the situation of each language, the Parties shall base their policies, legislation and practice on the following objectives and principles:

a. the recognition of the regional or minority languages as an expression of cultural wealth;

b. the respect of the geographical area of each regional or minority language in order to ensure that existing or new administrative divisions do not constitute an obstacle to the promotion of the regional or minority language in question;

c. the need for resolute action to promote regional or minority languages in order to safeguard them;

d. the facilitation and/or encouragement of the use of regional or minority languages, in speech and writing, in public and private life;

e. the maintenance and development of links, in the fields covered by this Charter, between groups using a regional or minority language and other groups in the State employing a language used in identical or similar form, as well as the establishment of cultural relations with other groups in the State using different languages;

f. the provision of appropriate forms and means for the teaching and study of regional or minority languages at all appropriate stages;

g. the provision of facilities enabling non-speakers of a regional or minority language living in the area where it is used to learn it if they so desire;

h. the promotion of study and research on regional or minority languages at universities or equivalent institutions;

i. the promotion of appropriate types of transnational exchanges, in the fields covered by this Charter, for regional or minority languages used in identical or similar form in two or more States.

2. The Parties undertake to eliminate, if they have not yet done so, any unjustified distinction, exclusion, restriction or preference relating to the use of a regional or minority language and intended to discourage or endanger the maintenance or development of it. The adoption of special measures in favour of regional or minority languages aimed at promoting equality between the users of these languages and the rest of the population or which take due account of their specific conditions is not considered to be an act of discrimination against the users of more widely-used languages.

3. The Parties undertake to promote, by appropriate measures, mutual understanding between all the linguistic groups of the country and in particular the inclusion of respect, understanding and tolerance in relation to regional or minority languages among the objectives of education and training provided within their countries and encouragement of the mass media to pursue the same objective.

4. In determining their policy with regard to regional or minority languages, the Parties shall take into consideration the needs and wishes expressed by the groups which use such languages. They are encouraged to establish bodies, if necessary, for the purpose of advising the authorities on all matters pertaining to regional or minority languages.

5. The Parties undertake to apply, mutatis mutandis, the principles listed in paragraphs 1 to 4 above to non-territorial languages. However, as far as these languages are concerned, the nature and scope of the measures to be taken to give effect to this Charter shall be determined in a flexible manner, bearing in mind the needs and wishes, and respecting the traditions and characteristics, of the groups which use the languages concerned.

Part III – Measures to promote the use of regional or minority languages in public life in accordance with the undertakings entered into under Article 2, paragraph 2

Article 8 – Education

1. With regard to education, the Parties undertake, within the territory in which such languages are used, according to the situation of each of these

languages, and without prejudice to the teaching of the official language(s) of the State:

a. i. to make available pre-school education in the relevant regional or minority languages; or

   ii. to make available a substantial part of pre-school education in the relevant regional or minority languages; or

   iii. to apply one of the measures provided for under i and ii above at least to those pupils whose families so request and whose number is considered sufficient; or

   iv. if the public authorities have no direct competence in the field of pre-school education, to favour and/or encourage the application of the measures referred to under i to iii above;

b. i. to make available primary education in the relevant regional or minority languages; or

   ii. to make available a substantial part of primary education in the relevant regional or minority languages; or

   iii. to provide, within primary education, for the teaching of the relevant regional or minority languages as an integral part of the curriculum; or

   iv. to apply one of the measures provided for under i to iii above at least to those pupils whose families so request and whose number is considered sufficient;

c. i. to make available secondary education in the relevant regional or minority languages; or

   ii. to make available a substantial part of secondary education in the relevant regional or minority languages; or

   iii. to provide, within secondary education, for the teaching of the relevant regional or minority languages as an integral part of the curriculum; or

   iv. to apply one of the measures provided for under i to iii above at least to those pupils who, or where appropriate whose families, so wish in a number considered sufficient;

d. i. to make available technical and vocational education in the relevant regional or minority languages; or

   ii. to make available a substantial part of technical and vocational education in the relevant regional or minority languages; or

   iii. to provide, within technical and vocational education, for the teaching of the relevant regional or minority languages as an integral part of the curriculum; or

   iv. to apply one of the measures provided for under i to iii above at least to those pupils who, or where appropriate whose families, so wish in a number considered sufficient;

e. i. to make available university and other higher education in regional or minority languages; or

   ii. to provide facilities for the study of these languages as university and higher education subjects; or

iii. if, by reason of the role of the State in relation to higher education institutions, sub-paragraphs i and ii cannot be applied, to encourage and/or allow the provision of university or other forms of higher education in regional or minority languages or of facilities for the study of these languages as university or higher education subjects;

f. i. to arrange for the provision of adult and continuing education courses which are taught mainly or wholly in the regional or minority languages; or

ii. to offer such languages as subjects of adult and continuing education; or

iii. if the public authorities have no direct competence in the field of adult education, to favour and/or encourage the offering of such languages as subjects of adult and continuing education;

g. to make arrangements to ensure the teaching of the history and the culture which is reflected by the regional or minority language;

h. to provide the basic and further training of the teachers required to implement those of paragraphs a to g accepted by the Party;

i. to set up a supervisory body or bodies responsible for monitoring the measures taken and progress achieved in establishing or developing the teaching of regional or minority languages and for drawing up periodic reports of their findings, which will be made public.

2. With regard to education and in respect of territories other than those in which the regional or minority languages are traditionally used, the Parties undertake, if the number of users of a regional or minority language justifies it, to allow, encourage or provide teaching in or of the regional or minority language at all the appropriate stages of education.

Article 9 – Judicial authorities

1. The Parties undertake, in respect of those judicial districts in which the number of residents using the regional or minority languages justifies the measures specified below, according to the situation of each of these languages and on condition that the use of the facilities afforded by the present paragraph is not considered by the judge to hamper the proper administration of justice:

a. in criminal proceedings:

i. to provide that the courts, at the request of one of the parties, shall conduct the proceedings in the regional or minority languages; and/or

ii. to guarantee the accused the right to use his/her regional or minority language; and/or

iii. to provide that requests and evidence, whether written or oral, shall not be considered inadmissible solely because they are formulated in a regional or minority language; and/or

iv. to produce, on request, documents connected with legal proceedings in the relevant regional or minority language, if necessary by the use of interpreters and translations involving no extra expense for the persons concerned;

b. in civil proceedings:

    i. to provide that the courts, at the request of one of the parties, shall conduct the proceedings in the regional or minority languages; and/or

    ii. to allow, whenever a litigant has to appear in person before a court, that he or she may use his or her regional or minority language without thereby incurring additional expense; and/or

    iii. to allow documents and evidence to be produced in the regional or minority languages, if necessary by the use of interpreters and translations;

c. in proceedings before courts concerning administrative matters:

    i. to provide that the courts, at the request of one of the parties, shall conduct the proceedings in the regional or minority languages; and/or

    ii. to allow, whenever a litigant has to appear in person before a court, that he or she may use his or her regional or minority language without thereby incurring additional expense; and/or

    iii. to allow documents and evidence to be produced in the regional or minority languages, if necessary by the use of interpreters and translations;

d. to take steps to ensure that the application of sub-paragraphs i and iii of paragraphs b and c above and any necessary use of interpreters and translations does not involve extra expense for the persons concerned.

2. The Parties undertake:

a. not to deny the validity of legal documents drawn up within the State solely because they are drafted in a regional or minority language; or

b. not to deny the validity, as between the parties, of legal documents drawn up within the country solely because they are drafted in a regional or minority language, and to provide that they can be invoked against interested third parties who are not users of these languages on condition that the contents of the document are made known to them by the person(s) who invoke(s) it; or

c. not to deny the validity, as between the parties, of legal documents drawn up within the country solely because they are drafted in a regional or minority language.

3. The Parties undertake to make available in the regional or minority languages the most important national statutory texts and those relating particularly to users of these languages, unless they are otherwise provided.

Article 10 – Administrative authorities and public services

1. Within the administrative districts of the State in which the number of residents who are users of regional or minority languages justifies the measures specified below and according to the situation of each language, the Parties undertake, as far as this is reasonably possible:

a. i. to ensure that the administrative authorities use the regional or minority languages; or

ii. to ensure that such of their officers as are in contact with the public use the regional or minority languages in their relations with persons applying to them in these languages; or

iii. to ensure that users of regional or minority languages may submit oral or written applications and receive a reply in these languages; or

iv. to ensure that users of regional or minority languages may submit oral or written applications in these languages; or

v. to ensure that users of regional or minority languages may validly submit a document in these languages;

b. to make available widely used administrative texts and forms for the population in the regional or minority languages or in bilingual versions;

c. to allow the administrative authorities to draft documents in a regional or minority language.

2. In respect of the local and regional authorities on whose territory the number of residents who are users of regional or minority languages is such as to justify the measures specified below, the Parties undertake to allow and/or encourage:

a. the use of regional or minority languages within the framework of the regional or local authority;

b. the possibility for users of regional or minority languages to submit oral or written applications in these languages;

c. the publication by regional authorities of their official documents also in the relevant regional or minority languages;

d. the publication by local authorities of their official documents also in the relevant regional or minority languages;

e. the use by regional authorities of regional or minority languages in debates in their assemblies, without excluding, however, the use of the official language(s) of the State;

f. the use by local authorities of regional or minority languages in debates in their assemblies, without excluding, however, the use of the official language(s) of the State;

g. the use or adoption, if necessary in conjunction with the name in the official language(s), of traditional and correct forms of place-names in regional or minority languages.

3. With regard to public services provided by the administrative authorities or other persons acting on their behalf, the Parties undertake, within the territory in which regional or minority languages are used, in accordance with the situation of each language and as far as this is reasonably possible:

a. to ensure that the regional or minority languages are used in the provision of the service; or

b. to allow users of regional or minority languages to submit a request and receive a reply in these languages; or

c. to allow users of regional or minority languages to submit a request in these languages.

4. With a view to putting into effect those provisions of paragraphs 1, 2 and 3 accepted by them, the Parties undertake to take one or more of the following measures:

a. translation or interpretation as may be required;

b. recruitment and, where necessary, training of the officials and other public service employees required;

c. compliance as far as possible with requests from public service employees having a knowledge of a regional or minority language to be appointed in the territory in which that language is used.

5. The Parties undertake to allow the use or adoption of family names in the regional or minority languages, at the request of those concerned.

Article 11 – Media

1. The Parties undertake, for the users of the regional or minority languages within the territories in which those languages are spoken, according to the situation of each language, to the extent that the public authorities, directly or indirectly, are competent, have power or play a role in this field, and respecting the principle of the independence and autonomy of the media:

a. to the extent that radio and television carry out a public service mission:

   i. to ensure the creation of at least one radio station and one television channel in the regional or minority languages; or

   ii. to encourage and/or facilitate the creation of at least one radio station and one television channel in the regional or minority languages; or

   iii. to make adequate provision so that broadcasters offer programmes in the regional or minority languages;

b. i. to encourage and/or facilitate the creation of at least one radio station in the regional or minority languages; or

   ii. to encourage and/or facilitate the broadcasting of radio programmes in the regional or minority languages on a regular basis;

c. i. to encourage and/or facilitate the creation of at least one television channel in the regional or minority languages; or

   ii. to encourage and/or facilitate the broadcasting of television programmes in the regional or minority languages on a regular basis;

d. to encourage and/or facilitate the production and distribution of audio and audiovisual works in the regional or minority languages;

e. i. to encourage and/or facilitate the creation and/or maintenance of at least one newspaper in the regional or minority languages; or

   ii. to encourage and/or facilitate the publication of newspaper articles in the regional or minority languages on a regular basis;

f. i. to cover the additional costs of those media which use regional or minority languages, wherever the law provides for financial assistance in general for the media; or

    ii. to apply existing measures for financial assistance also to audiovisual productions in the regional or minority languages;

g. to support the training of journalists and other staff for media using regional or minority languages.

2. The Parties undertake to guarantee freedom of direct reception of radio and television broadcasts from neighbouring countries in a language used in identical or similar form to a regional or minority language, and not to oppose the retransmission of radio and television broadcasts from neighbouring countries in such a language. They further undertake to ensure that no restrictions will be placed on the freedom of expression and free circulation of information in the written press in a language used in identical or similar form to a regional or minority language. The exercise of the above-mentioned freedoms, since it carries with it duties and responsibilities, may be subject to such formalities, conditions, restrictions or penalties as are prescribed by law and are necessary in a democratic society, in the interests of national security, territorial integrity or public safety, for the prevention of disorder or crime, for the protection of health or morals, for the protection of the reputation or rights of others, for preventing disclosure of information received in confidence, or for maintaining the authority and impartiality of the judiciary.

3. The Parties undertake to ensure that the interests of the users of regional or minority languages are represented or taken into account within such bodies as may be established in accordance with the law with responsibility for guaranteeing the freedom and pluralism of the media.

Article 12 – Cultural activities and facilities

1. With regard to cultural activities and facilities – especially libraries, video libraries, cultural centres, museums, archives, academies, theatres and cinemas, as well as literary work and film production, vernacular forms of cultural expression, festivals and the culture industries, including inter alia the use of new technologies – the Parties undertake, within the territory in which such languages are used and to the extent that the public authorities are competent, have power or play a role in this field:

a. to encourage types of expression and initiative specific to regional or minority languages and foster the different means of access to works produced in these languages;

b. to foster the different means of access in other languages to works produced in regional or minority languages by aiding and developing translation, dubbing, post-synchronisation and subtitling activities;

c. to foster access in regional or minority languages to works produced in other languages by aiding and developing translation, dubbing, post-synchronisation and subtitling activities;

d. to ensure that the bodies responsible for organising or supporting cultural activities of various kinds make appropriate allowance for incorporating the knowledge and use of regional or minority languages and cultures in the undertakings which they initiate or for which they provide backing;

e. to promote measures to ensure that the bodies responsible for organising or supporting cultural activities have at their disposal staff who have a full command of the regional or minority language concerned, as well as of the language(s) of the rest of the population;

f. to encourage direct participation by representatives of the users of a given regional or minority language in providing facilities and planning cultural activities;

g. to encourage and/or facilitate the creation of a body or bodies responsible for collecting, keeping a copy of and presenting or publishing works produced in the regional or minority languages;

h. if necessary, to create and/or promote and finance translation and terminological research services, particularly with a view to maintaining and developing appropriate administrative, commercial, economic, social, technical or legal terminology in each regional or minority language.

2. In respect of territories other than those in which the regional or minority languages are traditionally used, the Parties undertake, if the number of users of a regional or minority language justifies it, to allow, encourage and/or provide appropriate cultural activities and facilities in accordance with the preceding paragraph.

3. The Parties undertake to make appropriate provision, in pursuing their cultural policy abroad, for regional or minority languages and the cultures they reflect.

Article 13 – Economic and social life

1. With regard to economic and social activities, the Parties undertake, within the whole country:

a. to eliminate from their legislation any provision prohibiting or limiting without justifiable reasons the use of regional or minority languages in documents relating to economic or social life, particularly contracts of employment, and in technical documents such as instructions for the use of products or installations;

b. to prohibit the insertion in internal regulations of companies and private documents of any clauses excluding or restricting the use of regional or minority languages, at least between users of the same language;

c. to oppose practices designed to discourage the use of regional or minority languages in connection with economic or social activities;

d. to facilitate and/or encourage the use of regional or minority languages by means other than those specified in the above sub-paragraphs.

2. With regard to economic and social activities, the Parties undertake, in so far as the public authorities are competent, within the territory in which the

regional or minority languages are used, and as far as this is reasonably possible:

a. to include in their financial and banking regulations provisions which allow, by means of procedures compatible with commercial practice, the use of regional or minority languages in drawing up payment orders (cheques, drafts, etc.) or other financial documents, or, where appropriate, to ensure the implementation of such provisions;

b. in the economic and social sectors directly under their control (public sector), to organise activities to promote the use of regional or minority languages;

c. to ensure that social care facilities such as hospitals, retirement homes and hostels offer the possibility of receiving and treating in their own language persons using a regional or minority language who are in need of care on grounds of ill-health, old age or for other reasons;

d. to ensure by appropriate means that safety instructions are also drawn up in regional or minority languages;

e. to arrange for information provided by the competent public authorities concerning the rights of consumers to be made available in regional or minority languages.

Article 14 – Transfrontier exchanges

The Parties undertake:

a. to apply existing bilateral and multilateral agreements which bind them with the States in which the same language is used in identical or similar form, or if necessary to seek to conclude such agreements, in such a way as to foster contacts between the users of the same language in the States concerned in the fields of culture, education, information, vocational training and permanent education;

b. for the benefit of regional or minority languages, to facilitate and/or promote co-operation across borders, in particular between regional or local authorities in whose territory the same language is used in identical or similar form.

Part IV – Application of the Charter

Article 15 – Periodical reports

1. The Parties shall present periodically to the Secretary General of the Council of Europe, in a form to be prescribed by the Committee of Ministers, a report on their policy pursued in accordance with Part II of this Charter and on the measures taken in application of those provisions of Part III which they have accepted. The first report shall be presented within the year following the entry into force of the Charter with respect to the Party concerned, the other reports at three-yearly intervals after the first report.

2. The Parties shall make their reports public.

Article 16 – Examination of the reports

1. The reports presented to the Secretary General of the Council of Europe under Article 15 shall be examined by a committee of experts constituted in accordance with Article 17.

2. Bodies or associations legally established in a Party may draw the attention of the committee of experts to matters relating to the undertakings entered into by that Party under Part III of this Charter. After consulting the Party concerned, the committee of experts may take account of this information in the preparation of the report specified in paragraph 3 below. These bodies or associations can furthermore submit statements concerning the policy pursued by a Party in accordance with Part II.

3. On the basis of the reports specified in paragraph 1 and the information mentioned in paragraph 2, the committee of experts shall prepare a report for the Committee of Ministers. This report shall be accompanied by the comments which the Parties have been requested to make and may be made public by the Committee of Ministers.

4. The report specified in paragraph 3 shall contain in particular the proposals of the committee of experts to the Committee of Ministers for the preparation of such recommendations of the latter body to one or more of the Parties as may be required.

5. The Secretary General of the Council of Europe shall make a two-yearly detailed report to the Parliamentary Assembly on the application of the Charter.

Article 17 – Committee of experts

1. The committee of experts shall be composed of one member per Party, appointed by the Committee of Ministers from a list of individuals of the highest integrity and recognised competence in the matters dealt with in the Charter, who shall be nominated by the Party concerned.

2. Members of the committee shall be appointed for a period of six years and shall be eligible for reappointment. A member who is unable to complete a term of office shall be replaced in accordance with the procedure laid down in paragraph 1, and the replacing member shall complete his predecessor's term of office.

3. The committee of experts shall adopt rules of procedure. Its secretarial services shall be provided by the Secretary General of the Council of Europe.

Part V – Final provisions

Article 18

This Charter shall be open for signature by the member States of the Council of Europe. It is subject to ratification, acceptance or approval. Instruments of ratification, acceptance or approval shall be deposited with the Secretary General of the Council of Europe.

Article 19

1. This Charter shall enter into force on the first day of the month following the expiration of a period of three months after the date on which five member States of the Council of Europe have expressed their consent to be bound by the Charter in accordance with the provisions of Article 18.

2. In respect of any member State which subsequently expresses its consent to be bound by it, the Charter shall enter into force on the first day of the month following the expiration of a period of three months after the date of the deposit of the instrument of ratification, acceptance or approval.

Article 20

1. After the entry into force of this Charter, the Committee of Ministers of the Council of Europe may invite any State not a member of the Council of Europe to accede to this Charter.

2. In respect of any acceding State, the Charter shall enter into force on the first day of the month following the expiration of a period of three months after the date of deposit of the instrument of accession with the Secretary General of the Council of Europe.

Article 21

1. Any State may, at the time of signature or when depositing its instrument of ratification, acceptance, approval or accession, make one or more reservations to paragraphs 2 to 5 of Article 7 of this Charter. No other reservation may be made.

2. Any Contracting State which has made a reservation under the preceding paragraph may wholly or partly withdraw it by means of a notification addressed to the Secretary General of the Council of Europe. The withdrawal shall take effect on the date of receipt of such notification by the Secretary General.

Article 22

1. Any Party may at any time denounce this Charter by means of a notification addressed to the Secretary General of the Council of Europe.

2. Such denunciation shall become effective on the first day of the month following the expiration of a period of six months after the date of receipt of the notification by the Secretary General.

Article 23

The Secretary General of the Council of Europe shall notify the member States of the Council and any State which has acceded to this Charter of:

a. any signature;

b. the deposit of any instrument of ratification, acceptance, approval or accession;

c. any date of entry into force of this Charter in accordance with Articles 19 and 20;

d. any notification received in application of the provisions of Article 3, paragraph 2;

e. any other act, notification or communication relating to this Charter.

In witness whereof the undersigned, being duly authorised thereto, have signed this Charter.

Done at Strasbourg, this 5th day of November 1992, in English and French, both texts being equally authentic, in a single copy which shall be deposited in the archives of the Council of Europe. The Secretary General of the Council of Europe shall transmit certified copies to each member State of the Council of Europe and to any State invited to accede to this Charter.

9. Recommendation 1201 (1993) on an additional protocol on the rights of national minorities to the European Convention on Human Rights, adopted by the Parliamentary Assembly of the Council of Europe, 1 February 1993

[...]

Preamble

The member states of the Council of Europe signatory hereto;

1. Considering that the diversity of peoples and cultures with which it is imbued is one of the main sources of the richness and vitality of European civilisation;

2. Considering the important contribution of national minorities to the cultural diversity and dynamism of the states of Europe;

3. Considering that only the recognition of the rights of persons belonging to a national minority within a state and the international protection of those rights are capable of putting a lasting end to ethnic confrontations, and thus of helping to guarantee justice, democracy, stability and peace;

4. Considering that the rights concerned are those which any person may exercise either singly or jointly;

5. Considering that the international protection of the rights of minorities is an essential aspect of the international protection of human rights and, as such, a domain for international co-operation,

Have agreed as follows:

Section 1 – Definition

Article 1

For the purposes of this Convention the expression "national minority" refers to a group of persons in a state who:

a. reside on the territory of that state and are citizens thereof;

b. maintain longstanding, firm and lasting ties with that state;

c. display distinctive ethnic, cultural, religious or linguistic characteristics;

d. are sufficiently representative, although smaller in number than the rest of the population of that state or of a region of that state;

e. are motivated by a concern to preserve together that which constitutes their common identity, including their culture, their traditions, their religion or their language.

Section 2 – General principles

Article 2

1. Membership of a national minority shall be a matter of free personal choice.

2. No disadvantage shall result from the choice or the renunciation of such membership.

Article 3

1. Every person belonging to a national minority shall have the right to express, preserve and develop in complete freedom his/her religious, ethnic, linguistic or cultural identity, without being subject to any attempt at assimilation against his/her will.

2. Every person belonging to a national minority may exercise his/her rights and enjoy them individually or in association with others.

Article 4

Every person belonging to a national minority shall be equal before the law. Any discrimination based on membership of a national minority shall be prohibited.

Article 5

Deliberate changes to the demographic composition of the region in which a national minority is settled, to the detriment of that minority, shall be prohibited.

Section 3 – Substantive rights

Article 6

All persons belonging to a national minority shall have the right to set up their own organisations, including political parties.

Article 7

1. Every person belonging to a national minority shall have the right freely to use his/her mother tongue in private and in public, both orally and in

writing. This right shall also apply to the use of his/her language in publications and in the audiovisual sector.

2. Every person belonging to a national minority shall have the right to use his/her surname and first names in his/her mother tongue and to official recognition of his/her surname and names.

3. In the regions in which substantial numbers of a national minority are settled, the persons belonging to a national minority shall have the right to display in their language local names, signs, inscriptions and other similar information visible to the public. This does not deprive the authorities of their right to display the above-mentioned information in the official language or languages of the state.

Article 8

1. Every person belonging to a national minority shall have the right to learn his/her mother tongue and to receive an education in his/her mother tongue at an appropriate number of schools and of state educational and training establishments, located in accordance with the geographical distribution of the minority.

2. The persons belonging to a national minority shall have the right to set up and manage their own schools and educational and training establishments within the framework of the legal system of the state.

Article 9

If a violation of the rights protected by this protocol is alleged, every person belonging to a national minority or any representative organisation shall have an effective remedy before a state authority.

Article 10

Every person belonging to a national minority, while duly respecting the territorial integrity of the state, shall have the right to have free and unimpeded contacts with the citizens of another country with whom this minority shares ethnic, religious or linguistic features or a cultural identity.

Article 11

In the regions where they are in a majority the persons belonging to a national minority shall have the right to have at their disposal appropriate local or autonomous authorities or to have a special status, matching the specific historical and territorial situation and in accordance with the domestic legislation of the State.

Section 4 – Implementation of the protocol

Article 12

1. Nothing in this protocol may be construed as limiting or restricting an individual right of persons belonging to a national minority or a collective right of a national minority embodied in the legislation of the contracting state or in an international agreement to which that state is a party.

2. Measures taken for the sole purpose of protecting ethnic groups, fostering their appropriate development and ensuring that they are granted equal rights and treatment with respect to the rest of the population in the administrative, political, economic, social and cultural fields and in other spheres shall not be considered as discrimination.

Article 13

The exercise of the rights and freedoms listed in the protocol fully apply to the persons belonging to the majority in the whole of the state but which constitute a minority in one or several of its regions.

Article 14

The exercise of the rights and freedoms set forth in this protocol are not meant to restrict the duties and responsibilities of the citizens of the state. However, this exercise may only be made subject to such formalities, conditions, restrictions or penalties as are prescribed by law and necessary in a democratic society in the interests of national security, territorial integrity or public safety, for the prevention of disorder or crime, for the protection of health and morals and for the protection of the rights and freedoms of others.

Article 15

No derogation under Article 15 of the Convention from the provisions of this protocol shall be allowed, save in respect of its Article 10.

Article 16

No reservation may be made under Article 64 of the Convention in respect of the provisions of this protocol.

Article 17

The states parties shall regard the provisions of Articles 1 to 11 of this protocol as additional articles of the Convention and all the provisions of the Convention shall apply accordingly.

Article 18

This protocol shall be open for signature by the member states of the Council of Europe which are signatories to the Convention. It shall be subject to ratification, acceptance or approval. A member state of the Council of Europe may not ratify, accept or approve this protocol unless it simultaneously ratifies or has previously ratified the Convention. Instruments of ratification, acceptance or approval shall be deposited with the Secretary General of the Council of Europe.

Article 19

1. This protocol shall enter into force on the first day of the month following the date on which five member states of the Council of Europe have expressed their consent to be bound by the protocol in accordance with the provisions of Article 17.

2. In respect of any member state which subsequently expresses its consent to be bound by it, the protocol shall enter into force on the first day of the month following the date of the deposit of the instrument of ratification, acceptance or approval.

Article 20

The Secretary General of the Council of Europe shall notify the member states of the Council of:

a. any signature;

b. the deposit of any instrument of ratification, acceptance or approval;

c. any date of entry into force of this protocol;

d. any other act, notification or communication relating to this protocol.

10. Framework Convention for the Protection of National Minorities

(adopted by the Committee of Ministers of the Council of Europe, 8 November 1994)

opened for signature on 1 February 1995

Entry into force: 1 February 1998

The member States of the Council of Europe and the other States, signatories to the present framework Convention,

Considering that the aim of the Council of Europe is to achieve greater unity between its members for the purpose of safeguarding and realising the ideals and the principles which are their common heritage;

Considering that one of the methods by which that aim is to be pursued is the maintenance and the further realisation of human rights and fundamental freedoms;

Wishing to follow-up the Declaration of the Heads of State and Government of the member States of the Council of Europe adopted in Vienna on 9 October 1993;

Being resolved to protect within their respective territories the existence of national minorities;

Considering that the upheavals of European history have shown that the protection of national minorities is essential to stability, democratic security and peace in this continent;

Considering that a pluralist and genuinely democratic society should not only respect the ethnic, cultural, linguistic and religious identity of each person belonging to a national minority, but also create appropriate conditions enabling them to express, preserve and develop this identity;

Considering that the creation of a climate of tolerance and dialogue is necessary to enable cultural diversity to be a source and a factor, not of division, but of enrichment for each society;

Considering that the realisation of a tolerant and prosperous Europe does not depend solely on co-operation between States but also requires transfrontier co-operation between local and regional authorities without prejudice to the constitution and territorial integrity of each State;

Having regard to the Convention for the Protection of Human Rights and Fundamental Freedoms and the Protocols thereto;

Having regard to the commitments concerning the protection of national minorities in United Nations conventions and declarations and in the documents of the Conference on Security and Co-operation in Europe, particularly the Copenhagen Document of 29 June 1990;

Being resolved to define the principles to be respected and the obligations which flow from them, in order to ensure, in the member States and such other States as may become Parties to the present instrument, the effective protection of national minorities and of the rights and freedoms of persons belonging to those minorities, within the rule of law, respecting the territorial integrity and national sovereignty of States;

Being determined to implement the principles set out in this framework Convention through national legislation and appropriate governmental policies,

Have agreed as follows:

Section I

Article 1

The protection of national minorities and of the rights and freedoms of persons belonging to those minorities forms an integral part of the international protection of human rights, and as such falls within the scope of international co-operation.

Article 2

The provisions of this framework Convention shall be applied in good faith, in a spirit of understanding and tolerance and in conformity with the principles of good neighbourliness, friendly relations and co-operation between States.

Article 3

1. Every person belonging to a national minority shall have the right freely to choose to be treated or not to be treated as such and no disadvantage shall result from this choice or from the exercise of the rights which are connected to that choice.

2. Persons belonging to national minorities may exercise the rights and enjoy the freedoms flowing from the principles enshrined in the present framework Convention individually as well as in community with others.

Section II

Article 4

1. The Parties undertake to guarantee to persons belonging to national minorities the right of equality before the law and of equal protection of the law. In this respect, any discrimination based on belonging to a national minority shall be prohibited.

2. The Parties undertake to adopt, where necessary, adequate measures in order to promote, in all areas of economic, social, political and cultural life, full and effective equality between persons belonging to a national minority and those belonging to the majority. In this respect, they shall take due account of the specific conditions of the persons belonging to national minorities.

3. The measures adopted in accordance with paragraph 2 shall not be considered to be an act of discrimination.

Article 5

1. The Parties undertake to promote the conditions necessary for persons belonging to national minorities to maintain and develop their culture, and to preserve the essential elements of their identity, namely their religion, language, traditions and cultural heritage.

2. Without prejudice to measures taken in pursuance of their general integration policy, the Parties shall refrain from policies or practices aimed at assimilation of persons belonging to national minorities against their will and shall protect these persons from any action aimed at such assimilation.

Article 6

1. The Parties shall encourage a spirit of tolerance and intercultural dialogue and take effective measures to promote mutual respect and understanding

and co-operation among all persons living on their territory, irrespective of those persons' ethnic, cultural, linguistic or religious identity, in particular in the fields of education, culture and the media.

2. The Parties undertake to take appropriate measures to protect persons who may be subject to threats or acts of discrimination, hostility or violence as a result of their ethnic, cultural, linguistic, or religious identity.

Article 7

The Parties shall ensure respect of the right of every person belonging to a national minority to freedom of peaceful assembly, freedom of association, freedom of expression, and freedom of thought, conscience and religion.

Article 8

The Parties undertake to recognise that every person belonging to a national minority has the right to manifest his or her religion or belief and to establish religious institutions, organisations and associations.

Article 9

1. The Parties undertake to recognise that the right to freedom of expression of every person belonging to a national minority includes freedom to hold opinions and to receive and impart information and ideas in the minority language, without interference by public authorities and regardless of frontiers. The Parties shall ensure, within the framework of their legal systems, that persons belonging to a national minority are not discriminated against in their access to the media.

2. Paragraph 1 shall not prevent Parties from requiring the licensing, without discrimination and based on objective criteria, of sound radio and television broadcasting, or cinema enterprises.

3. The Parties shall not hinder the creation and the use of printed media by persons belonging to national minorities. In the legal framework of sound radio and television broadcasting, they shall ensure, as far as possible, and taking into account the provisions of paragraph 1, that persons belonging to national minorities are granted the possibility of creating and using their own media.

4. In the framework of their legal systems, the Parties shall adopt adequate measures in order to facilitate access to the media for persons belonging to national minorities and in order to promote tolerance and permit cultural pluralism.

Article 10

1. The Parties undertake to recognise that every person belonging to a national minority has the right to use freely and without interference his or her minority language, in private and in public, orally and in writing.

2. In areas inhabited by persons belonging to national minorities traditionally or in substantial numbers, if those persons so request and where such a
request corresponds to a real need, the Parties shall endeavour to ensure, as
far as possible, the conditions which would make it possible to use the
minority language in relations between those persons and the administrative
authorities.

3. The Parties undertake to guarantee the right of every person belonging to
a national minority to be informed promptly, in a language which he or she
understands, of the reasons for his or her arrest, and of the nature and cause
of any accusation against him or her, and to defend himself or herself in this
language, if necessary with the free assistance of an interpreter.

Article 11

1. The Parties undertake to recognise that every person belonging to a
national minority has the right to use his or her surname (patronym) and
first names in the minority language and the right to official recognition of
them, according to modalities provided for in their legal system.

2. The Parties undertake to recognise that every person belonging to a
national minority has the right to display in his or her minority language
signs, inscriptions and other information of a private nature visible to the
public.

3. In areas traditionally inhabited by substantial numbers of persons belonging to a national minority, the Parties shall endeavour, in the framework of
their legal system, including, where appropriate, agreements with other
States, and taking into account their specific conditions, to display traditional
local names, street names and other topographical indications intended for
the public also in the minority language when there is a sufficient demand
for such indications.

Article 12

1. The Parties shall, where appropriate, take measures in the fields of education and research to foster knowledge of the culture, history, language and
religion of their national minorities and of the majority.

2. In this context the Parties shall *inter alia* provide adequate opportunities
for teacher training and access to textbooks, and facilitate contacts among
students and teachers of different communities.

3. The Parties undertake to promote equal opportunities for access to education at all levels for persons belonging to national minorities.

Article 13

1. Within the framework of their education systems, the Parties shall recognise that persons belonging to a national minority have the right to set up
and to manage their own private educational and training establishments.

2. The exercise of this right shall not entail any financial obligation for the Parties.

Article 14

1. The Parties undertake to recognise that every person belonging to a national minority has the right to learn his or her minority language.

2. In areas inhabited by persons belonging to national minorities traditionally or in substantial numbers, if there is sufficient demand, the Parties shall endeavour to ensure, as far as possible and within the framework of their education systems, that persons belonging to those minorities have adequate opportunities for being taught the minority language or for receiving instruction in this language.

3. Paragraph 2 of this article shall be implemented without prejudice to the learning of the official language or the teaching in this language.

Article 15

The Parties shall create the conditions necessary for the effective participation of persons belonging to national minorities in cultural, social and economic life and in public affairs, in particular those affecting them.

Article 16

The Parties shall refrain from measures which alter the proportions of the population in areas inhabited by persons belonging to national minorities and are aimed at restricting the rights and freedoms flowing from the principles enshrined in the present framework Convention.

Article 17

1. The Parties undertake not to interfere with the right of persons belonging to national minorities to establish and maintain free and peaceful contacts across frontiers with persons lawfully staying in other States, in particular those with whom they share an ethnic, cultural, linguistic or religious identity, or a common cultural heritage.

2. The Parties undertake not to interfere with the right of persons belonging to national minorities to participate in the activities of non-governmental organisations, both at the national and international levels.

Article 18

1. The Parties shall endeavour to conclude, where necessary, bilateral and multilateral agreements with other States, in particular neighbouring States, in order to ensure the protection of persons belonging to the national minorities concerned.

2. Where relevant, the Parties shall take measures to encourage transfrontier co-operation.

Article 19

The Parties undertake to respect and implement the principles enshrined in the present framework Convention making, where necessary, only those limitations, restrictions or derogations which are provided for in international legal instruments, in particular the Convention for the Protection of Human Rights and Fundamental Freedoms, in so far as they are relevant to the rights and freedoms flowing from the said principles.

Section III

Article 20

In the exercise of the rights and freedoms flowing from the principles enshrined in the present framework Convention, any person belonging to a national minority shall respect the national legislation and the rights of others, in particular those of persons belonging to the minority or to other national minorities.

Article 21

Nothing in the present framework Convention shall be interpreted as implying any right to engage in any activity or perform any act contrary to the fundamental principles of international law and in particular of the sovereign equality, territorial integrity and political independence of States.

Article 22

Nothing in the present framework Convention shall be construed as limiting or derogating from any of the human rights and fundamental freedoms which may be ensured under the laws of any Contracting Party or under any other agreement to which it is a Party.

Article 23

The rights and freedoms flowing from the principles enshrined in the present framework Convention, in so far as they are the subject of a corresponding provision in the Convention for the Protection of Human Rights and Fundamental Freedoms or in the Protocols thereto, shall be understood so as to conform to the latter provisions.

Section IV

Article 24

1. The Committee of Ministers of the Council of Europe shall monitor the implementation of this framework Convention by the Contracting Parties.

2. The Parties which are not members of the Council of Europe shall participate in the implementation mechanism, according to modalities to be determined.

Article 25

1. Within a period of one year following the entry into force of this framework Convention in respect of a Contracting Party, the latter shall transmit to the Secretary General of the Council of Europe full information on the legislative and other measures taken to give effect to the principles set out in this framework Convention.

2. Thereafter, each Party shall transmit to the Secretary General on a periodical basis and whenever the Committee of Ministers so requests any further information of relevance to the implementation of this framework Convention.

3. The Secretary General shall forward to the Committee of Ministers the information transmitted under the terms of this article.

Article 26

1. In evaluating the adequacy of the measures taken by the Parties to give effect to the principles set out in this framework Convention the Committee of Ministers shall be assisted by an advisory committee, the members of which shall have recognised expertise in the field of the protection of national minorities.

2. The composition of this advisory committee and its procedure shall be determined by the Committee of Ministers within a period of one year following the entry into force of this framework Convention.

Section V

Article 27

This framework Convention shall be open for signature by the member States of the Council of Europe. Up until the date when the Convention enters into force, it shall also be open for signature by any other State so invited by the Committee of Ministers. It is subject to ratification, acceptance or approval. Instruments of ratification, acceptance or approval shall be deposited with the Secretary General of the Council of Europe.

Article 28

1. This framework Convention shall enter into force on the first day of the month following the expiration of a period of three months after the date on which twelve member States of the Council of Europe have expressed their consent to be bound by the Convention in accordance with the provisions of Article 27.

2. In respect of any member State which subsequently expresses its consent to be bound by it, the framework Convention shall enter into force on the first day of the month following the expiration of a period of three months after the date of the deposit of the instrument of ratification, acceptance or approval.

Article 29

1. After the entry into force of this framework Convention and after consulting the Contracting States, the Committee of Ministers of the Council of Europe may invite to accede to the Convention, by a decision taken by the majority provided for in Article 20.d of the Statute of the Council of Europe, any non-member State of the Council of Europe which, invited to sign in accordance with the provisions of Article 27, has not yet done so, and any other non-member State.

2. In respect of any acceding State, the framework Convention shall enter into force on the first day of the month following the expiration of a period of three months after the date of the deposit of the instrument of accession with the Secretary General of the Council of Europe.

Article 30

1. Any State may at the time of signature or when depositing its instrument of ratification, acceptance, approval or accession, specify the territory or territories for whose international relations it is responsible to which this framework Convention shall apply.

2. Any State may at any later date, by a declaration addressed to the Secretary General of the Council of Europe, extend the application of this framework Convention to any other territory specified in the declaration. In respect of such territory the framework Convention shall enter into force on the first day of the month following the expiration of a period of three months after the date of receipt of such declaration by the Secretary General.

3. Any declaration made under the two preceding paragraphs may, in respect of any territory specified in such declaration, be withdrawn by a notification addressed to the Secretary General. The withdrawal shall become effective on the first day of the month following the expiration of a period of three months after the date of receipt of such notification by the Secretary General.

Article 31

1. Any Party may at any time denounce this framework Convention by means of a notification addressed to the Secretary General of the Council of Europe.

2. Such denunciation shall become effective on the first day of the month following the expiration of a period of six months after the date of receipt of the notification by the Secretary General.

Article 32

The Secretary General of the Council of Europe shall notify the member States of the Council, other signatory States and any State which has acceded to this framework Convention, of:

a. any signature;

b. the deposit of any instrument of ratification, acceptance, approval or accession;

b. any date of entry into force of this framework Convention in accordance with Articles 28, 29 and 30;

d. any other act, notification or communication relating to this framework Convention.

In witness whereof the undersigned, being duly authorised thereto, have signed this framework Convention.

Done at Strasbourg, this 1st day of February 1995, in English and French, both texts being equally authentic, in a single copy which shall be deposited in the archives of the Council of Europe. The Secretary General of the Council of Europe shall transmit certified copies to each member State of the Council of Europe and to any State invited to sign or accede to this framework Convention.

11. Central European Initiative Instrument for the Protection of Minority Rights, adopted by CEI member states, 19 November 1994

The Member States of the Central European Initiative signatory hereto,

Recognising that questions relating to national minorities can only be satisfactorily resolved in a truly democratic political framework, which is based on the rule of law and guarantees full respect for human rights and fundamental freedoms, and equal rights and status for all citizens,

Reaffirming that protection of national minorities concerns only citizens of the respective States who will enjoy the same rights and have the same duties of citizenship as the rest of the population,

Convinced that national minorities form an integral part of the society of the States in which they live and that they are a factor of enrichment of each respective State and society,

Bearing in mind that a very effective way to achieve stability in the region is developing good relations between neighbours, and being conscious of the need to avoid any encouragement of separatist tendencies of national minorities in the region,

Confirming that issues concerning the rights of persons belonging to national minorities are matters of legitimate international concern and consequently do not constitute an exclusively internal affair of the respective State,

Considering that respect for the rights of persons belonging to national minorities, as part of universally recognised human rights, is an essential factor for peace, justice, stability and democracy in the States,

Convinced that international protection of the rights of persons belonging to national minorities, as enshrined in the present Instrument, does not permit any activity that is contrary to the fundamental principles of international law, in particular sovereignty, territorial integrity and political independence of States,

Recognising the particular importance of increasing constructive co-operation among themselves on questions relating to national minorities and that such co-operation shall promote mutual understanding and confidence, friendly and good neighbourly relations, international peace, security and justice,

Expressing their condemnation of aggressive nationalism, racial and ethnic hatred, anti-Semitism, xenophobia and discrimination against any person or group and of persecution on religious and ideological grounds,

Have agreed as follows:

Article 1

The States recognise the existence of national minorities as such, considering them integral parts of the society in which they live, and the States guarantee the appropriate conditions for the promotion of their identity.

For the purpose of this Instrument the term "national minority" shall mean a group that is smaller in number than the rest of the population of a State, whose members being nationals of that State, have ethnic, religious or linguistic features different from those of the rest of the population, and are guided by the will to safeguard their culture, traditions, religion and language.

Article 2

To belong to a national minority is a matter of free individual choice and no disadvantage shall arise from the exercise or non-exercise of such a choice.

Article 3

The States recognise that persons belonging to national minorities have the right to exercise fully and effectively their human rights and fundamental freedoms, individually or in common with others, without any discrimination and in full equality before the law. Those persons shall be able to enjoy the rights foreseen by the present Instrument, individually or in common with others, and to benefit from the measures ensuring those rights.

Article 4

The States guarantee the right of persons belonging to national minorities to express, preserve and develop their ethnic, cultural, linguistic or religious identity and to maintain and develop their culture in all its aspects.

Article 5

The adoption of special measures in favour of persons belonging to national minorities aimed at promoting equality between them and the rest of the population or taking due account of their specific conditions shall not be considered an act of discrimination.

Article 6

The States shall take effective measures to provide protection against any acts that constitute incitement to violence against persons or groups based on national, racial, ethnic or religious discrimination, hostility or hatred, including anti-Semitism.

Article 7

The States recognise the particular problems of Roma (Gypsies). They undertake to adopt all legal, administrative or educational measures as foreseen in the present Instrument in order to preserve and to develop the identity of Roma, to facilitate by specific measures the social integration of persons belonging to Roma and to eliminate all forms of intolerance against such persons.

Article 8

The States, taking measures in pursuance of their general integration policy without prejudice to democratic principles, shall refrain from pursuing or encouraging policies aimed at the assimilation of persons belonging to national minorities against their will and shall protect these persons against any action aimed at such assimilation.

Article 9

When modifying administrative, judicial or electoral subdivisions, the States should be aware that such modifications shall respect the existing rights of the persons belonging to national minorities and the exercise of those rights, among other criteria. In accordance with national legislation, they should consult with the populations directly affected before adopting any modification in the matter.

Article 10

Any person belonging to a national minority shall have the right to use his or her language freely, in public as well as in private, orally and in writing.

Article 11

Any person belonging to a national minority shall have the right to use his or her surname and first names in his or her language and the right to official acceptance and registration of such surname and names.

Article 12

Whenever the number of persons belonging to a national minority in an area reaches a significant level according to the latest census or other method of ascertaining its consistency, they shall have the right to use, whenever possible and in accordance with applicable national legislation, their own language in oral and written form in their contacts with public authorities of the said area. The authorities shall reply as much as possible in the same language.

Article 13

The States, in conformity with national legislation and bilateral agreements with other interested States, especially with neighbouring States, may allow the display of bilingual or plurilingual local names, street names and other topographical indications in areas where the number of persons belonging to a national minority reaches a significant level according to the latest census or other method of ascertaining its consistency. The display of signs, inscriptions or other similar information of a private nature in the minority language should not be subject to specific restrictions other than those generally applied in the relevant field.

Article 14

Any person belonging to a national minority, when exercising religious freedom, shall have the right to use his or her own language in worship, teaching, religious practice or observance.

Article 15

Whenever the number of persons belonging to a national minority reaches the majority of the population in an area according to the latest census or other method of ascertaining its consistency, the States will promote the knowledge of the minority language among officers of the local and decentralised state administrative offices. Endeavours should be made to recruit, if possible, officers who in addition to knowing the official language, have sufficient knowledge of the minority language.

Article 16

The States recognise the right of persons belonging to national minorities to establish and maintain their own cultural and religious institutions, organisations or associations, which are entitled to seek voluntary financial and other contributions as well as public assistance, in conformity with national legislation.

Article 17

The States recognise the right of persons belonging to a national minority to establish and maintain their own private pre-schools, schools and educational establishments and possibly obtain official recognition, in conformity with national legislation. Such establishments may seek public financing or other contributions.

Article 18

Notwithstanding the need to learn the official language of the State concerned, every person belonging to a national minority shall have the right to learn his or her own language and receive an education in his or her own language. The States shall endeavour to ensure the appropriate types and levels of public education, in accordance with national legislation, whenever the number of persons belonging to a national minority in an area reaches a significant level according to the latest census or other method of ascertaining its consistency. In the context of the teaching of history and culture in such public establishments, adequate teaching of history and culture of the national minorities should be ensured.

Article 19

The States guarantee the right of persons belonging to a national minority to support media in their own language with financial assistance, in accordance with relevant States regulations. In the case of public ownership of television and radio, the States will assure, whenever appropriate and possible, that persons belonging to national minorities have the right to freely access the media, including producing such programmes in their own language.

Article 20

The States shall guarantee the right of persons belonging to national minorities to participate without discrimination in the political, economic, social and cultural life of the society of the State of which they are citizens and shall promote conditions for exercising those rights.

Article 21

The States shall allow persons belonging to a national minority to establish political parties.

Article 22

In accordance with the policies of the States concerned, the States will respect the right of persons belonging to national minorities to effective participation in public affairs, in particular in the decision-making process on matters and create conditions for the promotion of the ethnic, cultural, linguistic and religious identity of certain national minorities by adopting appropriate measures corresponding to the specific circumstances of such minorities as foreseen in the CSCE documents.

Article 23

Every person belonging to a national minority, while duly respecting the territorial integrity of the State, shall have the right to have free and unimpeded contacts with the citizens of another country with whom he or she shares ethnic, religious or linguistic features or a cultural identity. The States shall not unduly restrict the free exercise of those rights. Furthermore, they will encourage transfrontier arrangements on national, regional and local levels.

Article 24

Any person belonging to a national minority shall have an effective remedy before a national judicial authority for any violation of rights set forth in the present Instrument, provided that those rights are enacted through national legislation.

Article 25

In any area where those who belong to a national minority represent the majority of the population, the States shall take the necessary measures to ensure that those who do not belong to this minority shall not suffer from any disadvantage, including those that may result from the implementation of the measures of protection foreseen by the present Instrument.

Article 26

None of these commitments shall be interpreted as implying any right to engage in any activity in contravention of the fundamental principles of international law or, in particular, the sovereign equality, territorial integrity and political independence of the States.

Nothing in the present Instrument shall affect the duties related to persons belonging to national minorities as citizens of the States concerned.

Persons belonging to national minorities will also respect, in the exercise of their rights, the rights of others, including those of persons belonging to the majority population of the respective State or other national minorities.

Article 27

This Instrument shall not prejudice provisions of domestic law or any international agreement which provide greater protection for national minorities or persons belonging to them.